Herman & Daphine

Carrollton, Texas –   1983

NEIL SPERRY'S
COMPLETE GUIDE
TO
TEXAS GARDENING

NEIL SPERRY'S
COMPLETE GUIDE
TO
TEXAS GARDENING

TAYLOR PUBLISHING COMPANY
Dallas, Texas

Editor:
Olivia Lane

Book Designer:
Kathleen Ferguson

Illustrations:
Frank Campagna
Linda Daboub
Paula Lawson
Louis Orrill
Jeff Sheppard
Jerry Sutton
Jackie Voigt

Library of Congress Cataloging in Publication Data

Sperry, Neil.
  Neil Sperry's Complete Guide to Texas Gardening.

  Includes index.
  1. Gardening — Texas. 2. Gardening. I. Title.
  II. Title: Complete guide to Texas gardening.
  SB453.2T4S63   635′ .09764   81-84757
  ISBN 0-87833-322-3   AACR2

Printed in the United States of America

In memory of my father,
Dr. Omer E. Sperry

and dedicated to
my mother, Lois
wife, Lynn
sons, Brian and Todd
and daughter, Erin

ACKNOWLEDGEMENTS

The author wishes to give special thanks to the following recognized horticulturists for their technical advice and review of the book: Philip Huey, Jr., Assistant Director Maintenance and Beautification Park and Recreation Department of Dallas, for his comments on the introduction to gardening, landscapes, trees, shrubs, vines, ground covers, lawns, annuals, perennials, insects and diseases (chapters 1 through 9, and 12); Kim Andersen, Andersen's Greenery, Arlington, Texas, William Welch, Ph.D., Landscape Horticulturist, Texas Agricultural Extension Service, Texas A&M University, Everett Janne, Landscape Horticulturist, Texas Agricultural Extension Service, Texas A&M University, for their comments on landscapes (chapter 2); Quinton A. Johnson, Golf Course Superintendent, Brookhaven Country Club, for his comments on lawns (chapter 7); Bluefford G. Hancock, Horticulture Project Group Supervisor and Extension Horticulturist, Texas Agricultural Extension Service, Texas A&M University, for his comments on fruit and nut crops (chapter 10); Samuel D. Cotner, Ph.D., Vegetable Specialist, Texas Agricultural Extension Service, Texas A&M University, for his comments on vegetables (chapter 11); H. A. Turney, Entomologist, Texas Agricultural Extension Service, Texas A&M University, for his comments on insects (chapter 12); Norman L. McCoy, Ph.D., Plant Pathologist, Texas Agricultural Extension Service, Texas A&M University, for his comments on diseases (chapter 12).

Photograph Acknowledgements

The photographs included in this book have been taken by the author with the exception of the following photographs for which permission to reproduce them has been kindly given: Chester Allen 344 (top left); Horticultural Printers 371 (top), 377 (top left, bottom left and right), 396 (top); Dr. Norman L. McCoy 486 (top left and right), 487 (top left and right); John Watson Landscape Illumination, photographs by John Watson, 79 (both).

Table of Contents

vii

Chapter 3: Trees . . . Texas' Best

Chapter 4: Shrubs

Chapter 8: Annuals

Chapter 9: Perennials

Chapter 10: Fruit and Nut Crops

Chapter 11: Vegetable Gardening

Chapter 12: Insects and Diseases

Texas has long been known for its outstanding landscapes and gardens. Horticulture is perhaps our state's leading hobby. Simply put, we appreciate fine plants.

However, it's not always easy to find reference help in growing those plants. All too often, the authors have aimed their works at other parts of the country. They're great books, but somehow they just don't fit our soils and our climates. That's bothered me since my formative years helping Dad transplant oak trees in Central Texas. Where could you find a complete gardening guide for our great state?

So here I am, 25 years later, still wondering. Sometimes you just have to do things yourself, and that's what you'll find in the 500-plus pages which follow.

I've spent the last 12 years helping people in our state with their plant problems. I've answered phone lines in metropolitan counties and traveled the state border to border talking to the gardeners of Texas. I do six hours a week of live call-in question-and-answer radio programming, and have presented over 1,000 gardening programs all across Texas . . . all of it to learn the joys and sorrows of gardening in the Southwest.

I've taken those experiences, and have laid them out like a roadmap . . . to guide you through plant growing in Texas. Everything you need to know to grow trees, shrubs, vines, ground covers, turfgrass, annual and perennial flowers, fruit and vegetables in your area is between these covers. All the important plants are included, along with details of how best to grow them.

The book has been years in the planning and over a year in the writing. Skilled artists have illustrated important points, and detailed photographs identify plants and show how to care for them.

The book has been reviewed by a group of professional horticulturists . . . the best the state has to offer, each a recognized expert in the field. Advice and guidance given is the most accurate and reliable that is available for all parts of Texas.

I have two major goals in offering this reference for your horticultural library:

1. To share my enthusiasm for the miraculous plant kingdom with gardeners of all ages, and

2. To provide, in one handy reference, all you'll need to be a successful gardener in Texas.

Here's hoping we'll accomplish both of those goals.

Happy reading . . .

and happy gardening!

Chapter 1

Getting Started in Gardening

How were things in Green Bay . . . Cleveland . . . L.A., or wherever it was you last lived? Well, no matter where, things are different in Texas! And those differences make Texas gardening an exciting challenge.

What follows are the fundamentals of landscaping and gardening here in the Southwest . . . the things you'll need to consider as you plan your first plantings.

If you're one of our new Texas residents, welcome! Though I'm a native Texan, I, too, have lived in the Northeast and the West. In returning to Texas, I faced the same adjustments you're making now. The suggestions in this chapter should help you bypass the stumbling blocks.

If, on the other hand, you're a veteran Texas gardener, you'll find lots of new ideas. There's always something to learn when you're dealing with such variables as climate and soil. New plants are hitting the market each day.

What follows will be the summation of 25 years of experience in Texas gardens . . . no, more than that. Let's include my dad's, too . . . I learned at his knee.

HOW TEMPERATURE AFFECTS YOUR PLANTS' GROWTH

While it's true that most places will support some type of plant life, it isn't necessarily true that every plant will grow in your landscape or garden. Plants, you see, are like humans and other animals. They have particular environmental requirements.

Temperature is one of the most important aspects of that environment. It's the logical starting point in choosing your plants because temperature is an element we can't control. We must choose plants that can survive what nature provides us.

Texas is a large state with widely varying weather conditions. You can add one week to each end of the growing season for every 100 miles you move south. That's only a generality, of course, but it illustrates the importance of knowing your locality.

And, as any veteran gardener can verify, conditions can even vary widely within the same landscape and garden.

Heat, cold, wind, drought and floods are common in each part of our state. This makes it all the more important to know all the facts and choose the most durable plants available.

The Texas Seasons . . . Through the Eyes of the Gardener

Spring: A delightful time marked by cool-to-warm breezes and a sizeable portion of the annual rainfall.

Summer: A challenge to gardeners. Extreme heat in many parts of the state, prolonged periods of drought. More moderate temperatures and higher humidity along the Gulf Coast.

Fall: Good growing conditions return. Temperatures drop gradually for two to four months. Rainfall becomes somewhat more frequent.

Winter: Varies from extreme cold in the Panhandle and North Texas to sub-tropical in southern regions. All areas, though, will have at least a few days of good gardening weather.

Texas at a Glance

Some years ago, in an effort to determine winter temperature extremes in the various parts of the country, the United States Weather Bureau evaluated 60 years of their records. They plotted the information, county-by-county, across the United States.

That information is invaluable to gardeners, because it gives us a handle on the plant types that could reasonably be expected to survive average winters. What you see next is our part of that map. Study it carefully, and remember your county's zone number as you read what follows, particularly the references to "minimum temperatures" and "hardy" plants.

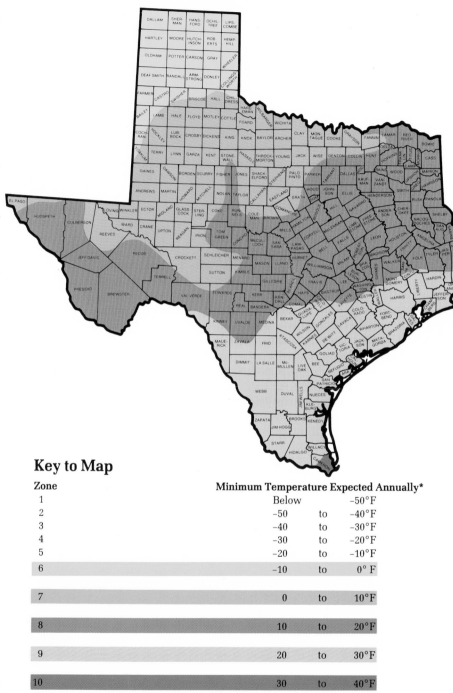

Key to Map

Zone	Minimum Temperature Expected Annually*		
1	Below		−50°F
2	−50	to	−40°F
3	−40	to	−30°F
4	−30	to	−20°F
5	−20	to	−10°F
6	−10	to	0° F
7	0	to	10°F
8	10	to	20°F
9	20	to	30°F
10	30	to	40°F

*Taken from United States Department of Agriculture Plant Hardiness Zone Map.

*Based on 60-year records of U.S. Weather Bureau. Temperature Zones 1 through 5 do not occur, in Texas.

Three Important Temperatures Which Make Up A Plant's "Acceptable" Range

Every plant that you grow will have three critical temperatures . . . minimum, maximum and optimum. Sometimes temperature ranges will be generalized. In all cases, the ranges will be important to the success or failure of your plants.

1. Minimum: All plants will have a certain temperature below which they cannot survive. For example, scheffleras (used for house plants in many homes) are actually large shade trees when they're grown in areas where it never freezes. If moved to an area where the temperature goes below 30°F, the plant will be killed. Pecan trees, on the other hand, are large shade trees that can survive temperatures of zero and below.

Minimum temperature is, then, one of your major criteria in evaluating a plant's suitability for a given location. While thumbing through your favorite garden magazine, notice that there will be a reference to a plant as being "hardy" in a particular zone. For example, let's say Zone 6. This means, according to our hardiness map, on page 3, that the plant can be expected to survive anywhere that temperatures don't fall below -10°F. That plant would be a good candidate, then for Zones 6-10.

2. Maximum: Few plants have a maximum temperature above which they cannot survive. The problem, instead, comes from prolonged extreme heat, when the plant must struggle to maintain life. Stored food is consumed faster than the plant can produce more . . . sort of like writing checks faster than you cover them with deposits. Eventually the plant runs out of stored reserves and dies.

3. Optimum: Every plant has a certain temperature range at which it grows best. Mountainous plants may thrive between 30 and 60°F, while seashore tropicals prefer 60 to 90°F. Move a plant to a wrong range and you're asking for trouble.

Two Terms Relating to Temperature

Hardy: As mentioned earlier, this term refers to a temperature at which you could reasonably expect a plant to survive. Dwarf gardenias, for example, are "hardy" to 20°F, which means they're hardy in Zone 8.

Hardened: Refers to a plant that has gradually been conditioned to cold (or hot) weather. Plants that normally would survive ("be hardy to") temperatures of 10°F may freeze at 20°F if that is the first subfreezing weather they encounter. Conversely, a plant that's been grown in a cool greenhouse will literally cook within minutes in the hot sun.

Five Things You Can Do to Protect Plants
From Temperature Injury

Don't send your plants out to battle the heat and cold unattended. Give them some help . . .

Apply fertilizers containing potassium (K). It promotes durability to heat and cold.

Avoid reflected heat for sensitive plants.

Water before hard freezes and during heat waves.

Mulch with compost, bark and straw to minimize soil temperature fluctuations and to conserve moisture.

Shelter cold-sensitive plants from winter winds.

MOST COMMON QUESTION

"How long is the growing season in my part of the state?"

I'll answer with a map:

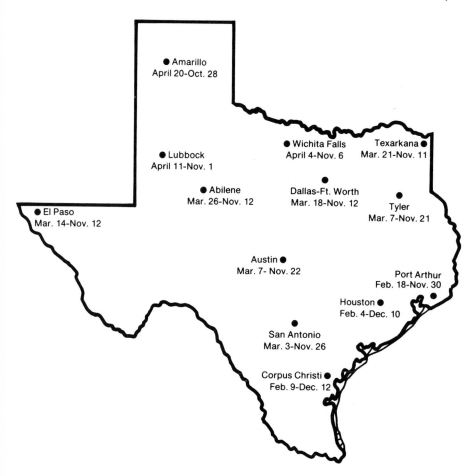

● Amarillo
April 20-Oct. 28

● Wichita Falls   Texarkana ●
April 4-Nov. 6   Mar. 21-Nov. 11

● Lubbock
April 11-Nov. 1

● Abilene   Dallas-Ft. Worth
Mar. 26-Nov. 12   Mar. 18-Nov. 12

●
● El Paso   Tyler
Mar. 14-Nov. 12   Mar. 7-Nov. 21

Austin ●
Mar. 7- Nov. 22   Port Arthur
Feb. 18-Nov. 30

Houston ●
Feb. 4-Dec. 10

●
San Antonio
Mar. 3-Nov. 26

Corpus Christi ●
Feb. 9-Dec. 12

From the U.S. Department of Commerce, Environmental Science Service Administration.

RULE OF GREEN THUMB: Acclimatize your plants gradually ... *harden* them progressively. If they're going to be growing in harsh conditions, let them get used to it step-by-step. Don't move them from protected spots directly out into the sun, wind, heat or cold. Let them get used to adversity a little at a time.

THE SOIL: PREPARING TO PLANT

Soil is to your garden as the foundation is to your house . . . the beginning for all that follows. Most of us are quite willing to spend extra money for a good foundation, and so it should be with our soil preparation.

Start by knowing your soil and its properties. Have your soil tested and learn the modifications you can make in the soil to improve its gardening potential. (More on soil testing follows.)

Soil Types: Their Strengths and Weaknesses

Clays: Smallest of all soil particles. High nutrient, water retention capacity. Help bond sands and silts into crumbs for better soil structure. Soils with high clay content, though, are difficult to work with.

Silts: Between clay and sand in size and properties. Important in loam soils, but not ideal by themselves.

Sands: Coarsest of all soil particles. Well aerated. Sands drain rapidly. Ideal for root growth, but moisture and nutrient retention are poor.

Loam: Soil that contains approximately equal amounts of clay, silt and sand, plus some organic matter. This is the ideal garden soil, since it has all of the advantages of each soil category.

Depth: How It Affects Plant Growth

Soil acts as a reservoir to hold moisture and nutrients. To a large degree, your plants' success depends on the depth of their soil.

Most trees do best when given a minimum of two to four feet of good loam topsoil. Shrubs will need one to three feet of topsoil, depending on the size of the plant. Vines, ground covers and annual and perennial flowers will need at least one foot of good soil. Turf grasses will require eight to 12 inches of topsoil.

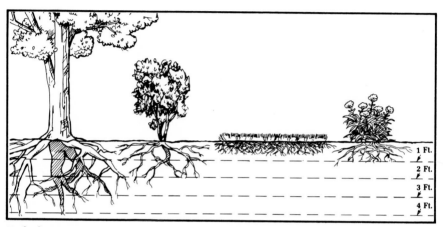

Each plant in your landscape and garden has a minimum amount of soil in which it can grow vigorously.

TEXAS TIP

Since Texas soils are often quite shallow, you may need to import soil into your landscape and garden just to meet the bare minimums. Ask a nurseryman to refer you to someone who can supply good soil. Specify that the soil you buy be free of serious weed pests such as nutgrass.

Remember too, that plants growing in shallow soil need more frequent watering and feeding because they have a more limited soil reservoir.

Soil pH: What It Is and How It Affects Plant Growth

The term "pH" is borrowed from chemistry and refers to the acidity or alkalinity of a solution. It ranges from 0 (extremely acid) to 14 (extremely alkaline), with a pH of 7.0 being neutral. Texas soils generally range from 5.5 to 8.5. Here is an illustration showing pH ranges and their best uses.

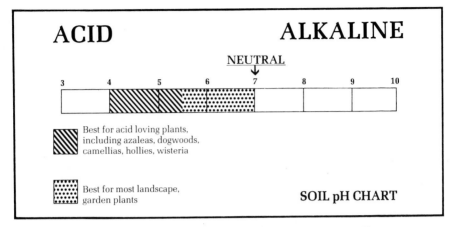

Though there are exceptions, soils in areas of higher rainfall (East Texas) will be acid, while soils in drier regions (western two-thirds of Texas) will be alkaline. High concentrations of organic matter, such as decaying tree leaves, help acidify soil.

Gardeners must be concerned with the acidity or alkalinity of their soil because pH affects the way plants grow. This factor also determines whether or not a plant will have a rich, dark green color. Several nutrients change form chemically as the soil pH changes. Iron, for example, is readily available in acid soils, but becomes unavailable chemically in alkaline soils. That is the reason why iron deficiency (chlorosis) is most obvious in alkaline soils of the western two-thirds of Texas.

How to Alter pH

To lower pH (make soil less alkaline):
  • Incorporate generous amounts of organic matter (peat moss, rotted compost or shredded bark, for instance) before planting.
  • Add sulfur-based soil acidifier. Your nurseryman will offer several varieties. Some will contain supplemental iron as well. Product directions will tell you how much to add to obtain desired results.
  • Use acid-form fertilizers such as ammonium sulfate whenever practical.

To raise pH (make soil less acid):
  • Incorporate finely ground limestone into soil. Add 50 to 75 pounds per 1,000 square feet for a pH increase of 1.0. For a pH increase of 2.0 double the amount of ground limestone.

RULE OF GREEN THUMB: Always use a soil test when altering pH. Over-correcting an acidity or alkalinity problem can be more damaging than the original problem.

Beware of the pH of the water you're using to irrigate. In many parts of Texas, water from municipal systems is even more alkaline than the local soils. Also, know if the water is contaminated with soluble salts, particularly sodium. For some of your plants, using rainwater may be necessary, to let you bypass these problems. Otherwise you'll simply have to water carefully, flushing and leaching the soil periodically by watering heavily. Contact your municipal water office for particulars of pH and soluble salts for your locale.

MOST COMMON QUESTION

"How can I improve my soil?"

Organic matter (peat moss, shredded bark, compost, etc.) isn't a cure-all, but it comes very close.
   Consider these advantages:
   • *Loosens tight clays.*
   • *Improves air circulation in clays, so they warm up faster in spring.*
   • *Increases water penetration by reducing run-off and erosion.*
   • *Makes soil less alkaline.*
   • *Helps sandy soils retain moisture and nutrients.*
   • *Improves friability of soil.*

Organic Matter and Its Role in Gardening

Organic matter is derived from things that were once living. Tree, shrub and grass leaves, decaying roots, micro-organisms, peat moss, compost, manure, shredded bark, straw . . . they're all organic matter.

Which type is best?

Organic matter improves the soil as it decays, so choose yours carefully. You're best off with a moderately active material such as well-rotted compost, shredded bark or brown Canadian peat moss.

Avoid types that decay too rapidly, since they can result in nitrogen deficiencies. Prime among these are fresh manures, corn cobs, pecan hulls, fresh grass clippings and fresh sawdust.

Stay away from the inactive organic materials, too. Domestic black muck peat moss from the northern United States (the type sold by weight, in bags), for example, has finished most of its decomposition. It offers little in soil improvement.

A Word of Caution: Beware of quack products.

There are no shortcuts to garden soil improvements. Yet every year here in Texas, tens of thousands of dollars are spent on miracle cures . . . products purported to improve the ground used for gardening.

Be suspicious of any bold claims made about a product. Look for verification from recognized testing facilities, especially major universities.

Texas is over-run with these useless products. Until we enact far more restrictive laws on what may and may not be claimed, we must put the quacks out of business by neglecting their products.

Fertility and How to Check It

How well your plants grow and develop depends largely on the fertility of the soil you provide for them. Generally, the darker the soil the more fertile it is.

Even that is variable, though. Only by testing can you determine your soil's fertility. Test through your local County Extension Service office, by a nurseryman or testing lab, or by using one of the do-it-yourself kits.

Things you'll want to have tested
• Nutrient content, including nitrogen, phosphorus and potassium.
• Organic matter content.
• Soluble mineral salts.
• pH (acidity or alkalinity).

What to do
• Sample representative areas. Take small portions from various parts of your landscape or garden, to make up one overall sample. That will minimize the chance of a biased sample from an atypical spot. Do at least one sample for your lawn and one for your flower and vegetable gardens, since their fertilizer needs will be different.

• Interpret your results accurately. Adapt them to the plants you'll be growing. Use your soil test as an aid in meeting the specific needs of the plants you'll be growing.

• If you're making changes in your soil's characteristics, monitor those changes with subsequent tests on six to eight month intervals. Otherwise, retesting will only be needed every couple of years.

Preparing Soil for Flowers and Vegetables

Good soil preparation is the first major key to success in any gardening effort. That's especially true when you're planting flowers, vegetables and ground covers . . . small plants that could easily be crowded and killed by weeds and other soil-borne problems.

Start by removing all the existing vegetation in the new bed area, either with a hoe or a square-bladed shovel. Be especially careful to remove bermuda grass runners and all nutgrass plants and roots. Next, rototill the area to a depth of eight to 12 inches. Go over it several times until all the soil particles are golf-ball sized or smaller. As rocks, roots and other debris surface, remove them.

The first time you prepare the soil, add organic matter such as peat moss, compost or shredded bark soil conditioner in a three to four-inch layer. If you rework the soil annually, add one to two inches of organic matter each year. For clay soils, add a one to two-inch layer of washed brick sand. Rototill all of this together, again to eight to 12-inches below the original soil grade.

Rake the area to establish the final grade, then fumigate to eliminate soil-borne insects, diseases, weeds and nematodes. Use a material such as vapam with a short residual effect (three weeks). Read and follow label directions for the best results, and you'll have a garden area fit to be tried!

Step 1: Remove existing turf and weeds.

Step 2: Rototill.

Step 3: Add organic matter and sand.
(Add organic matter alone
if you're working with sandy soil.)

Step 4: Rototill again.

Step 5: Rake smooth.

Step 6: Fumigate to
eliminate soil-borne pests.

Changing the Grade of Your Soil: Do It Right!

Thousands of landscape trees are killed every year by careless grade changing. Surprisingly, raising the level of soil around a tree can do even more damage to an established tree than lowering the grade. This is because the new soil compacts, providing the roots with less and less oxygen. The root system gradually dies and the tree declines over a period of six months to five years.

Consider all of the alternatives before making a substantial grade change. If you have to make a grade change, evaluate each of the trees that might be affected. Determine the practicality of trying to save a particular tree by considering the following:

1. How many other trees would remain to fill in the void?

2. What type of tree is involved? (Some trees are more valuable than others.)

3. What is the health and vigor of the tree?

TEXAS TIP

Trees are too valuable in Texas to waste. If there's any way to save a tree from the path of construction grade changes, make the effort!

Steps to Raise Grade

1. Install a tile drain system using four-inch agricultural clay tile or a four-inch perforated plastic pipe. Install six lines radiating from tree trunk like spokes, sloping gradually away from trunk.

2. Encircle these six lines with additional tile laid under tree's drip line. Provide drainage from a low spot in the line to a storm sewer or a drainage ditch.

3. Install vertical pipes to surface to permit good air circulation. Hold in place with coarse gravel.

4. Construct a well around the tree trunk (two to six feet from the trunk) using either brick or ledgestone. Slope sides of well gently outward, away from the tree trunk.

5. The top of the retaining wall should be even with the desired final grade. Cover the opening with wood decking or metal grating.

6. Begin filling with coarse gravel (six to 10 inches), then medium and fine gravel, and finally a sandy loam soil.

7. Fill vertical tiles with coarse gravel and cover with wire mesh to keep small animals out.

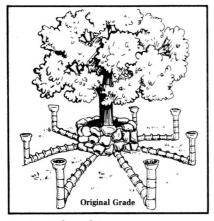

See steps 1 through 5

See steps 6 and 7

Steps to Lower Grade

In many respects, lowering a tree's soil grade is like transplanting it ... you cut away valuable roots. Not surprisingly, the remedies are about the same. You must thin the tree (not "top" it!) to compensate for the roots that were removed. You should apply a high-phosphorous, root-stimulating fertilizer (avoid high-nitrogen fertilizers for one to two years). You should water it frequently and deeply during hot weather, and you should avoid additional grading, trenching and other root-damaging construction.

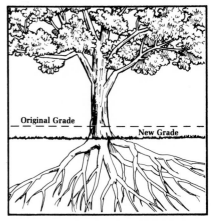

Large surface roots to be removed shaded in black.

Tree should be thinned to compensate for major roots lost during grade lowering.

FERTILIZER FACTS

No discussion of soils would be complete without an explanation of fertilizers. They're the "vitamin pills" of the soil . . . the source of extra pep for your plants. Few soils in Texas provide all the necessary nutrients. We gardeners, then, have to supplement those soils. We must provide the missing or deficient nutrients. For that we turn to fertilizers.

Fertilizers come in many forms. Some are liquids, others are granular. Some are organic (such as bone meal or manure), and others are inorganic, having been manufactured.

You must learn to read product labels carefully to choose the best fertilizer for your plants. In the state of Texas every product sold as a fertilizer must include a list of contents. Everything you will need to consider in choosing a fertilizer is listed on the product label. Get in the habit of reading labels before you buy and apply fertilizers.

Here's what you'll find on the label

Brand: Identifies manufacturer; may also indicate use of product.

Analysis: Tells the nutritional content of the product. Expressed as percentages. For example, 12 percent nitrogen (N), is used by plants to produce leaves, stems.

Four percent phosphorus (P), is used by plants to produce roots, flowers and fruit.

Eight percent potassium (K), is used by plants in developing heat and cold hardiness.

Contents: Product may or may not contain various trace elements, including iron (Fe), sulphur (S), zinc (Zn) and others.

Product may or may not contain insecticide.

Product may or may not contain herbicide (weed killer).

Inert Ingredients: Inert (inactive) ingredients include fillers and carriers . . . materials added to facilitate application.

Precautions: Product label may list special precautions you should take during application. Read and follow these directions for best and safest results.

Weight: Weight of product, including nutrients, additives and carriers.

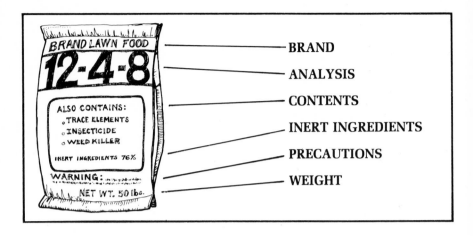

MOST COMMON QUESTION

"Which is better for my plants, an organic fertilizer or an inorganic one?"

Good question, with a tricky answer. Plants take nutrients into their roots as elements in a water solution. Plants have no way of differentiating between elements that came from manure and those which came from a fertilizer bag. To the plant, it's just nitrogen, phosphorus, or potassium. Add to that the fact that organic fertilizer sources such as manure contain very small amounts of nutrients (generally less than eight percent of the total product weight). That makes them relatively expensive compared to inorganic fertilizer.

However, organic fertilizers offer one distinct advantage over inorganic ones. Organic fertilizers improve soil. Much like peat moss and compost, organic fertilizers loosen tight clays and help sandy soils hold moisture and nutrients.

The answer? Why not use some of both? Organic fertilizers for their soil building and their long-term nutrient release, and the bagged, inorganic fertilizers to keep your plants happy on a day-to-day basis.

Ways Fertilizers Are Sold

Fertilizers are offered in a variety of ways, for a variety of applications. Each offers its own advantages and special uses. An almost endless selection of analyses is available, which means there is a fertilizer type for most any plant that you're growing.

BAG
Least expensive. Easy to distribute evenly over large area such as lawn. Depending on nutrient sources, can provide quick or timed release. Available with special additives (insecticides, weed killers and others).

WATER SOLUBLE
AND LIQUID
Quickly available for use by plants, since highly soluble. Good for container plants.

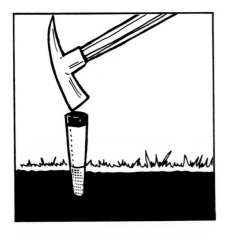

SPIKES

Allow placement of fertilizer in specific locations around trees and large shrubs.

CARTRIDGES

Allow saturation of soil with a fertilizer solution. Especially good on slopes where surface watering would run off. Do not insert too deeply ... eight to 12 inches is generally adequate.

ENCAPSULATED

Time-release fertilizers. Good for flowers and vegetables. Most commonly used with container plants. May release nutrients too rapidly in extreme heat.

How to Recognize and Treat Iron Deficiency

Tens of thousands of dollars are misspent annually by Texas gardeners in their attempt to control iron deficiency. Make sure you don't misdiagnose a shortage of iron in your plants . . .

MOST COMMON QUESTION

"How can I recognize iron deficiency?"

Look for two symptoms. Both should be present if your plant is truly iron deficient:

1. Yellow leaves with dark green veins. This contrast of color gives leaves a striped or netted appearance. Veins may eventually turn yellow, too. Leaves may even fade to white, then become brown and crisp.

2. Deficiency symptoms are most visible on newest growth . . . near the tips of twigs. Older leaves will retain darker green color.

Prime candidates for iron deficiency: azaleas, camellias, gardenias, hollies, slash and loblolly pines, dogwoods, wisteria, silver maple and Chinese tallow.

Iron deficiency is one of the most common nutrient shortages in Texas, especially in the alkaline soils of the western two-thirds of the state. There, iron chemically changes into a form the plants cannot take in through their roots.

That means that we can treat iron deficiency in three ways. For best results, use each method several times during each growing season.

1. Apply a soil acidifier such as sulfur, to allow iron already in the soil to return to an "available" form.

2. Apply a chelated (treatment to maintain solubility) iron material, or copperas (iron sulfate) to the soil.

3. Apply foliar spray of an iron compound. By bypassing the root zone, you'll get quick results. This must be done during periods of active growth, and it will have shorter residual action than the soil applications.

KEEP ALL IRON PRODUCTS OFF MASONRY AND PAINTED SURFACES . . . THEY CAN STAIN!

And . . . just for the record . . . nails driven into tree trunks and iron fillings used to correct iron deficiency will not work. Again, it's the wrong form of iron.

Iron deficiency shows yellowed leaves with dark green veins on newest growth first.

WHERE CAN I GET RELIABLE NURSERY HELP?

Looking for a source of good nursery advice? Work with a pro ... someone who really knows plants. Look for a reputable nurseryman near you. One of the best ways is to look for a member of the Texas Association of Nurserymen.

TAN is a strong and active trade organization which continues to upgrade the Texas nursery industry. Through its members' efforts, TAN has become one of the best educated and most progressive groups of nurserymen in America.

A recent development from TAN has been the Texas Certified Nurseryman training program. Both nursery owners and employees certified under the program have passed a very comprehensive exam on all aspects of horticulture. Those who succeed are awarded designation as a "Texas Certified Nurseryman." You know that their advice will be timely and reliable.

Shop where you see the signs of the Texas Association of Nurserymen and the Texas Certified Nurseryman program.

WAYS PLANTS ARE SOLD

There are only three ways that plants are sold in nurseries: (1) bare-rooted, which come in bags or paper boxes, (2) balled-and-burlapped, and (3) in containers. Each has its own advantages and disadvantages.

Always try to buy your plants in containers. If they're not available that way, try to get balled-and-burlapped. Use bare-rooted plants as the last possibility. The following chart tells why:

How Plants Are Sold

Bare-rooted

Balled-and-burlapped

Container-grown

Advantages	Disadvantages
Least expensive since labor and transportation costs are reduced. Main way of buying fruit and pecan trees, roses and spring-flowering shrubs.	Greatest setback following transplanting, since most small feeder roots are left behind. Limited to dormant season months.
Most common way of buying large shrubs and trees. If done properly, good chance of success. Good way of relocating plants already in your landscape. If plants have been properly held, can be planted almost year-round.	Larger plants may show signs of transplant shock for one to two years as they establish a new root system. Watch for "packaged" balls having soil balls formed around bare-rooted plants . . . this is not a desirable way of selling balled-and-burlapped plants.
All roots remain intact, so plant hardly knows it's been transplanted. Can be planted year-round, as long as you can work soil. Widest selection of plant material, since most nursery stock is sold this way.	Size of plant materials is limited to small and medium-sized trees and shrubs, though more and more nurseries now offer specimen-sized material.

TEXAS TIP

Plants are a lot like people. The younger they are, the better they transplant. That's especially true with balled-and-burlapped and bare-rooted plants where root systems are disturbed. It's particularly important in Texas, where hot, dry summer weather puts newly transplanted trees and shrubs under special strains. For balled-and-burlapped plants medium-sized plants are probably your best buy (six to 10-foot trees and three to four-foot shrubs), unless you have specific need of something larger (to match other existing plants, to landscape a large home or building). Small plants (one to three feet) are best for bare-rooted plantings.

MULCHES . . . NATURE'S SECURITY BLANKET

What on earth is a mulch? Basically, just that . . . a covering of the soil. Mulches come in two general types:

1. *Organic:* compost, bark, corn cobs, leaves, straw and others.

2. *Inorganic:* gravel, black polyethylene plastic and others.

Reasons for mulching:

• Minimize soil temperature fluctuations during hot and cold weather.

• Improve water penetration, reduce run-off and erosion.

• Reduce soil compaction from pounding rains.

• Reduce soil lost to wind erosion.

• Reduce weed problems.

• Improve the quality of fresh produce, such as strawberries and tomatoes, by keeping them off the ground.

To be effective, most mulches should be applied two to four inches thick. Black plastic film is the obvious exception. Its use should be restricted to areas with excellent drainage, since it inhibits evaporation of water from the soil. If you do decide to try it, overlap its seams by four to six inches to keep weeds from growing up through them. Black plastic film soaks up the sun's rays in the spring . . . an advantage. But that plus turns to a minus during the heat of the summer. In summer, cover plastic with some other type of mulch such as bark.

Looking for a cheap and easy temporary mulch, perhaps for the vegetable garden? Old newspapers work well. Apply them eight to 10 sheets deep and hold them in place with small amounts of soil or stones. The paper will gradually decay as the garden plants get big enough to stand on their own.

TEN STEPS TO TRANSPLANTING SUCCESS

Once the soil is prepared you're ready for planting. Of course, as you'll see in the chapters that follow, you should always have a plan for your plantings . . . some idea of what should go where. Let's assume for the moment that you've already done that. Let's take a walk, step-by-step, through the techniques of successful transplanting. Given are the tips for tree and shrub planting. Modify them ever so slightly and they'll fit any plant that you're using.

1. Know your plant's mature size and shape, its light requirements and any peculiar soil needs it might have. Be sure you've selected an appropriate location.

2. Dig the hole twice as wide as necessary, but no deeper than required.

3. Set the plant at the same height at which it grew in the nursery. Remove it from its metal or plastic container. Some fiber pots are manufactured to disintegrate in the soil. If you're in doubt, ask your nurseryman. If the plant is balled-and-burlapped, do not try to remove the burlap entirely. Lay it away from the soil ball once the plant has been set in the hole. If the plant's roots are bare, fill around them with soil, holding the plant at the same level at which it grew in the nursery.

4. Use a back-fill soil mix of one-half peat moss and one-half top soil that was taken out of the hole. Pack lightly as you fill.

5. When the hole is half full, water slowly. Allow excess water to drain away. Finish filling the hole with the soil-peat mix and water again. Make a shallow basin of soil (berm) to retain the water, unless you live in an area with poor drainage and high water tables. Remove the berm after the first year.

6. Apply a high-phosphorus, root-stimulating fertilizer to bare-rooted and balled-and-burlapped plants. Give container-grown plants half-strength applications of complete and balanced fertilizer.

7. Prune to the desired shape. Pruning also compensates for roots lost during the digging. Prune 40 to 60 percent for bare-rooted plants, 25 to 35 percent for balled-and-burlapped plants and as needed to shape container-grown plants.

8. Wrap the trunk to prevent sunscald and to retard borer invasion.

9. Stake and guy large plants to keep them vertical. Be sure at least one stake is on the side of the prevailing summer breezes for your area. Protect trunks and limbs with heavy cloth or by running the guy wires through a piece of old hose.

10. Post-planting care: Check soil moisture frequently. Water regularly during warm weather and any prolonged drought.

(See next page illustrating these steps.)

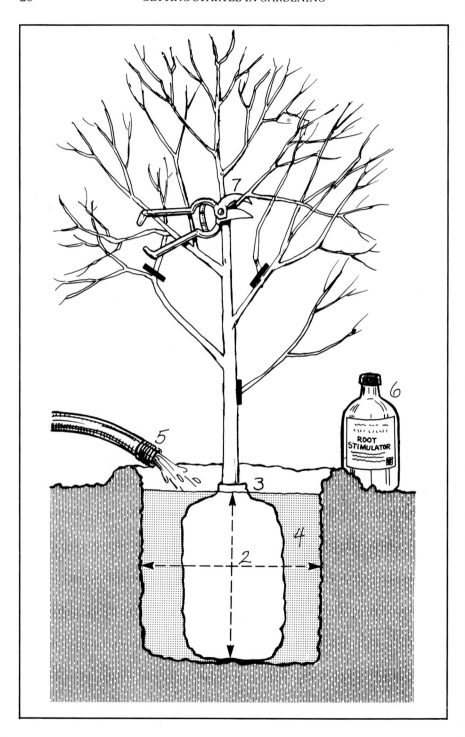

Root Pruning Pays

If you're planning on moving either native plants or established land-scape plants, better root-prune them four to 12 months in advance. Root-pruning allows the plant to develop a tighter, more compact root system. That helps hold the soil ball together, which increases chances of survival.

Native or established landscape plant has wide-reaching roots. Getting soil ball to hold together during digging could be difficult because of number of roots severed.

Several months prior to digging, use sharpshooter spade to cut through major lateral roots at a point six to 12 inches inside eventual transplanting cut. Do not cut tap root.

Numerous new roots will form where cuts are made, making transplanting much easier. Soil ball is more likely to hold together. Plant has more roots at time it's transplanted, for better chance of survival.

WATERING: YOUR MOST IMPORTANT GARDENING RESPONSIBILITY

Water is as important to plants as it is to us humans. It helps plants hold their leaves erect, to soak up the sun's rays. Water carries fertilizers into the root systems . . . all nutrients are absorbed in liquid solution. Manufactured foods are carried from the leaves to other plant parts in a water solution, too. Water even cools plants during the summer.

Water Comes in Two Forms . . .

1. *Soil-borne* water is taken in by plants' roots. Obviously, the better and deeper the soil is, the more water it can hold for eventual use by the plants. Sandy and shallow soils will require more frequent watering than deep clays. Mulches can help conserve soil-borne moisture.

2. *Air-borne* moisture is better known as humidity. Most plants are rather tolerant of fluctuations in humidity. Plants from arid areas may be more susceptible to leaf diseases when grown in humid regions. Conversely, plants from more humid beginnings may scorch and burn in drier environments. Generally, however, plants will adapt quite well to changes in humidity.

How to Know When to Water Your Plants

Learn to "read" your plants. They'll tell you when they're dry. Check them daily, and water as needed. Look for any or all of the following symptoms:

Wilting: This is the most obvious symptom, but it can also be evidence that the plant has been kept consistently too wet. Wilting merely indicates root damage. Always feel the soil to make sure it's not already too wet. If the plant is wilted and the soil is dry, water. If it's still wet, let it dry out before watering again.

Folding or cupping: Many plants merely fold up their leaves when they're dry. Lawn grasses are excellent examples. Their leaves either fold like a book or roll like a newspaper.

Subtle color changes: Some plants never wilt, fold or curl when dry. Their leaves simply lose their rich green coloration. Hollies are excellent examples. Their foliage, when dry, turns a dull, metallic green color.

Point to Remember: In the winter, when many of your plants are bare and your lawn may even be brown, it's tough to tell if they're dry or not. Just remember that roots keep growing all winter long, and if their soil dries out, the plant can suffer measurably. It's best to water at least every couple of weeks in the winter if you've not been blessed with rain. But to prevent damage to plumbing and equipment, don't leave your hoses and sprinklers out in freezing weather.

MOST COMMON QUESTION

"How often should I water my plants?"

There's no good answer to that. You don't take a drink by the clock . . . You drink when you're thirsty. It's the same with your plants. Too many variables can enter the picture: temperature, light, wind, rain and humidity.

Water your plants when they're dry, not before. Learn to recognize drought symptoms. Don't put any plant on a time schedule!

All Water Isn't Good Water

Soluble Salts: As essential as water is to good plant growth, not all water is good water. Some waters are overloaded with minerals, called "soluble salts." With prolonged use, these waters can actually cause burned roots and subsequent leaf scorching and die-back. The solution is to water deeply whenever you water, so the mineral salts will be dissolved and leached out of the root zone. If that fails, consider using rainwater for watering your more important plants.

Alkalinity: Water can also be extremely alkaline. This is why some gardeners in the western two-thirds of Texas go to great pains to grow acid-loving plants like azaleas, dogwoods, hollies and wisterias, only to see them yellow and die. Even though acid soil mixes have been prepared, alkaline municipal water used repeatedly overrides the gardener's good intentions.

TEXAS TIP
Fight back with a soil-acidifying material (generally sulfur-based) that can neutralize the water's alkalinity.

Why You Should Water Deeply

Deep watering encourages deep rooting. Shallow watering invites drought damage. Soak the soil thoroughly when you water, then allow it to dry slightly before watering again. Your plants' root systems will grow downward in search of the moist soil.

Do:

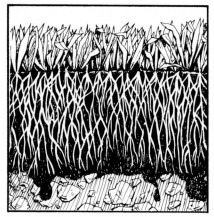

Plants watered less often, but more heavily develop deeper root systems. They become better able to withstand hot, dry weather.

Don't:

Frequent light waterings encourage shallow, fibrous root systems that are easily damaged by even short droughts.

Choose Your Watering Tools Carefully

Good watering equipment is one of your most important investments. Remember the requirements: whichever equipment you use must distribute water uniformly and efficiently, with a minimum of run-off and evaporation. What follows is a list of tools and their practical uses:

1. Automatic sprinkler systems offer all combinations of patterns and spray heads. Properly installed and maintained, they can provide regular, uniform watering.

2. Hose comes in three common sizes: ½-inch, ⅝-inch, and ¾-inch diameters. Larger sizes deliver water much faster, however, ¾-inch hose is heavy and hard to move. Good quality ⅝-inch hose is probably the best buy.

3. Water timers shut off water flow after a predetermined amount of water has been delivered. Especially helpful if you want to start water, then go to bed or leave for work.

4. Water breakers work like a shower head to send water in a fan or cone-like pattern. Since water flow is deflected, breakers allow you to water at full or nearly full volume without washing the soil.

5. Water bubblers slow water flow even more. They turn a full volume flow into a babbling brook. They are useful in watering new plants, container gardens. Note that both breakers and bubblers are attached to long-handled watering wands that let you stand out of the way of the overflow.

6. Drip irrigation equipment is the most efficient way of watering. Special fittings, called "emitters," drip slowly (as little as one-half to two gallons per emitter per hour), super-saturating the soil around them. Plant roots grow toward the moist soil. There is little evaporation and no run-off. They are good for shrubs, flowers, vegetables, orchards and patio plants.

7. Soaker hoses, generally made of canvas or porous rubber, allow water to drip through side walls along entire hose length.

8. Oscillating sprinklers allow soft, gentle watering over square or rectangular areas. They give good coverage to standard urban lots, which are generally rectangular. They are not good in windy areas and cannot water small areas in a hurry. Increasing the volume of flow merely increases area covered. They clog easily.

9. Circular sprinklers can be adjusted to cover any size area at any rate of flow. Droplets are relatively large, so wind is generally not a major problem. Their pattern is circular (pulsating types can be adjusted for semi-circles), which makes it difficult to get uniform coverage in square corners.

10. Travelling sprinklers move along garden hose that has been laid in a specific pattern. Most types are relatively expensive and are best used in large lawn areas.

11. Sprinkler hoses put water out in a fine mist covering long, narrow areas. Especially useful along driveways, in alleyways and between front walks and the street. Can also be inverted and used as a soaker hose, particularly if wind is causing uneven coverage.

(See pages 34 and 35 for photographs of these tools.)

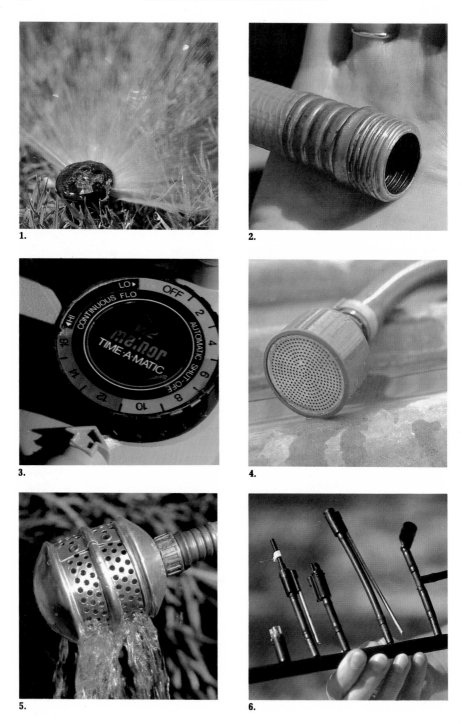

1.

2.

3.

4.

5.

6.

7.

8.

9.

10.

11.

MOST COMMON QUESTION

"What time of day should I water?"

Water when your plants are dry . . . morning, afternoon or night. Daytime watering may result in more loss to evaporation, but waiting until night to water may result in plant damage. Evening watering may promote turf disease problems, but that's mainly on St. Augustine, and primarily in the fall. Mildew on flowers and shrubs may be encouraged by evening watering. It bears repeating: if the plant is dry, water it . . . no matter what time of day or night!

PRUNE YOUR PLANTS WISELY

Discipline is important for any young, growing thing, whether it's a child, a puppy or a plant. You have to train them all, so they'll develop to your best expectations.

In the case of your plants, that discipline comes in the form of pruning. You guide the plant . . . You train it to conform to the shape and appearance you desire.

Pruning is a year-long responsibility that starts the moment you plant your first plant. For that reason, the topic belongs in any discussion of gardening basics.

Two Points to Remember: First, it's always best to avoid pruning as much as possible. Choose plants whose mature size and form meets your needs without formal shaping and shearing. There's no point in using an eight-foot shrub under a four-foot window, then trying to keep it pruned back. Ask a nurseryman to suggest the best plants for your needs . . . ones that will stay in bounds. Second, always prune with a purpose. Know why each cut is being made. Probably half of all the pruning we do is done needlessly or incorrectly.

These are some of the possible reasons for pruning:
- To modify direction of a plant's growth;
- To reduce total height or width of plant;
- To train to specific form or shape;
- To help plant recover from transplant shock;
- To repair storm, insect and disease damage;
- To increase quality or quantity of flower, fruit production;
- To improve visibility, making entryways and street intersections safer.

When to Prune Everything

Type of Plant	Best Time to Prune	Acceptable Time to Prune	Seasons to Avoid Pruning
Shade trees	mid-winter dormant season	all other seasons	
Evergreen shrubs	mid-winter dormant season	all other seasons	
Spring-flowering shrubs and vines	spring, following flowering	summer	fall, winter
Crepe myrtles and other summer-flowering shrubs	mid-winter dormant season	lightly in summer, to remove spent blooms	
Hedge plantings	severe pruning: late winter	prune to shape: all seasons	
Ground covers	late winter	all other seasons	
Fruit and nut trees	mid-winter dormant season	only as needed to repair damage other seasons	
Grapes	mid-winter dormant season		
Blackberries, dewberries, etc.	immediately after harvest		winter, spring
Roses (bush)	late winter, just before growth starts in spring	lightly during growing season to remove spent blooms	late fall, early winter
Roses (climbing)	immediately after spring bloom	lightly during growing season to keep in bounds	winter
Chrysanthemums	pinch monthly to keep compact, March through early August		after mid-August

What Happens When You Prune

Terminal buds . . . those buds at the ends of twigs and branches . . . produce a growth hormone (auxin) that directs most of the growth to occur at
the tips. Side shoots are reluctant to develop as long as the terminal bud is
in place. Pruning suddenly frees the side shoots from their growth inhibitor,
allowing them to grow. Generally the bud nearest the cut is the one that
develops most rapidly. Therefore, by choosing the position of your cut
carefully, you can direct the future growth of the plant just as you want it.
Here's what the different cuts look like:

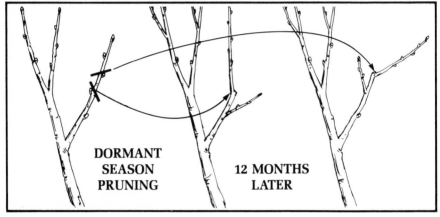

**DORMANT
SEASON
PRUNING**

**12 MONTHS
LATER**

In many plants, buds lay dormant along stem as long as terminal bud is actively
growing. Remove tip growth and bud closest to cut will usually develop. Choose bud
according to desired direction of growth.

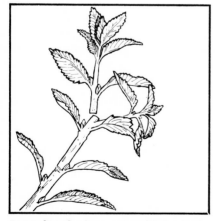

Prune directly above outward facing bud
to encourage more horizontal growth.

Prune directly above inward facing bud to
encourage more vertical growth.

Helpful Hints for Pruning:

We stated earlier that half of the pruning we Texans do is probably done incorrectly. Outlined below are some of the prime problem areas, and ways to avoid them.

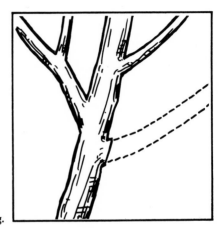

Close pruning promotes quick healing.

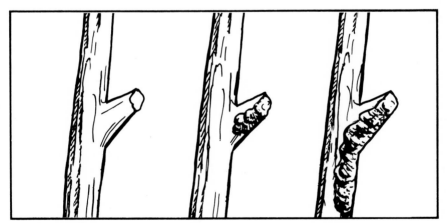

Don't leave stubs.

BEST   ACCEPTABLE   NOT ACCEPTABLE

Shaping a hedge . . .

Don't top that tree!

If you must prune a limb, prune flush with a remaining limb.

Pruning Tools: Choose the Right Tool for the Job

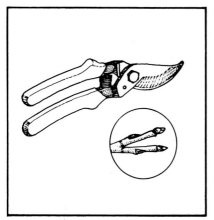

Hand shears. (Twigs less than one-half inch in diameter).

Lopping Shears. (Branches one-half to one inch in diameter).

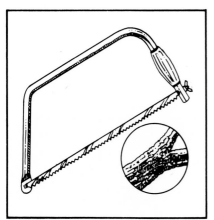

Pruning Saws. (Limbs over one inch in diameter).

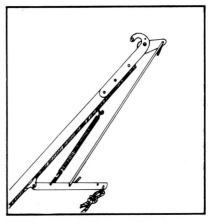

Pole Pruner. (Aluminum and wood models, extend to 14 to 24 feet. Do not use near power lines).

Chain Saw. (Electric models for light pruning, gasoline models for more rugged, remote jobs).

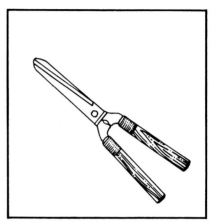

Hedge Shears. (For formal pruning and shaping).

Electric Hedge Shears. (Use care when using near wet plants and soil).

Seal all cuts over one-inch in diameter with black pruning paint.

Growing Espaliers

Espaliers are plants trained to grow flat against a fence or wall. They're particularly valuable to the cramped urban landscaper with little horizontal space to utilize.

Many types of plants are suitable for espaliering, including fruit trees, pyracantha, elaeagnus, hollies, junipers, magnolias, camellias, cotoneasters and ligustrums.

Know from the outset what pattern your espalier will take. Lay it out on the wall. Secure it with masonry nails and wires in brick walls. Espaliers against wood siding should be trained on hinged trellises that can be lowered when house painting time comes around.

Nurseries offer staked espaliers for instant landscaping. You can also grow your own, but be sure the pattern fills from the bottom up. Complete the lowest level before progressing upward.

Espaliers are fat plants gone flat! Shrubs and trees trained two-dimensionally against fences and walls. They take on many patterns and forms.

Chapter 2

Planning
Your Landscape

*And on the first day (in the new house) he created a landscape. And that
landscape grew and flourished and added to his love of his world and to
the value of his home.*

God gave us the plants. Spectacular plants! But what we do with the
plants is up to us. They're the tools of our trade. They're merely the building
blocks. It's the design that ties it all together.

Landscape design is the greatest part of gardening. It's a chance to show
your personality . . . to choose plants that please you. It's the chance to meet
your family's needs. It's the chance to combine plants and art forms, to mix
and to match. But most importantly, it's a chance to leave something behind
you besides footprints. Something functional and beautiful . . . a spot of
betterment. For you, your family and for all who pass by, take that chance!
Design for a better lifestyle.

The following pages will help plant seeds of ideas . . . and give you
landscaping principles, shortcuts and suggestions. You'll find basic
guidelines about plants and how to use them in landscaping, while later
chapters will include specific plant information. Check through them. I
think you'll find some profitable pointers.

WHO DOES THE PLANNING?

Good landscapes are great investments of time, effort and money. They're functional, they're beautiful and they're worth their weight in gold dust aucuba when it comes time to resell your house. In two words, landscaping pays!

The question inevitably arises though, "Shall I plan it myself, or shall I hire a pro?" Where do you turn for landscaping advice?

Do-it-yourself

To do your own landscape planning you need two things: (1) a feeling for good design principles . . . what looks good together, and (2) a knowledge of the various plants and what they can offer.

If you're confident of your ability in those two areas, try it yourself.

Or Work With . . .

Nurserymen

No one knows plant materials better than reputable retail nurserymen. They deal with them daily. Many are also skilled in design practices. If you choose this route, take measurements, drawing and photos in with you. Go during the week, when they'll have more time to spend with you. Ask about charges . . . many nurseries offer reduced fees for plans if you buy your plants from them.

Landscape Architects

They are the full-time professional planners of fine landscapes. Their fees aren't as great as you might expect, and their artistic talents can turn a lovely landscape into a showplace. They've been trained in the best design principles, and they know their plants well. Ask for references and examples of their work, then go take a look. You'll likely be excited by what they can offer.

When You're Doing It Yourself

You don't have to be a skilled artist to do your own landscape plan, but you do have to be thorough and patient. You must evaluate the site and your needs, then plot it all carefully. Follow these few simple steps:

1) Use graph paper and draw your plan to scale.

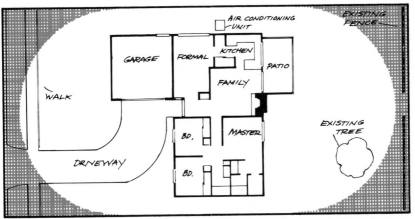

2) Measure the landscape's dimensions carefully. Make note of the locations of all permanent features (such as walks, drive, patio, windows, entries and utilities). Plot these on the plan.

3) Make a list of the prime objectives you have in landscaping . . . the things you want it to accomplish.

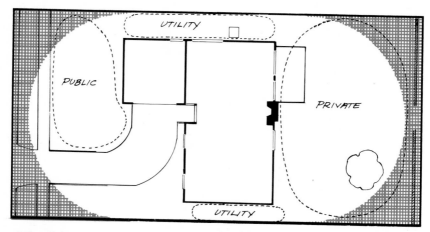

4) Plot all three parts of the landscape (public, private and service) in a rough plan of your grounds.

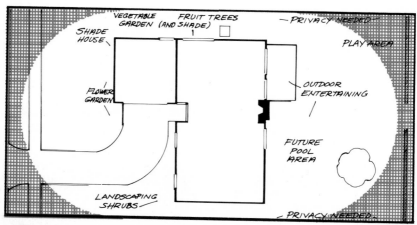

5) Mark each of your goals into the appropriate area.

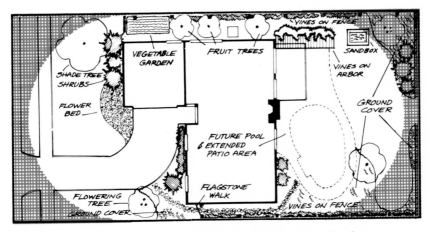

In the plan: VINES ON FENCE, VEGETABLE GARDEN, FRUIT TREES, SANDBOX, SHADE TREE SHRUBS, VINES ON ARBOR, FLOWER BED, GROUND COVER, FUTURE POOL & EXTENDED PATIO AREA, FLAGSTONE WALK, FLOWERING TREE, GROUND COVER, VINES ON FENCE

6) Using those goals and the precise measurements, fill in the plants. Use them to accomplish all of your goals. Know their mature sizes, and growth forms, and draw them to scale.

THE PARTS OF A LANDSCAPE

Almost all residential landscapes consist of three parts: the public portion (front yard), the private portion (back yard) and the work, or service area. Each of these fills a specific need. Plan them into your plantings.

Establish the locations and boundaries of the three parts of your landscape before you ever start planting.

1) The public area is what the general public sees when they pass by your home;

2) The service area acts as a utility space. It's where the garden, compost pile, clothesline, trash cans and storage building are. Hopefully, it's screened from public and private areas; and

3) The private area is everything else: back yard, side yards, obscured entries . . . landscaped space that's reserved for your family and friends.

RULE OF GREEN THUMB: Good landscapes are simple, yet tasteful.

Your landscape is to your house as a frame is to artwork. You wouldn't put a pink and purple frame around a fine piece of art, and you shouldn't put a gaudy landscape around your house. It's tough for a plant professional to admit, but after all the landscape must serve the house. It has to be complementary. Don't let it overwhelm.

Take a look around town. The best-looking landscapes are often some of the simplest.

Space and Scale

Two important features: In many respects, landscapes are like interior decorating. Things must relate, one to another. "Space" is an important feature indoors, and so it is outside. Each of us has a feeling for the space in our landscape. Do we want an enclosed or open feeling? We should let our landscape provide whichever we choose. Instead of walls, we plant shrubs or install fencing. Instead of ceilings, we use arbors, patio roofs and spreading trees.

Since all parts of the landscape must work together, it's important that they be compatible with relation to size. We use the phrase "in scale" in describing the relative sizes of landscaping materials. It's critical that all of our plants and construction materials be sized proportionate with the overall landscape.

PLANT PERSONALITIES IN LANDSCAPING

Just like the people who grew them, plants have distinct personalities. Some ward off attention, while others reach out and grab it. Professional landscape planners use these unique features in shaping a feeling. Consider them all, and you can use them, too.

Size is obviously the foremost concern when you choose plants for the landscape. The plant has to fit. Know its mature dimensions before planting.

Form refers to the plant's shape . . . is it upright or spreading? Is it erect or weeping? Knowing the form will tell you whether the plant will fit its surroundings. Spreading trees dare not be planted against houses, and vertical ones shouldn't go under power lines.

Color is important in many respects ... it provides the sparkle, the accent, the drama of the whole planting. Yet, using color is a bit like walking a tightrope. You have to know when to get off. Use too much or use it wrong and it's garish. You'll find much more on color in the pages that follow.

Texture is the overlooked characteristic, yet it really makes plants stand out. Large-leafed, bold-textured plants demand attention.

Fine-textured plants soften harsh walls. They provide a soothing, calming effect that tones down the entire landscape.

MOST COMMON QUESTION

"How much should I spend on my landscape?"

That may not be a question folks ask of those in the industry . . . but it's certainly a question they ask of themselves. The only problem: there's no good answer. It's a little like asking how much you should spend at the grocery. It depends entirely on what you need and how long you're planning for.

By the time you include a patio (and maybe a patio roof), fencing, extra walkways . . . and the turf, trees and shrubs, your landscape will have run into several thousands of dollars. One new West Texas house comes to memory . . . the landscape cost half again more than the house did!

Let's just say that the money you spend on your landscape should be carefully considered. Don't plant something unless it will improve the overall appearance. But, most importantly, know that dollars you spend landscaping will be returned several times over when it comes time to sell your house and move on. Landscapes are a great investment. Ask any realtor or prospective home buyer!

GOOD LANDSCAPING: STEP-BY-STEP

To build anything worth keeping you have to move one step at a time. And so it is with fine landscapes. There's a logical sequence that you'll want your plants to follow. It's important that you consider the order as you budget your time and funds for your landscape improvements.

1) **Trees** are a top priority. They're the main structural element of the design, and they take the longest to develop. Plant them early in your improvements.

2) **Turf** must go in immediately. Nobody wants to track mud and debris indoors for months. Plant the grass as soon as possible.

3) **Shrubs** also rate high, especially those most visible to the general public. Like trees, shrubs take several years to reach their best appearance. Plant them as soon as possible.

4) **Vines and ground covers** are less obvious, but very important parts of the landscape. Plant them as shrub beds are finalized.

5) **Fruit trees and the vegetable garden** can be planted as your time and space allow. Be sure you have a good idea of your general landscaping layout before you obligate areas to long-term food crop production.

6) **Color** is quick, easy and inexpensive. However, it's also fragile, so you

must complete your shrub and tree plantings before setting out flowers. One nice thing about flowering plants is that, because of their quick growth and good looks, they can make a new landscape appear much more mature within the very first season.

7) **Patio and other recreational additions** can be made as time and money allow. Where they occur in your overall landscape development is negotiable. If you entertain a great deal, your patio improvements may be an immediate need. Likewise for a pool, for new walks or for a greenhouse. Adapt your landscaping sequence to your own family's needs.

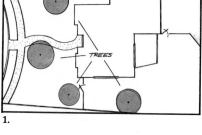

1.

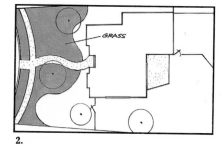

2.

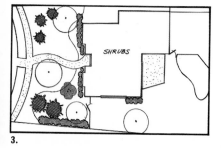

3.

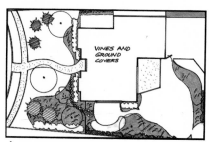

4.

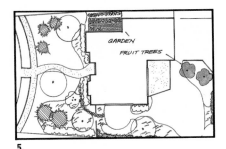

5.

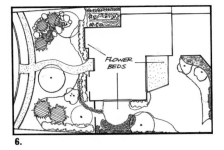

6.

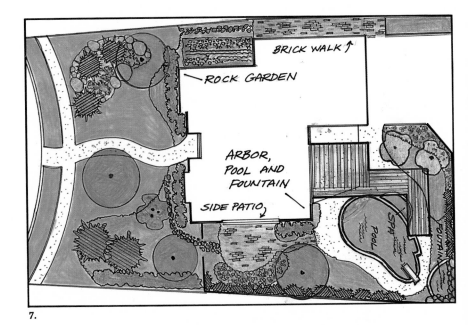

7.

Placing the Trees

Since trees are the largest plants in your landscape, you need to be careful in locating them. Know their mature size and growth form. In most cases it's best not to plant new trees where they will block the view of your house.

Also consider that your landscape is a sort of visual funnel. By planting taller plants to the sides and by tapering down toward the entry you'll guide your visitors' eyes right where you want them . . . toward the focal point of your landscape. Disrupting that visual flow may draw undue attention away from your house. Simply put, let the trees frame your house.

Trees enframe house.   **Trees block view of house.**

TEXAS TIP

Trees are the best living sources of shade. You should plan that into your placement. Get the most out of your trees. It may even mean that you have to violate other rules about planting, but shade is a crucial necessity in Texas landscaping. Plot the sun's summertime direction and plant to intercept it.

Trees can also be used as bold accents. Use their special features (color, growth form and texture) to highlight special parts of your plantings.

Consider a tree-form crepe myrtle in flower near your entry. Or . . .
Outline a curving drive with a row of vertical sweetgums.

MOST COMMON QUESTION

"I'd like to plant a tree on the west side of my house for shade, but it would have to be planted close to the foundation. What's the minimum distance it could be without damaging the foundation?"

You could probably plant within five or six feet, if you were planting a durable, long-lived, deep-rooted tree. Fast growing types like cottonwoods and many elms would simply have too many roots too near the surface. Same goes for plantings near sidewalks and drives.

You really shouldn't plant all that close anyway. Large limbs could end up rubbing your roof or damaging the house's wood trim. It's better to stay back 10 to 15 feet at a minimum. If you have to go closer, consider a fairly vertical type tree.

Entryway Landscaping

Does your house say a happy "Howdy!" or does it bark out "Stay away!"? Your guests' first impressions are formed at your entryway. Like the old saying suggests . . . you never get a second chance to make a good first impression. It's the wise landscape planner who spends extra effort near the front door. It's the next step in landscaping. Here are some simple idea starters . . .

Provide a smooth and direct access from the parking area to the front door. Flare the walk at the doorway to allow ample room for greeting your guests. If a step is required, provide adequate room for opening the door so guests won't be required to step back.

Keep it well-lighted. Not only does good lighting provide a cheerful greeting, but it also is safer, especially if there are steps.

Show color. Use your best flowering plants near your entry, where the greatest number of people can enjoy them. Provide for a full season of color. Use containerized plants to the maximum.

Use fragrances. Scented flowers and herbs provide special emphasis to any part of the landscape. Use them near the entryway where your guests will brush against them.

Vary the textures. Provide highlights where needed by growing bold, large-leafed plants. Soften stark walls with clinging vines, ferns and other fine-textured plants. Avoid thorny shrubs that might catch your visitors' clothes.

Entryway landscaping provides good first impression.

How Many Plant Types to Use ...
Continuity vs. Monotony

It's important that your landscape have some variety. A row of waxleaf ligustrum stretched across the front of your house like a green moustache doesn't offer much variety or interest. On the other hand, you don't want your place to look like some sort of botanic garden.

It's a fine line between variety and confusion. The best solution is to group your plants. Use three, five or more of a given type in a planting. Use another type with another texture and feeling somewhere else in the landscape. It will be a more natural, pleasant landscape to look at.

Provide continuity in your landscape by repeating plant types, but vary them enough to be interesting.

TEXAS TIP

Plant in natural clusters rather than long formal rows . . . what used to be called "foundation planting." You'll still hear reference made to the old style of covering the whole front of the house with shrubs. Check those sources and you'll usually find they're referring to old houses with tall pier-and-beam underpinnings. Modern houses are built differently, and that sort of landscaping isn't needed any more.

Repetitive landscaping lines *not* desirable.

Landscaping Color

Once the trees are all planted and the lawn is green and growing, it's time for the color. In fact, color is the artwork of landscaping. For most gardeners, it's the whole reason for being there . . . for planting plants in the first place. We deal with specific sources of color in our plant chapters (chapters 3 through 9: trees, shrubs, vines, ground covers, lawns, annuals and perennials). For now, let's look more at the concepts of color.

TEXAS TIP

In spite of increased awareness Texas still needs more color. We need to follow the lead of other parts of the country . . . places where color is a way of life. Set your goal to perk up your plantings, and do it today!

Following are some quick and easy tips to help you get more color for your time and effort.

Sources of color: Most folks think first of flowers when planning color into their landscapes. Don't forget the other sources, though. Leaves, fruit and even twigs all provide beautiful colors.

Green is the foundation: The more you depart from plain old basic green, the more dramatic the impact on your landscape will be. Simply put, green is the beginning. All other colors are additional. Remember that as you place your color. Be sure the attention is being drawn where you really want it.

Small plantings adequate: You don't have to have acres of color to make an attractive display. Small pockets of color, strategically placed as shown on top of page 60, can serve just as well . . . with far less effort.

Mass colors for best impact: If you're trying for the best possible show, plant a single color (two at the most) per bed. Landscape architects refer to it as "color massing," and they use it to achieve some fantastic results. Take a look sometime at what others have done. You'll likely agree. Most times a five-foot bed of one color will have more impact than a 50-foot bed of mixed colors.

Warm colors advance, cool colors recede: Bright colors, like yellow, white, orange and red, advance visually in landscapes. Your eye sees them first. Use them when you want impact from a distance. Let them make a large area seem smaller.

Cool colors, like green, purple, blue and dark red, appear more distant. Use them near entries, around the patio . . . somewhere close to the viewer. They'll create a feeling of openness and space.

Plant colors complement one another: Luckily, most plant colors look good together. That doesn't mean that you should purposely plant an artist's palette. It just means that you don't have to worry so much about clashes and conflicts.

Use containerized color: Flowering and fruiting plants grown and shown in containers offer some unique advantages. First, you can provide exactly the soil and the environment the plants need. Because they're portable, you can move them into and out of the sun at will. You can bring them indoors for the winter. You can move them to the most important spot in your landscape while they look good, then relegate them to the "outback" while they're rebuilding for another session of color. You can utilize otherwise unavailable spaces (patios, walks, entryway courtyards).

Container color adds the exclamation point to your plantings. Don't neglect it!

Plan for season-long color: It's no challenge at all to have color in the springtime. Flowering shrubs, trees, vines, annuals and perennials abound then. The *real* challenge is to have color during the heat of the summer and the cold days of winter. Plan for a succession of flowers, fruit and foliage.

Spring

Petunia

Summer

Multi-Colored Sunflower

Fall

Silver Maple

Winter

Possumhaw Holly

A GUIDE TO
COLOR THROUGH THE SEASONS

SPRING
February-May

Annual Flowers: calendula, California poppy, English daisy, pansy, petunia, pinks, snapdragon, sweet alyssum, viola, wallflower
Perennial Flowers: alyssum saxatile, anemone, crocus, daffodil, daisy, grape hyacinth, hyacinth, iris, oxalis, perennial candytuft, phlox, ranunculus, rose, tulip, violet
Vines: Carolina jessamine, climbing rose, honeysuckle, wisteria
Shrubs: azalea, bridal wreath, flowering quince, forsythia, gardenia, Indian hawthorn, viburnum, weigela
Trees: crabapple, dogwood, flowering peach, plum, pear, magnolia, redbud

SUMMER
May-September

Annual Flowers: ageratum, amaranthus, begonia, caladium, celosia, coleus, copper plant, cosmos, dusty miller, dwarf dahlia, flowering tobacco, gaillardia, geranium, gloriosa daisy, impatiens, marigold, moss rose, periwinkle, salvia, sunflower, verbena, zinnia
Perennial Flowers: canna, daylily, gladiolus, hollyhock, lantana, mallow, plumbago, spider lily
Vines: clock vine, cypress vine, Madame Galen trumpet vine, moonvine, morning glory
Shrubs: abelia, althaea, crepe myrtle, oleander, pomegranate
Tree: golden raintree

FALL
October-November

Annual Flowers: candletree, copper plant, Joseph's coat, marigold, zinnia
Perennial Flowers: chrysanthemum, fall crocus, Michaelmas daisy, (aster)
Vine: Boston ivy
Shrub: crepe myrtle
Trees: ashes, Bradford pear, Chinese pistachio, Chinese tallow, ginkgo, maples, red oak, sweetgum

WINTER
December-February

Annual Flowers: flowering cabbage, kale (both have colorful foliage)
Vine: wintercreeper euonymus
Shrubs: camellia, hollies, nandinas, photinia, pyracantha, mahonia

Colorful Leaves

Many trees and shrubs have colorful flowers. Many also have colorful fall foliage. What you see listed below, though, are trees, shrubs and other landscape plants with colorful foliage all through the growing season. Use these as contrasts, to draw attention to focal points in your plantings. The list isn't all inclusive . . . it's merely a beginning. You'll find many other, less common, plants that will also bring interesting variations from basic green. Use them all carefully. Don't let them overwhelm.

Trees	Red	Pink	Yellow	Silver-White	Orange-Bronze	Purple-Plum	Blue-Gray
Acer Japanese maples	X						
Cercis Forest Pansy redbud						X	
Cupressus Arizona cypress							X
Gleditsia Sunburst honeylocust			X				
Juniperus many varieties of juniper						X*	X
Shrubs							
Aucuba Golddust aucuba, others			X				
Elaeagnus variegated elaeagnus			X				X
Euonymus many varieties of euonymus			X	X			
Hydrangea Variegated hydrangea				X			
Juniperus many varieties of juniper						X*	X
Leucophyllum Texas purple sage (ceniza)							X
Ligustrum several varieties			X	X			
Nandina several varieties	X*						
Pittosporum variegated pittosporum				X			

* Color most intense during cold-winter months

	Red	Pink	Yellow	Silver-White	Orange-Bronze	Purple-Plum	Blue-Gray
Vines and Ground Covers							
Euonymus Wintercreeper euonymus						X*	
Juniperus several trailing junipers						X*	
Lonicera Purpleleaf honeysuckle						X*	
Trachaelospermum Variegated Asiatic jasmine				X			
Vinca Variegated vinca				X			
Annuals and Perennials							
Acalypha Copper plant	X		X		X		
Ajuga Variegated ajuga				X			
Alternanthera Joseph's-coat	X		X		X	X	
Begonia Charm begonia			X	X			
Caladium Caladium	X	X		X			
Canna Variegated canna						X	
Coleus Coleus	X	X	X	X		X	
Festuca Blue fescue							X
Liriope Variegated liriope				X			
Pelargonium Variegated geranium			X	X			
Stachys Lamb's ear							X

Landscaping Surfaces

If you've been walking through weeds and wading through mud, just because you thought it took an expert builder to put in new walks, then rejoice! You can add those walkways you've always needed — and add to the patio too. In fact, you can probably do the job yourself in one or two afternoons. Even if you decide to hire a contractor, do get the job done. There's no point in suffering the discomforts of an under-walked landscape.

Plan beforehand to be sure it's done right. Answer these few simple questions . . .

1. Where exactly is the walk needed? (Use direct routing as much as possible, or you'll find folks taking shortcuts.)

2. How wide should it be? (42 to 48 inches minimum for entry walks, 24 to 36 inches for backyard pathways.)

3. Will the walk change drainage patterns, and, if so, what corrections need to be made beforehand?

4. Will steps or ramps be needed? How many and where?

5. What will the surface be? (See later discussion for choices.)

6. What special skills will the installation require, and do you have those skills? (It may be cheaper to employ a pro if you're doing anything beyond your own abilities.)

There are many good walk surfaces. The ones listed below are among the most popular:

Concrete is the number one choice of most contractors, especially for the main entryway sidewalk. It's reasonably attractive and modestly priced. Properly installed it's virtually permanent. If you're handy you can do your own concrete work by setting your own forms and pouring and finishing it yourself. Be sure the final surface is slightly roughened, for better traction when wet.

You might also consider exposed aggregate concrete, where fine gravel is pressed into the surface as the concrete sets. It's later washed clean, leaving a beautifully natural looking walk surface. Unless you're really skilled, though, better leave the exposed aggregate to the folks with the tools and the experience.

As an option, you might want to use pre-poured concrete rounds or squares. Exposed aggregate types are also available in various shapes and sizes. These are all best suited to light traffic walkways . . . to the patio or out by the garage. They can be used either side-by-side or spaced several inches apart. Measure your stride carefully, though, in determining spacing. Place the stones improperly and you'll either do the quick-step or pull a hamstring.

Bricks are also good choices. They're perhaps the most beautiful of all landscaping surfaces and among the most permanent. One precaution: some bricks will absorb enough water that winter's freezing and thawing can cause them to deteriorate, especially in moist walkway conditions. Use hard-fired brick pavers for best durability. Be sure the brick surface won't be slippery when moist.

Bricks should always be placed on a two to three-inch bed of packed sand. They can be secured in mortar, or placed side-by-side with fine dry sand swept in between.

Several patterns are available for laying your bricks. If you're doing the job yourself you'll save many hours of frustration by using a simpler style. Even with the simplest of patterns, though, you'll still need to cut a few bricks to fit the odd spaces. Soak them several hours, then use a carbide masonry blade to cut them.

Flagstone is a natural surface, compatible with rock outcroppings in many parts of Texas. It provides good traction, in fact, to the point of being fairly rough in some instances. Mortaring flagstone is no small challenge, because of the various shapes, thicknesses and irregular surfaces. Be sure it drains well.

Wood Surfaces are most useful in conjunction with wood decks, and over irregular terrain. As with stone, be sure the surface will provide good traction when wet. Use preservative-treated, decay-resistant lumber for best durability. Anchor the wood securely to lessen warping and twisting. Wood rounds are also especially attractive in walkways.

Gravel is the overlooked surface. If you have small areas of infrequent traffic, fine washed gravel can be an ideal surface covering. Select a type that's easy to walk on. Some gravels shift and move underfoot, while others pack enough to provide a firm surface. Apply a pre-emergent weed killer before putting gravel in place (read label carefully to avoid damage to desirable trees and shrubs nearby).

TEXAS TIP

Don't place stepping stones directly into the lawn. Our southern lawn grasses produce runners that will quickly cover the stones. The only alternative then is time-consuming trimming and edging. It's better to place the stones within an edging strip, with fine gravel between the stones. Set potted flowering plants on the gravel or use clump-forming ground covers to break the straight lines of the edging strip.

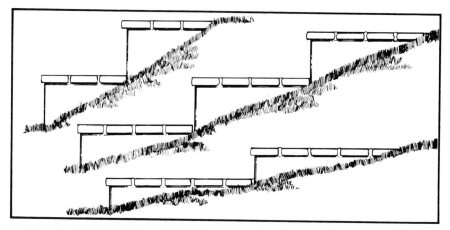

Steps should be convenient, safe and comfortable. Most popular sizing is 6-inch risers with 15-inch treads. As width of treads increases, height of risers must decrease. Other satisfactory combinations include:

riser	tread
4 in.	19 in.
5	17
7	11

PATIO PLANNING

Patios are as important to Texans as wildflowers and football. They're a natural transition, a step from indoors to outdoors. For many of us, they're another whole family room . . . the heart of outdoor recreational activities. They reflect our Latin American influences, but they're now part of a standard American lifestyle. Spend a little more time studying your patio, and what you might do to make it more functional.

Location. Properly designed, a patio is a place of beauty, one that should be seen from inside the house. Most commonly it's located off the family room or the kitchen. Small, intimate patios may be off the bedroom, study or bath. Sheltered and screened entryway patios are increasingly important in Texas, as smaller city lots make space more and more valuable. They're especially useful in apartments and town houses. All of which is to say, a patio can be anywhere . . . wherever people are.

Obviously, the patio should be convenient. It should also be sheltered from the wind, the sun and from unwanted eyes. Most of these are things you can modify through careful planning.

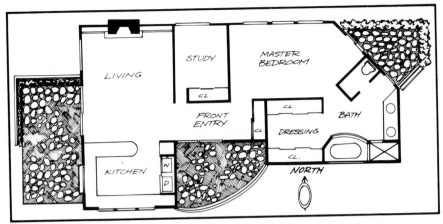

Patios can be added wherever they're needed. Accessibility is a prime concern.

Size. Your patio's size should be dependent on its intended uses. Build it large if you entertain frequently, or scale it down if it's primarily for you and your family. Size range: as a general rule, 50 to 100 square feet of patio for each family member.

Patios have become the center of the outdoor Texas lifestyle.

Enlarging an existing patio . . .

Home builders frequently bless us with picayune patios, too often of plain, uninteresting concrete. If they're to have any value at all, we have to expand them. One of the easiest ways to do that is to use pre-poured concrete sections around the perimeter of the existing surface. Brick can also be used, placed on packed sand and held in place by border strips of redwood or preservative-treated wood. Be sure all new patio surfacing drains away from your house.

If you're faced with an inadequate patio surface, you may not have to remove the old patio before installing the new concrete. Depending on the type and condition of the existing patio surface and the thickness of the new slab, you may be able to pour a new surface over the existing one. Special bonding agents are available that help new concrete adhere to old. However, you probably should call in a professional contractor to advise as to the best way of completing the job. You might also consider mortaring thin brick pavers over the existing surface if you have adequate space for the increased thickness.

Enlarging your patio needn't be a large scale task, Use of pre-poured concrete rounds and squares make the job quick, neat and easy.

Controlling Your Patio Temperature. Cooling can be accomplished in several ways:

• Locate patio a minimum of 20 to 25 feet from air-conditioner unit, preferably where house can provide afternoon shade.

• Plant shade trees overhead and to the sunny side of the patio.

• Train vines over patio roof.

• Use open style patio roof that allows free air movement. Closed roofs trap heat.

- Keep dense shrub and tree plantings away from patio.
- Use sound of moving water to provide psychological cooling effect.
- If a sheltered location is available, install an electric fan.

Warming is needed during late fall and early spring, when the patio might otherwise be useless. Check these guidelines:

- Locate patio on south or east side of the house, away from north winds.
- Block wind movement with shrub plantings or fence/screen on north side of patio.
- Use deciduous trees and vines to provide summer shading, so sun's rays can reach patio during cooler months.

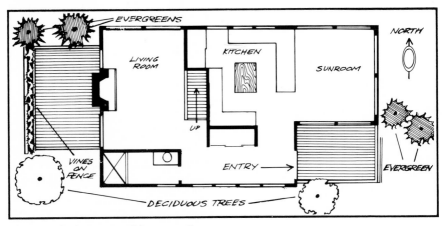

Plan patio for longest possible season of use.

Covering the Patio. To get the most out of your patio you may decide to cover it. Start by checking set-back requirements and building restrictions, to be sure all you want to do will be allowed. Obtain the necessary permits.

Today's materials offer you many possibilities, including wood (either solid or slats), fiberglass, bamboo and others.

Solid patio roofs give protection from rain, and they give total shading. However, they also block the free flow of air. You must also make sure you have adequate pitch for proper runoff of rainwater.

Wood slats give good shading, and they also allow air to circulate freely. Slats should be arranged on a general north-south direction (rather than east-west), so that each part of the patio will receive alternating sun and shade as the sun passes overhead.

Slatted wood patio roofs provide shade, yet permit good air circulation.

Whatever the covering you choose, make sure the supports will keep it air-borne. Figure in the weight of your prized hanging baskets (heaviest right after watering) and any snow you might expect in your part of the state. Use lumber appropriately sized. Generally, 4x4's, 4x6's and other large timbers are best.

While you're insuring that the cover stays up, be sure also that it stays down. Anchor it securely into concrete or bolt it to the existing slab. This is especially critical for solid roofs that restrict air movement. Similarly, be sure the top panels (especially fiberglass) are tightly secured. They blow off easily in gusty breezes.

Attach your patio roof either to the outside wall of your house or directly onto the eave of the roof. The roof attachment is the most preferable, but be careful not to damage the existing roof to the point of its leaking.

Providing Patio Color. Assuming your patio has a solid floor that prohibits planting directly into the soil, you can still landscape. Use container plants ... trees, shrubs, vines, annuals, perennials, vegetables and fruit crops ... all growing in patio pots. Select attractive pots (drain holes required) sized proportionate to the plants that will be growing in them.

Select the best potting soil available, preferably one high in organic matter. Keep the plants well watered, and feed them with every watering, using one of the water-soluble complete and balanced fertilizers.

Protect your containerized plants from cold weather extremes. Even woody types can be killed by unusually low temperatures because their roots are so much more exposed and vulnerable. Durability varies with species, but even the hardiest plants should be protected at temperatures under 20°F when grown in containers. Wheel 'em into the garage for a few days when the temperature plummets.

Finishing Touches for the Patio. Once the surface, the cover, the screens and the shade trees are all in place in your patio area, it's time to furnish the space.

Buy quality chairs, tables and other furniture. They'll last years longer, making your patio a family tradition in entertaining. Furnishings should be weather-resistant and heavy enough that they're not blown about by gusty winds.

DO FENCE ME IN!

In today's crowded urban lifestyle, fences have become as important as sidewalks. In fact, they perform some of the same roles as the walls of your house in providing privacy, sheltering out noise and giving security. If you're planning on fencing in part of your property, start with two visits: one to city hall to make sure you're in compliance with rules, and the other to your neighbors, to be sure it's a happy fence that's agreeable to both sides. They may even share in its cost.

Types of Fencing

Wood (solid). Several patterns are available. All look quite natural and blend well with the landscape. Posts should be treated with a preservative and secured in concrete. Slope the top of the concrete so it will shed water away from the post. Let the wood weather naturally rather than painting.

Wood Picket. Attractive, but requiring high maintenance for painting. Most useful in colonial style homes.

Split Rail. Most useful in property delineation and for landscape accents. Rustic wood texture blends well with western ranch-style homes.

Masonry. The ultimate in permanence and formality. Brick walls provide good sound screening and excellent privacy. They're especially good in patios and intimate gardens, also around pools. And, the bricks needn't be set solid. If air movement is needed, have openings left as they're laid.

Wrought Iron. Durable and lovely! Especially suited to formal landscapes and gardens. Openness allows good visibility ... good for use around pools. Can be tailor-made to fit most any opening.

Chain Link. Good for security and confinement of pets, but rather stark in the landscape. Undoubtedly the least natural fencing material. Use vines and upright shrubs to soften its harsh lines.

Woven Wire. A more subtle type of wire enclosure. Available in rolls from hardware stores and farm supply houses. Posts should be either redwood or pressure-treated pine. Use care in stretching the wire tightly between posts, to prevent wrinkles and sags.

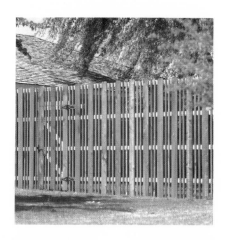

HOW TO BUILD A RETAINING WALL

Back East, Texas has the reputation of being as flat as a pancake. Well, that's not always true. Many parts of our state feature terrain changes, and some are even quite steep. For a landscaper, that's merely an opportunity . . . a chance to add personality and interest to his design.

That's where retaining walls step to the rescue. Rather than having steep, unmanageable slopes, the landscape can be levelled and flattened. Soil erosion is reduced and pedestrian traffic is often redirected.

Construction Materials

Most any building material that endures weather and soil conditions and that's strong enough to hold back tons of wet soil can be used as a retaining wall.

Some of the best: concrete, brick, ledgestone, railroad ties and other timbers.

Best way to select the material is to drive around town and see what others have used. Find a type that you like, then check supplies and costs. Look in your yellow pages under "lumber" and "stone-natural" headings. You can also check with wrecking yards for aged timbers. Be sure any creosoted lumber you use is well seasoned, since fresh creosote is toxic to plants.

Steps in Building the Wall

• Start at city hall. Be sure your new wall meets any applicable codes.

• Check water flow patterns. Be sure you won't be creating a lake in somebody's kitchen. Find where water accumulates. Wet soil is very heavy. Don't let it rupture your retaining wall.

• Shape the soil. Determine the lines you want your wall to follow, then remove excesses of soil. Always slope the top of the wall gently back into the hill to equalize the pressure of the earth behind it. If drainage is a real problem, you may even want to install a three to five-inch layer of medium-sized gravel behind the wall.

• Lay your stone or timbers carefully in place. If you intend to use brick or concrete, begin by pouring a solid concrete footing 15 to 20 inches wide. Depth of footing should be proportionate to height and weight of wall.

• As you put the wall pieces in place, be sure you leave weep holes near the base so excess soil moisture can escape from soil behind wall.

• If the wall is tall or unusually vertical, you can anchor it with a "dead man" every few feet (crosstie or timber placed perpendicular to the wall and extending into the slope).

Planting the Wall

You can soften the lines of your retaining wall by planting low-growing, cascading plants directly above it. Ground covers like Asian jasmine, potentilla, sedum, English ivy, mock strawberry and the trailing junipers are naturals. Include a few colorful annuals like verbenas, trailing lantanas and moss rose for added interest.

To make watering easier, use a soaker hose laid upside down, one of the drip irrigation systems or special narrow-throw heads for an automatic sprinkling system.

WATER IN THE LANDSCAPE

Nothing cools a hot summer day here in Texas like a rain shower, and nothing cools a landscape like the sound of running water. It may be in the forms of fountains, waterfalls, watercourses and pools. In any event, it's a feature that can make your landscape unique.

Fountains probably do more to cool a landscape than any other water source you can add, simply because they're so noisy. The water bubbles and spills . . . it's a great sound. There's an unlimited number of fountain types on the market, and you can even design your own. For best effect, position the fountain against a plain, dark background that will show the water droplets to their best advantage. Use stout streams of water in windy locations, fine mists in more protected spots. Provide a receiving pool for the falling water. Its size should be in keeping with the height of the spray.

Waterfalls and watercourses also provide the sound of moving water. However, they should look like they belong in the landscape. Free-standing plastic models that sit in the corner probably won't look too natural. It's better to use waterfalls and watercourses in sloping landscapes and to construct them out of native rock. Be sure they're proportionately sized with the rest of the landscape. You'll need a small recirculating pump and the necessary plumbing to keep your watercourse running. Use lots of tiny plants along it, preferably types you'd see along a marshy stream. Keep its sides slightly above the surrounding grade to keep debris from washing in.

Pools come in all shapes and sizes. Obviously, swimming pools would rate as the largest. Let's concentrate now on smaller landscaping pools. They can be made of brick, concrete, rock, fiberglass and even galvanized metal. The important thing is to blend the pool in, so it doesn't look contrived. Position the pool where it can be a focal point of your garden. Paint the bottom black to make it appear deeper. Use potted plants around the pool to help it fit into the landscape. They may be plunged into the soil around the pool to help make them appear to be growing there. Use sunken pots of water plants for the final touch.

LIGHTING YOUR LANDSCAPE

Night lighting your landscape can make it safer, more useful and much more attractive. Fact is, it's the perfect finishing touch to any urban landscape. You may choose to do it yourself with one of the modestly priced kits available from nurseries and garden centers (sometimes available from light supply dealers) or you may want something more elaborate, a system planned by a lighting professional. Either way, you'll be thrilled with the results. And, since it's all low-voltage equipment, it's inexpensive to operate. Consider the reasons:

Safety Landscape lighting can illuminate special hazards like steps, walks, drives, pools and slopes. Special fixtures are available for each purpose to allow you to put the extra light right where it's needed.

Security By illuminating your landscape you'll discourage prowlers, burglars and other undesirable visitors. Automatic time clocks allow you to set the lighting to come on whenever you want it.

Recreation Your outdoor activities, be they playing or working, will benefit most by the addition of landscape lighting. In the short days of winter it will extend your productive hours, and in summer's hot weather it'll give you a chance to get outside without being broiled to a crisp.

Moods Choose your feelings. Put on the bright lights so you can work. Turn on the artificial moonlight for quiet entertaining, or change to festive holiday lights. You can do it all with just the flick of a switch when you have the right landscape lighting. There's really no limit.

Some tips for your landscape light planning . . .

• Plan your lighting carefully. There are dozens of types of fixtures and special equipment. Take time to try your lights in various locations before you secure them permanently. Try a variety of sizes, colors and intensities before you decide.

• Accent the most interesting features of your garden . . . sculpture, pools, fountains, fences, buildings, trees or plants. Hide the less attractive parts by leaving them dark.

• Side or back lighting will produce interesting and dramatic results. Front lighting will be less interesting and flatter, though it may be the best way to light hazardous areas.

• Vary the strength of your light proportionate with its distance from the object being lighted. Restrain the amount of light that you use. Remember that you're not trying to give the feeling of daytime, you're just providing special accents.

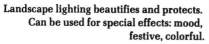
**Landscape lighting beautifies and protects.
Can be used for special effects: mood,
festive, colorful.**

• Make your system look natural. Hide all the fixtures and wires. Use indirect light whenever possible, reflecting it off some other surface rather than making it directly visible.

• Underground circuits are the most permanent and satisfactory, but they must be protected from insects and rodents. They should be encased in conduit or pvc pipe to protect them from digging.

• Use only special low-voltage equipment. Regular household current could easily be lethal in moist outdoor conditions.

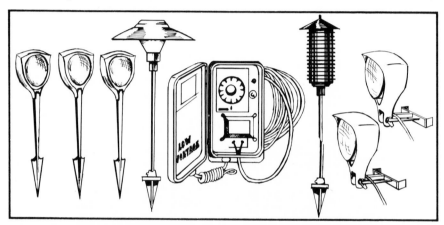

Outdoor lighting accessories include time clock, low-voltage transformer, lights, mounting fixtures, low-voltage line.

GARDEN ART ... THE FINISHING TOUCH

Simplicity is the watchword in garden art. That special sculpture or the striking sundial may just be the finishing touch for a fine landscape. Improperly used art can be distracting or downright disfiguring.

Statuary and Sculpture are available in many types and at all prices. Choose from cast concrete, marble and other stone, copper and brass. It should be in scale with its surroundings . . . large enough to be seen, yet not overwhelming. Place it at a focal point of your landscape.

Fountains, Waterfalls and Birdbaths are often forms of statuary, yet they deserve special attention since they introduce water to the landscape. Be sure the water looks natural . . . it mustn't look contrived. Waterfalls and trickling brooks are especially suited to rolling terrain. Birdbaths should be nestled into the shade and protection of trees and large shrubs. Nothing's more lonesome than a birdbath in the sunny middle of a hot Texas landscape.

Living Art comes in the form of specially trained plants. Whether it's espaliers, bonsai, poodle trees or a hand-manicured formal garden, shaped plants are special art pieces. Use them in moderation, though . . . they're real eye catchers.

ENERGY SAVINGS THROUGH LANDSCAPING

If you're tired of runaway utility bills, maybe it's time you put plants to work at your place. While efficient insulation and weatherstripping may still be the best means of cutting the bills, don't overlook what plants can do.

Plants Can Cool . . .

1. Large shade trees can reduce temperatures inside your home by 20 degrees or more.

2. Vines growing against sunny side of house cut summertime heat penetration.

3. Turf and other living ground covers cool better than concrete. Reduce reflected heat: allow room for planting of grass or other ground cover along the drive and walks.

4. Create comfort by training plants properly. Remove all airflow restrictions such as low-hanging limbs that keep air movement from your patio. Remove lower limbs of trees, up to eight to 10 feet, and you'll funnel the air in below them.

And, plants can warm . . .

5. Plant evergreen shrubs and trees to act as windbreaks during the winter.

6. Use deciduous plants (lose leaves in winter) to shade in summer. By being bare in winter they'll allow sun's warming rays to reach house.

1

2

STRETCHING YOUR LANDSCAPING DOLLARS

There's good evidence that your landscape will actually make you money when it comes time to resell your house. Still, there's no point in spending more money than necessary. Here are some tips to help you get the most for your money.

• *Buy larger shrubs and smaller trees.* By using larger shrubs (two, three and five-gallon sizes) you'll be less likely to plant them too close. More distant spacing means fewer plants required. Larger shrubs also have better root systems, for more durability during extremes of heat or cold.

• Smaller trees (six to eight feet) generally survive transplanting better and give shade years faster, since proportionately fewer of their roots are damaged during the digging.

• *Buy container-grown stock whenever possible.* You'll get all the roots, for quicker re-establishment. More and more plants, even large trees, are being grown and sold in containers.

• *Buy native plant species whenever practical.* They've already proved their durability to our state's soils and weather.

• *Prepare the soil carefully prior to planting.* The soil amendments may cost more than the shrub or tree you're planting (as in dogwood or azaleas planted in the western parts of the state), but you're wasting your money without them.

• *Protect your investment by keeping your plants healthy and vigorous.* Fertilize and water them regularly. Watch for early signs of insects and diseases. It will cost you less if you only plant once!

HOW MUCH IS MY LANDSCAPE WORTH?

Or, "Will I ever get my money back if I decide to sell the house?" The answer, a resounding "YES!" That's assuming the work you do in your landscape is tasteful (surely you wouldn't have it any other way!) and in keeping with the rest of the neighborhood.

Still, it's hard to predict value appreciation exactly. Everyone wants to know just two things from any investment: how much will I make and how long will it take me to make it? In the plant world, that's an impossible prediction. There are so many variables that you can deal only in generalities.

Let me speak from firsthand experience. We sold a house several years ago. We had lived there for seven years and had developed a functional, neat and simple landscape . . . good plants and basic planning. We kept track of our expenditures. Realtors consistently under-appraised (in our opinion) our house, and we continued to hold out for our price. We knew what we had spent and what it was worth.

Finally, in desperation and against our better judgment, we decided to sell it ourselves. We tidied it up, bought some colorful plants for containers and had a sign painted telling its virtues. Within three days we had four nibbles . . . and three contracts! We sold our house in three days, for within one percent of our asking price! Other houses on the block remained on sale for several months.

In addition to helping us sell our house in a hurry, and getting top dollar as well, our landscape also attracted attention. It got those folks to call in the first place!

You may not be able to affix the exact value of your landscape when you sell your house, but I'm here to tell you it's a moneymaker!

LANDSCAPING LABOR SAVERS

If you read this whole book cover to cover you'd come across every one of the 10 suggestions listed below at some time or other.

Here, summarized in one list, are 10 ways guaranteed to save you time, effort and/or money in landscaping and gardening. Admittedly, they're simple ... you might even take them for granted. Think through them carefully ... you're probably ignoring more than you'd imagine.

1. Use top quality tools. Cheap tools are no bargain. They're harder to use and they simply don't last. Spend the few extra bucks it takes. Buy the right tool for the job. You can't drive a nail with a screwdriver and you can't pull weeds with a leaf rake.

2. Use edging ... good edging. Wood, metal, concrete, brick, stone, or strong rubber edging ... anything durable enough to keep the grass in its place.

3. Mulch, to keep out the weeds ... and to prevent soil erosion, rapid freezing and thawing and other landscaping problems.

4. Avoid high-maintenance plants. Use types that are adapted. Don't plant trees or shrubs with known problems, whether those problems are insects, diseases or bad growth habits. Avoid those plants like a bad debt.

5. Utilize the best in irrigation equipment. Consider an automatic system. If that's out of the budget, at least buy the best sprinklers and hoses. They'll do a better job, and they'll last years longer.

6. Use drip, or trickle, irrigation whenever possible. It puts out small amounts of water over a long period of time, super-saturating the soil. You'll conserve water because it won't evaporate so readily. Plus, it's a lot easier.

7. Use ground covers to replace grass in the problem spots ... in shade, on slopes and in long, narrow areas like parkways and alleyways. See Chapter 6 for details on ground covers.

8. Plan for season-long color. You don't have to have large beds if you'll just plan for continuous color. Know when the plants will show that color and plan them into your plantings.

9. Mow frequently. Yes, it will save you work! Research has shown that if you mow often you don't have to catch the clippings, and that saves a good deal of time and effort. Too, the grass responds better, since it's less of a shock.

10. Watch for insects and diseases that do arise, and treat them promptly. It's a lot easier to control one small problem than to go after a crisis.

TEN WAYS TO BE A BETTER NEIGHBOR THROUGH LANDSCAPING

We Texans are known for being good neighbors, and there's no place where that shows more quickly than in the way we landscape our homes. Here are 10 easy ways to win the thanks of those who live and work near you.

1. Take pride in the way your place looks. Outline projects you can do yourself, and those with which you'll need help. Let your ideas expand to the block, the neighborhood, perhaps the whole city.

2. Clean up the debris. Get rid of the weed patch, the broken-down cars and the tumble-down shacks. It's amazing how much improvement you can make on a landscape just by cleaning it up.

3. Keep your landscape safe. Watch for low-hanging branches, cracked sidewalks and sharp-pointed shrubs. Trim limbs that obscure intersections.

4. Keep your landscape consistent with those around it. Let it blend and look natural. It needs to belong. It should be a part of the block plantings. Don't let it overwhelm.

5. Be careful when you plant trees near the property line, or near your neighbor's house. Be sure their roots and limbs won't cause any harm.

6. If you're putting up fences check with your neighbors first. Clear the style and the placement.

7. Keep your weeds . . . and your pests . . . and your pets . . . under control! Nobody wants to live next door to Typhoid Mary, and nobody wants to live next door to the world's source of crabgrass, either.

8. Co-op some costs. There's no point in everybody on the block owning a pressure spray rig. Buy as a group, then use it as needed. Assign the block mechanic the responsibility of storing and maintaining it in return for his share of the use. Use the same technique for other expensive and seldom-used pieces of equipment.

9. Keep your sprays to yourself. Nobody wants stray weed killer sprays. The chemicals you're using on your lawn and landscape may ruin the next guy's garden. Don't let that happen. Keep 'em under control.

10. Grow plenty of plants — flowers, fruit and vegetables. You'll be the most popular **neighbor** around when you start passing out surplus garden-fresh produce.

CIVIC BEAUTIFICATION

Texans have always been known for their civic beautification projects, and that's a good reflection on the pride we take in our state.

Once you've shown your neighborhood what a good residential landscape can do for the morale of the block, watch others near you join in. There's something infectious about landscaping neatness.

From your neighborhood that enthusiasm will spread to churches, schools and on to the business community. Before long you'll see landscaping in warehouse and industrial districts.

Plan your efforts, though . . . list these four things:

1. Outline your goals. What exactly are you trying to accomplish? Who is in charge of the planning? Have you considered hiring a professional landscape architect to make sure it's planned properly?

2. Make a list of potential supporters. 100 people working together can do more than 1,000 working separately.

3. Establish a budget. Volunteer labor is great, but some things will cost money. Know exactly how much you have.

4. Plan for the follow-through. Who will pull the weeds and drag the water hoses? This is the spot where most projects fail!

Whether your group is planting crepe myrtles or spring-flowering bulbs, beautifying downtown, the parks or the school or simply conducting a clean-up and fix-up campaign, make sure you have answers to all four of those categories before you ever get started.

Once you've done that you're on your way toward making Texas even better. Good luck!

Chapter 3

Trees...Texas' Best

Trees are as important to Texans as football and homemade ice cream. Probably nowhere else in this world do folks appreciate good shade any more than we here in Texas. But not all trees are created equal. Some are decidedly better than others. You have, at tree-planting time, control over the destiny of generations to come. Plant a good tree and you and those who follow will enjoy the results.

Trees are the ideal investment. The Texas Association of Nurserymen estimates that a good quality shade tree, properly planted and cared for, can increase in value by 400 percent in just five to seven years. Not a bad return, even with today's rapid inflation!

Add to that the benefits you gain in cooling, winter wind-breaking and just plain old beauty, and you've made a pretty strong case for tree planting. What follows will give you proper direction in planting and caring for the trees at your place.

TREES AT THE NURSERY . . . BUYING THE BEST

Of all the plant material you'll buy for your landscape, your trees will be the largest investment. It makes sense, then, to try to get the most for your money. Follow these few simple guidelines for starters:

• Take your time. Compare prices and quality. Tree prices may vary from one retail nursery to another. Compare the trees carefully, though, just to be sure they're equal products.

• Biggest isn't always the best. Large trees suffer more transplant shock, with more time required for the trees to re-establish. There's a higher chance of mortality with larger trees.

• There's another way to diminish the chance of losing the tree, and that's to buy one grown in a container, where you get all the roots. Container-grown plants suffer virtually no transplant shock . . . they just keep growing. And, even better, there's a trend now to larger container plants. Even landscaping-size trees are now available.

• If the tree is still dormant, scratch the bark and check the buds. The tissues should be both moist and green inside the bark. Buds should be plump and swollen. They also should be moist and crisp when flicked with your fingernail.

• If the tree is in leaf, check for normally shaped leaves of a reasonably good size for the species. Any tree that has been dug and transplanted will suffer some setback, and leaf size will be diminished. The tree should, however, show at least modest signs of vigorous new growth.

• Most importantly, buy from a reputable nurseryman — someone who will be around if your tree runs into problems. Texas is full of door-to-door tree peddlers who sell off the backs of trucks. Be cautious of them. Their prices may be attractive, but their merchandise may be far inferior.

MOST COMMON QUESTION

"Do nurserymen guarantee their trees? Should I look for one who does? Will it cost extra?"

Ask your nurseryman about his company's policy. They vary almost with every nursery.

One San Antonio nursery features a sign: "No Plant Life is Guaranteed. Neither is human or any other life on this planet."

That nurseryman probably has the most realistic approach to warranties. Fortunately, though, most nurseries offer some type of replacement policy, generally at a reduced price for the second tree. Often the guarantee requires that the nursery deliver and plant the tree, so they're sure it was done properly.

If you know the tree is healthy and vigorous when you buy it, and if you plant it promptly and care for it properly, the chance of its surviving are excellent, and you may decide not to pay extra for their delivery, planting and warranty.

Flowering Trees

Nothing puts more spring in your bloomers than flowering trees! They're a great source of color and, by including a few of the later-flowering types, you can extend the blooming season many months. Here in approximate order of blooming dates, are some of the best for general use in Texas:

Spring Blooming	Color of Bloom
Saucer magnolia	white-pink-purple blend
Flowering plum	white, pale pink
Flowering pear	white
Flowering peach	red, pink, white
Crabapple	rose-red, pink, white
Redbud	pink, white
Dogwood	white, pink, red
Texas mountain laurel	lavender
Southern magnolia	white

Summer Blooming	Color of Bloom
Mimosa (Silktree Albizzia)	pink
Golden raintree (northern)	yellow
Althaea (Rose of Sharon)	white, pink, lavender
Crepe myrtle	pink, red, white, lavender
Retama (Jerusalem thorn)	yellow

Fall Blooming	Color of Bloom
Golden raintree (southern)	yellow
Loquat	yellow-green . . . grown for its fragrance

Saucer Magnolia

Peppermint Flowering Peach

Flowering Peach

Saucer Magnolia

Flowering Crabapple

Best Trees for Fall Color in Texas

Fall color from trees may not be as plentiful in Texas as it is for our northern neighbors, but there's still plenty to go around. The trick comes in utilizing it. Plan your plantings for at least a few trees to provide color each autumn. Among the best:

Red	Yellow
Sweetgum	Ginkgo
Chinese pistachio	Silver maple
Chinese tallow	Arizona ash
Red oak	Green ash
Flowering pear	American elm
Sumac	Persimmon
Black gum	Pomegranate
Crepe myrtle	Western soapberry
Red Maple	
Dogwood	

To Get the Best Fall Color . . .

Fall color in your plants is brought on by cool weather that changes the sugars inside the plants' leaves and brings out the red, yellow and orange pigments.

RULE OF GREEN THUMB: You'll get the best fall color when your plants are kept just a little bit hungry and thirsty. If you feed them too late in the year with a high-nitrogen fertilizer you'll be left with only green leaves when the first frost arrives.

Sweetgum

Special Plants for Special Places

Trees to Use Under Power Lines: Best small trees for use in confined areas over most of the state include yaupon holly, Nellie R. Stevens holly, possumhaw holly, crepe myrtle, golden raintree, redbud, flowering crabapple, flowering (or fruiting) peaches and plums, tree-form ligustrums and photinias, loquat, Japanese black pine, and Japanese maple. For West Texas, in addition to these, consider retama (Jerusalem thorn) and Russian olive. For East Texas, add dogwoods, cherry laurel and American holly.

Upright Trees for Cramped Urban Landscapes: If horizontal space is at a premium in your landscape, yet you still want shade, consider one of these upright trees. Each grows at least half again as tall as it is wide.

For shade, plant cedar elm, Chinese tallow, sweetgum, Bradford and Aristocrat pears (other ornamental flowering pears also worthy of trial), bald cypress and, for East Texas, slash and loblolly pines.

Southern magnolias, eastern red cedars and Arizona cypress also grow rather upright, but lower limbs close to the ground make them less suitable to cramped landscapes.

MOST COMMON QUESTION

"What is the best fast-growing shade tree for our area?"

Don't be totally concerned about a tree's growth rate when you plan your plantings. Most quick-growing shade trees have a large list of serious problems such as insects, diseases, weak and brittle wood, and so on.

To carry the message one step farther, let's not just group trees into "fast" and "slow" categories. Let's also include an in-between: the "moderate" growers. Most of the really high quality trees such as the oaks and pecans will fit into the latter category. Magnolias, by comparison, are very slow growers.

Now at last, in answer to your question ... best fast-growing shade trees adapted over a large part of the state: Bradford pear, Chinese tallow and perhaps even fruitless mulberry. The old suggestion still holds: when in doubt, ask a professional nurseryman ... someone who really knows plants. Let your nurseryman suggest the very best plant for your place.

How Long Does That Tree Live?

Shade tree longevity should be a more common concern as we landscape our homes. All too often quick growth is the only consideration. Just because a tree lives a long time doesn't necessarily mean that it's a slow grower. There are thousand-year-old live oaks in Texas, but live oaks can grow fairly rapidly given good care and attention. And so it is with many other trees.

That means that trees' life spans should move toward the front as a major consideration as we develop neighborhood landscapes.

Listed are some of Texas' more common shade trees along with estimated *average* life spans. Bear in mind that some trees of a given species will survive decades and even centuries, while others will succumb within just a few years. Figures given are simply guidelines of what you might expect.

Short Life Span (under 25 years)	Medium Life Span (25-50 years)	Long Life Span (over 50 years)
Fruitless mulberry	Crabapple	Live oak
Arizona ash	Chinese tallow	Red oak
Mimosa	Redbud	Water oak
Willow	Hackberry	Bur oak
Siberian elm	Silver maple	Pecan
Catalpa	Cottonwood	Cedar Elm
Sycamore	Loquat	Sweetgum
Boxelder	Deodar cedar	Bradford pear
Chinaberry		Chinese pistachio
Lombardy poplar		Slash pine
		Loblolly pine
		Bald cypress
		Magnolia
		Yaupon holly
		Crepe myrtle
		Dogwood
		Red cedar

Plan Tree Plantings to Conserve Energy

Trees are some of the best energy savers in landscaping. Generous amounts of research have shown the importance of shade trees in these several functions.

A) Trees planted in strategic locations shade the house from afternoon sun. This can reduce the temperature inside by 10 to 20 degrees, plus cut the number of hours the indoor temperature exceeds 75°F.

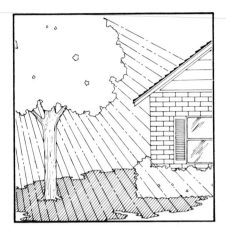

B) By removing lower limbs you can encourage air flow to split, with good movement coming in under the trees. Coordinate your hedge and fences accordingly, so they also allow free air movement.

C) Trees properly placed can cool an air conditioning unit outdoors for increased efficiency.

D) Evergreen trees can be used as windbreaks, particularly in open rural areas. Note that windbreaks do not stop the wind, they merely redirect it. The windbreak should be 1½ to two times the height of the building, and ideally should be located several times as far away from the building as the windbreak is tall. Tree windbreaks, according to research on the Great Plains, are of limited value in urban areas, simply because there isn't adequate space.

How to Transport a Tree From the Nursery

You no doubt will spend a good deal of time selecting your new tree at the nursery. Protect that tree as you carry it to and from your car. Transport it cautiously, to keep it intact. Follow these guidelines:

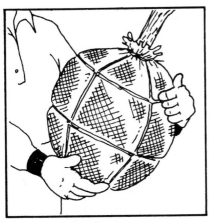

Always carry by soil ball, never lift or carry by tree's trunk.

Brace soil ball securely, then tie trunk lid in place. Drive slowly . . . wind "burns" leaves.

Get help with heavy loads. Handle soil ball carefully.

HOW TO TRANSPLANT A TREE

Trees are among the largest investment in landscaping. Their success, to a large degree, depends on how you plant them — no matter what type you select or where you decide to place them. Follow these transplanting tips:

Select a proper planting site for your tree. Know the tree's mature growth form and size. Be sure the location provides adequate room. Locate water and sewer lines that might be nearby, and don't plant tall-growing species under power lines.

Hole should be dug twice as wide as tree's rootball, *but not deeper than necessary* (digging deeper results in loose soil under ball ... potentially allowing settling of the tree too deep into hole). Tree should be set in hole at same depth at which it grew in nursery. Container-grown trees should be removed carefully from the containers. Do not attempt to remove wrapping from balled-and-burlapped plants. If it is secured with a piece of nylon twine or wire, clip or remove it so it won't girdle expanding tree trunk years later. Prune broken roots of bare-rooted trees before planting. Fill around the tree with a mixture containing equal parts of: (1) the topsoil removed from the hole, and (2) brown Canadian peat moss, shredded bark soil conditioner or well-rotted compost.

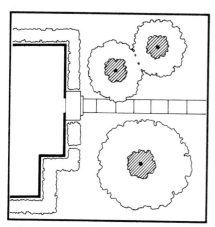

Select a proper planting site.

Dig the hole twice as wide as tree's root ball.

Water the tree immediately after planting. Apply a high-phosphorus root-stimulating fertilizer according to label directions. Prune balled-and-burlapped trees to compensate for roots lost during the digging (generally 25 to 40 percent of top growth removed). Bare-rooted trees should be pruned 40 to 60 percent. Container-grown trees should be pruned only as needed to develop proper shape. Wrap the trunk with paper tree wrap to protect against borers and sunscald. Stake and guy medium and large trees for first year. Keep tree well watered until it's established.

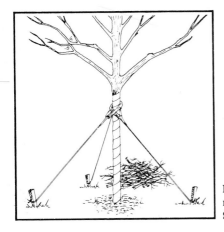

Prune to compensate for
roots lost during digging.
Stake and guy tree.

Tree Planting Tricks ... for Wet or Dry Soil

Good drainage is essential to the success of most any shade tree. Yet, there are times when modifications must be made in normal planting procedures to allow for better root growth.

In soils with a high water table, where water frequently stands, plant your trees "high" ... a few inches above the surrounding grade. This is common practice along the Gulf Coast. It's amazing how just a couple of inches of rise encourages water to drain away quickly. The soil remains well aerated, and the tree roots respond favorably.

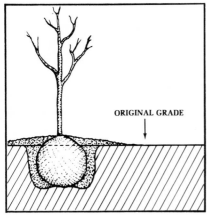

ORIGINAL GRADE

Tree planted in wet soil.

In areas where dry spells can be prolonged, it's a good idea to provide some type of watering reservoir for your new tree. Plant the tree at the same depth at which it grew in the nursery. Construct a four to five-inch soil berm 16 to 24 inches away from the trunk. Then fill the basin each time that you water. If prolonged rainy weather risks drowning the plant, open the berm temporarily.

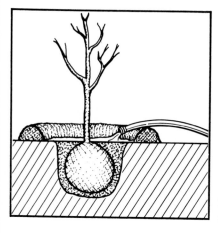

Berm allows more thorough
watering during prolonged drought.

Staking a Young Tree

Newly transplanted trees will require staking against the strong Texas breezes. This is especially important as the tree develops a new root system . . . to keep the new roots from being broken away by the motion. Depending on the size and vigor of the tree, the stakes should generally be left in place one to two years.

Insert stakes on each side of tree.
Be sure one is on side of prevailing
summertime breezes, generally
south in most parts of Texas.

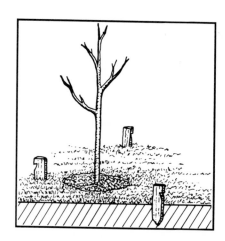

Protect tree trunk with short section of old garden hose or scrap of burlap wrapped around trunk.

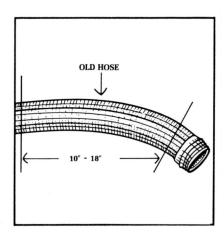

Use rope, stout twine or fine cable to secure tree. Do not attempt to pull tree into vertical position if it is out of plumb. Dig and reset it prior to staking.

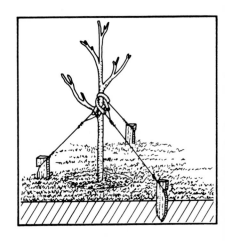

Another option is to drive two strong stakes well into ground opposite one another, one on the side of the prevailing summertime wind. Make a ring of old rubber hose and attach pieces of flexible chain from it to each post. This technique is particularly useful with small and medium-sized trees.

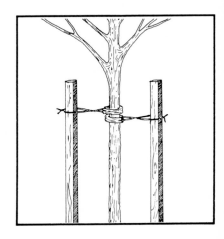

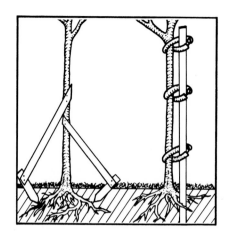

Alternate ways of staking trees. Driving nails through boards into tree trunk does hold tree erect, but opens small wounds for borer and disease invasion. Single stake provides minimal support, particularly for medium and large trees with heavy canopies.

TRAINING YOUR TREES . . . BRING THEM UP RIGHT!

Your trees' ultimate growth habit and shape depends a lot on the initial care you give them after planting. Start from the outset with regular pruning and shaping. Get your trees off to a good start.

A) Newly transplanted trees, especially those that were dug bare-rooted or that were balled-and-burlapped, will need pruning to compensate for roots lost in the move. Aim to remove 25 to 35 percent of the top growth for balled-and-burlapped trees and 40 to 50 percent for those dug bare-rooted.

B) Buds and twigs emerge from tree limbs in all directions. By pruning directly above one facing away from the center of the tree you can encourage lateral, spreading growth.

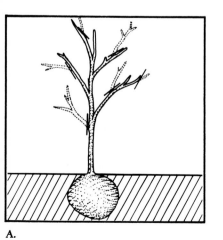

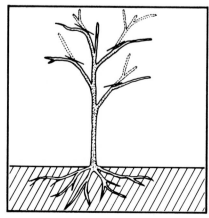

A.   B.

C) Prune above a bud facing the center of the tree and you'll encourage more vertical growth. That's true at least to a degree . . . you can't make major changes in the genetic direction of a tree's growth habit.

D) By leaving lower limbs on small trees for a year or two, you encourage a thicker trunk development. This is especially noticeable in oaks and pecans, but will be true for almost any species. The limbs can be removed once the trunk is stout enough to support the top growth.

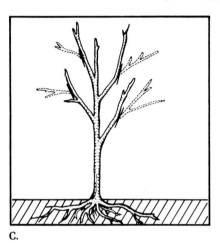

C.

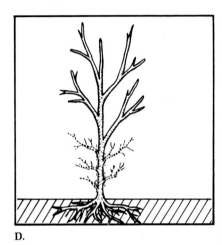

D.

Watering Your Trees

Water is the key to success in Texas tree growing. Few trees would survive their first summer without supplemental watering. Established trees would cease growth . . . they would thin and weaken . . . if it weren't for the hose. Watch all your trees daily. If the soil dries three to four inches deep, or if the leaves start to wilt, it's time to water.

If your trees are growing in lawn areas they're probably getting enough water, at least if the grass is healthy and vigorous. To be sure, though, and to provide water to other trees in less developed landscaping areas, plan on special care during prolonged heat and drought. Keep the hose handy!

A) Water your trees slowly and deeply. Take the sprinkler off the end of your hose and let the water dribble slowly for several hours in a location. Move it to other locations and repeat the process. It would be difficult to over-water established trees during a hot Texas summer. Soak them deeply! It may take a day or two to do the job right, but your trees will appreciate your effort.

A.

B) If you water your trees regularly by method A, you might consider making a special ring out of drip irrigation equipment. Install the emitters at 12-inch intervals and make a 15 to 25-foot section of the drip equipment. That will allow you to water an entire root zone without moving the hose.

C) If you have a watering rod, insert it six to 10 inches into the soil and let it run slowly. Move it from location to location until the ground is saturated. *Remember to water your trees during the fall, winter and spring, too ... any time that the soil is dry.*

B.

C.

MOST COMMON QUESTION

"Why do my fruitless mulberries and cottonwoods drop so many leaves in early summer each year?"

Large-leafed trees shed leaves in the first hot days of summer because they can't pull water through fast enough. The great growing conditions of spring result in an abundance of large, succulent foliage. Nature protects the trees against the ravages of summer by allowing them to drop some of that responsibility. Additional watering may help temporarily, but you can still expect a certain amount of leaf drop as long as it's hot. Prime candidates, in addition to the two already mentioned, include catalpas, sycamores and silver maples.

Tree Feeding . . . How, When and Why

Fertilizing your trees should present no special problems. Many different products are available just for that purpose. Here are three alternatives:

Spikes allow you to fertilize the tree exactly where you want to, without run-off or over-drift onto patios and sidewalks. Like the old art of driving a rod into the ground and filling the holes with fertilizer, spikes provide very concentrated spots of fertilizer separated by non-fed areas, a minor drawback. Read label directions and use prescribed number of spikes.

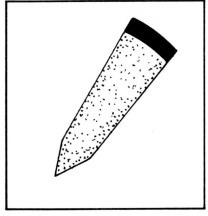

Spikes

Watering rods ensure ample moisture is supplied with your fertilizer ... no chance of burning the roots with fertilizer salts. Runoff is unlikely provided you keep the water turned to a slow volume. Don't insert rods too deeply into the soil or you'll miss most of the roots — six to 12 inches is sufficient.

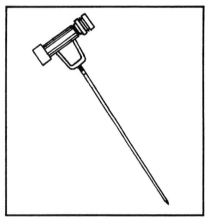

Watering rods

Dry, bagged fertilizer such as you would use on your lawn also works well. Apply it with your fertilizer spreader under the tree's canopy, then water it in thoroughly. Since the tree's roots are near the soil surface, they will compete favorably with grass and ground cover roots for the nutrition. You may find it easier just to make an extra pass or two under your trees with your fertilizer spreader while you are feeding the grass. Just be sure your fertilizer doesn't contain weed killer that might harm your trees.

Dry, bagged fertilizer

TEXAS TIP

Because of our long growing season, feed your trees several times per year . . . small amounts each time, rather than one big dose in the spring. How much to apply? If you are using a complete and balanced plant food such as 12-12-12, apply two pounds per inch of trunk diameter at ground level. For multi-trunked trees, add diameters of the several stems together and use the combined total in figuring amounts of plant food to apply. Make adjustments to the rate as needed for plant foods containing more or less nitrogen. For spikes and for water-soluble cartridges designed for the watering rods, read and follow label directions.

Timing the Feedings

Anticipate the growing season by fertilizing your trees two to four weeks before they break bud in the spring.

Make the second application six to eight weeks later . . . once the trees have reached peak spring growth.

Fertilize again in six to eight weeks . . . in early summer . . . to take advantage of the last weeks of the spring growth spurt.

Research has shown that trees also respond to feedings in late fall, about the time of the average first frost date.

Special Exceptions

New trees: for the first year following the root loss of transplanting, balled-and-burlapped and bare-rooted trees will need a high-phosphorus, root-stimulating fertilizer. Several fine brands are available.

RULE OF GREEN THUMB: Do not apply high-nitrogen fertilizers until new trees have developed good root systems capable of supporting vigorous top growth.

Flowering and fruiting trees: these will respond to additional phosphorus. Apply 10-20-10 or some other high-phosphorus material two to four months prior to flowering.

Pecans: research has shown these respond to high-nitrogen plant foods, unlike most other flowering and fruiting plants. Apply a lawn-type fertilizer in late winter, one month before the average last killing frost for your area. Make a second application just as the leaves are expanding. Pecans will also need zinc when grown in the western two-thirds of the state. Include it with your pecan sprays (see p. 388 for more details).

Iron deficiency: certain trees in certain soils can develop extreme iron deficiency problems. Classic examples are dogwoods and slash pines in alkaline soils of the western two-thirds of Texas . . . also silver maples and Chinese tallows growing in shallow, rocky outcroppings . . . and the list goes on and on.

Consider just one fact before you try to correct iron deficiency in any tree. If the tree is reasonably small, and if the problem will just recur as the tree gets larger and larger, you might be better off simply to replace the tree now. Sure, you can solve iron deficiency in trees. It gets very costly when the tree is fully grown.

With trees, as with most other plants, a healthy and vigorous specimen wards off insects and diseases. Good fertilization helps provide that. Keep your trees well fed and active!

Trees . . . Where the Roots Are

There's something fascinating about things we cannot see — like tree roots. You might be surprised to find out exactly where they are located. More importantly, you might want to change your feeding techniques.

A) Regardless of the tree species and the type and depth of the soil it's growing in, 90 percent of almost any tree's roots are in the top foot of soil. That becomes very important when we water and feed the tree. For example, if you are using a root-feeding rod, don't insert it too deeply into the soil or you'll miss most of the roots. Note, too, that the tree's roots generally extend slightly beyond the outermost limbs — the drip line.

B) Don't add soil on top of the existing grade around trees, or you'll suffocate their roots. Even an addition of two to three inches of soil could cause harm. No longer will the majority of the tree's roots be in the top foot . . . they'll be much lower. See tips on creating tree wells, page15.

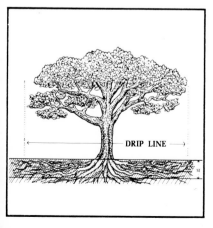

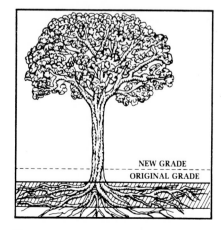

A.

B.

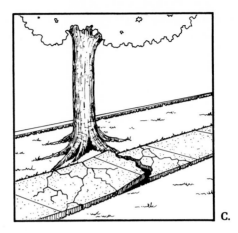

C.

C) Some trees regularly produce large roots quite near the soil surface, even when they're growing in deep, fertile soils. Chief among them: fruitless mulberries, cottonwoods, willows, silver maples, Siberian ("Chinese") and American elms. For this reason do not plant these near existing driveways, walks or the foundation of your home.

MOST COMMON QUESTION

"How often does a tree have to be pruned? Is it done on regular intervals?"

Most of the tree pruning we home gardeners do here in Texas is done improperly. Better than half isn't needed at all. Realistically, there's no way to tell you how often to prune. It depends on the type of tree, its growth rate, the space available and the ultimate size you desire. Basically, you're better off to leave the tree alone until you see a real need for pruning. It's like answering the question, "How often do you change a light bulb?"

REMOVING LARGE LIMBS FROM TREES

Occasionally it becomes necessary to remove large limbs from trees. Either they cause excessive shade, they block desirable views, or they become damaged or misshapen through improper management. Whatever the reason, the limbs must go.

However, large limbs are heavy. Improperly cut, they can be hazards to people, to property below and even to the tree itself.

If you're in doubt, and if you don't have all the necessary equipment, you may find it easier simply to hire a professional tree service company to remove the limbs for you.

If you do intend to do the job yourself, however, follow these few important guidelines.

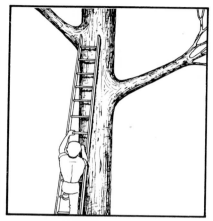

Check the limb for soundness before doing any work on it, especially before climbing on or against it.

Remove as much of the smaller growth as possible before trying to remove the major portion near the trunk of the tree.

Use heavy ropes to hold any parts of the limb that might damage property below. Let other limbs support the limb being removed, but be sure that they, too, are secure. Remove the limb in manageable pieces.

Undercut the limb by one-third at a point two to three feet out from the main trunk.

At a point six to 12 inches out from the undercut, cut through the limb from the top. As the weight of the limb causes it to crack and split, the undercut will stop the splitting from spreading back to the main trunk.

Remove the rest of the limb by cutting flush with the main trunk. Leave no stub!

Seal the wound with pruning paint.

DON'T TOP THOSE TREES!

Proper pruning is essential to every plant in your landscape, but most especially to your shade trees. You can ruin in minutes what it has taken nature many years to produce.

Tree topping, or pollarding, fits right into that category. It's been a Texas tradition for decades. Only in the past few years have some folks seen its folly.

Alleged reasons for topping trees include confinement of tall-growing trees under power lines, elimination of flowers and seed pods and "to stimulate new growth." Well, gardener, it just doesn't work that way! Consider the disadvantages . . .

Top a tree and it will regrow, with three to four times as many shoots as before. Those new limbs will be weak and easily broken by ice and wind storms.

The tree will be more subject to insect and disease invasion. Decay may set in, causing the ultimate death of the entire tree.

All of which ignore the real case against topping: it ruins the natural shape and beauty of the tree.

RULE OF GREEN THUMB: Simply put . . . there's never any reason . . . at any time . . . to top any tree! No exceptions!

CABLING TREES FOR SUPPORT

Should major tree limbs pose hazards to people or property, they can be braced against one another with strong cables. The work is rather precise and does involve a certain element of risk. You probably should hire a professional tree service company . . . someone with the crews, the equipment and the experience. Here are some guidelines, however, should you do the work yourself.

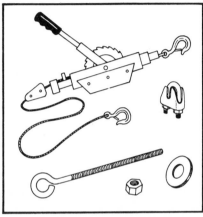

Use only heavy-duty supplies: cable, clamps, eyebolts.

Climb carefully . . . be sure limbs are sound before putting weight on them.

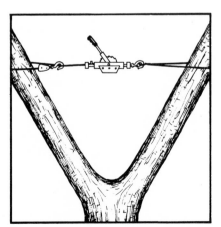

Pull limbs together slightly with portable winch. Use fabric or burlap scraps to protect bark on limbs.

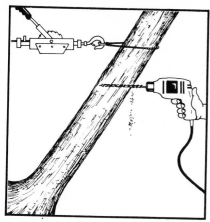

Drill through each limb. Drill bit should be aimed along line to be followed by cable. Holes drilled should be very slightly smaller than diameter of bolts.

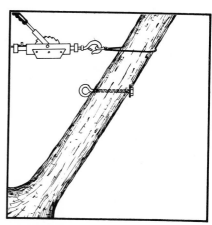

Insert eyebolts. Use large washers on outsides of limbs to keep bolts from pulling through.

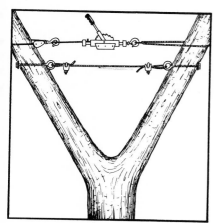

Attach cable using appropriate clamps. Tighten securely.

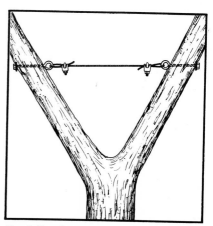

Carefully release winch. If cable does not draw tight, repeat the process and shorten the cable slightly. Install additional cables as needed.

REPAIRING A SPLIT TREE TRUNK

Ice, wind and heavy fruit loads can cause major limbs, even trunks, to split and break. Many of these trees could be repaired, but only through prompt attention.

Strong branching pattern. Limbs form at right angles to main trunk, for good union of strong internal tissues.

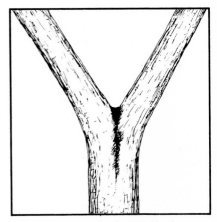

Weak branching pattern. Dead bark, moisture and debris are caught within narrow angle of branches. This type of branching is characteristic of many fast-growing shade trees.

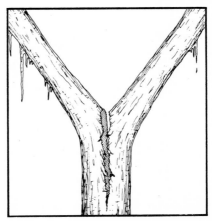

Split trunks often result from narrow limb angles. Chief causes include wind, ice and fruit load.

Should this happen to your trees, follow these guidelines:

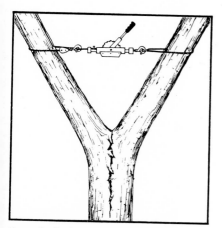

Draw the limbs back together using clamps or a portable winch. Work as quickly as possible, to prevent drying of the tree's internal tissues. This is especially important if the tree is leafed out and growing actively during warm weather.

Assemble the repair materials: a drill and bit, all-thread rod (slightly larger in diameter than the bit), large washers and nuts to fit the rod, a sharp knife, pruning paint and a borer control material.

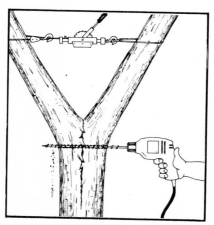

Drill completely through the trunk at right angles to the split. Several holes will be needed for a larger tree.

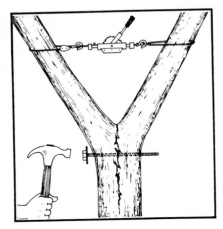

Put washer and nut on one end of all-thread rod, then drive it through hole in trunk.

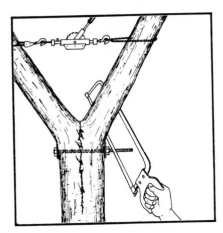

Put washer and nut on other end of all-thread, then cut to desired length. Repeat for other holes.

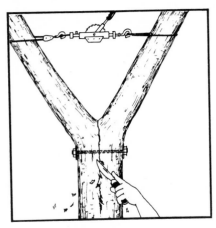

Trim any damaged wood or loosened bark, and treat exposed wood with pruning paint.

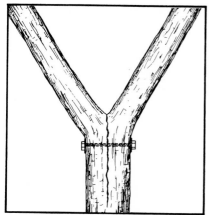

Carefully remove winch. If trunk does not appear strong enough to support weight of limbs, prune to reduce total weight or consider cabling limbs together.

Protect injury from borer invasion by treating monthly with borer spray until wound is completely healed over. Tree will gradually grow to cover all-thread rod and nuts.

FILLING CAVITIES

Decay occasionally invades tree trunks as the result of insect or disease problems, storm damage or improper pruning. That decay can seriously weaken trees, causing potential hazards to the tree and to all that surrounds it. Decay should be dealt with immediately.

Clean all rotted wood out of the wound. Use a sharp knife or mallet and chisel. Clean back to healthy, sound wood.

Taper the wound so water will drain out. Do not leave pockets that can trap and retain water. You may prefer to install copper tubing into the bottom of the wound. Aim the tubing slightly downward to permit flow of moisture.

Allow the wound to air-dry for a day or two, then spray with a combination of fungicide and borer preventative. Allow spray to dry for an additional day or two.

Seal small wounds with pruning paint.

If the wound is extensive, fill it with mortar. Use chicken wire wadded up as a support for the wet mortar. Use roofing paper or pliable sheet metal to make a form for the mortar. Trowel the mortar smooth and flush with the surrounding bark. The bark will grow over the mortar over a period of years, completely covering and sealing the wound.

HOW TO DETERMINE THE VALUE OF YOUR TREE

Assessing the actual value of a tree is a difficult thing. In fact, even skilled arborists won't always agree. For that reason some general guidelines have been set up to aid in accurate, repeatable evaluations.

Three things are considered in evaluating shade trees:

1) First you must establish the tree species. Some trees are more valuable than others. Live oaks, due to their permanence, landscaping beauty and inherent value, command a much higher price than equally sized cotton-woods. If you're not familiar with the various types of trees, take samples to a local nurseryman for identification.

2) Next you must consider the tree's size. Most arborists measure a tree at chest height (4½ feet above the ground). In most cases, the larger the trunk diameter, the more valuable the tree.

3) Finally, you must evaluate the tree's overall condition. Trees in prime health and vigor are worth far more than damaged or diseased trees. The tree must be measured against the best possible tree of its type . . . is it less perfect, and if so, by how much?

If you're trying to prove the worth of a tree that was damaged by storm, automobile accident, vandalism or whatever, you probably should call in the help of a professional. Look for a trained arborist, perhaps one employed by a tree service company. Nurserymen can also be a great help, since they deal with trees daily and are well acquainted with replacement costs.

Best advice of all: If you have a tree that is either extremely valuable or extremely vulnerable, better take photos to establish its "before" value. Knowing the exact placement and condition of the tree can be a great aid in estimating its value.

Assume, for example, that a valuable tree is destroyed by vandalism during the winter, when it had no leaves. How can you prove its condition at the time of its death. Recent photographs can establish that it had a full complement of leaves during the past growing season . . . a major point in evaluation.

THREE OVERLOOKED NATIVES

Want a plant that will survive in your area? One that likes your climate and soil? Consider a native, a plant that's already growing there, one that's proved its adaptability in the Lone Star State. Listed here are three Texas natives that grow over much of our state, yet find infrequent use in our landscapes. Each should be planted far more often.

Possumhaw holly *(Ilex decidua)*: resembles yaupon holly in many respects, except this one is bare during the winter. That exposes all the brilliance of its bright red berries (female plants only) that persist into the spring. Plant is very attractive during growing season as well. Generally grown multi-trunked and as a small tree to 12 to 15 feet. Native through the central third of the state.

Mexican plum *(Prunus mexicana)*: small spreading tree with peeling bark. Bright white flowers in early spring followed by small edible fruit in early fall (good for preserves). Tree offers interesting texture. Better adapted to various Texas soils than other stone fruits. Mature height: 10 to 15 feet. Native over central and eastern portions of state.

Western soapberry *(Sapindus drummondii)*: vigorous upright tree with light green compound leaves much like pecan foliage, only smaller. Attractive bark character. Fruit in winter resembles chinaberry, but tree overall is far superior. Good shade tree to 30 to 40 feet. Native over much of Texas.

STARS ON THE HORIZON

Looking for something unusual . . . a "new" tree to Texas landscapes? Consider the following:

Chinese pistachio *(Pistacia chinensis)*

Oklahoma redbud *(Cercis canadensis* cv. Oklahoma)

Bradford pear *(Pyrus calleryana* cv. Bradford)

All are described in detail in the tree listings that follow. Each is just starting to receive common acclaim, yet all are outstanding trees for general use in the state. Give 'em a try!

TEXAS' TOP 25 TREES

Several hundred trees of varying descriptions are adapted to at least some part of Texas. Many are native trees to the hillsides and woodlands of our state, of little or no landscape importance.

Eliminating those with undesirable growth habits, major insect and disease problems and poor adaptability, we're left with several dozen types that are commonly used in landscaping. Here are 25 of the best.

Not all of these trees will be adapted in your area. Read the descriptions carefully and ask the help of a local nurseryman in making your final selection.

Zone hardiness listings refer to map on page 3. Locate your county and its corresponding zone. Any tree with a number equal to or greater than that of your county's zone should be expected to survive average winters in your landscape.

Carya illinoensis   Zone 5
PECAN

Rounded large tree to 60 to 70 feet tall, 50 to 60 feet across. Moderate rate of growth. Adapted over entire state, though certain varieties are better adapted to certain portions. Check with local nurserymen or with your county Extension agent for the best types for your area. (Also check variety suggestions in Chapter 10, *Fruit and Nut Crops*.) Plant the newer, improved types for better disease and insect resistance. Do not plant pecan seeds or seedlings, since you'll have no way to predict their habits and problems. Pecans do best given deep soil, preferably at least 5 to 6 feet. Trees in western two-thirds of Texas will benefit from addition of zinc to each spray application. Zinc deficiency results in terminal die-back of shoots, called "rosette." Pecans are outstanding large shade trees provided they're given adequate room ... ideally 30 to 35 feet in all directions. As nut-producing trees, pecans will need regular spraying (see Chapter 10, *Fruit and Nut Crops*). As shade trees, however, pecans require little more spraying maintenance than other ornamentals. Generally sold bare-rooted and packed in moist sawdust or moss in late winter. This is the Texas State Tree, and one of the most popular trees in Texas landscapes.

Cedrus deodara   Zone 7
DEODAR CEDAR

Large pyramidal tree, to 40 to 50 feet tall, 25 to 35 feet across at base. Allow ample room in landscape, as tree spreads far and wide. Moderate growth rate. Foliage an attractive blue-green. Adapted in most regions of state. Can show iron deficiency symptoms, however, in rocky, alkaline soils. Bagworms and cotton root rot occasional problems. Resembles Colorado blue spruce, yet far more dependable in most parts of Texas.

DEODAR CEDAR

PECAN

Cercis canadensis   Zone 4
REDBUD

Small rounded tree to 25 to 35 feet tall, 20 to 30 feet across. Moderate rate of growth. Native over much of Texas and well adapted to a variety of soils and climates. Outstanding spring color, with pink being most common. White and deep wine-red forms also available. Flowers hold several weeks, much longer than most flowering trees. Deciduous. Two improved varieties of note: Oklahoma (glossy green leaves, dark wine-colored flowers) and Forest Pansy (purplish-green leaves all season long, rose-pink blooms spring). Somewhat weak wooded, with occasional die-back of twigs and limbs. Subject to leaf spots and leafrollers, though neither is terribly weakening. All things considered, an excellent source of spring color.

Cornus florida   Zone 4
DOGWOOD

Small rounded tree, to 20 to 30 feet tall, 15 to 25 feet across. Moderate rate of growth. Adapted to eastern third of state, in other regions with extensive soil preparation (beds consisting of pure Canadian peat moss). Must have acid soil. Responds well to azalea-camellia-gardenia foods with supplemental iron and soil acidifier. Prefers afternoon shade. "Flowers" are actually showy bracts, in early spring. Pure white is most common, but pink and red forms also available. Named and improved white forms are available, as are (occasionally) dwarf and weeping types. Deciduous, with deep red fall color. Attractive and showy.

Eriobotrya japonica   Zone 7
LOQUAT (Japanese plum)

Small rounded tree, to 20 to 25 feet tall and 20 to 25 feet across. Moderate rate of growth. Adapted to southern four-fifths of state. Evergreen, with large, tropical-looking leaves. Blooms late fall-early winter. Flowers are not showy, but are extremely fragrant. Fruit may follow, depending on winter weather conditions. Somewhat susceptible to fire blight and cotton root rot. Good specimen or small accent tree.

Fraxinus pennsylvanica   Zone 2
GREEN ASH

Rather upright tree, to 40 to 50 feet tall, 20 to 30 feet across. Moderate-to-fast rate of growth. Native to much of eastern half of Texas and adapted to a variety of soil and climatic conditions in all regions of the state. Deciduous. Dark green foliage during growing season. Bright yellow fall color. Somewhat susceptible to borers, but less so than more common Arizona ash. Erect, attractive growth.

Ilex vomitoria   Zone 7
YAUPON HOLLY

Small rounded tree, to 15 to 20 feet tall, 10 to 15 feet across. Moderate rate of growth. Native over eastern third of state, but adapted in all regions. Evergreen foliage is small, without spines

LOQUAT

REDBUD

DOGWOOD

GREEN ASH

of any kind. Fruit is small, bright red (yellow-fruiting type seen rarely in nursery trade). Fruit persists all winter. Only female plants bear fruit. Buy only plants with fruit to be sure you're getting females. Plant one male plant for each 10 females to insure pollination if you have no others nearby. As with most hollies, adapted to sun or shade. Weeping yaupon holly also available, making distinctly vertical tree with weeping branches.

Other hollies are generally sold in shrub form. Many, however, can easily be trained into attractive landscaping trees. Consider Nellie R. Stevens holly, Burford holly, possumhaw holly, and Wilson's holly among many others.

Koelreuteria paniculata   Zone 5
GOLDEN RAINTREE

Small rounded tree, to 25 to 30 feet tall, 20 to 25 feet across. Moderate rate of growth. Adapted over most of state. Blooms in early summer with large sprays of brilliant buttery yellow flowers. Tan seed pods follow. In southern third of state (zones 9 and 10) species *K. formosana* (Formosan golden raintree) is preferred, blooming mid-to-late summer, and with large showy pink seed pods resembling Chinese lanterns. Both types deciduous. Best bought in containers, as somewhat difficult to transplant successfully. Excellent small flowering shade trees.

Lagerstroemia indica   Zone 7
CREPE MYRTLE

Small upright tree to 12 to 20 feet tall, 10 to 15 feet across. Moderate growth rate. Adapted over entire state. Showy flower sprays from early summer to frost, in shades of red, pink, lavender and white. Keep seed heads trimmed off to encourage additional blooming, Deciduous, with good fall color (orange-red and yellow) if powdery mildew is kept under control. Attractive slick bark becomes real asset during winter. Best used as small specimen tree or as flowering accent. Can be used to shade small spaces such as patios. Actually is large shrub that must be trained into tree form by regular removal of shoots emerging from base of plant.

Best current tree-form types include: (red) Country Red, Dallas Red, William Toovey, Durant Red and assorted types generally labelled simply as "watermelon red"; (pink) Potomac; (lavender-purple) Majestic Orchid; and (white) Glendora White and Natchez.

Continuing interest in the plant has sparked considerable research into new and improved types. Scientists and nurserymen are breeding our familiar type *L. indica* with other species of crepe myrtles in attempts to obtain better color, quicker growth, still better bark character and mildew resistance.

Ligustrum lucidum   Zone 7
GLOSSY PRIVET
(commonly known as Japanese ligustrum)

Small rounded tree, to 20 to 25 feet tall, 15 to 20 feet across. Moderate-to-rapid rate of growth. Adapted to southern two-thirds of state. Evergreen, with glossy leaves 2 to 3 inches long. White flowers late spring, not showy. Purplish-black berries borne in fall, persist through winter. Generally grown as large shrub. Requires pruning and stem removal to train as tree. Used in tree form increasingly in small urban landscapes.

JAPANESE LIGUSTRUM

CREPE MYRTLE

GOLDEN RAINTREE

YAUPON HOLLY

Liquidambar styraciflua   *Zone 4*
SWEETGUM

Upright tree, to 60 to 70 feet tall, 30 to 45 feet across. Moderate rate of growth. Adapted to eastern half of Texas, in soils ranging from acid to very slightly alkaline. Shows iron deficiency yellowing in highly alkaline soils. Does best in deep, well-drained soils. Deciduous, with outstanding fall color in shades of red, wine, orange, rust and yellow, often on same tree. Bark is coarse and corky, adding interest during winter months. Fruit a spiny ball which can be objectionable under foot. Outstanding shade tree for cramped urban landscapes. Improved, named varieties available.

Magnolia grandiflora   *Zone 7*
SOUTHERN MAGNOLIA

Upright tree, to 60 to 70 feet tall, 30 to 45 feet across. Slow rate of growth while young; moderate as tree becomes established. Large, dark green evergreen leaves. Very large (8 to 12 inches) white flowers in late spring and early summer, fragrant. Stately and durable tree adapted to eastern half of state and elsewhere where soils are not extremely shallow or alkaline. Responds well to addition of iron and nitrogen. Lower limbs should be left in place whenever possible, both to maintain characteristic magnolia appearance and to shade the tree's shallow root system. No serious insect and disease problems. Leaves may show wind burn and scorch in late winter and early spring in northern regions. A spectacular tree where it grows well.

Malus sp.   *Zone 3*
CRABAPPLE

Spreading tree, to 20 to 25 feet tall and 20 to 30 feet across. Moderate growth rate. Adapted over most of state, but most types flower best in northern half of Texas where winters are adequately cold to satisfy chilling requirements. Flowers early spring: white, pink, rose-red. Fruit red, occasionally yellow. Fruit size varies, generally less than two inches diameter. Deciduous. Require good drainage. Susceptible to cotton root rot fungus.

Morus alba "Fruitless"   *Zone 6*
FRUITLESS MULBERRY

Medium-sized spreading tree, to 25 to 35 ft. tall, 30 to 40 ft. wide. Rapid growth rate when given optimum growing conditions. Deciduous. Large dark green leaves. Best used as quick-growing shade tree. Shallow surface roots require planting at least 6 to 10 ft. from walks, foundations and curbs. Premature leaf drop during prolonged summer heat and drought can be an annoyance. Heavy shade under canopy may make it difficult to keep grass established. In spite of problems, an acceptable fast-growing tree.

SOUTHERN MAGNOLIA

SOUTHERN MAGNOLIA

CRABAPPLE

FRUITLESS MULBERRY

SWEETGUM

Pinus taeda
LOBLOLLY PINE
Zone 6

Pinus elliottii
SLASH PINE
Zone 7

Upright trees, to 50 to 100 feet tall, 20 to 40 feet across. Moderate-to-fast rate of growth. Adapted to acid soil areas of East Texas only. Severe iron deficiency occurs when these are grown in alkaline soils. Evergreen, grown for their showy habit. Loblolly pine, native to much of East Texas, is susceptible to damage of the pine tip moth. Slash pine, a similar species, is susceptible to fusiform rust, another damaging pest problem. With reasonable care, and in good growing environments, either can develop into an attractive specimen. Neither, though, should be planted in the western two-thirds of the state. (See Japanese black pine for a suitable replacement.)

Pinus thunbergii
JAPANESE BLACK PINE
Zone 7

Rounded small tree, to 20 to 30 feet tall and 20 to 25 feet across. Can be kept somewhat smaller by regular and careful pruning. Moderate rate of growth. Adapted over entire state. Especially useful in alkaline soils where other pine species would develop severe iron deficiency symptoms. Evergreen with long dark green needles. Trees develop erratic, multibranched shapes, not the characteristic vertical shape of loblolly and slash pines. Few serious insect or disease problems. Well adapted to a variety of soil conditions and suitable for use as small accent tree or large screen.

Pistacia chinensis
CHINESE PISTACHIO
Zone 6

Rounded tree to 40 to 50 feet tall, 30 to 40 feet across. Moderate-to-fast rate of growth. Adapted to all of state. Deciduous, with brilliant red (also yellow) fall color. Female specimens bear clusters of small red inedible fruit in fall. Male selections, when available, offer better overall plant habit. Insects and diseases not a major concern. A very attractive tree of increasing importance and popularity.

Pyrus calleryana
CALLERY PEAR
(including Bradford and Aristocrat)
Zone 4

Upright ornamental tree to 30 to 40 feet tall, 20 to 25 feet across. Moderate-to-fast rate of growth. Adapted to all of state, but may show iron deficiency yellowing in alkaline soils. Outstanding early spring color with bright white flowers. Bloom best in northern two-thirds of Texas because of chilling requirements. Fruit is small and inedible. Deciduous, with brilliant coppery-red foliage in very late fall. Tree grows vertically first several years, then gradually broadens. Very symmetrical habit. Resistant to fire blight disease. Callery pear is used as rootstock for edible types. When their tops die back to bud union, callery rootstalk begins

BRADFORD PEAR

BRADFORD PEAR

CHINESE PISTACHIO

JAPANESE BLACK PINE

SLASH PINE

growing and often develops into useful tree in its own right. Bradford and Aristocrat, among others, are improved selections of callery pear. Unlike callery, they have no thorns. Improved forms are becoming quite popular all across the country.

Quercus macrocarpa — Zone 3
BUR OAK

Rounded tree to 50 to 60 feet, 40 to 60 feet across. Slow-to-moderate rate of growth. Adapted over entire state, including alkaline soil areas. Large, dark green leaves and rough bark give this oak a coarse, distinctive texture. Deciduous, with fall color yellow to brown. Increasingly available in Texas nursery trade, or can be started from specimens collected in wild or from acorns (large, may attain size of golf balls). Insect and disease problems rare. An outstanding tree that should be more widely planted.

Quercus nigra — Zone 6
WATER OAK

Slightly upright tree to 50 to 60 feet tall, 30 to 40 feet across. Moderate rate of growth. Adapted to eastern third of state . . . acid and neutral soils only. Shows extreme iron deficiency yellowing in alkaline soils. Deciduous, but holds leaves well into winter. Fall color yellow to brown. Closely resembles another acid-soil oak, willow oak *(Q. phellos)*. Readily available in nursery trade in areas where it's adapted. An outstanding and attractive shade tree.

Quercus shumardii — Zone 3
SHUMARD RED OAK

Rounded tree to 50 to 60 feet tall, 40 to 60 feet across. Moderate rate of growth. Adapted over entire state. Particularly well suited to alkaline soils where other similar oaks show iron deficiency. Summertime foliage a lustrous dark green on stately, formal trees. Deciduous, with brilliant red (sometimes yellow) fall color. Grows well in a variety of soil conditions, from deep loams to shallow rocky outcroppings. Insect galls may disfigure foliage and twigs slightly, but do no appreciable damage. An outstanding tree. Texas red oak *(Q. texana)*, also sold as Spanish oak, is another similar species, though it is somewhat smaller at maturity.

Quercus virginiana — Zone 7
LIVE OAK

Spreading tree to 30 to 40 feet tall, 40 to 50 feet across. Moderate rate of growth. Adapted over entire state, including all types of soils. Totally evergreen in southern two-thirds of state, may show some winter burn in northern regions during extreme cold. Trees in all regions will shed old leaves in late winter, before new growth begins in the spring. Live oaks exhibit a great deal of genetic variability from one tree to the next: in leaf size, growth habit and rate of growth. Several growers offer seedlings of selected trees in attempts to reduce the variability. Insect galls may disfigure leaves, but do no permanent damage. Only disease of consequence is live oak decline, an uncommon but serious problem. All things considered, live oaks remain some of the finest of all tree investments in landscaping.

BUR OAK

RED OAK

LIVE OAK

WATER OAK

Sapium sebiferum   Zone 7
CHINESE TALLOW TREE

Upright tree to 30 to 40 feet tall, 20 to 25 feet across. Fast growth rate. Adapted to eastern half of Texas, as far north as Red River. Not adapted to shallow, highly alkaline soils. Deciduous, with brilliant red, wine, yellow and orange fall color, often all on the same tree. One of best trees for fall color in southern portions of state. Trees produce small white berries resembling popcorn that persist during winter. No major insects or diseases. Trees leaf out late in spring, often showing 4 to 8 inches of terminal die-back from winter. New growth soon overcomes it. One of the few highly acceptable fast-growing trees.

Taxodium distichum   Zone 4
BALD CYPRESS

Upright tree, to 60 to 70 feet tall, 30 to 45 feet across. Moderate rate of growth. Adapted to much of state, though may show iron deficiency in extremely alkaline soils. Tree shape pyramidal while young, rounded with maturity. Deciduous, though a cone-bearing plant. Foliage is a medium-green, soft-textured and ferny. Bagworms may be a problem some years, but can be controlled with one or two sprayings. Fall color a dark rust-red, sometimes attractive. Interesting winter twig character. Trunk heavily buttressed near base. Adapts well to variety of soil conditions, from normal upland landscapes to boggy river bottoms. Should be more widely planted.

Ulmus crassifolia   Zone 6
CEDAR ELM

Upright tree to 50 to 60 feet tall, 30 to 40 feet across. Moderate rate of growth. Native to broad band of Central Texas, but adapted to entire state. Especially useful in alkaline soils of western two-thirds of Texas. Deciduous. Fall color generally not notable, yellow. Winter bark characteristics good: fine twiggy growth gives interesting silhouette. Generally sold as balled-and-burlapped specimens collected from nature. One of the few really good elm species for Texas landscapes.

CHINESE TALLOW TREE

BALD CYPRESS

CEDAR ELM

OTHER COMMON TEXAS TREES

Sycamore

Weeping Willow

Cottonwood

Chinaberry

Purple Plum

Hackberry

Siberian Elm

Silver Maple

Arizona Ash

THE OTHER COMMON TREES ... WHY THEY'RE SCORED DOWN

No listing of landscape plants for Texas would be complete without men
tioning all of the common fast-growing, less desirable trees ... the ones w
see on every street in our state. Many of these, in special situations, can b
acceptable landscape additions. Check their faults first, though, to be sur
you can live with them.

	Insects	Diseases	M Ha
Acer saccharinum SILVER MAPLE	X	X	
Acer negundo BOX ELDER	X	X	
Albizzia julibrissin MIMOSA (Silktree)	X	X	
Catalpa sp. CATALPA	X	X	
Celtis sp. HACKBERRY,SUGARBERRY	X	X	
Fraxinus velutina ARIZONA ASH	X	X	
Gleditsia triacanthos HONEYLOCUST	X	X	
Liriodendron tulipifera TULIP TREE	X	X	
Melia azedarach CHINABERRY	X	X	
Platanus sp. SYCAMORE, PLANETREE	X	X	
Populus sp. COTTONWOOD, POPLAR	X	X	
Prunus sp. ORNAMENTAL PLUMS	X	X	
Salix sp. WILLOWS	X	X	
Ulmus americana AMERICAN ELM	X	X	
Ulmus pumila SIBERIAN ELM*	X	X	

* most commonly, but improperly, referred to as "Chinese" elm

Weak Wood	Poorly Adapted (soils, climate)	Potential Damage (sewers, concrete)	Short Life Span
	X	X	
X		X	
		X	X
	X	X	
X		X	
X		X	X
X		X	
	X	X	
X		X	X
		X	
X		X	X
X	X		X
X	X	X	X
		X	
X	X	X	X

Chapter 4

Shrubs

Shrubs are the heart of the landscape. In fact, they do much of the work. They beautify, they screen, they shade and they protect. They're about a versatile as any group of plants could possibly be.

Best of all, we here in Texas are blessed with hundreds of types of shrub ... all shapes and sizes, all colors and textures. You name the need, there' a shrub waiting to help.

We've devoted a whole chapter to this important group of plants. You'l find special sections on selecting and planting shrubs, flowering and fruiting shrubs, hedges and screens, and care of them all, including watering, pruning and feeding shrubs.

Finally, to aid in specific shrub selection, you'll find an encyclopedi listing of the most common shrubs grown in Texas ... their plusses and their minuses.

Out of that collection of hundreds of shrubs suited to Texas it's your job t select the ones that best suit your purposes. What follows will help.

SHRUBS IN THE LANDSCAPE

Shrub placement in landscaping is one of the most important parts of creating a good design. Chapter 2, *Planning Your Landscape*, deals with that in great detail . . . just exactly how you go about using shrubs in your plantings. Where do they go, and why do they go there? How far apart do you plant them? Those are landscaping specifics we've already covered.

Let's spend some time, now, on the details of shrubs.

The Ways Shrubs Are Sold

As with trees, shrubs are sold in three basic ways: container-grown, balled-and-burlapped and bare-rooted. Each has its own purpose, and each has advantages and drawbacks.

Container-grown: Most landscaping shrubs today are grown and sold in containers. It's easier for the nurseryman (space, labor and transportation costs are reduced compared to the older methods of selling most shrubs balled-and-burlapped) and it's better for the consumer (plants retain all their roots for less transplant shock).

Container size varies from one quart to 15 gallon, so you can buy most any size of plant you might need.

Balled-and-burlapped: Still a popular way of producing nursery stock, particularly larger sizes. There is some damage to root systems during digging, but plants dug and planted promptly and properly shouldn't be set back too much.

Bare-rooted: Used primarily for digging small spring and summer-flowering shrubs such as flowering quince, bridal wreath, forsythia and crepe myrtles, among others. Plants dug this way lose almost all of their tiny feeder roots. You must prune them back considerably to help offset the loss. If at all possible, you're better off to plant container or balled-and-burlapped specimens.

RULE OF GREEN THUMB: *Size to Buy:* **You'll save money in the long run if you buy medium-sized shrubs (2, 3 and 5-gallon sized). Since they'll be 12 to 24 months ahead of one-gallon-sized plants, you'll have a much quicker impact on your landscape. You'll be able to tell more about the mature shape and size of these larger plants. You also won't have the temptation to crowd them close together like you would with the smaller plants, so you'll end up buying fewer plants. Their roots will immediately be deeper into the soil, so you'll have greater margin for error when summer drought and watering time come.**

    "Bigger" isn't always "better," but in the case of container-grown shrubs, it generally is.

HOW TO PLANT SHRUBS

Since shrubs are a relatively permanent part of the landscape, you need to know exactly where each one should go. Ideally you have some sort of master plan to use as a roadmap.

As for the best planting season, the advent of containerized nursery stock (where the plant loses none of its roots during transplanting) made it possible to landscape every day of the year. If the soil can be worked, you can plant shrubs. You can plant any time it's convenient!

The only two exceptions to that rule would be for tender plants that might be damaged by extreme winter cold or blazing summer sun. Give those plants an extra margin of safety by planting two to four months ahead of the stress season.

Put Shrubs to Bed

Your shrub plantings will look better and will be much easier to maintain if they're in beds rather than being a part of the lawn. Allow yourself a four to five week headstart . . . get the beds ready before planting.

1. Have a plan for the bed's shape and size. Measure and stake it out.

2. Spray the staked area with a short-lived weed killer to eliminate established weeds. Allow weed killer two weeks to complete its work.

3. Rototill to a depth of eight to 12 inches. Remove roots, rocks and building debris.

4. Incorporate a four to five-inch layer of peat moss, shredded bark or compost and till again.

5. Fumigate the newly prepared soil with vapam or similar material and wait three to four weeks before planting. Read and follow label directions carefully to avoid damage to desirable plants nearby.

6. Dig holes in newly prepared soil large enough to accommodate soil balls. Remove plants carefully from containers. Plants in plastic nursery cans will generally slip out given gentle tapping. To hold soil balls together, make sure soil is moist, not wet and not dry, when you remove plants from containers. Metal cans should be cut at the nursery, then removed immediately prior to planting. Set plants at same depth at which they grew in container. Cover soil ball immediately and water thoroughly. Apply root-stimulator fertilizer for one to two months before beginning regular fertilization program.

7. Balled-and-burlapped and bare-rooted plants should be planted essentially the same way. However, they will need to be pruned 25 to 50 percent to compensate for the roots they lost during the digging. Use root-stimulator fertilizer once a month for entire first growing season.

8. Use some type of edging material to define turf and non-turf areas. Metal edging, timbers, brick and masonry all work well. The edging may not physically stop spread of grass into bed . . . it merely provides a boundary to run your edger along.

9. Use mulches and weed killers as necessary to retard weed growth under shrubs. Read and follow weed killers label directions carefully to avoid damage to desirable plants.

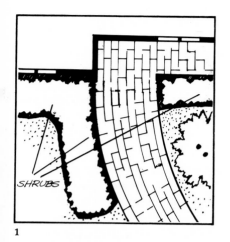

1

2

3

4

5

6

7

8

9

HOW TO WATER YOUR SHRUBS

In many cases your shrubs will be watered as you water your lawn. When you have them in special beds, though, your sprinklers may not reach them completely. That's the time to turn to special techniques to get water to them. Each is intended to soak the soil deeply and, at the same time, to keep the water off the foliage where it could promote disease and ruin flowers.

Drip irrigation systems put small amounts of water in shrubs' root zones. These are also an excellent way of keeping the soil around your house's foundation uniformly moist.

Soaker hoses allow slow, penetrating watering. Some types "leak" along entire length, while others can be used as lawn sprinklers or, upside down, as soakers for shrub beds.

Root-watering rods are effective, but only if they're not inserted too deeply, preferably only six to eight inches deep. That's where most of your plants' roots will be.

Automatic sprinkler systems can include special heads for watering shrub beds.

TEXAS TIP

Don't let heat and drought ruin your plantings. One or two strategically timed waterings may mean the difference between live, vigorous and valuable plants and a pile of dried sticks. Protect your investment!

HOW TO FEED YOUR SHRUBS

There basically are two considerations when you're feeding your shrubs: are you growing them for flowers or for foliage? That answer will determine your fertilization techniques, both in type and in timing.

Spring-flowering shrubs: Apply a high-phosphorus fertilizer such as 10-20-10 in late summer to promote good bud set for following spring's bloom. Apply a complete and balanced fertilizer such as 12-12-12 immediately after blooming. Both can be applied at the rate of one pound per inch of total trunk diameter at ground level.

Summer-flowering shrubs: Apply a complete and balanced fertilizer such as 12-12-12, one pound per inch of trunk diameter at ground level, as growth starts in early spring and again before blooming season. A third application could be made in late summer to stimulate additional growth during the fall.

Evergreens: Apply a high-nitrogen fertilizer (lawn foods work well) before growth begins in early spring, in late spring and again in late summer or early fall. Use one pound per inch of total trunk diameter at ground level.

Types of Shrub Fertilizers

There are many brands of shrub and tree fertilizer available, and most will keep your plants well satisfied. Nonetheless, there are some decisions to be made:

Granular types can be applied quickly over large areas. They must be watered into the soil to become effective, and there is a chance of run-off if heavy rains hit before you've finished watering. These are perhaps the least expensive means of feeding your shrubs.

Specialty granular fertilizers are available
for plants such as azaleas, camellias,
gardenias, hydrangeas and others. Many
times these offer soil acidifiers and iron
that other shrub foods don't have.

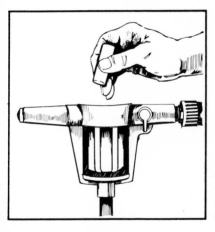

Cartridges for root-watering rods allow
you to inject the plant food directly into
plant's soil environment. Don't insert it too
deeply, though, or you'll miss the plant's
roots.

Plant food spikes provide concentrated
amounts of fertilizer in specific areas.
They dissolve over a period of time,
reducing the risk of their leaching
too rapidly.

HOW TO PRUNE YOUR SHRUBS

Few shrubs grow to a neat and tidy mature habit without regular pruning. Most need your care and attention at least a time or two during the growing season. Still, much of the pruning we do is done incorrectly.

When you do have to prune: do it with an eye toward the plants' natural shape and beauty. Whenever possible, prune with hand tools. They'll allow you to trim limb by limb, rather than the mass cutting that hedge shears and electric hedge trimmers give. Make each cut flush with a remaining limb. Don't leave stubs. It may take a few extra minutes, but the results will be worth the extra effort.

Hand pruning, limb-by-limb, gives more natural appearance to finished pruning job. Waxleaf ligustrum shown before and after pruning.

MOST COMMON QUESTION

"When's the best time to prune my shrubs?"

The answer depends on the shrubs:

Spring-flowering shrubs: *prune immediately after blooming season (forsythia, flowering quince, bridal wreath, weigela, azaleas, camellias, viburnums and Indian hawthorns, among others).*

Summer-flowering shrubs: *prune during winter, while dormant; minor pruning as needed during growing season (crepe myrtles, althaeas, oleanders and others).*

Evergreens, nonflowering deciduous shrubs: *major pruning midwinter, light pruning at any time (junipers, arborvitae, also broadleafed evergreen shrubs except those listed in spring-flowering category).*

RULE OF GREEN THUMB: Buy a plant that grows to the size and shape you want, then leave it alone. Choose one that doesn't require excessive pruning. Don't trim your shrubs into boxy square shapes. Let 'em go natural! They'll give your place a more relaxed look.

MOST COMMON QUESTION

"My shrubs are overgrown. How far back can I prune them?"

Some shrubs, including ligustrums, hollies, photinias and many of the other vigorous broadleafed types, can be pruned back 40 to 50 percent or even more. Evergreens such as junipers and arborvitaes have a harder time rejuvenating new growth and shouldn't be pruned back more than 10 to 30 percent.

Any heavy pruning of this type should be done during late winter, just before spring growth begins. Make all the cuts flush with remaining limbs. Try to leave as much foliage as possible on the plant to nurse it back to vigorous growth.

Obviously you'd be better off to avoid the problem by (1) planting varieties that don't grow out of hand or (2) pruning more often, removing less at a time.

SIX STEPS TO WINTER SURVIVAL

No matter where you live, there are plants that will be marginally hardy to your locale's winters. Damage ranges from leaf scorch and twig die-back to complete loss of the plant.

Follow these simple suggestions to protect the plants at your place:

Know the plant's hardiness. The U.S.D.A. zone hardiness map on page 3 will tell you expected minimum temperatures for your county. Plant descriptions, at the end of this chapter, will tell you various plants' hardiness zones. If you're careful to choose plants that are hardy at least in your zone and northward, they will have a good chance of surviving your winters.

Placement. Plants suffer winter damage in two major ways: 1) from exposure to continuous hard winds, and 2) by prolonged exposure to low temperatures. Shelter tender plants against the south or east sides of your home, out of the gusty north winds. Utilize overhangs, alcoves and other protected spots where temperatures may be a critical few degrees warmer.

Plant tender species in protected alcoves, preferably on south or east sides of your home.

Covering. If it's impossible to plant tender species in protected locations, cover them during extreme cold. Use quilts, blankets or large pieces of burlap draped and secured over plants' canopy to retain natural heat generated by the plant and released by the soil. Do not wrap tightly. Do not use plastic, since it can heat up the following morning and actually do a great deal of damage by itself. Remove the cover once temperatures leave the danger range.

Use fabric covering to shelter tender plants
from cold, drying winds. Wrap lightly, to
provide buffer of "dead" air, and secure.

Mulches. Covering the soil with bark chips, compost or other mulch doesn't keep the soil from freezing. What it *does* do is prevent rapid fluctuation of soil temperatures. The gradual freezing and thawing lessens cold injury. Apply mulches three to four inches deep for best results.

Mulches prevent rapid freezing, thawing
of soil in plants' root zone.

Watering. Cold damage is worse when soils are allowed to dry out. Water all of your plants, particularly those that are cold-sensitive, prior to expected cold snaps. Again, by conserving soil moisture, mulches will reduce freeze injury.

Water prior to expected hard freezes to lessen chance of cold damage to plants.

Late Fall Feedings. Avoid high-nitrogen fertilizers that would stimulate excessive leaf growth late in the fall. Soft, succulent growth is far more susceptible to cold weather injury. Shift instead to a plant food with a high proportion of potassium (third number of the fertilizer analysis), the element that stimulates winter and summer hardiness.

Potassium, the final number of fertilizer analysis, promotes cold (and heat) hardiness. Include it in your fall feedings.

FLOWERING SHRUBS

Shrubs provide a substantial portion of Texas' landscaping color. Here are some of the best and their general season of bloom:

Plant	Height*	Color	Blooming Season
Abelia (Abelia)	2 to 8 feet	white, pink	early summer
Bottlebrush (Callistemon)	10 to 18 feet	red	generally summer
Camellia (Camellia)	5 to 15 feet	red, pink, white	late fall-spring
Flowery Senna (Cassia)	6 to 10 feet	golden yellow	late summer-fall
Flowering Quince (Chaenomeles)	3 to 6 feet	red, pink, white, orange	early spring
Pampas Grass (Cortaderia)	6 to 7 feet	white, sometimes pink	fall
Forsythia (Forsythia)	5 to 7 feet	yellow	early spring
Gardenia (Gardenia)	2 to 8 feet	white	spring-early fall
Althaea (Hibiscus)	8 to 12 feet	white, red, violet, pink	late spring-summer
Hydrangea (Hydrangea)	4 to 12 feet	pink, blue, white	late spring-summer
Hypericum (Hypericum)	2 to 3 feet	yellow	spring
Jasmine-Italian and Primrose (Jasminum)	4 to 8 feet	yellow	late winter-spring
Purple Sage (Leucophyllum)	4 to 7 feet	lavender-pink, white	summer-fall
Winter Honeysuckle (Lonicera)	6 to 8 feet	white	late winter
Oleander (Nerium)	6 to 20 feet	red, white, pink, yellow	spring-summer

Plant	Height*	Color	Blooming Season
Pomegranate (Punica)	2 to 12 feet	orange-red, cream	spring-summer
Crepe Myrtle (Lagerstroemia)	3 to 20 feet	red, pink, purple, white	summer-early fall
Indian Hawthorn (Raphiolepis)	3 to 8 feet	pink, white	spring
Azalea (Rhododendron)	2 to 8 feet	red, pink, white, purple	spring
Mountain laurel (Sophora)	8 to 12 feet	purple	spring
Bridal Wreath (Spiraea)	2 to 6 feet	white, purple	spring-summer
Snowball (Viburnum)	5 to 15 feet	white	spring
Weigela (Weigela)	6 to 8 feet	red, pink, white	spring

*Heights vary according to species. Dwarf forms of many are available.

Azaleas

MOST COMMON QUESTION

"What are the best shrubs for low borders? Something under two feet?"

*For sun I'd suggest dwarf yaupon holly, dwarf Chinese holly, trailing
junipers, dwarf nandina, boxwood and santolina.
For shade consider dwarf yaupon holly, dwarf Chinese holly, Carissa
holly, dwarf pittosporum and dwarf azaleas.*

SHRUBS WITH COLORFUL FRUIT

Although the beauty of flowering shrubs may be the perfect choice for
parts of your landscape, consider fruiting shrubs for additional color:

Plant	**Fruit Color**
Barberry (Berberis)	red, purple
Cotoneaster (Cotoneaster)	red
Euonymus (Euonymus)	red
Holly (Ilex)	red, occasionally yellow, black
Honeysuckle (Lonicera)	red
Indian Hawthorn (Raphiolepis)	purple
Mahonia (Mahonia)	blue, black, red
Nandina (Nandina)	red
Photinia (Photinia)	red
Pomegranate (Punica)	red
Pyracantha (Pyracantha)	red, orange, rarely yellow
Redwing (Heteropteris)	red
Viburnum (Viburnum)	black, red

Yaupon Holly

Oregon Grape Holly *(Mahonia)*

MOST COMMON QUESTION

"What are the best shrubs for shade in Texas?"

There are many, including aucubas, azaleas, camellias, cleyera, fatsia, fatshedera, gardenias, hollies, hydrangeas, mahonias, osmanthus (false hollies) and viburnums.
Some plants that normally tolerate nearly full sunlight will look better given some shade. Wheeler's dwarf pittosporum is a classic example.

A HEDGE AGAINST INVASION

Hedges are some of the more functional parts of our landscapes. Though some gardeners refer to any planting of shrubs as "their hedges," let's reserve the term for its pure horticultural meaning . . . a cluster or row of plants intended for one of these very utilitarian purposes:

Protect Against Intrusion

Dense and thorny shrubs deter prowlers, pedestrians. Best types for Texas include pyracantha, photinia, hollies.

Provide Privacy

Evergreen hedges give year-round privacy, especially important in urban areas. Some of the best for most of Texas include the various hollies, photinia, junipers, glossy privet and waxleaf ligustrum.

Screen Unsightly Views

Well-placed shrubs can block views of streets and highways, schoolyards, vacant lots and businesses. Be sure you use evergreen types.

Delineate Boundries

Hedges can be placed merely for visual separation of parcels of property, or to delineate parts of a single landscape.

Break flow of wind

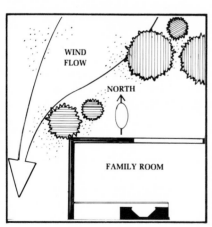

Shrubs can also act as windbreaks, particularly when they're planted reasonably close to the house. Again evergreen types are essential. See Chapter 3, *Trees . . . Texas' Best* for more details on windbreaks.

HOW TO SELECT THE HEDGE

Not every shrub is suited for use as a hedge. Some do the job better than others. There are some tips, though, that will help you get the best plant for the purpose:

• Determine your exact objective in planting the hedge. Are you trying to screen, protect, beautify . . . just what's the reason for making the planting?

• Buy the best plant for the job. Choose one that grows to approximately the height you want your hedge to be . . . don't buy a green giant where a dwarf is required. Excessive pruning is tough on you and the plant! Also, the plant probably should be evergreen to provide year-round screening.

• Buy the largest plants possible, ideally 5-gallon size minimum. That will give a more immediate impact and a quicker screening. You'll also be able to space the plants farther apart and still get a good effect.

Pruning The Hedge

Hedge should be slightly wider at base than at top to allow all foliage to receive sunlight. Informal pruning retains natural shape. Shearing would require more constant care and attention, would look more stiffly formal.

TEXAS TIP

Give a native a chance. Shrubs that grow wild in our state are suited to our soils and our climate. If they weren't they wouldn't already be growing here. You're probably familiar with hollies such as yaupon, possumhaw and, in East Texas, the lovely American holly. You no doubt have seen Texas sage (ceniza), and perhaps you're familiar with agarita, a sister of the various mahonias. All of these are native to the Lone Star State.

Many other fine native shrubs wait to be tried. Watch for them coming out of the nursery industry during the next decade, as we try for plants that are more resistant to hot and dry weather. And, until they're available through your local nurseries, dig them from nature. You'll be surprised at how lovely many will become.

BEST HEDGES TO BUY

Looking for the best possible plants for a hedge here in Texas? You'll find several sure winners below.

Plant	Trained Height	Comments
Arborvitae	5 to 20 feet	Old favorite, less popular now
Azaleas	2 to 6 feet	Spectacular color in spring
Cherry Laurel	10 to 20 feet	Dark green, best in acid soils
Elaeagnus	4 to 6 feet	Extremely heat and drought-tolerant
Euonymus	3 to 6 feet	Many types; some brightly colored
Glossy Privet	10 to 25 feet	Also called "Japanese Ligustrum"
Hollies	2 to 10 feet	Best types include yaupon, Nellie R. Stevens, willowleaf, Burford, Chinese, Wilson's and Foster
Indian Hawthorn	3 to 12 feet	Colorful, durable shrubs. Height varies with varieties. "Majestic" is tallest.
Junipers	3 to 10 feet	Many types, growth habits, colors
Oleander	6 to 15 feet	Bright flowers, cold-tender
Pampas Grass	6 to 8 feet	Large grassy clumps; white flowers
Photinia		
Chinese	8 to 15 feet	Colorful, upright, red berries
Fraser	8 to 12 feet	Bright coppery-red new growth
Pittosporum	5 to 12 feet	Green and variegated types
Privet	4 to 10 feet	Old fashioned, less refined
Pyracantha	6 to 12 feet	Great barricade, bright berries
Sweet Viburnum	6 to 12 feet	Glossy green, upright
Waxleaf Ligustrum	4 to 8 feet	Over-used, but dependable

SHRUBS FOR TEXAS LANDSCAPES

Hundreds of species and cultivars (varities) of shrubs are adapted to Texas landscaping. Some do well in most of the state, while others require very specific soil or climatic conditions and will survive only in localized regions. Consider your choices carefully. Read the descriptions and ask questions of your local nurseryman.

What follows are several dozen of the best shrubs for the South and Southwest. Unless otherwise noted, you can assume that any shrub listed will require standard soil preparation (see Chapter 1, *Getting Started in Gardening*) and post-planting care.

For zone hardiness ratings refer to the U.S.D.A. map on page 3 (See Chapter 1). Begin by locating your county. If the shrub you're considering has a zone rating equal to or smaller than the zone of your county you can assume it will not freeze in normal winter conditions.

Abelia sp.   *Zone 6*
ABELIA

Sun or part sun. Spreading shrubs to 2 to 8 feet. Evergreen in warmer regions, semi-evergreen farther north. Blooms in summertime: bright white (also pink) bell-shaped flowers. Used as landscape accent, rock gardens, low hedges. Can develop severe iron deficiency in alkaline soils.

Varities:
A. grandiflora (Glossy Abelia): Height 6 to 8 feet. White flowers. Spreading habit. Prostrate form also available.

A. hybrid Edward Goucher (Edward Goucher Abelia): Height 2 to 5 feet. Pink flowers. Spreading habit.

Agave sp.   *Zone 6*
CENTURY PLANT AGAVE

Sun. Blooms after 6 to 10 years of growth, sending spikes 10 to 20 feet high. Mother plant dies after blooming, but offshoots (pups) will emerge in all directions around the mother plant. These can be dug and divided for additional plants. Clumping perennials grown for their striking foliage and unusual flowers.

A. americana is most common species. Evergreen, with gray-green foliage. Agaves are used for accents and as barricade plants. All types require perfect drainage. CAUTION: leaves of most agave varieties are pointed and extremely sharp. They should not be planted near pedestrian areas or where children are likely to be playing.

Aucuba japonica   *Zones 6 and 7*
AUCUBA

Shade. Upright shrubs to 2 to 8 feet. Evergreen, with large, often colorfully variegated leaves. Good source of color in shady spots (leaves turn sunburned black in bright light). Good specimen and accent plant.

Varieties:
A. j. "Dwarf Female": low-growing dark green shrub noted for its bright red berries. Zone 6.

A. j. Picturata: small plant with yellow blotch in center of leaves, surrounded by dark green. Striking. Zone 7.

A. j. Sulphur: small plant, dark green leaves with bold yellow band along edges. Zone 7.

A. j. variegata: Gold Dust plant, grows to 6 to 8 feet. Leaves green flecked with bright gold. Zone 6.

Berberis sp.   *Zone 6*
BARBERRY

Sun or part sun. (Red-leafed types must have sun to develop good color.) Low arching shrubs to 2 to 6 feet. Mostly deciduous, some types semi-evergreen to evergreen in warmer climates. Most types spiny, with leaves either intense purplish-red or bright green. Most types bloom spring, bright yellow flowers. Durable shrubs that tolerate minimum maintenance better than most. Use as low borders, colorful accents. Prune out dead twiggy growth to keep plants attractive.

Varieties:
B. julianae (Wintergreen barberry): height 4 to 6 feet. Very spiny, excellent barrier hedge. Evergreen, dark green foliage.

B. mentorensis (Mentor barberry): height 4 to 6 feet. Dark green foliage turns red in fall. Dark red fruit. Compact, good hedge.

B. thunbergii (Japanese barberry): height 4 to 6 feet. Arching branches with deep green leaves, red in fall. Red fruit fall and winter.

B. t. atropurpurea (red-leafed Japanese barberry): height 4 to 6 feet. Foliage remains red all summer long.

B. t. atropurpurea nana Crimson Pigmy: height 1½ to 2 feet. Dwarf red, useful for small accents, low borders.

Buxus sp.   *Zones 5 and 7*
BOXWOOD

Sun or part sun. Small rounded shrubs to 2 to 4 feet. Evergreen, glossy foliage. Most commonly used as sheared low borders, edging. Susceptible to nematodes, spider mites, cold weather leaf burn.

Varieties:
Buxus microphylla japonica (Japanese boxwood): bright green, most susceptible to winter damage. "Green Beauty" selection more cold hardy. "Richard" more vigorous, taller. "Korean" boxwood is hardiest of all selections. Zone 7.

Buxus sempervirens (English boxwood): dark green, hardy to more cold than other boxwoods. Not adapted to hot sites, alkaline soils. Zone 5.

JAPANESE BOXWOOD

CENTURY PLANT AGAVE

AUCUBA

ABELIA

BARBERRY

Callistemon citrinus   Zone 9
BOTTLEBRUSH

Sun. Large upright shrub to 10 to 18 feet, shorter in northern extremities of its zone, where winter damage keeps it pruned back. Evergreen with medium-green strap-shaped leaves. Flowers very showy, scarlet-red, spring and again through the season. Flowers resemble fluffy bottle brushes. Dramatic hedge or screen plant for warmest parts of Texas. Protect from winter winds.

Camellia sp.   Zones 7 and 8
CAMELLIAS

Rounded-to-upright shrubs to 5 to 15 feet. Evergreen with glossy dark green foliage. Showy flowers, single, semi-double and double, are produced from late fall through mid-spring, depending on variety.

Camellias require essentially the same site selection, soil preparation and post-planting care as azaleas, though they're generally less cold-tolerant than azaleas. They should be planted in an acid soil mix (totally Canadian sphagnum peat moss in the western two-thirds of the state), preferably in a raised planting bed that insures good drainage. They should be given bright light but protection from afternoon sun. In areas with alkaline soils and tap water, the planting bed should be given 3 or 4 applications of a soil acidifier and iron additive per growing season. Plants will need to be sprayed regularly to prevent accumulations of tea scale insects on the foliage, thrips and botrytis disease in the flowers.

Camellias can also be grown successfully in containers, where their soil conditions and lighting can be more carefully manipulated. Plants in containers, however, will be far less cold hardy, and will likely require winter protection indoors.

Varieties:

C. japonica: among the showiest of the entire camellia group. Generally bloom winter and spring, depending on variety. Most types have larger leaves and flowers than other species. Less tolerant of cold and poor soils. Zone 8.

C. sasanqua: more dependable shrub with attractive small foliage and lovely flowers in late fall and early winter. More durable to cold, poor soils and alkalinity. Zone 7.

Chaenomeles japonica   Zone 5
FLOWERING QUINCE

Sun or part sun. Rounded shrubs to 3 to 6 feet tall. Deciduous. Leaves are preceded in spring by brilliant blossoms that cover the plant. Rather coarse, stemmy shrubs when not in flower, so best used away from the house, in shrub beds and backgrounds. Flower colors: red, pink, white, orange. May show iron deficiency in really alkaline soils.

Varieties:

Apple Blossom: pink and white, 4 to 6 feet.
Coral Beauty: red-orange, 4 to 6 feet.
Orange Delight: orange-red, 3 to 5 feet.
Pink Beauty: rosy pink, 4 to 6 feet.
Snow: white, 4 to 6 feet.
Texas Scarlet: intense red, 3 to 5 feet.
(many other varieties also available)

Cortaderia selloana   *Zone 6*
PAMPAS GRASS

Full sun. Large clumping grass to 6 to 7 feet, taller when blooming. Evergreen, but clumps may freeze back in North Texas. Long narrow sharp-edged leaves. Flowers showy white plumes in late summer, fall, last for months. Pink variety less common, less showy. Flowers can be cut and brought indoors to dry. Good screen to be used in place of sheared hedge. Good specimen accent plant. Do not plant too near house because of ultimate size.

Cotoneaster sp.   *Zones 5 and 6*
COTONEASTER

Sun or part sun. Large group of shrubs, some upright and many spreading. Height varies with varieties, from 1 to 2 feet to 8 to 12 feet. Some types are evergreen, others semi-evergreen, others deciduous. Leaves of many are dark green and glossy, though gray-leafed types also exist. Flowers are white, sometimes pink. Fruit is generally red or orange-red and showy. Larger types are used as specimen plants in landscape, also in backgrounds. Shorter types are used as ground covers and in rock gardens. All types require good drainage and air circulation. All types are relatively susceptible to fire blight and will require copper spray in spring, at time of bloom.

Varieties:

C. glaucophyllus (Gray Cotoneaster): Gray-green small shrub to 3 to 4 feet. Semi-evergreen, depending on temperatures. Orange fruit. Especially susceptible to fire blight, leaf rollers, cotton root rot, occasionally borers.

C. horizontalis (Rock Cotoneaster): Low spreading, to 1 to 2 feet tall, 4 to 6 feet wide. Briefly deciduous. Bright green leaves, red fruit. Good in rock gardens, bank plantings.

C. lacteus (Parneyi): Large evergreen shrub to 10 to 12 feet. Foliage deep green above, white and hairy below. Larger leaves than most cotoneasters. Arching habit. Well suited to background plantings, espaliers. Fire blight and leaf rollers major problems.

Elaeagnus sp.   *Zones 2, 6 and 7*
ELAEAGNUS (silverberry)

Sun or part sun. Spreading shrubs, most to 4 to 10 feet. Evergreen, most types with gray-green foliage with silvery under-surface. Rapid growth and good heat and drought tolerance. Fragrant flowers in late fall are inconspicuous. Fruit pungent but edible. Excellent low screen or bank plant, specimen. Striking when planted against contrasting dark background. Somewhat susceptible to cotton root rot.

Varieties:

E. macrophylla Ebbengi: more upright, silvery foliage marked with brown scales. Excellent screen. Height 8 to 10 feet. Zone 7.

E. pungens fruitlandi: spreading plant with dark green leaves marked silvery underneath. Vigorous. Height 6 to 8 feet. Zone 6.

E. clemsoni aurea variegata (Clemson variegated Elaeagnus): resembles other elaeagnus varieties in habit. Leaves' centers are yellow with darker green margins. Height 3 to 5 feet. Zone 7.

E. angustifolia (Russian Olive): large gray-leafed deciduous elaeagnus occasionally used for windbreaks and for large specimen plants. Rather informal. Height 15 to 20 feet. Zone 2.

FLOWERING QUINCE

BOTTLEBRUSH

CAMELLIA

ELAEAGNUS

PAMPAS GRASS

COTONEASTER

Euonymus sp.   *Zones 5 and 6*
EUONYMUS

Sun or part sun. Upright and rounded shrubs and trailing vines, depending on species. Heights: 1 to 12 feet. Mostly evergreen, though some types are deciduous. Most types grown for attractive, often glossy foliage. Several types used for brightly variegated foliage. Best landscape uses: ground covers, low borders, hedges, specimen accent plants. Susceptible to euonymus scale, a devastating insect pest that is most prevalent on upright types, also powdery mildew. Require frequent attention to keep those pests under control.

Varieties:

E. fortunei colorata (purple wintercreeper euonymus): low-growing 12 to 18-inch ground cover, dark green during summer and plum-red in winter. Good in sun, few pests.

E. fortunei Emerald Gaiety: small dense shrub with dark green leaves with white margins.

E. fortunei Golden Prince: low-growing evergreen with brilliant golden yellow new growth contrasted with dark green older growth.

E. fortunei Sarcoxie: upright, to 4 feet. Glossy green leaves.

E. fortunei Silver Queen: low spreading type with dark metallic green leaves with white margins. Evergreen and popular.

E. japonica aureo-marginata (golden euonymus): medium sized, compact shrub with dark green leaves with golden margin.

E. japonica aureo-variegata (goldspot euonymus): popular medium-sized variety with dark green leaves with yellow blotch in centers. Has tendency to revert to solid green ... those reversions must be pruned out.

E. japonica microphylla (boxleaf euonymus): low growing dwarf, to 1 to 2 feet. Most commonly used as low border. Dark green foliage.

E. japonica Silver King: upright shrub with large green leaves bordered with white.

E. kiautschovica (patens) Manhattan: upright shrub commonly used as hedge. Dark green glossy leaves.

Fatsia japonica   *Zone 8*
JAPANESE ARALIA

Shade or part shade. Rounded shrub to 6 to 8 feet. Huge star-shaped leaves (evergreen) give lush tropical appearance, even though plant is hardy even beyond southern half of Texas. Flowers white in spring followed by clusters of shiny black fruit. Use for landscape accent, for dramatic impact. Will bleach and sunburn in afternoon sun.

Feijoa sellowiana   *Zone 8*
PINEAPPLE GUAVA

Full sun. Large rounded shrub or small tree to 15 to 18 feet. Evergreen, oval gray-green foliage. Flowers waxy white with red stamens. Fruit tasty, with slight pineapple flavor. Used as large screen or small accent tree with moderate growth rate. Special varieties may be available through nurseries.

Forsythia sp.   Zone 5
FORSYTHIA (Golden Bells)

Sun. Rounded shrubs to 5 to 7 feet. Deciduous with rather rank growth habit. Brilliant yellow flowers very early each spring, before leaves emerge. Very showy when in bloom, but not terribly attractive rest of year. For that reason, best used as background shrub, away from house. Best suited to northern half of Texas, where flower production is greater.

Varieties include Lynwood Gold (deep golden yellow), Spring Glory (paler yellow), Spectabalis (deep yellow on tall plants), among many others. A weeping form (*F. suspensa*) is also available.

Gardenia sp.   Zone 8
GARDENIA

Part shade or shade. Rounded shrubs to 2 to 8 feet tall. Evergreen with dark, glossy green leaves. Very fragrant white flowers, mostly during late spring. Attractive shrubs for landscape use, especially in acid soils of East Texas. Grown by most gardeners, however, for the delicious fragrance of the blooms. Require the same general soil preparation and care as azaleas and camellias. Plant in raised beds of Canadian peat moss. Apply iron and soil acidifier regularly during year. Feed with acid-type azalea-gardenia fertilizer 3 to 4 times during growing season. Keep plants well watered. Prune in early spring to remove freeze damage, again after bloom to shape plant. Protect against temperatures below 20 degrees by covering plants temporarily with heavy quilting (no plastic, please). Plants suffer from iron deficiency in alkaline soils. Plants are susceptible to nematodes. Whiteflies can also be a serious problem. Their honeydew excretions can give rise to sooty mold invasion. Best control for the mold is to control the whiteflies by regular spraying with general-purpose insecticide.

Varieties:

G. jasminoides August Beauty: 4 to 6 feet, blooms late summer, fall.

G. jasminoides Mystery: 6 to 8 feet, blooms late spring, again during late summer, fall. Requires regular pruning.

G. jasminoides radicans (dwarf): 1 to 2 feet, small pointed dark green leaves. Flowers are smaller, but perfectly formed and just as fragrant. More winter-tender than others.

G. veitchi: 3 to 4 feet, compact and reliable bloomer.

Hesperaloe parvifolia   Zone 6
RED YUCCA

Sun. Clumping perennial to 4 to 6 feet when blooming. Leaves resemble yucca, though are less spiny than most yuccas. Flowers are deep pink and yellow, summer and fall. Attractive large rock garden plant. Adapts well.

SILVER KING EUONYMUS

GOLDEN EUONYMUS

VARIEGATED CREEPING EUONYMUS

JAPANESE ARALIA

FORSYTHIA

GARDENIA

RED YUCCA

Hibiscus syriacus   Zone 6
ROSE OF SHARON, ALTHAEA

Best in full sun. Upright shrub to 8 to 12 feet. Deciduous. Blooms summer in shades of white, pink, lavender and red. Both single and double-flowering types available. Single types give better floral display. Good background plant or small specimen tree. Often used in irregular rows to delineate property boundaries, much as tree-form crepe myrtles. Susceptible to cotton root rot.

Varieties:
Ardens: light purple double flowers
Bluebird: large pale lavender-blue flowers, single
Collie Mullens: double purple-lavender with red eye
Diana: USDA release with huge single white flowers
Helene: USDA release, large single white flowers with red centers
Red Heart: pure white with deep red center
Woodbridge: rose-pink with red eye

Hydrangea sp.   Zones 4 and 6
HYDRANGEA

Do best along north or east side of house or in other partially shaded location. Small rounded shrubs to 4 to 12 feet. Deciduous, most with large coarse-textured leaves. Grown mostly for spectacular flower heads (actually bracts) in late spring and summer. Good sources of color at a season when few other shrubs are blooming. Prune after flowering, removing stems that have bloomed and leaving vigorous stems that did not.

Varieties:
H. macrophylla (Garden Hydrangea): height 3 to 6 feet. Flowers pink in alkaline soils, blue in acid soils. Though it's best to leave the color to nature, you can attempt to change pink to blue by adding aluminum sulfate. To change blue to pink, add agricultural lime or super-phosphate to the soil. Start treatment months ahead of flowering. Zone 6.

H. paniculata grandiflora (PeeGee Hydrangea): height 8 to 15 feet. Large shrub or small tree with white flower heads later turning to pinkish bronze. Large leaves, coarse texture. Zone 4.

H. quercifolia (Oakleaf Hydrangea): height 4 to 6 feet. Durable type blooming in early summer with white flower clusters. Large oak-like leaves. Zone 4.

Hypericum sp.   Zone 6
HYPERICUM (St. Johnswort, Gold Flower)

Sun or part sun. Sprawling low shrub or woody perennial flower. Grows to 2 to 3 feet. Evergreen or semi-evergreen, depending on temperature. Foliage light green. Flowers 2½ inches across, late spring, bright yellow. Good low border or rock garden plant. Subject to iron deficiency in alkaline soils.

ROSE OF SHARON

HYDRANGEA

HYPERICUM

Ilex sp.
HOLLIES

Zones 5, 6 and 7

Hands down, hollies are among the best shrubs in the landscape. They're durable, colorful and almost maintenance-free. Depending on the variety selected, they're small border shrubs, larger accent shrubs and even small trees. There's one (or more) just right for your place!

Varieties:

I. altaclarensis Wilsoni (Wilson's Holly): Large shrub or small tree with large dark green leathery leaves and bright red berries. Very bold. Male and female plants. Zone 6.

I. cornuta (Chinese Horned Holly): Large and dense shrub with spiny leaves. Impenetrable, excellent security hedge to 6 to 10 feet. Red berries winter. Male and female plants. Zone 6.

I. cornuta Berries Jubilee (Berries Jubilee Holly): Mounded growth, somewhat dwarf. Foliage resembles Chinese Horned Holly. Berries are extraordinarily large. Zone 6.

I. cornuta burfordi (Burford Holly): One of most functional of all hollies. Dark evergreen foliage with one lone spine at leaf tips. Red berries on all plants. Excellent hedge or specimen, to 6 to 10 feet. Sun or shade. Zone 6.

I. cornuta burfordi nana (Dwarf Buford Holly): All the fine traits of Burford on a smaller plant. Somewhat upright, to height of 4 to 6 feet. Can be maintained at 3 to 4 feet. Red berries on all plants. Sun or shade. Zone 6.

I. cornuta Carissa (Carissa Holly): Extra low, to 2 to 3 feet, with habit of dwarf Chinese holly. Dense, spreading. No berries. Shade or part shade. Zone 6.

I. cornuta Dazzler (Dazzler Holly): Large spiny holly leaves with multitudes of berries. Good upright type. Zone 6.

I. cornuta rotunda (Dwarf Chinese Holly): Outstanding landscape tool. Slow growing with rounded habit, to 2 to 3 feet with extreme age. Spiny leaves, no berries. Sun or shade. Zone 6.

I. cornuta Willowleaf (Willowleaf Holly): Resembles Burford holly, but leaves are more pointed, narrower. Lovely when mature. Height: 6 to 10 feet. Good production of bright red berries on all plants. Zone 6.

I. crenata (Japanese Holly): Attractive small dark green plants. Several varieties available, most staying under 3 to 4 feet. All need good drainage and protection from afternoon sun. Require slightly acid soil. Zone 6.

I. decidua (Possumhaw Holly, also known as Deciduous Yaupon): Upright large shrub or small tree. Rarely seen in nursery trade, but native over much of eastern half of Texas. Should be more widely planted. Deciduous, displaying bright red berries to their best during the winter. Male and female plants. Zone 5.

I. hybrid Blue Prince, Blue Princess (Blue Prince and Blue Princess Hollies): Upright habit, though plants remain small. Extremely dark foliage, a purplish-green. Require afternoon shade in most parts of Texas. Blue Prince is pollinator, while Blue Princess produces berries. Allow one pollinator for every 10 female plants. Zone 5.

I. hybrid Nellie R. Stevens (Nellie R. Stevens Holly): One of the most attractive of all hollies. Vigorous rounded growth habit to 6 to 12 feet. Dark green leaves resemble Burford. Also suitable as small tree. Zone 6.

I. opaca (American Holly): Large tree-form species native to acid soils of East Texas. Selected cultivars including East Palatka available in nursery trade. Zone 5.

J. vomitoria (Yaupon Holly): Outstanding, native over much of East Texas, and well adapted throughout the state. Small spineless leaves and multitudes of small bright red berries. Easily trained as hedge, shrub or small tree. Mature height: 8 to 15 feet. Male and female plants. Look for fruit on the plants when you buy them, to be sure you're getting a female. Weeping and yellow-fruited types also available. Zone 7.

I. vomitoria nana (Dwarf Yaupon Holly): Low spreading type to 24 to 30 inches. Small spineless leaves. Well adapted to sun or shade. Excellent low border plant. No berries. Zone 7.

MOST COMMON QUESTION

"Why don't my hollies have berries?"

Several causes should be evaluated:

    1. You may have a male plant.

    2. You may have a female plant with no male pollen plant nearby, or male plants may flower at different times.

    3. Buds or flowers may have been damaged by late frosts.

    4. You may have pruned improperly, removing buds, flowers or immature fruit.

    5. Cold, rainy weather may have prevented good distribution of pollen by insects.

DWARF CHINESE HOLLY

DWARF YAUPON HOLLY

YAUPON HOLLY

DWARF BURFORD HOLLY

YAUPON HOLLY FRUIT

NELLIE R. STEVENS HOLLY

Jasminum sp.   Zones 7 and 8
JASMINE

Sun or part sun. Gracefully arching shrubs to 4 to 8 feet tall. Evergreen in warmer climates, semi-evergreen in northern half of state. Foliage bright green to dark glossy green. Flowers yellow in winter, spring. Good accent plant, large rock garden or bank planting shrub. Somewhat cold tender in northern third of Texas.

Varieties:

J. humile (Italian Jasmine): height 4 to 6 feet, spread 6 to 8 feet. Dark glossy green leaves cover attractive sprawling shrub. Flowers are small but bright yellow. Zone 7.

J. mesnyi (Primrose Jasmine): height 4 to 8 feet, spread 6 to 10 feet. Bright green leaves cover arching shrub. Flowers are 2 to 2½ inches across, bright yellow, in winter, spring. Requires occasional pruning to keep in good shape. Zone 8.

J. nudiflorum (Winter Jasmine): height 3 to 4 feet, spread 4 to 5 feet. Arching deciduous shrub with late winter yellow flowers. Glossy dark green foliage. Useful in covering banks and to stop erosion. Zone 7.

Juniperus sp.   Zones 3 and 5
JUNIPERS

All junipers do best in full sun. Evergreen trees, shrubs and ground covers. Fine textured, needle-like foliage in colors ranging from dark green to bright green and steel-blue. Some types, primarily the blue-green varieties, take on intense purple-red color in winter. Some varieties have conspicuous and colorful fruit (cones).

Junipers tolerate cold, heat and drought. In that measure, they're some of the most useful plants available for Texas landscapes. They require good drainage and, for that reason, they may suffer root damage in plantings along the Gulf Coast.

For best growth, fertilize your junipers every 6 to 8 weeks during the growing season. Use a high-nitrogen tree and shrub fertilizer. Water after feeding, and regularly throughout the year. In spite of their durability, junipers respond well to attention.

Spider mites may cause junipers to dry, usually from the bottom, or crown, of the plant upward. Control with miticide.

Bagworms will attack most junipers, especially the upright types, in late spring and early summer. Control with general-purpose insecticides, but spray as soon as feeding starts.

Ground Covers

Shore, Blue Pacific, Bar Harbor, Andorra, Wiltoni (Blue Carpet, Blue Rug), Buffalo, Tamarix (Tam) and others.

Shrubs

Blue Vase, Hetz, Pfitzer, Blue Pfitzer, Golden Pfitzer, Mint Julep, Table Top Blue, Hollywood Twisted and others.

Columnar

Keteleer, Spartan, Wintergreen, Pathfinder, Skyrocket, Manhattan Blue, Hillspire and many others.

Trees

Eastern redcedar.

SEA GREEN JUNIPER

TABLE TOP BLUE JUNIPER

ITALIAN JASMINE

Lagerstroemia indica
CREPE MYRTLE

Zone 7

Does best grown in full sun in areas with good air circulation. Shrub or small tree grown for its attractive habit and colorful red, pink, white and purple flowers during the summer and early fall. Deciduous. Trunks of upright types develop slick, smooth appearance, particularly attractive during winter. Fall color good, ranging from red and orange-red to yellow.

Powdery mildew is a recurring problem, but can be managed by repeated applications of benomyl, Acti-dione PM or karathane.

Keep plants well watered. Fertilize every 6 to 8 weeks during the growing season with a complete and balanced analysis plant food.

Little regular pruning is required for crepe myrtles. You will want to remove seed heads as soon as petals fall, to encourage additional blooming. During the winter, prune off all remaining dried seed heads and all twigs smaller than a pencil in diameter. Don't pollard, or "top," your crepe myrtles or you'll end up with large, floppy flower heads and unattractive plants.

If you're trying to convert a shrub-form crepe myrtle into a tree, merely remove all but 3 to 5 of the main trunks. Remove basal side shoots that develop.

Variety Listings

Variety	Color
weeping miniature types* . . . 18 to 24 inches)	
Baton Rouge	Deep Red
Cajun Red Beverly	Rose-Red
Cordon Bleu	Lavender
Lafayette	Light Lavender
Mardi Gras	Violet
Snow Lace	White
Delta Blush	Pink
(dwarf types . . . 4 to 5 feet)	
Crepe Myrtlettes**	Mixed Colors
Petite Embers	Rose Red
Petite Red	Crimson Red
Petite Snow	White
Petite Pinkie	Pink
Petite Orchid	Dark Orchid
(intermediate types . . . 5 to 8 feet)	
Catawba	Dark Purple
Cherokee	Red
Conestoga	Lavender
Potomac	Pink
Seminole	Bright Red
Peppermint Lace	Pink, Edged White

Variety	Color
(large types . . . over 8 feet)	
Watermelon Red	Deep Red
Country Red	Bright Red
Durant Red	Red
Dallas Red	Bright Red
Fire Bird	Bright Red
Near East	Orchid Pink
Shell Pink	Pink
New Snow	White
Glendora White	White
Natchez	White
Majestic Orchid	Orchid Purple

*Weeping miniature types: hardy to 15°.

**seed-grown selection of George Park Seed Company, Greenwood, South Carolina

An important note: Though many crepe myrtles are sold merely by color ("red", "white", "pink", etc.), there are decided differences between varieties. Whenever possible you're better off to buy known varieties or to purchase your plants in bloom, so you can see exactly what you're getting.

And, equally important: New varieties are being introduced each year, the result of extensive research by the U.S.D.A. and by the nursery industry. Watch for types that are faster growing, showier bloomers, and more mildew resistant, to name just a few of the future features. Work aimed at making a great plant greater!

CREPE MYRTLE

CREPE MYRTLE

Leucophyllum frutescens   Zone 8
TEXAS SAGE, CENIZA

Full sun. Rounded shrub to 4 to 7 feet. Evergreen in southern half of Texas, semi-evergreen in colder regions. Small leaves are a striking gray all season long. Flowers varying shades of orchid and lavender, occasionally white. Plants bloom in summer, generally 3 to 4 days after shower . . . not easily fooled by water hose. Very drought-resistant and tolerant of poor soils.

Ligustrum sp.   Zone 7
LIGUSTRUM, PRIVET

Sun or part sun. Upright shrubs, to 6 to 20 feet tall. Most types are evergreen in Texas climates. Bold, dark green foliage is waxy, sometimes glossy. Creamy white flowers in late spring followed by purple-black berries fall and winter. Popular food for birds. Because of their good looks and durability, several of the ligustrums are over-used in landscapes. Susceptible to cotton root rot, also iron deficiency in alkaline soils.

Varieties:

L. japonicum (Waxleaf Ligustrum): Glossy-leafed shrub to 6 to 10 feet. Good for massed planting in landscape, also for intermediate screen. Variegated type "Silver Star" also available.

L. hybrid (Suwannee River Ligustrum): Small hybrid ligustrum with dark green foliage tightly clustered against stems. Results in rather stiff upright growth habit.

L. lucidum (Glossy Privet): Large shrub or small tree to 20 to 25 feet. Excellent large screen, patio tree. Commonly known in nursery trade as "Japanese ligustrum."

L. amurense (Amur River Privet): Old-fashioned hedge plant of Texas, still occasionally planted. Rather rangy without shearing. Grows to 10 to 15 feet, but can be held at 5 to 6 feet. More cold hardy than other Privets (Zone 4).

L. vicaryi (Vicary Privet): Bright golden-green foliage provides striking contrast to darker foliage nearby. Best color in full sun and when left unsheared.

Mahonia sp.   Zone 5
MAHONIA

Shade, part shade and sun. Small upright shrubs to 3 to 6 feet. Evergreen. Leaves bold, often spined. Related to nandina, with similar growth habits. Yellow flowers in spring are followed by blue-purple fruit fall and winter. Excellent in massed plantings and for colorful accents. Versatile.

Varieties:

M. aquifolium (Oregon Grape Holly): height 3 to 5 feet. (compact form available). Glossy dark green leaves are bright coppery-red when young. Improved forms also available, including OranGEE Flame, with brilliant orange new growth. Bright yellow flowers. Very attractive and much underplanted!

M. bealei (Leatherleaf Mahonia): height 4 to 6 feet. Gray-green leaves are extremely spiny. Excellent barricade plant, specimen. Fruit steel blue.

Nandina sp.   *Zone 6*
NANDINA (Heavenly Bamboo)

Plant in sun for best color. Upright or rounded plants, ranging from 1 to 6 feet tall. Evergreen, grown especially for their brilliant midwinter color in shades of red, orange, purple and yellow. Insignificant flowers, but one variety bears brilliant orange-red berries. Used as specimen plant, border, ground cover and massed planting. Very adaptable, but may show iron deficiency in extremely alkaline soils. Prune upright varieties late each winter by removing one-third of the canes at ground level. By choosing the tallest canes for removal each year, you can keep the plants compact.

Varieties:
   N. domestica: most common type, grown for its winter color, bright red berries. Height 4 to 6 feet.
   N. domestica compacta: as above, but more compact.
   N. domestica Harbour dwarf: most compact of all, with typical nandina foliage on 12 to 18-inch plants.
   N. domestica nana: small rounded plant to 12 to 18 inches. Grown for its brilliant winter color.

Nerium oleander   *Zone 8*
OLEANDER

Sun. Large rounded shrub to 20 feet. Evergreen. Leaves dark green, long and pointed. Brightly colored red, pink, white and pale yellow flowers late spring, summer. Good large specimen shrub, large screen. All parts of plants are poisonous. Subject to freeze damage in northern half of Texas, with subsequent die-back. New regrowth following freeze will not bloom well. Single red is hardiest, followed by single pink. White and yellow are most tender.
   Varieties include Single Hardy Red, Single Hardy Pink, Cherry Ripe, Isle of Capris (yellow), Mrs. Roeding (double, salmon-pink), Sister Agnes (white). Dwarf types (Zone 9) also available, including Petite Pink and Petite Salmon.

Osmanthus sp.   *Zones 6 and 7*
FALSE HOLLY

Protect from afternoon sun. Upright shrub 4 to 6 feet tall and 3 to 4 feet wide. Evergreen with holly-like spiny leaves, some varieties brightly variegated. Fragrant flowers small, not showy, early fall. Fruit rare. Special accent shrubs requiring good soil preparation, ample moisture. Shade and part shade.

Varieties:
   O. heterophyllus Gulftide (Gulftide False Holly): green-leafed type with compact habit, glossy green foliage with twisted margins. Well-branched. Good for small hedge. Zone 6.
   O. heterophyllus variegatus (variegated False Holly): leaf margin marked with broad creamy-yellow band. Striking and colorful accent. Zone 7.
   O. fragrans (Fragrant Tea Olive) is another false holly best adapted to the eastern third of Texas. It is a large shrub, to 6 to 10 feet, with fragrant inconspicuous flowers in the fall. Requires addition of considerable organic matter to planting soil in western two-thirds of state. Zone 6.

TEXAS SAGE FLOWERS

WAXLEAF LIGUSTRUM

MAHONIA

VICARY PRIVET

NANDINA

NANDINA BERRIES

FALSE HOLLY

NANA NANDINA (WINTER COLOR)

OLEANDER

Various species   Zones 7 through 10
PALMS

Sun. Tropical shrubs and trees commonly grown in southern third of Texas, less frequently farther north. Some types, as noted in the chart below, are hardy over fairly large portions of the state. Provide rich, well drained soil. If you're growing a cold-tender type, plant it on the south or east side of your house, out of the winter wind. Larger, more mature plants will also survive extreme cold better than younger specimens. Consider factors such as adjacent fences, trees overhead, radiated heat from buildings, pavement . . . anything that might modify the environment enough that tender types could survive. Plant palms in warm weather (late summer-early fall) for best recovery from transplanting shock.

hardy in zone 7 and southward:
    (Fan Palms — palmately leafed)
    Needle palm *(Rhapidophyllum hystrix)*
    Louisiana palmetto *(Sabal louisiana)*
    Dwarf palmetto *(Sabal minor)*
    Cabbage palmetto *(Sabal palmetto)*
    Texas palmetto *(Sabal texana)*
    Windmill palm *(Trachycarpus fortunei)*
    California fan palm *(Washingtonia filifera)*
      (Feather Palms — pinnately leafed)
    Pindo palm *(Butia capitata)*

hardy in zone 8 and southward:
    (Fan Palms)
    European fan palm *(Chamaerops humilis)*
    Fountain palm *(Livistonia australis)*
    Chinese fountain palm *(Livistonia chinensis)*
    Saw cabbage palm *(Paurotis wrightii)*
    Scrub palmetto *(Sabal etonia)*
    Hispaniolan palmetto *(Sabal umbraculifera)*
    Mexican fan palm *(Washingtonia robusta)*
    (Feather Palms)
    Chilean honey palm *(Jubaea spectabilis)*
    Canary Island date palm *(Phoenix canariensis)*
    Date palm *(Phoenix dactylifera)*
    India date palm *(Phoenix sylvestris)*

hardy in zone 9 and southward:
    (Fan Palms)
    Lady palm *(Rhapis excelsa)*
    (Feather Palms)
    Queen palm *(Arecastrum romanzoffianum)*
    Senegal date palm *(Phoenix reclinata)*
    Pigmy date palm *(Phoenix roebelenii)*

Photinia sp.   *Zone 6*
PHOTINIA

Best in full sun, where colors are most intense. Upright shrubs to 8 to 15 feet. Evergreen, with large dark green leaves. New growth pronounced coppery-red, especially during cool weather. Creamy white flowers (unpleasant aroma). Red clusters of fruit on Chinese photinia late fall, winter. Attractive to birds, both for feeding and nesting. Excellent large shrubs for tall screens and accents. Can be espaliered or trained as small patio tree. Susceptible to aphids in spring, mildew all season long.

Varieties:
P. fraseri (Fraser's photinia): More refined, growing to 10 to 12 feet tall. Has intense spring color and is mildew resistant.
P. serrulata (Chinese photinia): Coarser texture, taller plant, to 15 to 20 feet. Heat and drought resistant. Highly susceptible to mildew. Red berries.

Pittosporum tobira cv.   *Zones 8 and 9*
PITTOSPORUM

Sun to part sun. Spreading shrubs of varying heights. Evergreen with glossy foliage and dense habit of growth. Fragrant flowers inconspicuous.

Varieties:
P. tobira (Green Pittosporum): Largest and hardiest of the varieties. Glossy foliage. Grows to 10 to 15 feet in South Texas, remains shorter in north. Zone 8.
P. tobira variegata (Variegated Pittosporum): White, gray and light green variegation make this a refreshing looking plant. Tender to temperatures below 15 to 18 degrees. Prefers afternoon shade. Mature height: 4 to 6 feet. Hardy southern half of Zone 8 and southward.
P. tobira Wheeler's Dwarf (Wheeler's Dwarf Pittosporum): Low growing, to 2 to 3 feet. Best appearance in partial shade. Requires protection from temperatures below 20 degrees. Zone 9.

Podocarpus macrophylla   *Zone 7*
JAPANESE YEW (Yew Podocarpus)

Protect from afternoon sun. Upright evergreen shrub, to 10 to 25 feet, shorter in northern half of state. Leaves are 3 to 5 inches long, bright green and flattened. Fruit, when present, a bright blue berry (cone). Soft textured accent shrub with a very pleasing habit of growth. Can be trained, espaliered. Does best in acid, well-drained soils. Worthy of more common use.

Prunus caroliniana   *Zone 7*
CAROLINA CHERRY LAUREL

Sun or part sun. Large rounded-to-upright shrub, to 12 to 18 feet. Evergreen, with dark glossy green foliage. Creamy white flowers in spring followed by black berries summer and fall. Can be used as tall hedge, as specimen plant, or as small tree. Requires acid soil to prevent iron deficiency symptoms. Susceptible to cotton root rot fungus and, occasionally, borers. Variety "Bright 'n Tight" is decidedly upright, more compact.

VARIEGATED PITTOSPORUM

GREEN PITTOSPORUM

JAPANESE YEW

CAROLINA CHERRY LAUREL

PHOTINIA FRASER

Punica granatum   *Zone 7*
POMEGRANATE

Requires sun for best flowering. Upright shrub or small tree. Height varies with variety, but ranges from 2 to 12 feet. Deciduous. Leaves dark glossy green, turning bright yellow in the fall. Drought and heat tolerant. Colorful orange-red or creamy flowers late spring and early summer are followed by fruit in certain varieties. Good accent shrub, also used for deciduous hedge.

Varieties:

P. granatum Alba Plena (Flowering Pomegranate): height 6 to 9 feet. Flowers large creamy yellow. Ornamental, fruit rare.

P. granatum Chico (Dwarf Pomegranate): height 18 to 24 inches. Looks exactly like regular pomegranate, just in miniature. Orange-red flowers. Good for small accent shrub. Small fruit (inedible) persists through fall and well into winter. May show freeze damage in Zone 7.

P. granatum Double Red (Flowering Pomegranate): height 8 to 12 feet. Flowers large orange-red, resembling carnations. No fruit.

P. granatum Wonderful (Wonderful Fruiting Pomegranate): height 8 to 12 feet. Attractive large shrub bearing orange-red flowers followed by edible fruit. Best fruiting variety for Texas conditions. (See Chapter 10, Fruit and Nut Crops.)

Pyracantha sp.   *Zones 5, 6 and 7*
PYRACANTHA (Firethorn)

Sun or slight shade. Large upright and rounded shrubs, most types to 6 to 12 feet unless sheared. Dwarf types also available. Evergreen in most parts of Texas, semi-evergreen in extreme cold. Foliage dark green, narrow, to 1 to 2 inches long. Flowers creamy white spring, followed by showy orange, red or yellow fruit in fall and winter. Fruit is not poisonous, and can actually be used in jellies. One of best sources of mid-winter landscape color. Because of extremely sharp thorns, an excellent barricade plant when used as hedge. Also used as colorful accent. Twigs are supple when young, making the plant easily trained for espaliers and topiary. Subject to fire blight, cotton root rot, lace bugs and leaf rollers, so regular spraying will be required.

Varieties:

P. coccinea: among the hardiest of all pyracanthas. Orange-to-red berries, depending on cultivar. Most common types: Kasan (medium-sized, orange-red berries), Lalandei (large plant, orange berries), Lowboy (low spreader, orange fruit), Wyattii (upright, medium-sized, orange-red berries). Zone 5.

P. koidzumi: showy strong growers bearing intensely red fruit in large clusters. Most common types include Victory (large shrub with outstanding fruiting habits) and Santa Cruz Prostrate (low spreading type, also with bright red fruit in fall and winter). Zone 7.

Pyracantha (Mohave): introduced by the National Arboretum, this is one of the hardiest orange-reds available. Also shows fire blight resistance. Zone 6.

Pyracantha (Red Elf): dwarf mounding habit. Dark green foliage, bright red berries. Good for low border or massed plantings. Zone 7.

PYRACANTHA

CHICO DWARF POMEGRANATE

DOUBLE RED POMEGRANATE

PYRACANTHA

Raphiolepis indica   *Zone 7*
INDIAN HAWTHORN

Best in full sun or part shade. Spreading shrubs to 3 to 8 feet. Evergreen with dark leathery foliage. Dense growth requiring little shearing. Flowers spring pink, rose and white. Purple fruit follows flowers. Excellent low shrub for massed plantings, low borders and hedges. Has become one of most popular landscaping shrubs. Buy named and labelled varieties to be sure you're getting best shape and flowering habits.

Variety	Color	Relative Height*
Ballerina	deep rosy pink	low
Clara	white	medium
Coates Crimson	crimson-pink	medium
Enchantress	pink	low
Fascination	deep rosy pink	low
Jack Evans	bright pink	medium
Majestic Beauty	light pink	very tall
Rosea	light pink	medium
Rosea dwarf	light pink	medium
Snow White	white	medium
Springtime	deep pink	tall

*As a general rule, Indian hawthorn leaf size is proportionate to mature plant height for a given variety. Smaller types have smaller leaves. Conversely, Majestic Beauty has leaves 4 to 6 inches long.

Rhododendron sp.   *Zones 6 and 7*
AZALEAS

Most azaleas do best in filtered shade . . . with protection from the hot afternoon sun. No plant is any showier! But success with azaleas takes care and attention. Start by choosing the best location possible. Be sure your variety choice is adapted to your local climate. Plant and care for it properly.

Location

Ideally, azalea plantings should be in areas of high visibility. Basically, the thicker the leaf, the more direct sun that azalea variety can tolerate. They do well under tall shade trees and on eastern exposures. Azalea roots are rather tender, so perfect drainage is a must.

Variety Selection

(See planting chart at the end of this section)

Planting

Raised planting beds are preferable, especially where drainage may be a problem. Dig the bed 8 to 12 inches below the surrounding grade, then use landscaping ties or masonry to provide for the rise. Construct a 6 to 10-inch retaining wall around the bed.

Prepare the planting medium carefully. Since azaleas respond well to acid soils, let Canadian peat moss be at least half of the mix. Use compost or finely shredded bark soil conditioner as the remainder. If native soils are alkaline, the peat moss should be used for the entire planting mix. Do not include any native soils in the planting bed.

Plant close together for the quickest show. If roots are matted together inside the can, cut through the outer layer with a sharp knife. Set the plants in the peat-bark mix ½ to 1 inch higher than they grew in the container, again, to ensure good drainage.

Apply root-stimulator fertilizer after planting. Water thoroughly. Wait 2 to 3 weeks to begin the regular fertilization schedule.

Mulch the soil with coarse bark to conserve moisture and to prevent washing.

Post-Planting Care

Water your plants regularly. Don't allow the mix to dry completely or you'll have a tough time re-wetting it. Adding a few drops of a spreader-sticker surfactant will improve penetration of water into the mix.

Feed the plants monthly during the growing season with an azalea-camellia-gardenia food: 2 weeks after bloom, mid-summer and early fall. The early fall feeding should be at half the rate used at the two earlier fertilizations.

Apply a soil acidifier 3 to 4 times during the year if your native soil or water is alkaline.

Prune azaleas as needed, but do it after they finish flowering. Minor reshaping is generally all that's needed. Do no pruning between June 15 and the next year's blooming season, or you'll be cutting off buds.

Should iron deficiency show up, treat at once. Apply one of the several iron supplements, along with a soil acidifier. Keep iron products away from painted and masonry surfaces (they can stain).

Plants to Grow With Azaleas

Take advantage of the special site and soil preparation you've made for your azaleas. Add other compatible plants to their bed, including camellias, mahonias, cleyera, hollies, aucubas, Japanese maples and dogwoods.

Azaleas Planting Chart

Variety	Bloom Color	Flower Size	Bloom Time	Plant Habit
Christmas Cheer	red	medium	midseason	medium, spreading
Coral Bells	coral	small	midseason	dwarf, low spreading
Delaware Valley	white	medium	midseason	tall
Fashion	red-orange	medium	midseason	medium, upright
Formosa	magenta	medium	midseason	upright, tall
Glory	peach pink	medium	late	medium, spreading
Gumpo	white w/pink	small	late	dwarf, spreading
Gumpo Pink	pink	small	late	dwarf, spreading
Hampton Beauty	red w/darker blotch	medium	midseason	medium, spreading
Hersey Red	bright red	medium	midseason	medium, spreading
Hexe	violet-red	medium	midseason	dwarf, spreading
H.H. Hume	white	medium	midseason	medium, erect
Hino Crimson	red	medium	midseason	low spreading
Hinodegiri	red (less intense than Crimson)	medium	midseason	low spreading
Judge Solomon	deep pink	medium	late	tall, upright
Kate Arendall	white	medium	midseason	tall, upright
Mother's Day	red	medium	midseason	medium, upright
Orange Cup	orange-red	small	early	dwarf, upright

Variety	Bloom Color	Flower Size	Bloom Time	Plant Habit
Pink Pearl	pink	medium	midseason	dwarf, upright
Pink Ruffles	bright pink	medium	midseason	tall, vigorous
Pride of Mobile	deep pink	medium	late	tall, upright
Red Ruffles	deep red	large	midseason	medium
Salmon Beauty	salmon	medium	midseason	medium upright
Sherwood Red	orange-red	medium	midseason	low spreading
Snow	white	medium	midseason	medium, upright
Sweetheart Supreme	pink	medium	late	medium, spreading
Wakaebisu	medium pink	medium	late	dwarf, low spreading

AZALEA

INDIAN HAWTHORN

INDIAN HAWTHORN

AZALEA

Rosmarinus officinalis   *Zone 8*
ROSEMARY

Sun, part sun. Low spreading shrub 2 to 4 feet. Evergreen. Dark green leaves are fragrant, used in seasoning. Blue-violet flowers spring. Rugged appearance makes rosemary suitable for rock gardens, as medium border shrub. Endures heat and drought well, but must have good drainage. Requires winter protection in northern parts of state.

Santolina sp.   *Zones 7 and 8*
SANTOLINA (Lavendercotton)

Sun. Low spreading sub-shrub, to 1 to 2 feet. Evergreen. Fragrant foliage is either intense gray (*S. chamaecyparissus*, Zone 7) or bright green (*S. virens*, Zone 8). Flowers yellow in early summer, but should be removed while still in bud stage to keep plants compact. Commonly used in rock gardens and as low border shrubs. Shear plants several times during year to keep them compact. Plants must have perfect drainage.

Sophora secundiflora   *Zone 7*
MESCAL BEAN, TEXAS MOUNTAIN LAUREL

Sun. Rounded shrub or small multi-trunked tree, to 8 to 12 feet, taller in southern regions. Evergreen with deep glossy green foliage. Purple bloom clusters in spring resemble wisterias, heavily fragrant. Slow growing. Requires good drainage, and does best in alkaline soils. Well adapted to western two-thirds of Texas. Native to Southwest Texas.

Spiraea sp.   *Zone 5*
SPIRAEA (Bridal Wreath)

Best bloom occurs in full or nearly full sun. Spreading plants to 2 to 6 feet. Deciduous. Flowers spring or summer: white, pink or red. Plants are generally covered with blooms for several weeks. Larger types are best used as background plants, since they're relatively unattractive when out of bloom. Smaller types are often used in low borders and rock gardens. Iron deficiency can be a problem in extremely alkaline soils.

Varieties:
  S. bumalda Anthony Waterer: short plant, to 2 to 3 feet, reddish-pink flowers in summer.
  S. cantoniensis: upright, to 4 to 6 feet. White flowers early summer.
  S. prunifolia: rather rounded, to 6 feet. Double white flowers in mid-spring.
  S. vanhouttei: masses of snow-white flowers in spring. Mature height: 4 to 6 feet.

GRAY SANTOLINA

SPIRAEA ANTHONY WATERER

TEXAS MOUNTAIN LAUREL

SPIRAEA BRIDAL WREATH

Ternstroemia gymnanthera   Zone 7
CLEYERA

Does equally well in shade and sun. Rounded-to-upright shrub to 6 to 8 feet, but usually shorter. Extremely glossy evergreen foliage. New growth bright copper-orange. Good specimen plant, also good in small masses. Plants seem to vary somewhat in shape and size, so not as well-suited to large-scale plantings. May show iron deficiency in alkaline soils. Otherwise, almost problem-free.

Viburnum sp.   Zones 7 and 8
VIBURNUM (Snowball)

Excellent shrub for shade, also suited to part shade and sun. Rounded to upright shrubs to 5 to 15 feet, depending on variety. Mostly evergreen, most types having dark green, often glossy foliage. Flowers spring, most types in showy white clusters. Some types bear showy fruit, though it's not generally the main reason for planting. Good landscape specimens, accents, hedges. Should be planted far more often in the South. Few if any insect and disease pests.

Varieties:

V. odoratissimum (Sweet Viburnum): upright, to 10 to 15 feet. Large, very glossy green leaves. Flowers white, fruit red, then black. Showy large hedge or screen. Zone 8.

V. suspensum (Sandankwa Viburnum): rounded shrub to 4 to 8 feet. Leaves dark green, oval. Flowers spring, pink and fragrant. Commonly used in southern landscapes. Zone 8.

V. tinus: small to medium-sized shrub to 4 to 8 feet. Leaves dark green. Flowers white tinged pink, spring. Variety "Spring Bouquet" commonly sold in nursery trade. Compact form and taller type called "Robustum" also available. Zone 7.

(Many other viburnums are occasionally available in the Texas nursery trade. As a general rule, they're highly dependable.)

Weigela sp.   Zone 4
WEIGELA

Sun. Rounded shrubs to 6 to 8 feet. Deciduous plant with rather coarse-textured foliage. Eye-catching flowers red, white and pink, rarely yellow. Good background shrub. Attractive when in flower, less showy when not. Prune immediately after flowering to keep plant compact. Several varieties are available, though seldom seen in the Texas nursery trade.

Yucca sp.   Zones 4 to 7
YUCCA, SPANISH DAGGER

Sun. Shrubby perennials growing from clumps and shortened stems. Evergreen, grown for striking leaf character and showy flowers. Good barricade plants, also used as accents. Commonly grouped with cacti and succulents in rock gardens. All types require good drainage, though they don't have to be given totally arid conditions.

Varieties:

Y. *aloifolia* (Spanish Bayonet): Upright, rapid growth. Develops clumps with age. White flowers summer. Green foliage. Zone 7.

Y. *filamentosa* (Adam's Needle): Striking rosette of dark green leaves with bluish cast. Showy white flowers summer. Several improved varieties. Zone 4.

Y. *recurvifolia* (Pendula, Soft-Leafed): Clumping type with soft, harmless leaves with lovely blue-green cast. White flower spikes summer. Tolerant of most garden conditions. Zone 7.

Red Yucca: See "Hesperaloe."

CAUTION: Leaves of most yucca varieties are pointed and extremely sharp. They should not be planted near pedestrian areas or where children are likely to be playing.

YUCCA, SPANISH DAGGER

CLEYERA

VIBURNUM SPRING BOUQUET

Chapter 5

Vines

Vines deserve more attention in Texas landscapes and gardens. They perform functions no other plant can approach. They shade, screen, shelter and obscure. They're sources of color, fruit and vegetables. They're multi-functional plants that deserve a spot in your landscape.

Still, using vines requires careful planning. You have to know how large they'll grow and how they attach themselves to supports. You'd like to know whether they're deciduous or evergreen and whether they have flowers or fruit . . . the color and season.

You'll find all of that in this chapter. It's a chapter you can contribute to . . . by planting and growing vines in your Texas landscape and garden. Read on for details!

LANDSCAPING USES FOR VINES

Vines are unique landscaping plants . . . they do their jobs just as effectively as trees and shrubs, yet they take almost no lateral space. That makes them ideal for our shrinking urban landscapes, for a variety of reasons:

• vines provide color, from foliage, flowers and fruit;

• they're effective as windbreaks;

• they can be used as sunscreens, both overhead on patios and also grown flat against sunbaked walls;

• they're fast growing, an advantage if you're trying to fill in voids and gaps cheaply and quickly. Annual vines are especially useful;

• vines soften stark fences and walls, making them more attractive visually; and

• they can be sources of cut flowers (roses, trumpet vine and others) and fruits and vegetables, including grapes, beans, peas, cucumbers, melons and others.

Recent years have seen a trend toward the use of more and more vines in landscaping. Plan some into your plantings!

Vines perform many vital landscaping functions.

MOST COMMON QUESTION

"Will vines hurt my house . . . the brick, the mortar and the wood?"

That's a tough question to answer, because of the variables. Vines that cling to brick will not normally harm the mortar and should never hurt the brick (especially hard-fired clay bricks). There may be staining, however, where dust and moisture collect behind the vines. That can usually be removed by scrubbing should you ever remove the vines. There is also a possibility that evergreen vines which trap moisture in the winter might aid in the freezing and cracking of the mortar joints, but that's exceedingly rare.

As for wood surfaces, vines should not be allowed to adhere directly to them. It makes painting difficult and it also leads to decay and deterioration because of the moisture trapped continuously against the wood. Use hinged trellises for those vines.

HOW TO START AND MAINTAIN VINES

Most woody perennial vines are sold in one-gallon containers, with some being offered in a larger five-gallon size. Spring is an excellent time to plant vines, since nurseries offer the best selections then.

Vines are generally sold in one-gallon nursery containers, often trained and tied to poles. Remove from cans and plant against permanent support.

TEXAS TIP

Spring is also the best season for planting vines to cover a hot sunny exposure, since it allows the plants to become established before really hot weather arrives.

Follow these basic guidelines for planting and maintenance:

1. Measure the space to be covered and buy the appropriate number of plants to fill it.

2. Prepare a good planting bed using a generous amount of peat moss, compost or other organic matter prior to planting. Remove the plants from their containers and set them out at the same depth at which they grew in the nursery. If they are wrapped and tied together against a stake, remove the ties. If they're attached to the stake by tendrils or holdfast growths, leave the stake intact and place it against the permanent support (such as a wall or trellis) provided for the plants.

RULE OF GREEN THUMB: Vines should be planted rather close together for quickest cover. Though the encyclopedic listing of vines that follows lists maximum mature heights, most vines can be planted three to five feet apart. Exceptions: the really vigorous types such as trumpet vine, wisteria and grapes. All of these require six to 10-foot spacings.

3. Provide some type of trellis or wire support if needed. If the plants climb by their root structures, be sure they're kept in contact with the wall until the roots can form.

4. Prune and train your vines to encourage thick branching close to the ground. By removing the terminal buds every month or two you'll encourage branch formation from the base upward. Once the plants are established and have covered the desired area merely prune to maintain the proper shape. Grapes are the main exception, as regular pruning is needed for good fruit production (see Chapter 10, *Fruit and Nut Crops* for details).

5. Water your vines as you would any other landscape plant material, when their soil is dry to the touch.

TEXAS TIP

Vines grown against hot western exposures will require more water than almost any other plant in your landscape. Use drip irrigation, both to soak their soil deeply and to protect your foundation during drought.

6. Fertilize vines according to their landscape function. Vines grown for foliage should be fed in early spring and again in early summer with a high nitrogen plant food (16-4-8, 15-5-10, etc.). Flowering and fruiting vines should be given a complete and balanced fertilizer such as 12-12-12 in early

spring and again in early summer. Spring-flowering vines should also be given a high-phosphorus fertilizer such as 10-20-10 in early fall. Apply the appropriate fertilizer at the rate of one to two pounds per 100 square feet of ground space. Water thoroughly after feeding.

If you're starting annual vines such as morning glories, moonflower, cypress vine or clock vine, start with the same good soil preparation. Next, set either started transplants or seed directly into the prepared soil. Water and fertilize them regularly to encourage germination and growth. Plant as early in the season as possible for best growth.

MOST COMMON QUESTION

"What vines grow best in the shade?"

Best perennial vines for shady areas include English ivy (and its varieties), Algerian ivy, Carolina jessamine (jasmine), fatshedera, and Virginia creeper. Most vines, however, will tolerate shade for at least half a day daily, since most were originally native to shaded areas underneath trees in forests. Some blooming types such as wisteria, trumpet vine and climbing roses will not flower well in heavy shade.

TRAINING VINES . . . HOW THEY CLIMB

How a vine holds itself upright will do a lot toward determining how you train it. Know how the plant grows!

1. Some vines produce special rooting structures that enable them to adhere to flat surfaces. These can resemble tiny suction cups, as in this Boston ivy. They may also resemble shortened roots. This group requires little special attention . . . they climb on their own.

2. Other vines ascend by twining around their support. Some even produce tendrils to help in the twining, as this grape is doing. Provide some type of pole or wire for support.

3. Some plants provide themselves no means of support, yet they can't stand alone. These are the leaners of plant life, and the group includes fatshedera, climbing roses and several others. Provide a trellis, masonry anchors or some other type of support, and train the plants to it by tying them in place with plastic plant ties. Prune and shape as needed to direct plant growth.

MOST COMMON QUESTION

"Will English ivy hurt my tree if I let it climb up the trunk?"

Not until it forms a canopy over the top of the tree. The vine is not a parasite. It takes no water or nutrition from the tree. The only way it could cause harm would be if it formed a dense canopy that shaded the tree. It's easy enough to prune it once or twice a year to keep it out of the tree's limbs and confine it to the trunk.

GARDENER'S DOZEN ...
THE BEST FLOWERING VINES FOR TEXAS

Name	Flower Color	Perennial, Annual	Deciduous, Evergreen	Blooming Season
QUEEN'S WREATH, CORAL VINE (Antigonon)	pink	P*	D*	late summer, fall
TRUMPET VINE (Campsis)	orange, red, yellow	P	D	summer, fall
BOUGAIN-VILLEA (Bougainvillea)	purple, red, white, gold	P**	E	spring-fall
MOON VINE (Ipomoea)	white	A	-	late spring, summer, fall
CLEMATIS (Clematis)	white, blue, red	P	E	spring, some summer, fall
CAROLINA JESSAMINE (Gelsemium)	yellow	P	E	spring
MORNING GLORY (Ipomoea)	blue, white, red	A	-	summer, fall
HONEY-SUCKLE (Lonicera)	white, red, pink, yellow	P	mostly E	spring, some summer, fall
CYPRESS VINE (Ipomoea)	red, white	A	-	summer, fall
CLIMBING ROSES (Rosa)	yellow, pink, red, white	P	mostly E	mostly spring, some fall bloom
BLACK-EYED SUSAN, CLOCK VINE (Thunbergia)	yellow, white	A	-	summer, fall

Name	Flower Color	Perennial, Annual	Deciduous, Evergreen	Blooming Season
STAR JASMINE (Trachaelo- spermum)	white	P***	E	spring
WISTERIA (Wisteria)	purple, white	P	D	early spring

*Tops die to ground with first killing freeze. Plants grow back following spring from bulbous roots.

**Damaged or killed by sub-freezing weather. Adapted outdoors only in extreme southern portions of state.

***Requires winter protection in northern half of state.

MOST COMMON QUESTION

"Why won't my wisteria bloom?"

That's a very common problem brought on by one or more unrelated situations:

• too much shade (wisterias need full or nearly full sunlight);

• too much nitrogen (often caused by locating wisterias too close to adjacent lawn areas) . . . remember that high-phosphorus fertilizers promote flowering;

• too much moisture, causing plant to produce only leaves;

• pruning during fall or winter . . . wisterias set buds then for following spring's bloom. Prune only after blooming season has passed.

• there also is theory that some wisterias may have been propagated from nonflowering types and won't ever bloom. If possible, always buy them in bloom to be sure you're getting plants that do have the potential.

If you've had a problem getting your wisteria to bloom you might try root-pruning it in the early fall. Use a sharpshooter spade to cut through the lateral roots vertically some 24 to 36 inches away from the trunk. By cutting those roots you'll slow the vegetative growth. Often that encourages flower bud formation.

PATIO SHADE FROM VINES

Vines offer some decided advantages over solid roofs when it comes to shading a patio.

• First, they're less expensive. It doesn't cost much to buy a young vine. Fertilizer and water are comparatively inexpensive. Before you know it, the patio is covered.

• Vines are more natural . . . they're more pleasing to look at. Many even flower, for added appeal.

• Vines provide shade without stopping air movement entirely. Solid patio roofs can create hot spots that are unusable during the summer.

• Many vines drop their leaves in the winter, allowing the sun's warming rays to reach the patio. A permanent roof won't offer that.

Vines important method of shading patios, decks and other outdoor recreational areas.

Best Vines for the Job

Consider the following when choosing a vine to cover a patio:

• It should be attractive (perhaps even bloom);
• It should be neat and free from constant litter; and
• It should adapt well and grow quickly to a large size.

Evaluating all of that, you should consider these as some of the best vines for covering your patio in Texas:

• grapes (see variety recommendations, Chapter 10, *Fruit and Nut Crops*)
• wisteria
• trumpet creeper
• Lady Banksia rose
• Carolina jessamine (jasmine)
• Confederate star jasmine

VINES FOR TEXAS

To aid in your selection what follows are the best of the vining plants suited to Texas conditions. Any special care instructions are included as needed. Otherwise, assume the plant requires standard soil preparation and post-planting care.

Use of the term "perennial" indicates that the vine survives from year to year with woody stems. "Annual" vines must be replanted each year.

Zone hardiness notations refer to the minimum temperature map on p. 3. Locate your county on the map and determine its hardiness zone, Try to choose only those plants listed for that or more northern zones.

Antigonon leptopus   *Perennial, Zone 8*
CORAL VINE, QUEEN'S WREATH, Rosa de montana

Stands heat and sun very well. Fast growing vine to 35 to 40 feet. Bright pink flower clusters (late summer and fall) are very showy. Foliage dark green, evergreen in frost-free areas. Freezes to ground most other areas. Mulch root systems if prolonged periods of subfreezing weather are expected. Comes back vigorously from roots the following spring. Climbs with tendrils. Good cover for patio, excellent screen over large brick walls. Space plants 4 to 8 feet apart and keep well watered during hot summer weather.

Bougainvillea sp.   *Perennial, Zone 10*
BOUGAINVILLEA

Sun or part sun. Fast-growing tropical vine to 15 to 18 feet. Flowers (actually bracts) brightly colored, raspberry-red, pink, orange, red and white. Foliage dark green, stems thorny. Used in patio containers, hanging baskets and, in tropical areas, outdoors. Plants should be fed and watered regularly during growing season. Best flowering will be attained, though, if high-nitrogen fertilizers are avoided after early summer. Container plants will bloom better if kept slightly rootbound.

Varieties:
   single flowering:
   Barbara Karst — brilliant red
   California Gold — pale yellow
   Hawaii — red (variegated foliage)
   Jamaica White — white
   San Diego Red — deep red
   Texas Dawn — pink

   double flowering:
   Cherry Blossom — rose-red
   Manilla Red — bright red

Campsis radicans   Perennial, Zone 5
TRUMPET VINE, TRUMPET CREEPER

Sun. Quick-growing deciduous vine to 20 to 30 feet. Summer flowers are long and tubular, trumpet-shaped, in shades of orange, yellow and red. Foliage is dark green and robust. Climbs by aerial roots. Good for patio cover, on large fences and walls. Native Texas species root sprouts frequently, becomes a weedy pest. Improved types such as variety "Madame Galen" are far more refined. Flower size of Madame Galen 2½ to 4 inches. Space 5 to 8 feet apart. Keep moist throughout season, but do not apply high-nitrogen fertilizer nearby or you will decrease flower production.

Clematis sp.   Perennial, Zone varies
CLEMATIS

Sun or part sun. Group of showy vines, to 8 to 15 feet. Flowers red, purple or white, depending on variety. Bloom season also varies, spring for many, early fall for some. Most types are deciduous. All do best given bright light, deep rich soil and ample moisture and fertilizer. Showy northern hybrid types will require much more care and attention (mulching, careful watering, etc.) and still may not perform as well in Texas as they will in cooler climates. Concentrate, instead, on types such as C. texensis (Texas clematis — red flowers) and C. dioscoreifolia (sweet autumn clematis — white flowers).

Cucurbitaceae family   Annuals
ORNAMENTAL GOURDS

Grow gourds in full sun. Vigorous vines to 10 to 20 feet. Grown primarily for their unusual and long-lasting fruit. Sow seed in early spring, after danger of frost has passed. Thin plants to stand 2 to 3 feet apart, and grow either flat on mulched ground, or from fence or other support. Water frequently during hot summer weather, and control squash bugs and spider mites as needed. Apply a complete and balanced plant food such as 12-12-12, one pound per 100 square feet, once a month during the growing season. Harvest gourds when fully ripened and place in warm, bright, well-ventilated location out of direct sunlight. Once outer skin has toughened, coat gourds with shellac. Dried fruit should remain good for several months.

Important note: gourds do not cross-pollinate with cucumbers, watermelons and other cucurbits as some gardeners will allege. If cucumbers develop bitter flavor, it's because their growth was slowed as they matured, either from heat or drought.

Fatshedera lizei   Perennial, Zone 8
FATSHEDERA (Botanical Wonder)

Shade or part shade. Leaning vine-shrub, to 6 to 10 feet. Result of cross between Fatsia japonica (Japanese Aralia) and Hedera helix (English ivy), showing traits of each. Evergreen, with star-shaped dark glossy green foliage. Plant must have support to climb. Tropical appearing, even suited for use indoors. Outdoors use as special accent, in protected corner or against wall. Space plants 3 to 4 feet apart if planting in grouping. May show winter burn in northern half of zone 8. Variegated form available.

BOUGAINVILLEA

TRUMPET VINE

CLEMATIS

FATSHEDERA

CORAL VINE

Ficus pumila   *Perennial, Zone 9*
CLIMBING FIG, FIG IVY

Does best on southeast or east exposure, away from hot afternoon sun. North exposures work well where winter temperatures are fairly warm. Clinging vine to 20 to 30 feet and taller. Leaves are small when plants are young, though mature foliage may be 3 to 4 inches long. Dark green, evergreen. Attaches tightly to its support. Space plants 18 to 24 inches apart against wall to be covered. Hand train initial growth to be sure it starts climbing.

Gelsemium sempervirens   *Perennial, Zone 7*
CAROLINA JESSAMINE, CAROLINA JASMINE

Very adaptable: sun, part sun or shade. Compact, bushy vine to 10 to 25 feet. Evergreen in southern half of Texas, semi-evergreen farther north. Flowers in early spring, bright yellow single, tubular (double form also available). Flowers delightfully fragrant. Foliage is bright green, but shows iron chlorosis when plants are grown in alkaline soils. Climbs by twining. Good on fences, over patios, trailing over rock walls. Space plants 6 to 10 feet apart, and provide means of climbing (wires, etc.) to get the growth started upward.

Hedera canariensis   *Perennial, Zone 9*
ALGERIAN IVY

Shade or part shade. Vigorous grower, to 15 to 25 feet. Large leaves resemble English ivy, though 2 to 3 times as large. Evergreen, with dark leathery foliage. Clings to tree trunks, walls. Space plants 15 to 20 inches apart against walls. Provide uniform moisture. Plant in sheltered locations where winter temperatures do not drop far below freezing for extended periods.

Hedera helix   *Perennial, Zone 5*
ENGLISH IVY

Shade or part shade. Do not plant against hot, reflective walls that receive afternoon sunlight. Clinging vine, to 25 to 35 feet. Evergreen with dark green leathery leaves. Immature leaves, particularly those growing flat on ground, are triangular. Mature foliage on high branches becomes almost rounded. Excellent vine for covering masonry walls. Space plants 12 to 18 inches apart, planting them as close to wall as possible. Also used as espalier plant. Several selections are available, though few are as durable as the species.

Ipomoea alba   *Annual*
MOONFLOWER

Sun or part sun. Very fast growing relative of morning glories, to 8 to 15 feet. Flowers are similar to morning glories, but generally pure white, 4 to 6 inches wide. Blossoms open in evening and remain open until sun hits them the following day. Delightful fragrance and striking appearance when illuminated at night. Flowers best in relatively infertile soils. Do not plant adjacent to lawn areas where high-nitrogen plant foods might wash and result in lush top growth at the expense of flowering. Grown from seed, which is very hard. File through seed coats individually, or soak the seeds for 2 to 5 hours before planting.

CLIMBING FIG

CYPRESS VINE

ENGLISH IVY

CAROLINA JESSAMINE

Ipomoea quamoclit   *Annual*
CYPRESS VINE (Cardinal Climber)

Sun or part sun. Fast growing vine to 12 to 16 feet. Flowers red or white during summer and fall, generally 1 to 1½ inches across. Foliage resembles ferns, very soft textured, bright green. Climbs by twining. Very attractive. Sow seed directly into well-prepared soil in early spring. Allow plants to develop 12 to 15 inches apart.

Ipomoea tricolor   *Annual*
MORNING GLORY

Sun or part sun. Vigorous plant, to 8 to 15 feet. Flowers sky-blue, rosy-red and white, distinctly tubular, summer and fall. Blooms best when not heavily ferilized and watered. Good quick cover for new fences and walls. Blooms open in morning, remain open much of the day, depending on temperature. Grow from seed sown directly into good garden soil. Soak seed or file lightly to encourage quicker, more uniform germination.

Best varieties:
Heavenly Blue (sky blue), Scarlet O'Hara (red) and Pearly Gates (white).

Lonicera sp.   *Perennial, Zones 4 through 6*
HONEYSUCKLE

Sun or part sun. Group of deciduous and semi-evergreen vines to 8 to 12 feet tall. Bloom primarily in spring, sporadically throughout remainder of growing season. Flower color ranges from white and yellow to pink and rose-red. Climb by twining. Excellent for covering fences, arbors and trellises. Attract hummingbirds. Space 18 to 24 inches apart for most solid cover.

Varities:
L. heckrotti (Coral honeysuckle): coral-red flowers all season long. Rounded blue-green leaves are held tightly against stems. Refined grower that should be planted more often. Requires good air circulation to retard powdery mildew.

L. japonica Halliana (Hall's Japanese honeysuckle): bright green, fast-growing vine with fragrant white flowers (shade to yellow as they mature). Vigorous cover for fences. Escapes aggressively.

L. japonica purpurea (purpleleaf honeysuckle): leaves tinged dark purple, more dramatically in winter. Often used as ground cover, can also be used as vine provided weak growth is removed periodically. Flowers white laced with yellow and purple.

Parthenocissus quinquefolia   *Perennial, Zone 4*
VIRGINIA CREEPER

Sun to shade. Quickly growing vine to 20 to 35 feet. Deciduous, with dark green 5-parted leaves that turn to bright fall colors when exposed to cooler weather. Growth not as flat as Boston ivy, so more useful as trailing vine over brick walls, fences. Can also be used adhering to walls. Native to much of state, so well adapted.

BOSTON IVY

BOSTON IVY

CORAL HONEYSUCKLE

PURPLELEAF HONEYSUCKLE

VIRGINIA CREEPER

Parthenocissus tricuspidata   *Perennial, Zone 4*
BOSTON IVY

Sun or part sun. Vigorous and durable clinging vine, to 25 to 40 feet. Deciduous. Leaves are bright green in spring, dark leathery green in summer and turn a brilliant scarlet red in the fall. In winter bare twigs trace the wall in interesting patterns. Excellent energy conserver, since deciduous leaves soak up heat in summer, let sun's rays through in winter. Variety "Barbara Brooks" has larger leaves, "lowii" has smaller.

Passiflora caerulea   *Perennial, Zone 8*
BLUE PASSIONFLOWER

Sun. Showy tender evergreen vine adapted to southern portions of Texas. Plants will die to ground in winter in central part of Texas, may come back from roots following spring. Grown for its unusual multi-petalled blue flowers. Do best given loose garden soil and ample moisture. Plants climb by tendrils to 10 to 20 feet. Good for trellises, over fences and walls.

Polygonum aubertii   *Perennial, Zone 4*
SILVER LACE VINE

Sun. Rapid growing deciduous or semi-evergreen vine to 30 to 40 feet. Summer and fall flowers are small and white, borne in fluffy masses. Vine is used for its quick cover, but requires a great deal of growing room. Infrequently seen in retail nurseries, but available from national mail-order houses.

Thunbergia alata   *Annual, Tender Perennial, Zone 9*
CLOCK VINE, BLACK-EYED SUSAN VINE

Part sun. Fast growing, to 12 to 18 feet. Flowers yellow, orange, white, often with contrasting "eye" in center. Foliage medium-green. Climbs by twining. Useful for quick cover, hanging baskets, patio pots. Subject to spider mites, leaf miners. Space 18 to 24 inches apart.

*Trachaelospermum jasminoides**   *Perennial, Zone 8*
STAR JASMINE, CONFEDERATE JASMINE

Sun or part sun. Attractive vine to 12 to 18 feet. Evergreen, but may suffer winter burn in northern half of zone 8. Foliage very glossy dark green. Flowers spring, bright white, one inch across, shaped like small pinwheel and deliciously fragrant. Climbs by twining. Useful in covering fences, over arbors, patio roofs, also as low vining ground cover. Space plants 24 to 36 inches apart.

Note: *T. mandaianum* (Yellow Star jasmine) is less common, but hardier (zone 7). Its leaves are smaller, resembling Asiatic jasmine. Flowers are less showy than star jasmine, but equally fragrant.

*Sometimes sold as *Rhynchospermum jasminoides*.

Vitis sp.   *Perennial, Zones 5 and 6*
GRAPES

Sun or part sun. Large and vigorous vines, to 15 to 25 feet. Grown primarily for edible fruit (see Chapter 10 *Fruit and Nut Crops*), but many types are also attractive when used as landscaping materials. Deciduous. Climb by tendrils and wrapping. Grapes are commonly grown on overhead patio roofs for shade, also to soften impact of long fences. Provide good soil preparation and regular attention.

Wisteria sinensis   *Perennial, Zone 5*
WISTERIA

Best bloom occurs in full or nearly full sun. Very vigorous vine to 30 to 45 feet. Often trained, with support, as small tree. Deciduous, with flowers before foliage emerges in early spring. Blooms borne in clusters like bunches of grapes, most commonly lilac-purple. White variety also available. Flowers very fragrant. Foliage is dark green, but yellows badly (even turns white) from iron deficiency in alkaline soil. Climbs vigorously, often covering nearby trees.

Wisteria failing to bloom? See page 208

WISTERIA

BLUE PASSIONFLOWER

STAR JASMINE

Chapter 6

Ground Covers

One of the landscaping trends the last several decades has been to ground covers ... low-growing plants that hug the earth. And it's a great trend. They're some of the most versatile, useful plants in our plantings. There are types that thrive in shade. Others flourish in the heat of a Texas summertime sun.

Ground covers are transitional plants. We use them between shorter turf grass and taller shrubs. For the most part they're there for appearance, but in some cases we can walk on them. Many times they grow where the grass won't grow, or where it's simply difficult to maintain turf grass.

All things considered, ground covers need a place in your landscape. You'll be pleased with the work that they do!

GET THE MOST FROM YOUR GROUND COVERS

Many folks look to ground covers as labor-savers in landscaping, and that can be the case. However . . .

RULE OF GREEN THUMB: If grass will grow in an area, it will be the easiest plant to maintain in that area. In most cases, you're better off to save ground covers for these special locations . . .

Shade: all Texas turf grasses do best in full sun. Even St. Augustine, our most shade-tolerant grass, will run into problems if it doesn't get three to five hours of direct sunlight a day. At that point you have two options: either prune the trees so they allow more light to reach the grass below, or plant something that requires less light. Best shade ground covers include: English ivy, ajuga, monkeygrass, liriope, vinca, pachysandra and, to some degree, Asian jasmine.

Slope: feeding, watering and mowing hillsides can be a challenge. In fact, it can even be hazardous. Rather than going to all that trouble, it might be easier simply to plant some type of deep-rooted species that could hold the soil permanently, with less regular attention. Best types for such use include: liriope, purpleleaf honeysuckle, Asian jasmine and daylilies for sun and liriope, monkeygrass, English ivy and Algerian ivy for shade. Drip irrigation systems can facilitate watering.

Long, narrow areas: again, watering, mowing and edging can all be problems. Neatly trained beds of ground covers such as Asian jasmine, trailing junipers, mock strawberry, liriope, monkeygrass, sedum and verbena can add beauty and subtract maintenance.

Shade-loving ground covers can replace turf grass under trees, on north side of house.

Ground covers on slopes are more easily maintained than lawn grasses.

Edging, mowing and watering are difficult in odd shaped lawn spaces. Ground covers may save work.

Hot spots: looking for a ground cover to use against a light-colored wall or next to the pavement? Trailing junipers, purpleleaf honeysuckle, sedums, Asian jasmine and Peruvian verbenas all measure up.

Rock gardens: trailing plants that will cascade over raised plantings and retaining walls include wintercreeper euonymus, Carolina jessamine, English ivy, trailing junipers, potentilla, Asian jasmine and Peruvian verbena. Many low-growing perennials would also be useful.

And, all of this bypasses one of the most important reasons for using ground covers ... the aesthetics. They look fantastic! They're a transition from shrubs to turf grass ... sort of a middleman. They can be used in long, flowing curves to soften harsh architectural lines. Many types bloom, for a broad band of landscaping color.

Whatever the purpose, ground covers have become, in the last several decades, some of the most used plants.

Reflected heat may weaken lawn grasses against house. Heat-loving ground covers may be better solution.

Trailing ground covers add graceful touch to rock garden beds.

HOW GROUND COVERS ARE SOLD

Ground covers are sold in different sizes of containers. Your choice depends on several things: how fast you need coverage, soil type, exposure to heat and sun, possibility of erosion and time of year. Obviously, bigger sizes of a species can stand adversity better than smaller plants.

Most ground covers are sold in small (2½ to 3-inch) pots. Nurseries generally offer volume discounts for buying these small plants in quantities. This is generally the most economical way of getting ground covers started.

Many types are also offered in one-gallon cans. These give a more immediate impact and they can be spaced somewhat farther apart. They're rooted more deeply, so the soil is less likely to erode. The deep rooting also gives a greater margin of error in watering . . . they dry out more slowly.

A few ground covers are also sold bare-rooted, or as clumps. These are generally the flowering perennial types such as daylilies, Shasta daisies, iris, thrift, violets and oxalis.

MOST COMMON QUESTION

"How can I figure the number of plants I need to buy? I know the suggested spacing, but please take it from there."

You'll be planting ground covers on a checkerboard pattern, with the rows the same distance apart in each direction.

That means that if you plant the ground cover plants one foot apart in the rows, each plant will have one square foot of space. If the bed is five feet by 15 feet, you have 75 square feet, and you'll need 75 plants to fill it. Other spacings will require a little more math . . .

8 × 8 inches	2.25 plants/sq. ft.
10 × 10	1.44
14 × 14	.73
15 × 15	.64
16 × 16	.56
18 × 18	.44
20 × 20	.36
24 × 24	.25

Using those figures, then . . . if you have that same 75 square foot bed and want to plant on 18 × 18 inch spacings, you'll need (75 × .44) or 33 plants.

TEXAS TIP

If you're going to succeed with ground covers in Texas you have to get rid of two of our worst weed problems prior to planting. The culprits? Bermuda grass and nutgrass. They're invasive, tenacious and ugly. Not exactly the best thing to have in your ground cover beds. After you've prepared the soil, fumigate with vapam or similar material several weeks prior to planting. Otherwise you'll end up with an impossible war with the weeds.

PREPARING TO PLANT

Since they're small plants, ground covers are less able to crowd out weeds than larger landscape plants would be. They also have shallower root systems. It all adds up to a need for good soil preparation.

Steps to Take

1. Apply appropriate weed killers to eliminate existing grasses and weeds. Allow two to three weeks for complete kill.

2. Rototill or spade soil to a depth of six to 10 inches. Work soil less deeply under trees, where shallow surface roots might otherwise be damaged.

3. Incorporate a four to six-inch layer of organic matter into the soil.

4. Fumigate soil with vapam or similar material, to kill soil-borne insects, diseases, weeds and nematodes. Apply with sprinkling can to freshly turned soil, water heavily and cover with sheet of plastic film to hold in the fumigant's vapors. Allow two weeks before removing cover. Re-till and aerate soil for one additional week before planting. *A word of caution:* vapam cannot be used adjacent to desirable plants. Read and follow label directions carefully.

1.

2.

3.

4.

NINE STEPS FOR PLANTING GROUND COVERS

Once the soil has been properly prepared and fumigated you can start planting your ground cover.

Steps to Take

1. Begin by installing some type of edging material, to keep the grass in its place.

2. Measure the bed carefully. Determine how many square feet you'll be planting and calculate the number of plants needed to fill it. Buy a few extra plants just to be sure . . . you'll always be able to work them in.

1.

2.

3. Rake the bed smooth, then position the plants (still in their pots) on it. Use marked string to ensure accurate placement. Plants should be set in a checkerboard pattern.

4. Carefully tap plant out of pot.

5. Plant at same depth at which plants were growing in pots.

6. Water thoroughly immediately after planting. Include root stimulator fertilizer with watering, to get plants off to a quick start.

3.

4.

5.

6.

7. Mulch bed with compost or shredded bark to conserve moisture, reduce erosion, retard weeds.

8. Use erosion-control netting on slopes, to slow flow of water. Soil should be very smooth under netting so that water will form sheets over top of netting during heavy rains. Low spots and trenches encourage erosion, defeating purpose of netting.

9. Begin fertilizing the new planting two to three weeks later, using a complete and balanced plant food analysis for best total growth.

7.

8.

9.

MOST COMMON QUESTION

"I'd like to start English ivy. Can I dig up some that has already been planted, from my neighbor's bed and start it myself?"

You can do it, but it's not the best way of getting English ivy (or any other ground cover) started. You'll set the ivy back by transplanting it. You'd be months ahead to use small nursery transplants, and the cost shouldn't be excessive. If you'd really like to try your hand at starting your own plants, you'd be better off to start them in a florist's flat filled with a good potting soil mix, and then, once they've formed roots, to pot them up into 3-inch flower pots (2 to 3 plants per pot).

FERTILIZING GROUND COVER PLANTINGS

Your chief objective in growing a ground cover is to have foliage covering the soil. Generally, you use the same type of fertilizer to promote foliage in ground covers that you'd use on your lawn.

What to use: choose a plant food relatively high in nitrogen, the first number of the analysis (15-5-10, 12-4-8, 16-4-8 are examples). If you're using a turf fertilizer, though, be careful if it also contains a weed killer. Many are harmful to ground cover plants. It's generally safer to apply the materials separately. Apply with hand-held spreader or by hand.

When to use it: in early spring, just before growth begins; also in late spring, several weeks before summer's really hot weather; and, finally, in early fall, to stimulate one last round of growth before cold weather.

PRUNING AND TRAINING GROUND COVERS

Most plants selected as ground covers have low-growing habits. That means they'll require a minimum of pruning and special training.

If new plants become lanky and leggy and don't show tendencies to creep, they should be pruned lightly, to encourage basal branching and spreading growth.

If your established plants grow too tall, if they're ravaged by insects, or if they're burned back by a harsh winter, you may want to trim them back. Use either pruning shears, grass shears or electric hedge shears. Some folks even use their lawn mowers, adjusted to the highest setting possible, to trim plants like monkeygrass and Asian jasmine early each spring.

HOW TO CONTROL WEEDS IN YOUR GROUND COVER

Weeds are the most serious threat to ground cover plantings. That's simply because the weeds are often too closely related to the ground covers themselves to allow spraying. Chemicals that would kill weeds will kill the ground cover.

That's all the more reason to use a soil fumigant such as vapam prior to planting . . . to get rid of the weeds and their seeds before you ever plant the ground cover. That's also ample reason to use a mulch such as compost or finely shredded bark to retard weed growth as the ground cover gets started. Spot treat or hand-dig any weeds that do get a root-hold . . . don't let them encroach.

Should some weeds show up, though, you still have hope. If they're annual weeds (ones that die at the end of their growing period, and come back the next year from seed), then you can use one of the pre-emergent weed-killers such as Balan, Betasan, Dacthal or Eptam to control them. These must be applied before the weeds start to grow. You have to anticipate the problem and step in to stop it. Also, one or two of these will have precautions against use in certain ground cover plantings. Read and follow the label directions.

Perennial weeds (also those annuals that escape the pre-emergent weed killers) will be more of a problem. Few post-emergent weed-killers can be used in ground cover beds. Additional research may provide label clearance for the use of certain herbicides in such settings. For now, though, you're faced basically with either spot treating or hand digging.

COMMON TEXAS GROUND COVERS

Any plant that grows in a sprawling or prostrate habit might be considered as a ground cover. Obviously, that list could include many low-growing shrubs as well as perennial and even annual flowers. The listings that follow are confined solely to those plants not mentioned in other chapters. They are the specialists . . . the best plants for permanent ground cover plantings.

Unless otherwise noted, each ground cover included requires standard soil preparation and post-planting care, as recommended earlier in the chapter.

Zone hardiness listings in the upper right-hand corner of each description refer to the U.S.D.A. expected minimum temperature map of page 3. (in Chapter 1, *Getting Started in Gardening*.)

Ajuga reptans   Zone 3
AJUGA (Carpet Bugle)

Shade. Height 2 to 6 inches. Evergreen, low-growing rosetting plant with spoon-shaped leaves, dark green, often with purplish tint, variegated in some varieties. Intense blue flowers on spikes in early spring. Started from small transplants set out on eight to 10-inch centers. Will not tolerate direct afternoon sun. Requires good drainage. Subject to root knot nematodes and soil-borne diseases. Best used in small plantings, between stepping stones, as very low borders. Many varieties available, varying in leaf color and size. Very attractive.

Duchesnea indica   Zone 6
MOCK STRAWBERRY (Yellow Strawberry)

Sun or part sun, will tolerate shade. Height 4 to 8 inches. Dark green evergreen leaves resemble strawberry leaves exactly. Sends out runners profusely, covering quickly. Flowers bright yellow, up to ½-inch in diameter, followed by bright red marble-sized fruit (flavorless). Started from small nursery transplants or by transplanting of runners. Set plants 12 to 16 inches apart. Susceptible to rust disease (control with zineb). Trim with mower set at highest setting in early spring to keep foliage even.

Euonymus fortunei   Zone 6
WINTERCREEPER

Sun or part sun. Height 1 to 2 feet. Trailing evergreen with glossy green (some variegated) leaves summer, many types turning purplish-red in winter. Does not root along stem as freely as many other ground covers. Plants cover by multitudes of long branches that intertwine. Start from small pots or one-gallon containers. Space plants one to two feet apart, depending on the variety and plant size. Prune tall-growing shoots as needed to encourage basal branching. Not as susceptible to euonymus scale as upright shrubby types.

WINTERCREEPER

VARIEGATED AJUGA

AJUGA (FLOWERS)

MOCK STRAWBERRY

Varieties:

E. fortunei Azusa: Prostrate growth. Small, dark green leaves with purple winter coloration.

E. fortunei coloratus (purple wintercreeper): Height 12 to 18 inches. Bright green leaves about size of quarter turn plum red in winter.

E. fortunei gracilis: More compact growth habit. Best used in small plantings. Several varieties available, most with silver variegation.

E. fortunei kewensis: Very low and slow growing. Useful for small and very special areas.

E. fortunei radicans (common wintercreeper): Low trailing plant with long, dark green leaves.

E. fortunei vegetus (bigleaf wintercreeper): More upright, to 3 to 4 feet. Large, durable leaves. Attractive fruit with orange seeds.

Festuca ovina glauca   Zone 5
BLUE FESCUE

Sun or part sun. Height 6 to 10 inches. Thin blue-green evergreen foliage in small clumps. Flowers not showy, should be removed following blooming. Started from small potted transplants or one-gallon containers. Space plants 8 to 12 inches apart. Best in rows, but can be used over an entire bed area. Requires perfect drainage! Will not tolerate soils that are waterlogged for prolonged periods, especially clays. May need rejuvenation or replacement after several years.

Fragaria sp.   Zone 2
STRAWBERRIES (fruiting)

Morning sun, afternoon shade best for most parts of Texas. Height 6 to 10 inches. Attractive dark green three-parted foliage. White flowers spring and sporadically through summer followed by edible red fruit. Started from bare-rooted or potted nursery transplants or from divisions from existing plants. Space plants 12 to 15 inches apart for ground cover plantings. Provide particularly good soil mix and regular care and attention for plants being used for fruit production as well as ground covers. (See Chapter 10, *Fruit and Nut Crops* for additional details.)

Gelsemium sempervirens   Zone 7
CAROLINA JESSAMINE (Jasmine)

Sun or shade. Height 18 to 24 inches when used as ground cover without support. Glossy dark green leaves, evergreen or semi-evergreen, depending on temperature. Deliciously fragrant butter-yellow flowers in early spring. Started from one-gallon nursery containers spaced 24 to 30 inches apart. Requires supplemental iron in western two-thirds of Texas. Develops informal tufted appearance after several years as its growth piles upon itself. Somewhat coarse for most ground cover uses, but good for isolated plantings in rock gardens and retaining walls, where it can cascade down.

Hedera helix   Zone 6
ENGLISH IVY

Shade or part shade (morning sun, afternoon shade). Scorches in full summer sun. Height 6 to 10 inches when used as ground cover. Very dark green evergreen foliage on trailing vines. Plants have tendency to climb when grown adjacent to tree trunks and walls, but easily pruned. Started from small pots or one-gallon containers. Space small plants on 12-inch centers, gallon cans on 18 to 24-inch centers. Provide ample moisture during hot, dry weather. Fungal leaf spots (black spot on leaves) not rare, easily controlled with general-purpose fungicide. Varieties include Hahn's Self-Branching and Baltica, both with smaller green leaves and more profuse branching. Many other fancy-leafed and variegated types (most are slow growing) are also available. Entire group comprises some of the finest shade-loving ground covers available.

Hedera canariensis   Zone 9
ALGERIAN IVY

Shade or part shade. Height 8 to 12 inches. Leaves resemble English ivy foliage except 2 to 4 times larger (variegated form also available). Aggressive grower with much coarser texture than English ivy. Start from rooted cuttings, small potted transplants or one-gallon containers. Space small plants 12 inches apart, larger plants 18 to 24 inches apart. Same care as English ivy. Cold-tender in northern half of Texas.

Note: *H. colchica* (Persian ivy) resembles Algerian ivy, yet is considerably more cold hardy. It is occasionally seen in the Texas nursery trade.

Juniperus sp.   Zones 2 through 6
TRAILING JUNIPERS

Sun or part sun. Height 4 to 24 inches (other shrubby varieties much taller). Fine-textured evergreen foliage varying both in actual shape and color. Started from one, two and five-gallon containers. Space plants 2 to 4 feet apart, depending on variety and size of plant. Require good drainage. Not well-suited to wet soils and high humidity along Gulf Coast, but excellent inland. Bagworms and spider mites may be occasional problems.

Varieties for Texas include:

J. chinensis sargentii (Sargent juniper): 12 to 18 inches tall, gray-green foliage.

J. conferta (Shore juniper): 12 inches tall, bright green with unusual needles. "Blue Pacific" is more intensely blue-green.

J. horizontalis: several varieties, including "Bar Harbor" (blue-gray in summer, plum-red in winter, to 12 inches); "Andorra" (gray-green summer, plum-red in winter, to 18 to 24 inches); "Wiltoni," or "Blue Rug" (silver-blue-green, to 4 inches); and many others.

J. sabina: several varieties, including "Tamarix," or "Tam" (dark blue-green, to 18 inches) and "Buffalo" (bright green, to 12 to 14 inches).

ENGLISH IVY

TRAILING JUNIPER

CAROLINA JESSAMINE

BLUE FESCUE (Foreground)

Liriope muscari   Zone 6
LIRIOPE

Shade, part shade or nearly full sun (green varieties tolerate more sun than variegated types). Height 12 to 18 inches. Dark green grass-like leaves, clumping plants. Some types variegated white or pale yellow and green. Flowers generally lilac, some types white, on spikes 12 to 20 inches tall. Blooms last for several weeks during summer, followed by shiny black berries. Start from transplants or one-gallon sized nursery stock. Space clumps 15 to 18 inches apart, closer if small divisions are being used. Trim off dead foliage in late winter, just as new growth emerges. Excellent ground cover and low border edging. Best and boldest types, with most dramatic foliage and showiest flowers include Majestic and Big Blue. Silvery Sunproof is one of better variegated types.

Lonicera japonica varieties   Zone 5
HONEYSUCKLE

Sun or part sun. Height 12 to 24 inches. Dark green foliage (Hall's honeysuckle), or with purplish cast (Purpleleaf honeysuckle). Latter type is decidedly purple during winter. Spring flowers white, turning yellow as they age. Purpleleaf honeysuckle flowers have purplish-red tint. All are fragrant. Started from small potted plants or one-gallon containers. Space small potted plants 12 to 15 inches apart, those from gallon cans 18 to 24 inches apart. Fertilize generously to encourage vigorous growth. Prune severely in late winter, as needed to reduce overall height when plants become lanky. Of the two types, Hall's honeysuckle is perhaps the better vine, purpleleaf honeysuckle the better ground cover. Neither is highly refined and both should probably be reserved for rough-use areas.

Lysimachia nummularia   Zone 4
MONEYWORT

Part shade or shade. Height 2 to 4 inches. Small round light green leaves on long stems that grow rapidly, hug ground tightly. Started from small potted nursery transplants. Space plants 12 to 15 inches apart. Keep well watered at all times . . . tolerant of moist surroundings. Fertilize regularly. Attractive and unusual.

Ophiopogon japonicus   Zone 7
MONDOGRASS, MONKEYGRASS, LILY TURF

Shade, part shade, sun (does not thrive in hot spots with reflective heat). Height 6 to 10 inches. Leaves dark green, grass-like, borne in thick clumps. Flowers not as showy as plant's first cousin, Liriope. Started by division of existing plants, from small nursery pots or from larger one-gallon cans. It's often possible to divide full gallon cans into four or more clumps. Space plants 10 to 18 inches apart. Mow planting in late winter, before growth begins, to remove foliage damaged by cold. Use highest setting on lawn mower, then rake out dead stubble. A very dependable and aggressive ground cover.

LIRIOPE (MAJESTIC)

VARIEGATED LIRIOPE

MONDOGRASS

PURPLELEAF HONEYSUCKLE

Pachysandra terminalis   Zone 6
PACHYSANDRA (Japanese Spurge)

Shade only. Height 6 to 8 inches. Interesting medium-green leaves on small fleshy stems. Spreads to make tight ground cover layer. Started from small potted nursery plants. Space plants on 10 to 14 inch centers. Popular ground cover in the North, but hurt by intense heat in Texas summers. Provide uniform moisture supply. Try in small area on experimental basis before making large scale plantings.

Potentilla tabernaemontanii   Zone 4
POTENTILLA (Cinquefoil)

Sun or part sun. Height 2 to 4 inches. Three-parted leaves look somewhat like strawberry leaves, but are smaller and a lighter green. Spreads quickly by vigorous runners. Small bright yellow flowers throughout growing season, but heaviest in spring. Started from small potted nursery transplants. Space plants 12 to 18 inches apart. Requires good drainage. Often used between stepping stones, on sloping berms. Susceptible to spider mites. Among the fastest growing ground covers.

Sedum sp.   Zones 4 through 7
SEDUM, STONECROP

Sun or part sun. Height 3 to 8 inches. Unusual thickened succulent leaves in shades of blue-gray and green. Stems short and upright to creeping. Flowers generally bright yellow, spring. Started from small nursery transplants or stem cuttings. Space plant 6 to 12 inches apart. Sedums tolerate hot, dry locations better than most ground covers. Require perfect drainage and protection from pedestrian traffic. Many varieties.

Trachaelospermum asiaticum   Zone 7
ASIAN JASMINE

Sun, part sun or shade. Height 6 to 12 inches. Glossy green evergreen leaves about nickle-sized. Spreads rapidly by long, trailing runners. Started from small potted nursery transplants or one-gallon containers. Space small plants 12 to 15 inches apart, one-gallon cans 18 to 24 inches apart. Plant as early in growing season as possible, since much of plants' growth occurs in spring. Will suffer winter damage in extreme cold in Zone 7, generally coming right back with first warm days of spring. Perhaps the finest ground cover for almost all parts of Texas. Selection called "Longleaf Asian jasmine" offers less gloss to foliage, coppery tint to new growth. Variegated form also available, less tolerant of heat, cold.

Trachaelospermum jasminoides   Zone 8
CONFEDERATE STAR JASMINE

Sun or part sun. Height 12 to 18 inches when used as ground cover. Taller growing relative of Asian jasmine. Leaves are larger than Asian jasmine, dark glossy green. Stems ascend more,

POTENTILLA

STAR JASMINE

ASIAN JASMINE

SEDUM

will climb on one another and on any other means of support in their vicinity. Showy white pinwheel-like spring flowers are extremely (and delightfully) fragrant. Started from one-gallon nursery cans (occasionally from small pots). Space ground cover plantings on 18 to 24 inch centers. Cold-tender in northern half of state.

Verbena peruviana   *Zone 8*
PERUVIAN VERBENA

Sun. Height 3 to 5 inches. Small, fine-textured leaves topped by brilliant red flower clusters all season long. Perennial, started from small potted nursery transplants. Space plants 10 to 15 inches apart in well-prepared beds. Very durable to heat and to a modest amount of dry weather, but tender in cold winter weather. Plants will spread by runners that root into the ground. Eventually the parent plants will die out and the runners will have moved on to other locations. Excellent rock garden, low border flower. Use in small quantities. Other verbenas are also available. Most will grow taller than the Peruvian verbenas, but they're all just as attractive.

Vinca major   *Zone 7*
PERIWINKLE (trailing)

Shade or part shade. Height 12 to 18 inches. Dark green leaves on upright stems. Essentially evergreen, though somewhat sparse in late fall and winter. New growth in spring is intensely bright green. Flowers are purple-blue in spring, resemble annual periwinkles. Started from small nursery plants or one-gallon containers. Require protection from leaf rollers during sum-mer (Diazinon, Malathion, other general-purpose insecticides applied as worms first start to feed). Stubble should be mowed down in late winter, to encourage basal branching.

Varieties include variegated form, also V. *minor,* the trailing myrtle that resembles Asian jasmine. Both of these will require more protection from sun and heat than the green trailing periwinkle.

PERIWINKLE

PERUVIAN VERBENA

Chapter 7

Texas Lawns

Lawns are an integral part of every landscape. In fact, surveys of realtors have shown a well maintained lawn to be worth at least two thousand dollars in the resale value of an average home.

Perhaps even more importantly, a good lawn is the foundation of a good landscape. It is to the rest of your plantings what the carpet is to your furniture. It's the living surface your family will use for relaxation and recreation.

Texas lawns offer some unusual challenges, both in selection of grasses and in their care. The pages that follow will pinpoint all the specifics you'll need to know to keep your Texas turf healthy and vigorous.

EIGHT STEPS FOR
GETTING YOUR LAWN STARTED

Establishing a new lawn need not be a confusing, frustrating experience. Follow these few simple guidelines for the best possible results:

Step 1. Select Your Lawn Grass Carefully
Each type has its own advantages and drawbacks. Make sure that the one you choose best suits your needs. Each type adapts well to Texas soils.

Bermuda grass is durable and well suited to high traffic areas. It's also drought-tolerant, and since seed can be used, inexpensive to plant. However, it must have full, or nearly full sunlight. Unless bermuda grass is kept back, it can become a weed by invading gardens and ground cover beds. Subject to bermuda mite invasion and leaf diseases.

St. Augustine is also aggressive, with deep green luxuriant growth. Though it is best in the sun, St. Augustine will tolerate shade better than any other southern lawn grass. It is somewhat sensitive to cold in the northern half of Texas. It does not tolerate repeated pedestrian traffic. Established from sod or sprigs, St. Augustine is moderately costly. Susceptible to chinch bugs, St. Augustine decline virus and brown patch disease.

Bermuda grass

St. Augustine

Hybrid bermudas (several varieties, often called "Tif") are the golf green grasses. They're really spectacular when well-kept. They can be a maintenance nightmare, though, requiring special mowing equipment and much more frequent attention than other lawn grasses. All of the dwarf types of bermuda must have full sun to succeed. Must be planted from sod or sprigs or by hydromulching. Moderately costly.

Zoysia is the subject of thousands of questions each spring, as advertisements selling plugs of sod and claiming its great merits are carried in newspapers all across Texas. It *is* a good grass, but it's extremely slow to cover ... like two or more years! It cannot compete with existing lawn grasses, and it's quite expensive to establish. All things considered, you're probably better off with another lawn grass. If you do decide to try zoysia, at least buy it locally. Don't send your good money to out-of-state turf companies.

Hybrid bermuda

Zoysia

Fescue is another grass that's getting more and more attention in Texas. Basically, it's a cool season grass, which means it grows best in spring and fall. It is planted from seed sown in early fall. It stays green all winter long, and it goes virtually dormant during the summer. The fescues may one day, through continuing research, become satisfactory permanent lawn grasses for much of our state; but for now they're best suited as a replacement for St. Augustine in shady locations.

Buffalo grass is a drought and heat-tolerant plant that's native to much of Texas and the arid West. Though not the most luxuriant of lawn grasses, it's well suited to rough-use landscapes where low maintenance is a requirement. It is compact and low-growing, doing best in full sunlight and well drained locations. Requires infrequent feedings, less water than most other types.

Fescue

Buffalo grass

Step 2. Rototill The Soil

Rototill the lawn area to a depth of six to eight inches. If you have a heavy clay soil you can till a two to three-inch layer of sandy loam topsoil into the ground. Incorporate 20 pounds of 10-20-10 (or similar fertilizer) per 1,000 square feet into the soil. Rototill again to blend the materials.

Step 3. Rake to The Desired Grade

Rake out all the stones and roots to leave a smooth seedbed. You should slope the soil gently away from your home. Be sure the entire lawn area drains properly. It's much easier to change now than after the lawn is established.

Step 4. Plant the Grass

Sow the grass seed (use "hulled" bermuda grass seed for best germination), plant the sprigs or sod or have the lawn hydromulched. Hydromulching costs a bit more, but it offers a wood fiber mulch that protects the young grass as it gets started.

Step 5. Water the Lawn

Water the new planting frequently and lightly at first, since its roots will be shallow and quite vulnerable to moisture extremes. Gradually reduce the frequency and increase the dosages. Letting the soil dry to a depth of several inches will help the grass develop deep roots.

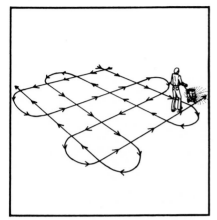

Sow seed (and apply fertilizer) by applying half going one direction, the remainder going at right angles.

Checkerboard sod plugs for quicker cover.

Step 6. Fertilize Your New Lawn

Fertilize your lawn with a complete and balanced plant food three to four weeks after it starts to grow (generally after the first or second mowing). Apply the material at half the recommended rate.

Note: Should your new bermuda grass seedlings develop a deep purple coloration, feed them at once with a high-phosphorus plant food, preferably one that's quickly soluble. For this one-time special treatment you might consider one of the special water-soluble fertilizers intended for flowering house plants.

Step 7. Mow Your Lawn

Mow at the recommended height from the outset. Don't let the grass get long and lanky.

Step 8. Don't Worry About Weeds . . . Yet

Use no weed killers for 10 to 15 weeks; for some, even longer. Most young grass is very sensitive and it's safer simply to wait. Mowing will eliminate many of the weeds.

Planting Chart for Southern Grasses

Grasses	Planting Season
Bermuda	April through mid-September
St. Augustine	April through August
Hybrid bermudas	April through mid-September
Zoysia	April through August
Fescue	September through October
Buffalo	April through August

MOST COMMON QUESTION

"How can I get grass to grow in the shade?"

All grasses do best in full sunlight. Some types, however, such as St. Augustine and fescue, will tolerate moderate shade. If you've tried these and failed, you have two options: (1) remove your trees' lower limbs, so more light can come in from the side, or (2) choose a ground cover such as English ivy, monkeygrass, liriope or vinca that requires less light to survive. Remember that failure of grass to grow in the shade comes from a lack of light . . . adding water and fertilizer may help a bit, but they're not the real solution to the problem.

Fall Lawn Plantings

A quick look at the planting chart will tell you that most of our permanent lawn grasses should be planted in spring or early summer. If you move into your house in mid-fall you probably don't want to track mud all winter long.

Ryegrass, or winter rye, is a good solution. Sown at six to eight pounds per 1,000 square feet anytime before winter's really cold weather it will germinate and grow into a temporary thick turf.

How Started	Seeding Rate and Sod Spacing
seed, sod	1 to 2 lbs. per 1,000 square feet, solid sodding or 6-inch blocks on 18-inch centers
sod	solid sodding or 6-inch blocks on 18-inch centers
sod	solid sodding or 4-inch blocks on 15-inch centers
plugs, sod	2 to 3-inch plugs on 12-inch centers
seed	6 to 8 lbs. per 1,000 square feet
seed	½ to ¾ lbs. per 1,000 square feet

Then when spring arrives, you can apply a foliar herbicide to kill out the ryegrass. Give the chemical a couple of weeks to do its work, then scalp the dead grass and rototill lightly as needed to establish a final grade. You'll then be at the perfect season to plant the permanent turf.

WATERING ... THE KEY TO SURVIVAL

No lawn can survive a hot Texas summer without extra watering. Fact is, you'll need to water your lawn during other seasons as well. Grass roots remain alive during the winter, and a good soaking every few weeks may be the key to pulling the grass through in prime condition.

How to Recognize Drought Symptoms

• Most grasses will turn a darker metallic green when they're dry. They'll lose their brilliance and gleam.
• Leaves will either fold or roll.
• As you walk across dry areas the grass just won't have the resilience. It won't spring back. You'll see your footprints.
• You'll probably also have particular spots that will dry out faster than others ... areas with shallow soil, slopes or space along sidewalks and curbs.

"Read" your grass. It will tell you when it's time to water.
Watch for folded or rolled leaves and other symptoms.

When and How Much You Should Water

Check your lawn every day during the summer and at least weekly at other seasons. When it shows signs of drying out, water it promptly and water it deeply. But don't water by the calendar. The grass will dry out at varying rates depending on rainfall, wind, temperature, humidity and a host of other variables. Wait until it's dry, then water it.

If you want to measure the amount of water you are applying set several straight-sided cans on the grass while the sprinkler is running. Measure the water depth with a standard ruler. You'll be amazed at how long you'll have to water to deliver just one inch. (Don't leave the cans on top of the grass once the water is shut off or you'll have burned dead spots.)

RULE OF GREEN THUMB:
- During summer apply one to two inches of water per week.
- During spring and fall apply one to two inches of water every two weeks.
- During winter apply one to two inches of water per month.
  (These amounts include rainfall totals.)

Create your own "rain" gauges to measure amount of water sprinkler delivers to lawn. It may take many hours just for one inch of water.

MOST COMMON QUESTION

"What time of day should we water our lawn?"

Water when the grass is dry . . . morning, noon or night. Realistically, early morning is the best time, since the grass will have the best chance of drying quickly (reduces chance of disease invasion), and since there will be minimal water lost to evaporation. However, if noon arrives and the grass has turned dry, better water then. Waiting could cause serious damage.

THE BEST WAY TO FERTILIZE YOUR LAWN

Choosing a fertilizer that will meet the needs of your lawn grass is the number one challenge. Fortunately, there are dozens available, most of them highly acceptable.

TEXAS TIP

Research shows that a high-nitrogen fertilizer is best for regular feedings of Texas turf. Choose a 3-1-2 or 4-1-2 ratio fertilizer (15-5-10 and 16-4-8 are examples, respectively). The first number (nitrogen) promotes the green leaf growth you want. The middle number (phosphorus) helps the turf develop deep roots, and the last number (potassium) promotes heat and cold hardiness. So long as you have this general content, your fertilizer will be entirely adequate. Many other similar analyses are available.

Many lawn fertilizers also contain insecticides and weed killers. They're an added convenience, in that you have only one trip to make over the lawn. Be sure the product will do your lawn good, though. There's no point in adding an insecticide if there aren't any insects, and there's no point in adding pre-emergent weed killers if weeds are already established and growing.

Fertilize your lawn regularly to help maintain its color and vigor. Watch for the following hungry-grass symptoms and deal with them promptly:

1. Grass loses its dark green appearance, takes on pale yellowish-green color.

2. Seed heads conspicuous.

3. Grass grows slowly, requires mowing less frequently.

Six Factors Which Affect How Frequently You Should Fertilize Your Lawn

1. *Temperature:* Warm-season lawn grasses do most of their growing during the late spring, summer and early fall. That's the time at which they need the heaviest feedings.

2. *Rainfall:* Moisture dissolves nutrients and carries them away from the plant roots.

3. *Soil Type:* Clay soils retain nutrients best. Sandy soils will require more frequent attention.

4. *Grass species:* Bermuda and St. Augustine, for example, require more fertilization than buffalo grass.

5. *Type of Fertilizer:* Some types of plant food contain a quick-release type of nitrogen, while nitrogen in other plant foods will be released over a longer period of time. Ammonium-form nitrogen is generally gone within four to six weeks, while the urea-form types last many weeks, even months.

6. *Clippings removed?:* Research has shown that leaving the clippings on the soil returns up to one-third the fertilization requirements. Be careful, though, that you're not encouraging thatch formation.

Lawn Feeding Schedule for Texas Turf

Fertilize warm-season lawn grasses at eight to 10-week intervals during the growing season. First application should be made two to four weeks after the last freeze, and the last application should be made six to eight weeks before the first expected killing frost.

For SOUTH TEXAS, then, applications should be made:
early March, early May, early July, early September and, perhaps, early November for deep South Texas.

For NORTH TEXAS, apply fertilizer:
late March, late May, mid-to-late July and mid-September.

Apply a 3-1-2 or 4-1-2 ratio fertilizer at each of these times. Rates of application will be listed on the package. Obviously, excessive rainfall and other climatic factors can result in need for more frequent feeding.

How to Apply Fertilizer

Use a rotary spreader for the best coverage. Apply the fertilizer in early morning or evening to lessen the chance of "burned" grass. Soil should be moist, but the grass blades should be perfectly dry. Calibrate the spreader to deliver the precise amount. Aim to apply half the material with your first pass. Make the second application travelling at right angles to the first, to minimize the chance of missed spots or overlaps.

Rotary spreader fans fertilizer out in broad pattern, for more uniform application. Double coverage and missed streaks are minimized.

Mark your path carefully. If the spreader wheels leave distinct tracks you can use them as your guide. Otherwise, use stakes or other landmarks to direct you.

Water the fertilizer into the soil immediately after it's applied. Leaving the plant food on top of the ground increases the chances of chemical burn to the plants.

MOWER SELECTION AND PROPER USE

You don't cut hair with a hand ax, and you can't cut wood with a screwdriver. It's the same with your lawn. You have to have the right equipment . . . a mower that does the job properly, safely and, one hopes, easily. Make your selection a considered one. A good mower can last and give good service for many years.

Types of Mowers

The type of lawn grass you're growing will, to a great degree, determine the type of mower you should buy.

Rotary: Rotary mowers are preferable for St. Augustine, common bermuda, fescue and other rather coarse grasses.

How it works: Mower blade travels parallel to ground and cuts like a knife. Available in push and self-propelled, walk-behind and rider. Because of high engine speed and method of cutting, rotary mowers can handle tall, thick grass. Special attachments are available with most models for collecting clippings and for mulching them finely.

Rotary mower provides best all-around service, most versatility, has capability to cut thick and tall turf.

Reel: Most reel mowers can be set quite low, making them the choice for tif and other dwarf bermuda lawns. However, most reel mowers lack the strength to pull through thick stands of St. Augustine or common bermuda.

How it works: Mower blades travel circularly over the lawn, like a paddlewheel travels through water. Reel mowers give a very precise scissorlike cut if their blades are kept sharp and aligned. Adjustments should be done by professional mower service firms, not a job for an amateur.

Reel mower gives smoothest, most precise cut. Essential for fine-bladed dwarf hybrid bermudas, but has difficulty handling thick, tough grasses like St. Augustine.

Tips For Selecting A Mower

Today's lawn mowers offer tremendous features. But to take advantage of all those features, you need the help of a pro ... someone who really knows the equipment he's selling.

Tell him your exact mowing conditions: size of your lawn; type of grass; terrain; number of trees that interfere with your mowing and so on. If you have particular physical needs that might dictate a rider or self-propelled model, tell him that.

Let him show you his complete line, from the least expensive to his top model. Shopping costs nothing and you may find that the few extra dollars it takes to get the top of the line to be money well spent.

Above all, buy quality. It's entirely possible that a mower that costs twice as much may last four times as long.

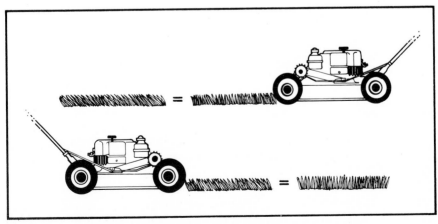

Mow your lawn in different directions to keep grass from developing a "grain."

Best Mowing Heights

The specific heights at which you mow your lawn will depend on the type of grass, the season, and any special conditions such as heavy shade or high traffic density. Here are general guidelines for average conditions:

Type of Grass	Best Mowing Height
Bermuda:	
Common	¾ to 1½ inch
Hybrids	¼* to ¾ inch
Buffalo	2 to 3 inches
Tall Fescue	3 to 4 inches
Rye	1½ to 2 inches
St. Augustine	1½ to 2 inches
Zoysia	1 to 1½ inches

*requires special golf green mower (reel type).

A Word of Caution:
Don't Let Your Mower Nip at the Trees!

Lawn mowers can be serious tree enemies. Repeated "de-barking" by mower wheels and discharge chutes invites insects and diseases. It also reduces tree vigor by disrupting flow of water and nutrients up and down in the trunk.

Protect the tree trunk, either with wrap or by keeping grass several inches away.

Paper tree wrap protects trunk against minor injuries from lawn equipment, also reduces sunscald to trunk, borer invasion.

Gravel or bark mulch around trunk keeps grass safely away.

Rather than running mower right up to trunk, trim grass by hand or with power filament line trimmer.

Maintain That Mower!

Protect your investment by practicing routine lawn mower maintenance. Your owner's manual will give you exact details. Here's a review check list:

☐ Check the oil level before each mowing. Change it at the recommended intervals, or more often if you're mowing in dry, dusty conditions.

☐ Clean or replace the air filter as recommended. Do not clean in gasoline!

☐ Sharpen the blade regularly. Watch the grass for brown, frayed tips. Check the blade each time that you mow. Don't tip your lawn mower over on your lawn to check or change the blade. Take it to your driveway, so any gasoline that might spill won't kill the lawn grass. Disconnect the spark plug wire when you're removing the blade, so the mower can't start accidentally. Tie the wire back, away from the plug. File the blade carefully, being sure to remove equal amounts from each side of the blade. Blades that are out of balance can damage a mower severely.

☐ Change the plug once a year, or as recommended in the owner's manual.

☐ Never store gasoline in your mower over the winter. Run it dry last thing in the fall. Old, deteriorated gasoline can foul an engine.

☐ Keep the housing under the mower clean all through the mowing season. Clean it by rinsing or scraping after each mowing, to prevent accumulations of grass clippings and mud.

SOLVING COMMON (AND NOT SO COMMON) LAWN PROBLEMS

Not every lawn looks like a golf green. Most of us run into problems at some time during the year. The grass won't grow . . . or it grows where it's not supposed to. The insects and diseases move in and start feeding . . . the weeds crowd the grass out.

Fortunately, most problems can be solved. Here are some you're likely to face, along with tips to their cures.

MOST COMMON QUESTION

"I've given up on our lawn . . . the grass is just too weak. Can I just plant new sod or seed in the bare spots, or do I need to rototill it and start over completely?"

Few lawns are so badly depleted that you'd have to start over from scratch. I'd try one more year. Put the lawn on a high-nitrogen diet during the growing season. Feed it more often than you have been. Keep it well watered. If weeds are present, combat them with weed-killing sprays. Chances are pretty good you can get the grass to cover back over.

If you do decide to replant, sod can be planted into the existing lawn, but seed would require rototilling and starting over. Little seedlings just can't compete in a world of established grasses and weeds.

How to Stop Turf Grass

Tired of invading turf grass? You can keep it from covering up your shrubs, flowers and ground covers by using one of the tricks shown here, or a combination of them. These bed edgings can provide an interface . . . a line of definition for your power edger or herbicide.

• Preservative-treated posts cut and placed vertically.

• Galvanized or baked enamel metal edgings. Use only heavy-duty, long lasting materials. Durable plastic and rubber types are also available.

• Bricks laid on side flush with soil surface.

You can also stop turf grass with:

• Weed killer sprays (read and follow label directions carefully.)

• Bark or gravel mulches to keep grass from rooting into ground. This provides the area for weed killer application without harming adjacent plants.

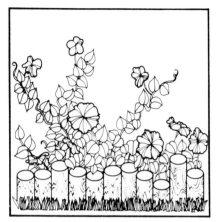

Preservative-treated posts.

Weed killer spray.

Metal edging.

Bark or gravel mulches.

Brick.

Guide for Controlling Lawn Insects

Insect	Symptoms	Controls
Bermuda Mites (Bermuda)	Grass appears dried in patches, runners are stunted, clubby	Diazinon
Chinch Bugs (St. Augustine)	Grass appears dried in irregular patches. Appears first in hottest part of lawn . . . full sun, along walks, drives	Aspon, Diazinon, Dursban
White Grubworms (all grasses)	Grass is dead or weak in irregular patches. Turf lays on top of ground like rug, lifts easily, runners and leaves remaining attached. Most evident spring, also fall.	Diazinon* Dursban*
Misc. Worms (sod webworms, armyworms and others)	Most types strip foliage, leaving dry grass stems. Will likely see moths, butterflies hovering over grass.	Diazinon Dursban Sevin
Ticks, Fleas, Chiggers	Irritating pests that cause human and pet discomfort, spread disease.	Diazinon or Dursban on lawn, low shrubs. 5% Sevin dust on pet, in his quarters.
Ants, Crickets, Earwigs	Nuisance insects, do little real damage. Fire ants are obvious exception, with painful infectious sting. Treat ant mounds directly.	Diazinon Dursban

*For homeowner use, granular materials are most effective in controlling white grubworms. Should be applied 6 weeks after main emergence of June beetles. Timing varies year to year, but generally is in early summer South Texas, mid-summer in Central Texas and late summer in North Texas.

MOST COMMON QUESTION

"What are the gray patches that look like cigarette ashes? They're all over our lawn?"

That's slime mold, a fungal organism. It lives off the decaying organic matter in the soil. What you see are merely its fruiting structures. It does no damage to any living plants. If desired, it can be removed with a forceful stream of water from the hose or by treating with a fungicide. (If all of our problems could only be as minor!)

How to Control Weeds

Even the best lawns have weeds. They're as inevitable in Texas landscapes and gardens as dry soil and bugs.

MOST COMMON QUESTION

(In fact, perhaps the NUMBER ONE QUESTION of all time in Texas landscapes and gardens.)

"How do I get rid of the weeds?"

For starters, don't pull them. Hand-pulling those weeds is a thing of the past. Today there's a better way. Special weed-killing products (herbicides) are available in granular and spray form. Most common lawn weeds can be controlled through their use. To get maximum effectiveness, though, you need to understand the products and the weeds you will be using them on. The following will help.

Types of Weeds

Weeds are either annual (have one-year life cycle, reseed themselves every year) or perennial (plant remains alive from one year to the next, often dying back to fleshy storage root). Beyond that, weeds can be broken into two major categories:

Group One: Grassy Weeds

Plants (annual or perennial) that are members of the grass family. Generally have long, narrow leaves with veins running parallel to leaf margins.

Dallisgrass. Perennial grass, dark green. Dense, low-growing, clumping. Seed heads arise soon after mowing.

Johnsongrass. Perennial grass, light green. Tall growing when unmowed, otherwise low and clumping.

Nutgrass (nut sedge). Perennial weed, not actually grass. Narrow glossy dark green leaves. Plants interconnected with nutlets in root systems. Flowering stems triangular.

Crabgrass. Annual warm-season grass. Spreading runners, light green foliage. Conspicuous seed heads.

Dallisgrass

Johnsongrass

Nutgrass

Crabgrass

Grassburs (sandburs). Annual grassy warm-season weeds. Spreading, with sharp, spiny seeds.

Winter grasses. Annuals. Many types, including rye, fescue, and annual bluegrass. Noticeable winter and in spring in dormant permanent lawn grasses.

Group Two: Broadleafed Weeds

Plants from families other than the grass family . . . these are the weeds that aren't grasses. Most types have wider leaves, many have showy flowers. Many types are annuals, some perennials.

Clover. Broadleafed weed, either annual or perennial depending on type. Most prevalent during cooler weather.

Grassburs

Clover

Winter grass

Dandelions. Perennial broadleafed weed. Bright yellow flowers early spring followed by fluffy white seed heads. Large dark green leaves.

Henbit. Annual broadleafed weed. Rounded small leaves and purplish-pink flowers. Most visible in the spring.

Chickweed. Spreading annual broadleafed weed. Bright green small leaves. Most visible in the spring.

Roadside Aster. Annual broadleafed weed. Foliage extremely fine. Flowers purplish-white in fall. Most visible in neglected turf areas.

Dandelions

Henbit

Chickweed

Roadside Aster

Types of Weed Killers

Modern technology has given us weed killers for just about any type of unwanted plant. Sometimes, however, it's hard to know just which type of weed killer is best for the task. Know the weed, its growth habits (annual or perennial) and the type of lawn grass it's growing in. The guidelines below can help pinpoint the best choice.

Pre-emergent: Attack weed seeds at germination. Effective only on annual weeds, and must be applied before seed sprouts. Two seasons to apply this type of weed killer in Texas.

1. Late winter — to control warm-season weeds, (repeat application in late spring), and;

2. Early fall — to control winter and early spring weeds.

Most types control annual grasses better than broadleafed weeds. Most are granular. The list includes: Atrazine, Balan, Betasan, Dacthal and Simazine. Waiting period before re-seeding varies: two to six months.

Post-emergent: Attack existing plants. Here are the three main types:

1. *Non-selective Weed Killers* — Control all vegetation, both grass and broadleafed. Some types kill by contact, destroying the plant parts on which they're sprayed. Other types are systemic, killing entire plant, roots and all. Some types have little or no soil residue (cacodylic acid, glyphosates and others), while some persist in the soil for up to a year or more (pramitol and others).

2. *Broadleafed Weed Killers* — Control non-grassy weeds in lawn. Most types can be used on any warm season lawn grass (bermuda, St. Augustine, hybrid bermudas, zoysia), though some types urge caution during extreme heat, particularly on St. Augustine. Most types are sprays, and most are at their best while weeds are actively growing. Weeds will gradually become distorted. Death will occur within 10 to 14 days. However, you may occasionally need to respray stubborn species.

3. *Grassy Weed Killers* — Attack existing grasses, either annual or perennial, without permanent damage to bermuda lawns. The most common types are sold under chemical abbreviations, DSMA, and MSMA. Not safe for use on St. Augustine and other broad-bladed grasses.

A Word of Caution: Protect your desirable lawn and landscape plants. Weed killers are intended to kill plants. Used according to label directions they'll not harm your permanent plantings. Read and follow the label directions implicitly! Be especially cautious of the broadleafed post-emergent weed killers that could cause harm to your trees and shrubs.

RULE OF GREEN THUMB: The best weed killers of all may be a bag of lawn fertilizer and a functioning lawn sprinkler. Vigorous turf discourages weeds. Keep the lawn well fed, watered and regularly mowed.

Thatch and Compaction . . . The Root Ruiners

Thatch is the layer of undecomposed organic matter that can accumulate on the soil surface, under your lawn's runners. Like old-time thatch roofs, it prevents penetration of water (also nutrients) into the soil. All types of turf grass are susceptible. In extreme cases the thatch layer can be an inch or more thick and as woody as fiberboard.

Roots fail to grow through thatch, leaving them vulnerable near top of ground.

Dethatchers flail the lawn, removing dead grass and thatch accumulations. They are most effective on bermuda lawns, since bermuda produces underground runners (rhizomes). St. Augustine lawns can be damaged by dethatchers set too low. To solve thatch problems in a St. Augustine lawn, use an aerator to encourage water and air movement into the thatch. That will promote decay of the thatch layer.

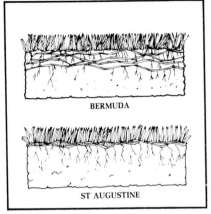

Flailing blades of dethatcher comb dead grass loose.

Dethatcher blades can cause damage to St. Augustine, since all of its runners (stolons) are on top of the thatch layer. Bermuda has runners both above and below the soil surface.

Soil compaction results from repeated traffic over a particular part of your lawn. Dog runs, kids' play areas and edges of driveways are common problem spots. The soil is repeatedly compressed until much of its air space is actually squeezed out.

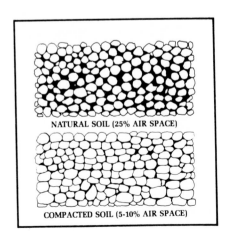

Rental companies offer lawn aerators that poke holes into the soil. The better types of aerators actually remove a small plug of soil, depositing it on top of the turf grass. Air and water can then penetrate into the soil and root growth increases almost immediately.

Power lawn aerator actually punches closely-spaced holes in turf, pulls small plugs out and leaves them laying on lawn surface. Holes permit air, water and nutrients to penetrate into soil, help thatch layer decompose.

Power lawn aerator

If you live in a part of Texas where grasses go dormant in the winter, scalp your lawn early each spring, before the grass begins to grow actively. Set the blade one or two notches lower to remove any leaf growth that was browned by the winter. Rake or bag the clippings and transfer them to the compost pile.

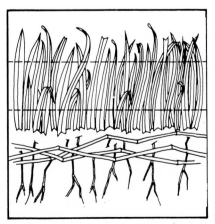

Regular mowing height would merely trim dead blades. Scalping removes all winter-killed blades.

MOST COMMON QUESTION

"What causes mushrooms, and will they hurt our lawn?"

Mushrooms are fungal growths that develop from decaying organic matter. Though they may cause temporary yellowing as they tie up the available nitrogen, there's no residual damage. Don't plan on eating them though . . . many are deadly poisonous.

LEVELING THE LAWN

Try to establish a smooth soil surface prior to planting your lawn grass. Should it develop low spots or ruts after the grass has covered, though, use washed brick sand to fill them in. Many folks use sandy loam topsoil for this purpose, only to discover it contains nutgrass and other serious weed problems.

Best time to apply the sand is in late spring, once the grass is actively growing. Apply a one-inch layer over the low area, then water the lawn thoroughly to help it filter through the grass leaves and runners. Add additional sand in two to three weeks if needed, to a maximum of two to three inches. For fills of greater depth, dig the sod, fill below it and replace it.

Do not, under any circumstance, use sand or sandy loam soil as a top dressing over an entire lawn. That neither stimulates nor fertilizes the existing grass, contrary to what some will tell you.

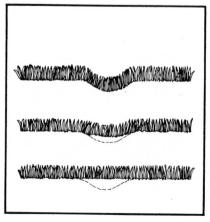

Use washed builder's sand (same type you'd use in sandbox) to fill minor depression. So long as it's not too deep or too wide, grass will grow across it and still retain good appearance.

MOST COMMON QUESTION

"Should I leave the tree leaves on the lawn over the winter ... to protect the grasses from the cold?"

No. What benefits you gain by the protection are more than offset by the chance of disease. And, if a sudden strong wind blows the leaves down the block just before record cold, you could lose big parts of your lawn. Rake 'em, and take 'em ... to the compost.

Chapter 8

Annuals

If it's true that color is an important and exciting element of our indoor environment...

And if it's true that landscapes are just extensions of our indoor living space...

Then doesn't it also follow that color would be important to the landscape as well?

Well, indeed!

Yet color remains the most overlooked part of southwestern landscaping. There *are* colorful plants that do well here. There *are* plants that provide season-long color.

Many of these cheerful contributors are annual flowers. They're quick and they're easy. They'll dazzle and delight! But only if you give them a chance.

We all have our goals in life. Mine is to share the joy and excitement of flowering plants in the landscape. What follows is threefold: (1) guidelines, (2) pep talk and (3) sales pitch.

Here's hoping it'll help.

Let's put some zip in our bloomers!

WHAT IS AN ANNUAL?

An annual completes its life cycle (seed to plant and back to seed) in one growing season, at which time the plant dies.

HOW TO PLANT ANNUALS

There are certain specific guidelines you need to follow in planting your annual color to realize the best show for your efforts. Pick the best spot, prepare the soil carefully and plant the seed or transplants properly. Though planting seasons will vary with the many different types of plants, the planting requirements are almost universal among them. Follow them carefully.

Selecting the Site

Since both sun and shade-loving annuals are available, almost any well drained garden location will be usable for annual color. Ideally it should be highly visible and situated where it can lend maximum impact to your home and its landscape. If you intend to grow specific types of flowers, you need to know their light requirements ahead of time, so you can plan and plant accordingly. (See listing at the end of this chapter.)

Preparing the Soil for Beautiful Color

Whether you're planting your annual flowers from seed or transplants, they're tender little things that deserve special soil preparation. Unlike trees, shrubs and other larger, woodier plants, they need just a little extra boost at the outset. Given that good soil preparation and regular attention thereafter, they'll perform like champions. Follow these guidelines:
1) Remove all sod, weeds and other undesirable vegetation;

2) Rototill to a depth of eight to twelve inches. Go over the area repeatedly, until soil clods are no larger than golf balls. Rake to remove roots, rocks and other soil-borne debris;

3) Spread a four to six-inch layer of peat moss, shredded bark, compost, well-rotted manure or other form of organic matter over the entire area. If you're preparing a clay soil, you may also want to include a two to three-inch layer of brick sand. Sand alone cannot do the job, but by mixing it in with the organic matter you'll end up with a sandy clay loam ... the best possible soil for gardening;

4) If soil tests show your native soil to be deficient in phosphorus, add super phosphate or other high-phosphorus fertilizer according to label directions;

5) Rototill again, to incorporate the organic matter, sand and fertilizer into the soil;

6) Apply soil fumigant such as vapam to freshly tilled soil, to eliminate soil-borne insects, diseases, weeds and nematodes. Best results will be obtained when vapam is applied to warm soil, and when treated area is covered with plastic immediately. Allow vapam 10 to 15 days to complete its fumigating effects. Uncover area. Rototill again and wait one week for proper aeration. *Caution:* read and follow label directions carefully. Do not use vapam where it could come into contact with roots of desirable plants;

7) Rake soil to establish smooth grade prior to planting. (To establish finest and smoothest seedbed, first rake with tines downward to remove clods and rocks, then smooth with rake upside down ... tines upward.)

See step 1.

See step 2.

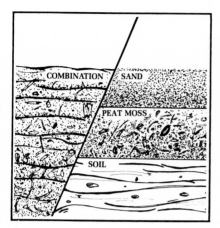

See step 3.

See step 4.

See step 5.

See step 6.

See step 7.

TEXAS TIP ⌐⟨⟩

Tired of flowers that fade away when it gets hot? Try the "heat-beaters." The list includes: periwinkles, moss rose (portulaca), marigolds, zinnias, lantana, verbena, gaillardias, gloriosa daisies, cosmos, gomphrena, cleome and cockscomb for flowers. For foliage: copper plants, Joseph's coat and amaranthus. For color in shady areas plant coleus, caladiums, begonias and impatiens, also scarlet sage and flowering tobacco. (And don't confine yourself just to this list . . . many other plants merit a trial.)

Ways Annuals Are Sold

Seed: Many annuals can be sown directly into the flower garden. In most cases, however, better results will be obtained if the transplants are started indoors on a bright windowsill or under greenhouse conditions.

Seedling flats: Small transplants grown and sold in communal pot or flat. Plants must be dug to be planted, resulting in transplant setback. It's better to buy plants individually potted whenever possible.

Cell-packs: Four to twelve seedlings are sold in a molded container. Each plant is individually potted within the pack, for minimal transplanting shock.

Individually potted: Transplants are sold in pots ranging in size from 1½ to six inches in diameter. Larger pot sizes provide more mature plants for quicker impact. Plant retains all its roots, for quickest re-establishment. Pots may be clay, plastic, compressed peat moss, paper or any of a number of other materials.

Have a Plan for Your Plantings

Know flowers' mature heights and widths, and plant for maximum visibility.

Setting the Transplants

Determine plant spacing.

Remove plant carefully by inverting, tapping against hard surface.

Set at same depth as plant was growing in pot.

If planting from peat pots . . .
break off portion of pot wall extending above soil line so it won't act as wick and dry out plant's root ball.

**Apply plant starter
(high-phosphorus content fertilizer).**

TEXAS TIP

Plant larger (three to five-inch) transplants for quicker color in flower beds. If you're trying for a full season of color, this will reduce the time the bed is out of bloom. Larger plants are also more established than small transplants, hence are better able to withstand trials of the Texas climate.

WATERING THE FLOWER GARDEN

Use surface application or fine mists whenever possible, to avoid damage to flowers.

Water deeply and regularly. Watch for signs of water stress ... wilted plants with dry soil ... then water immediately.

Water Breaker

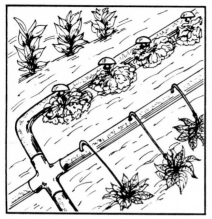

Drip Irrigation

Soaker Hose

FEEDING THE FLOWERS

Fertilize annual plants every four to six weeks all through their growing season. First feeding should be made two weeks after planting.

High-phosphorus fertilizers promote flowers (in addition to roots and fruit). For most annual flowers, then, you need to select a fertilizer having a relatively high middle number in its analysis. Most chemical companies offer one or more types labelled specifically for use on flowering plants.

For annuals with colorful foliage (copper plants, Joseph's coat, coleus, caladiums and others), use a complete and balanced plant food ... one where all three numbers in the analysis are relatively equal. Though you're growing the plants for their leaves, prolonged use of high-nitrogen fertilizers will likely cause excessive greening.

High-phosphorus fertilizer best for
flowering annual plants.

Complete and balanced plant food needed
for colorful foliage.

**RULE OF GREEN THUMB: Keep seed heads picked off annual
plants whenever practical. Formation of seed slows production of
additional flower buds. Remove spent flowers as soon as they fade.**

PEST PROBLEMS PREVENTABLE

Choose your annuals properly and care for them regularly and insect and
disease pests should be minor concerns. Listed below are some of the more
common ones to watch for.

Pillbugs, Snails and Slugs: Attack tender young seedlings, chewing
leaves or succulent stem tissues. Primarily a problem in cooler, early spring
months. Control with special baits or sevin dust sprinkled on ground.

Damping-off: Stem disease caused by combination of fungal organisms.
Young plants topple over, almost as if they'd been pinched with hot
tweezers. Older plants develop decayed spots in stem, usually at ground
line. Plants wither and die. Control by rotating crops ... don't plant same
type of flower in same area continuously for several years. Fumigate area
with vapam prior to planting. Use captan as soil drench prior to planting,
and again should problem arise.

Spider mites: Near-microscopic pests that attack leaves during warm
and hot weather. Singly, the worst pest problem of Texas landscaping.
Leaves turn tan mottled color. Marigolds, verbenas, impatiens and certain
other annuals will be affected. Treat with kelthane or other miticide spray.

Nematodes: Microscopic worms that sting plant roots, causing galls and
other root distortions. Control with soil fumigant such as vapam prior to

planting. Vapam cannot be used around existing plants. If you're unsure of whether your plants are affected by nematodes have a soil test run by the nematode diagnostic lab at Texas A&M. Your county Extension office can supply the necessary mailing materials and instructions for collecting the sample.

White Grub Worms: Larval form of May beetles or June bugs. In addition to damaging lawns, grubs can also devour roots of annual flowers. Control with applications of diazinon or dursban granules (six to seven weeks after major beetle flights) in late spring-summer.

MOST COMMON QUESTION

"Rabbits keep eating my young flower plants. What can I do to keep them out?"

There are four things, all about equally effective.

Sprinkle mothballs in flower bed, but not touching plants. Repeat every five to 15 days, as mothballs lose their potency (as measured by smell).

Sprinkle blood meal. It repels rabbits, but it attracts dogs.

Tie a big dog near the bed.

Talk it over with the rabbits, ask them to move on.

If all else fails you might try to cover the bed with bird netting (see Chapter 10 Fruit and Nut Crops) long enough to discourage the rabbits.

CONTAINER COLOR

Whether you live in a house or apartment, there's plenty of room for landscaping color. Grow 'em in pots, baskets and tubs. Containerize your plantings!

Be sure the container you choose has a drain hole. If it doesn't, drill one. Make certain, too, that it's large enough for the plants you'll be growing. Best pot sizes for most plants: six to 12 inches in diameter. Best basket sizes: eight-inch and larger. Use strawberry jars and halved whiskey barrels . . . any kind of container that will hold soil and drain.

RULE OF GREEN THUMB: When growing color plants in containers use the best possible potting soil. Generally it's best to avoid native Texas soils entirely. They're just too variable. Either buy a specially prepared potting soil mix or blend your own.

Choose a loose, well-drained potting soil mix, preferably one with a high percentage content of organic matter such as peat moss or shredded bark. Do not use native soils since results are generally poor. Nurseries offer specially prepared mixes, or you can blend your own. Start with 60 percent peat moss (brown Canadian peat moss is best), 20 percent either perlite or vermiculite, and 20 percent washed brick sand (available from lumber yards, sand and gravel companies). Modify the blend as needed to fit your plants and your care practices.

Include several plants in larger containers, for the best possible effect in the shortest length of time. If you're planting wire hanging baskets, plant some of your transplants in through the sides.

Since your container plants will have far less soil reservoir, you'll have to water and feed them much more often. When you water, water deeply and thoroughly. You may even want to water twice, back-to-back, to be sure you've saturated the soil mix. Most veteran gardeners feed their plants with a dilute water-soluble fertilizer with each of the waterings. That keeps the plants consistently fed, for the most uniform growth.

Remember that your container plants will be more vulnerable in cold, heat and wind than they'd be if they were growing out in the ground. Plants that would normally grow quite well in full sun may benefit from afternoon shade during the extreme heat of midsummer.

Finally and most importantly, feature your color. Highlight those plants currently blooming. If they're resting, put them back out of sight. Take advantage of their portability . . . move 'em around!

Container color provides special and portable show for landscape.

Coleus provides full season of container color.

Geraniums benefit from portability of containers for protection from summer sun.

Joseph's coat at home in pots.

Hybrid portulaca brightens drab corners.

Copper plant stands up to summertime heat, even when grown in container.

MOST COMMON QUESTION

"I have geraniums, coleus, impatiens and copper plants and I'd like to save them from the freezing winter weather. Can I grow them indoors until spring?"

Yes, but only if you have a bright windowsill or garden room. Give them less water and fertilizer than you did outside. If they're growing out in the ground (not in containers) you may find it easier to root cuttings of the plants and over-winter the smaller plants.

GROW YOUR OWN TRANSPLANTS

Interested in saving some bucks? Want to try an unusual flower variety no one seems to stock? Better grow 'em yourself. It's easy to start your own plants. Just be sure you have a bright sunny windowsill, a greenhouse or a coldframe, or some source of abundant light.

Select a shallow florists' flat or flowerpot.

Choose a sterile potting soil mix ... preferably one containing a high proportion of peat moss. Do not use any native Texas soils! They introduce the possibility of soil-borne disease problems. Moisten the mix, then smooth it. Firm it slightly, then make shallow depressions with the edge of a pot label or knife.

Sow seed in rows, and *sow thinly*. Overcrowding is the worst thing you can do to tender young plants. Put a crease in the seed packet, then tap the seeds out one at a time.

If the seeds are smaller than b-b's, do not cover them. If they're larger, cover them with more of the same potting soil mix. This top layer of mix should be twice the thickness of the seed.

Mist the planting, preferably with a fine atomizer, to help "wash" the seeds into the planting mix.

Cover the flat or pot with a sheet of plastic or glass to hold in the moisture. Leave a small crack, to be sure the moisture won't cause decay problems. Remove the cover entirely when the seeds have started to germinate.

Transplant the seedlings as soon as you can conveniently hold them. Always grasp young plants by their leaves ... not by the stems. If you damage a leaf, the leaf dies. If you damage the stem, the plant dies.

Use the same potting soil mix for the plants' first transplanting. Use a relatively small pot, so the plant won't be overpotted. Apply a plant starter to get the seedlings off to a quick start.

Keep your seedlings in bright light. Expose them to outdoor conditions gradually, so they'll be hardened before planting. Pay particular attention to frosts and wind ... the two most devastating problems for young seedlings. Make sure they're mature enough to stand on their own before you plant them outside.

HYBRID SEEDS WORTH THE COST!

Would you pay one or two extra cents for a seed that would produce twice as many blooms per plant? Perhaps with greater insect and disease resistance? Perhaps with larger flowers, or more intense colors? With measurably more vigorous plants?

You bet you would! And that's exactly what you're getting when you buy hybrid seeds or hybrid seedling transplants.

Plant breeders work long years developing new and improved forms of flowers (and vegetables). Their skill and patience is reflected in the many new and wonderful plants we now enjoy. True, you may pay a little more, but it's a great investment.

Here's How It Works

Let's use the old royal lines of Europe as examples. As families intermarried and became more and more inbred, weaknesses in the offspring showed up. The more inbreeding, the more problems.

It's the very same with plants. Inbreeding weakens a line. However, when you cross two less related lines you end up with what's called a "hybrid." That plant carries the better traits of each of its parents. It is simply more vigorous.

However, in most cases, hybridization requires careful hand pollination. That is the reason that hybrid seeds are more expensive, and now you see why they're worth it!

ALL AMERICA WINNERS

Royal diners of old had food tasters ... folks who ate first. If they survived, then royalty ate too.

There's a similar service available to flower growers. It's called the *All America Selections*. New flowers (also vegetables and roses) are tested against other similar existing varieties. Comparisons are run at several dozen test gardens across America ... all soils and all climates. Those new varieties that measure up as significant improvements are granted special AAS recognition. Only a few new plants are so honored each year, but you have the assurance that those plants bearing the All America designation will outperform anything previously available.

Watch garden publications and seed catalogs for listings of the newest and most recent AAS winners. Give 'em a try in your plantings!

WILDFLOWERS FOR TEXAS GARDENS

No book of gardening in Texas would be complete without a mention of the state's beautiful wildflowers, and how they can be brought into our landscapes. The truth is, any plant is fair game. If it looks good and grows in our soils and our climate, it's worthy of trial in our landscapes. There are some basics, though, that will make it all more rewarding.

Select a Good Site

Wildflowers are just like any other plant ... they enjoy the best possible growing location. Most types need good drainage and bright sunlight. While they don't need prime garden soil, most types shouldn't be expected to survive steep rocky slopes, heavily shaded bogs and other less desirable sites. If that's the type of setting you have, try to find varieties native to similar surroundings. In general, try to simulate what you see where they're growing in nature.

If you're planning on naturalizing them, try to find a spot that's not covered with lawn grass. The two plant groups usually aren't compatible, simply because rules and tradition say we have to keep the lawn mowed.

The ideal solutions would be either to naturalize the flowers in vacant lots, parks, schoolyards and other public places where turf grass is less highly maintained, or to provide the wildflowers a special bed in your landscape, where you can cultivate their beauty and feature them, all through the seasons. Though we've included wildflowers in our annual listings, many types are perennials and will enjoy the protection of a designated flower bed.

Preparing the Soil

Soil requirements vary with the different wildflowers, but most will do well given eight to 12 inches of native Texas earth.

If you need to mix compost or peat moss (perhaps even sand) to improve a clay soil, they'll surely not complain. That's especially important if you're growing them in a special landscaping bed, where you want maximum show for your efforts. Tip: don't try to develop an overly rich soil. Most wildflowers grow in poor and depleted soils and will "go all to leaves" if they're given too fertile a growing ground.

In naturalized plantings, you must work the soil lightly before planting. Otherwise, the seeds will lay on the hard-packed surface like birdfeed. Exactly like birdfeed! Rototill to a depth of two to three inches and rake the area lightly, just to keep it relatively smooth.

Planting the Seed

Once the soil is prepared you're ready for planting. Important thing here is the timing. Again, you need to simulate nature. If the plant blooms in the spring, it probably ripens its seeds in the summer. Sow them in late summer or early fall, just as nature would do. Let fall's cooler, (hopefully) moist weather help break through the seed coats and get the plants growing.

Broadcast the seed over the freshly worked soil. Plant varieties that are compatible together (same relative heights and complementary colors). Unless the seed is extremely fine, rake the soil gently (use back side of garden rake . . . upside down) to cover the seed lightly. Water deeply with some type of gentle sprinkler that won't wash the seeds away.

Caring for the Plantings

They wouldn't be "wild" flowers if they couldn't grow without a lot of care and attention. However, you may still need to pull the competing weeds. Just make sure you can tell the weeds from the wildflowers! Keep them well watered and fertilize lightly once or twice with a high-phosphorus plant food. Otherwise, leave them alone. And keep the mower away from them, at least until they've dried and reseeded.

Seed Sources

More and more seed houses now offer Texas wildflowers. One or two growers within the state specialize in their full-time production. You can even gather your own out in nature.

Watch your area for wildflower types you especially like. Make note of their locations, and pay close attention to the plants' appearance (they'll look different when the flowers are gone). When the seed heads start to ripen, generally within a month of blooming, clip off the heads, stem and all, and place them in paper sacks or envelopes. Store the seed cool (75 to 80°F) and dry while they finish ripening.

Special note: if you're collecting seed from private property, always ask the owner's permission. And don't ever take more than 10 to 20 percent of the supply . . . leave plenty for nature's use.

Bluebonnet Tips

Our State Flower is, by far, the most popular Texas wildflower. Seed is readily available, both in small packages and in bulk.

A hard seed coat protects the tender embryo, but also makes germination erratic unless you do something to break through it prior to planting. Some growers offer scarified seed (specially processed to cut through seed coat). Otherwise, you'll have to do the job yourself by freezing the seeds for two days, then pouring boiling water over them, and finally soaking for two to three additional days (drain and add more hot water daily).

Plant bluebonnet seeds in the fall, in prepared soil. Cover them lightly and water deeply. Water as needed during their growing season. Allow pods to dry completely before mowing the following season.

Other Flowers Worth Trying

Don't stop with bluebonnets. There are many other, equally spectacular native flowers . . .

Beard tongue *(Penstemon)* Perennial; pink, white, lavender, red; bloom spring through fall.

Black-eyed Susan *(Rudbeckia)* Annual, yellow daisy-like flower with brown center; bloom late spring through fall.

Butterfly weed *(Asclepias)* Perennial; vivid orange, bloom late spring through summer.

Cardinal flower *(Lobelia)* Perennial; bright red spikes to 5 feet; blooms late summer, fall; do not cover seeds.

Engelmann daisy *(Engelmannia)* Perennial; bright yellow; blooms spring, summer and fall; withstands mowing.

Evening primrose *(Oenothera)* Perennial; pink type most common, also yellow, white; blooms spring through fall; invasive in flower beds.

Firewheel *(Gaillardia)* Annual; red, yellow, orange and mahogany; blooms spring and summer.

Gayfeather *(Liatris)* Perennial; rose-purple; blooms late summer, fall.

Golden Wave *(Coreopsis)* Annual, perennial; yellow, marked maroon or brown; blooms spring and early summer.

Indian paintbrush *(Castilleja)* Annual (others perennial); mostly red, also pink, yellow, purple; blooms spring. Annual type difficult to establish.

Maximilian sunflower *(Helianthus)* Perennial; bright yellow flowers on spikes; blooms fall.

Mexican hat *(Ratibida)* Perennial, yellow often marked maroon; blooms late spring-summer.

Phlox *(Phlox)* Annual, perennial; pink, red, white, purple, often marked with contrasting colors; bloom spring.

Purple cone flower *(Echinacea)* Perennial; pink-purple; blooms late spring-summer.

Rain lily (many genera) Perennial; white, yellow, pink, lavender; bloom late spring through fall, after rains.

Standing cypress *(Ipomopsis)* Biennial, bright red; blooms spring.

Texas bluebell *(Eustoma)* Annual; generally purple, may be white, pink, yellow; bloom summer through early fall.

Verbenas *(Verbena)* Annual, perennial; lavender, purple, white, pink; bloom spring through fall.

Winecup *(Callirhoe)* Mostly perennial; reddish-purple, white, pink; bloom spring, early summer.

Texas Bluebell

Maximilian Sunflower

Bluebonnet

Indian Paintbrush

Mexican Hat

Golden Wave

PLAN FOR COLOR

Color up, Texas! Plant those flowers! There's no greater testimony to your love of life, beauty and Texas than to plant something to brighten your world. Choose from the various hues on this natural palette, with the assurance that all are tried and proved in Texas conditions.

Amaranthus (Amaranthus)	Four O'Clock (Mirabilis)	Nasturtium (Tropaeolum)
Begonia (Begonia)	Foxglove (Digitalis)	Pansy (Viola)
Chenille Plant (Acalypha)	Gaillardia (Gaillardia)	Petunia (Petunia)
Cockscomb (Celosia)	Geranium (Pelargonium)	Pinks (Dianthus)
Coleus (Coleus)	Hollyhock (Alcea)	Scarlet Sage (Salvia)
Copper Plant (foliage) (Acalypha)	Impatiens (Impatiens)	Snapdragon (Antirrhinum)
Cypress Vine (Ipomoea quamoclit)	Joseph's Coat (foliage) (Alternanthera)	Verbena (Verbena)
Flowering Cabbage, Kale (Brassica)	Morning Glory (Ipomoea)	Zinnia (Zinnia)
Flowering Tobacco (Nicotiana)	Moss Rose (Portulaca)	

Moss Rose (Portulaca)	Verbena (Verbena)	Four O'Clock (Mirabilis)
Periwinkle (Catharanthus)	Zinnia (Zinnia)	Foxglove (Digitalis)
Petunia (Petunia)	Begonia (Begonia)	Geranium (Pelargonium)
Pinks (Dianthus)	Cockscomb (Celosia)	Globe Amaranth (Gomphrena)
Snapdragon (Antirrhinum)	Coleus (foliage) (Coleus)	Iceland Poppy (Papaver)
Spider Flower (Cleome)	Cosmos (Cosmos)	Impatiens (Impatiens)
Stock (Matthiola)	English Daisy (Bellis)	Larkspur (Consolida)
Sweet Alyssum (Lobularia)	Flowering Tobacco (Nicotiana)	Morning Glory (Ipomoea)

Calendula (Calendula)	Gloriosa Daisy (Rudbeckia)	Moss Rose (Portulaca)
California Poppy (Papaver)	Iceland Poppy (Papaver)	Nasturtium (Tropaeolum)
Clock Vine (Thunbergia)	Impatiens (Impatiens)	Pansy (Viola)
Cockscomb (Celosia)	Joseph's Coat (foliage) (Alternanthera)	Snapdragon (Antirrhinum)
Cosmos (Cosmos)	Lantana (Lantana)	Zinnia (Zinnia)

Clock Vine (Thunbergia)
Cockscomb (Celosia)
Coleus (foliage) (Coleus)
Cosmos (Cosmos)
Four O'Clock (Mirabilis)

Gloriosa Daisy (Rudbeckia)
Hollyhock (Alcea)
Iceland Poppy (Papaver)
Joseph's Coat (foliage) (Alternanthera)
Lantana (Lantana)

Nasturtium (Tropaeolum)
Pansy (Viola)
Petunia (Petunia)
Snapdragon (Antirrhinum)
Zinnia (Zinnia)

Periwinkle (Catharanthus)
Petunia (Petunia)
Pinks (Dianthus)
Snapdragon (Antirrhinum)
Spider Flower (Cleome)
Stock (Matthiola)
Sweet Alyssum (Lobularia)
Verbena (Verbena)
Zinnia (Zinnia)

Geranium (Pelargonium)
Globe Amaranth (Gomphrena)
Hollyhock (Alcea)
Iceland Poppy (Papaver)
Impatiens (Impatiens)
Lantana (Lantana)
Larkspur (Consolida)
Moonflower (Ipomea)
Morning Glory (Ipomea)
Moss Rose (Portulaca)
Pansy (Viola)

Ageratum (Ageratum)
Begonia (Begonia)
Calendula (Calendula)
Clock Vine (Thunbergia)
Coleus (foliage)(Coleus)
Cosmos (Cosmos)
English Daisy (Bellis)
Flowering Cabbage, Kale (Brassica)
Flowering Tobacco (Nicotiana)
Foxglove (Digitalis)
Four O'Clock (Mirabilis)

Petunia (Petunia)
Plumbago (Plumbago)

Morning Glory (Ipomoea)
Pansy (Viola)

Ageratum (Ageratum)
Larkspur (Consolida)

Sweet Alyssum (Lobularia)
Verbena (Verbena)

Larkspur (Consolida)
Petunia (Petunia)
Pinks (Dianthus)
Pansy (Viola)

Ageratum (Ageratum)
Globe Amaranth (Gomphrena)
Hollyhock (Alcea)
Impatiens (Impatiens)

ANNUALS A TO Z

If you're looking for the best . . . the plants that will give the most color for your money, time and effort, then look no farther, gardener. You're about to enter the world of Texas winners . . . plants that will perform! Look through them and you'll be excited by all the possibilities.

Acalypha
COPPER PLANT

Sun. Height: 2 to 4 feet. Heat-tolerant background plant grown for its colorful foliage, a coppery-red. Leaf color intensifies with first cool weather of fall, making copper plants ideal background material. Especially effective used in contrast with light-colored flowers such as mums, marigolds and lantana. Most popular in bed plantings, but well suited to large patio pots. Grown from started nursery transplants (from cuttings only). Pinch out plants' growing shoots to keep them more compact. Plant in mid-spring, once night temperatures are well above freezing. Space plants 12 to 18 inches apart.

Note: Other types of acalyphas offer different variegations, including foliage marked with yellow. Chenille plants produce bright green foliage with long trailing flower catkins resembling bright red pipe cleaners. All are adapted to bright, sunny locations.

Ageratum
AGERATUM, FLOSS FLOWER

Sun or part sun. Height: 8 to 12 inches. Low rounded plants cover themselves with clustered heads of fluffy light blue or white flowers. Grown from seed, but usually planted from small nursery transplants set out in spring. Best used in small groups or as border flower. Set plants 10 to 12 inches apart. Spider mites are frequent visitors.

Alcea
HOLLYHOCK

Sun or part sun. Height: 2 to 8 feet. Vertical spikes on robust plants. Actually a biennial or short-lived perennial, but shorter types are commonly grown as annual flowers. Grown from seed or started nursery transplants. Colors: red, pink, yellow, white, purple, variegated. Some types are single-flowering, (one row of petals), but most are double-flowering, resembling carnations. Best used as a background flower. Shorter, single-colored varieties can be used in massed plantings. Select rust-resistant strains.

Alternanthera
JOSEPH'S COAT

Sun. Height: 12 to 18 inches. Spreading plant grown for its brightly variegated foliage. Several types available, most offering shades of red, yellow, orange and maroon. Colors intensify in fall's cooler weather. Good companion plant for copper plants, mums, marigolds, lantana. Grow in massed bed plantings or in pots and hanging baskets. Stands heat well. Easily grown from cuttings rooted in moist potting soil, or available in spring as nursery transplants. Plant after danger of frost has passed. Space plants 12 to 18 inches apart.

Amaranthus
AMARANTHUS

Sun. Height 4 to 6 feet. Upright plants grown for their truly spectacular summertime foliage. Intense reds, purples and yellows on large, spreading leaves. Variety names like "Flaming Fountain" and "Molten Fire" indicate brilliance of foliage. Growth is somewhat erratic, both in height and color, making massed plantings somewhat risky. Excellent plant for backgrounds, though flamboyant colors may dominate entire landscape. Planted from started nursery transplants.

Antirrhinum
SNAPDRAGON

Sun. Height: 6 to 42 inches, depending on variety. Showy upright bloomer used for bed edgings (dwarf types), massed plantings (dwarf and intermediate types) and for tall background plantings (taller types). Plants can survive hard freezes in much of the state provided they're not allowed to dry out during the cold. Bloom best in temperatures of 70-90°F, so best planted in fall in southern two-thirds of Texas, or in very early spring in all areas. Colors: red, yellow, pink, orange, bronze, white. For most effective landscape display, plant beds of single colors, saving mixed colors for cut-flower plantings. Start from nursery transplants. Space plants 6 to 12 inches apart.

Begonia
BEGONIA (wax, or fibrous-rooted begonias)

Shade or part shade. Height 6 to 12 inches. Small rounded plants well suited to low borders, massed plantings, hanging baskets and patio pots. Foliage color varies from bright glossy green to a waxy bronze. Variegated types are also available. Flowers contrast beautifully, in shades of red, pink and white. Plant in spring, after danger of frost has passed. Seed is extremely fine and difficult to germinate, even under greenhouse conditions. Buy started transplants and plant into well-prepared soil on 10 to 12 inch centers. One of the best shade flowers for season-long bloom!

Bellis
ENGLISH DAISY

Sun. Height: 6 to 8 inches. Less common flowering plants. Grown for their pastel pink, white, rose and lavender blooms, depending on the variety. Cold-resistant, so can be planted in fall in most areas, for bloom the following spring. Flowers resemble small asters or strawflowers. Plant started transplants, and space them 6 to 8 inches apart.

COPPER PLANT

AGERATUM

HOLLYHOCK

JOSEPH'S COAT

AMARANTHUS

FLORAL CARPET SNAPDRAGON

FLORAL CARPET SNAPDRAGON

BEGONIA

SNAPDRAGON

Brassica
FLOWERING CABBAGE, FLOWERING KALE

Sun. Height: 12 to 15 inches. Unusual annual plants grown for their richly colored foliage. Inner leaves may be red, white, rose or pink, against darker green outside leaves. Plants are tolerant of hard freezes. Transplants should be set out in the fall for best coloration and size. Plants will bolt (produce bloom stalks) in late spring. Cabbage loopers may chew foliage. Best used for accent beds. Can be grown in patio pots. Start plants from seed sown indoors in pots, or buy nursery transplants. Space plants 15 inches apart.

Caladium
CALADIUM

Shade or part shade. Height: 1 to 2 feet. Warm weather plant grown for its colorful foliage. Many varieties, leaf styles and colors, including red, pink, and white. White types are most tolerant of sunlight, followed by pink. Most red varieties sunburn and scorch easily. Useful massed in single-color beds or in patio pots. Grown from fleshy tubers. Leaf size is proportionate to size of the tuber. Plant late, once soil has warmed, generally 3 to 4 weeks after last killing frost. Plant tubers into well prepared garden soil with leaf sprouts facing upward. Keep plants well watered during growing season. Do not apply high-nitrogen fertilizers to caladiums (cause excess greening). Remove flower buds as they develop. In fall, once temperatures fall into the 50's and leaves start to droop and wither, gradually withhold water to plants. After most of their leaves have fallen over, dig and air-dry the tubers on newspapers for one week. Dust them with a fungicide and store them in dry perlite or sawdust at 55 to 60°F over winter. Allow no two tubers to touch during storage. Plant them out the following spring once the soil temperatures have warmed.

Calendula
CALENDULA (pot marigold)

Sun. Height: 1 to 3 feet. Cool-season plant, should be set out in fall in South Texas, in very early spring in north. Flowers resemble zinnias, in shades of yellow, orange and white. Plant from started nursery transplants. Showy annual flower that's well suited to backgrounds and massed plantings. Space plants 12 to 15 inches apart.

Catharanthus (Vinca)
PERIWINKLE

Sun. Height: 4 to 16 inches, depending on the variety. Among our most heat-tolerant annual flowers. Blooms are about size of quarters, in shades of rose, pink and white, resemble small pinwheels. Many have interestingly contrasting "eyes." Plant from small pots in spring. Good as ground cover (low-spreading types), with more upright types being used for border and massed color plantings, as well as in containers. Keep well watered in bright, full sun locations. Should flower size diminish and plant vigor fail, apply a complete and balanced plant food. The nitrogen in it, interestingly, will help rejuvenate the plants and their flower size. Space plants 10 to 12 inches apart.

Celosia
COCKSCOMB

Sun. Height: 6 to 24 inches. Two basic types of celosia are available: the plume, or feathery, type and the crested, or cockscomb, type. Bloom heads last for many weeks. Colors range from intense dark red to pink, orange and yellow. Foliage is green, often with deep reddish tint. Set out nursery transplants in spring, after danger of frost has passed. Best used as low border flower or showy specimen background plant. Keep plants vigorous and actively growing. Slowing of growth can lead to premature flower formation, with less spectacular displays. Space plants 8 to 16 inches apart, depending on the variety.

Cleome
SPIDER FLOWER

Sun. Height: 3 to 5 feet. Vigorous, upright background plant with wispy white, pink or purplish-pink flowers. Best used in wide beds, where plants can be spaced 2 to 3 feet apart. Provides softening texture, very compatible with lattice work. Transplants work well, but are seldom available in nurseries. Can be sown directly into garden, but must be thinned to proper spacing after germination. Warm season annual. Reseeds abundantly.

Coleus
COLEUS

Shade. Height: 1 to 3 feet. Colorful foliage in shades of red, pink, yellow, white and green. Best used in shady flower beds, patio pots and, for the trailing types, in hanging baskets. Require moist soils because of succulent foliage. Avoid high-nitrogen fertilizers that could lead to excessive greening of foliage. Remove flower buds to encourage more leaf production. Grown from seed sown in pots indoors, from cuttings, or from started nursery transplants. Space plants 8 to 12 inches apart.

Cosmos
COSMOS

Sun. Height: 2 to 6 feet. Large, open plants with dozens of daisy-like blooms. Colors range from orange and yellow to pink, purple and white. Single and double-flowering types available. Stand heat well. Best used as background plant, or as massed planting in large, open beds. Start from seed sown directly into garden, or start your own transplants by sowing seed in pots indoors several weeks before the last killing freeze for your area. Space plants 15 to 24 inches apart.

Dianthus
PINKS

Sun or part sun. Height: 6 to 15 inches. Small rounded plants with fragrant blooms resembling single carnations. Cold-hardy, so can be planted in mid-to-late fall in southern two-thirds of Texas, in very early spring in the north. Plant from started transplants. Excellent in borders

FLOWERING KALE

CALENDULA

CALADIUM

PERIWINKLE

COCKSCOMB

SPIDER FLOWER

COSMOS

COLEUS

PINKS

and massed plantings. Intense colors: red, pink, white and orchid, many with bicolored blooms. Should be planted far more often! Space plants 10 to 15 inches apart.

Digitalis
FOXGLOVE

Sun or part sun. Height: 2 to 6 feet. Interesting vertical-flowering annuals (older types required second year to produce flowers). Good background plants that bloom April through June. Plant in fall from seed or started nursery transplants. Flowers hang downward, creating graceful spikes of white, yellow, pink, rose and red, many with contrasting spots. Plant 16 to 24 inches apart.

Gaillardia
GAILLARDIA (Indian Blanket)

Sun. Height: 12 to 24 inches. Though generally grown as a perennial, several annual forms of gaillardias are available. All are ideal for massed plantings. Colors range from orange and red to yellow and brown. Both single and double-flowering types are available. Start plants from seed sown indoors or from nursery transplants. Well suited to hot, dry locations. Plant in spring, once danger of frost has passed. Space plants 10 to 15 inches apart, depending on the variety.

Note: See (Chapter 9, *Perennials*) for details of other gaillardias.

Gomphrena
GLOBE AMARANTH

Sun. Height: 2 feet. Free-flowering "strawflower" that not only survives hot weather well, but also can be dried for winter bouquets. Blossoms are marble-sized, in shades of pink, white, purple and lavender. Plant from seed or started transplants in early spring, after danger of frost has passed. Space plants 12 to 15 inches apart.

Impatiens
IMPATIENS (Sultana)

Shade or part shade. Height: the spreading plants grow to 6 to 24 inches tall, depending on variety. One of most popular sources of color in shady locations. Plants bloom freely, in shades of red, orange, pink, white, purple and lavender. Many are attractively variegated. Plants require ample moisture, and may need protection from spider mites during summer. Best used in massed plantings, as borders, in pots and baskets. Flower production will decrease during extreme heat, but plants will return to full bloom during fall. New plants may be started from seed or cuttings, but transplants should be used for planting into the flower garden. Space plants 8 to 15 inches apart, depending on the variety.

Note: Balsams are a closely related species producing double flowers in shades of red, pink and white. Though more upright and less showy, they are still good background or tall border flowers. Will tolerate more sun than sultanas.

Ipomoea
MORNING GLORIES, MOONFLOWER, CYPRESS VINE

Sun. Height: 8 to 15 feet. All are closely related, and all can provide quick cover and color for fences and walls. Seed germinates quickly, but will be hastened by scratching with a knife or sandpaper, to break through the seed coat. All require warm, rather infertile soil and ample moisture. Morning glories bloom from daybreak through early afternoon (flowers are open longer in fall's cooler weather). Colors: blue, white and pink, also two-toned. Moonflowers bloom from early evening into the next morning. Flowers are large, white and fragrant. Cypress vine produces smaller blooms, generally red, contrasting nicely against soft ferny foliage. All types will require support. Each should be planted on 2 to 4-foot spacings.

Lantana
LANTANA

Though commonly grown as an annual flower, lantana is actually a tender perennial. For details, refer to it in, (Chapter 9), *Perennials*.

Lobularia
SWEET ALYSSUM

Sun or part sun. Height: 2 to 4 inches. Low-spreading growth. Good for low borders and small patio pots. Cold-resistant: plant in very early spring in northern two-thirds of Texas, in fall or spring in southern portions. Flower color: white, rose and violet, depending on variety. Very fragrant. Grown from seed or, preferably, started nursery transplants. Set plants 6 to 10 inches apart.

Matthiola
STOCK (Gilliflower)

Sun. Height: 12 to 18 inches. Cool season flower producing spikes of fragrant blooms in shades of pink, lavender and white. Dwarf types better suited for use as bedding plants in Southwest. Grown from seed or, preferably, started nursery transplants. Plants are cold-resistant, so plant in fall in southern parts of state, in very early spring over all areas. Keep plants well watered and fertilized to keep them vigorous. Allowing them to stop growing will likely cause them to come into bloom prematurely. Best used in massed color plantings in flower beds, or for use as cut flowers. Space plants 8 to 12 inches apart.

Mirabilis
FOUR O'CLOCK

Shade or part shade. Will grow in sunny locations given ample moisture. Height: 2 to 3 feet. Brightly colored tuberous-rooted annual flower (often dies to ground but overwinters, coming back from fleshy root, particularly in southern two-thirds of state). Fragrant blooms open in late evening. Plant in spring, for blooms summer to frost. Reseeds freely. Colors: red, pink, white, yellow, and variegated. Easily grown from seed or transplanted seedlings. Space plants 15 to 20 inches apart.

IMPATIENS

IMPATIENS

GLOBE AMARANTH

SWEET ALYSSUM

FOXGLOVE

GAILLARDIA

Nicotiana
FLOWERING TOBACCO

Shade or part shade. Height: 12 to 20 inches. Novel group of warm season shade flowers. Rather upright habit. Fragrant star-shaped blossoms are produced in quantity. Many varieties offer soft pastel flower colors (including green), while others are far more intense, including bright red and hot pink. Plant in spring, after danger of frost has passed. This plant will be gaining in popularity in upcoming years . . . well worth trying! Plant from started transplants. Space plants 10 to 12 inches apart.

Papaver
POPPIES

Sun. Height: 1 to 3 feet. Though many perennial poppies are grown in Texas, especially in more northern landscapes, there are several strains that are either annuals or that are grown as annuals. Two in particular are Iceland poppies (pastels: yellow, white, orange, pink) and California poppies (actually Eschscholzia . . . in shades of yellow and orange). Both can be planted from seed sown directly into well-prepared garden soil in the fall, or from started transplants in very early spring. Space plants 6 to 12 inches apart.

Pelargonium
GERANIUM

Sun during spring and fall; part shade during summer. Height: 10 to 20 inches. Popular low shrubby annual flower grown from cuttings or seed. Seed types are special hybrids and offer the advantage of being free of stem diseases common in the cutting-grown types. Flowers borne in large heads. Colors range from bright red to pink, purple and white, some two-toned. Leaves of many types, especially the darker flowering varieties, attractively zoned with dark markings. Geraniums prefer cooler temperatures than most parts of Texas offer during the summer. While they're grown in full sun in northern climates, they do better in morning sun and afternoon shade in Texas. They're well suited to container culture, to allow portability during the changing seasons. Must have well drained soils, and old flower heads should be kept picked off to prevent seed formation. Start from nursery transplants in spring, once danger of frost has passed. Space plants 10 to 16 inches apart.

Other types of geraniums: Trailing (ivy-leafed) and Martha Washington (both heat-sensitive). Scented-leafed types: well adapted, but many grow quite large. Allow ample room.

Petunia
PETUNIA

Sun. Height: 8 to 12 inches. One of most popular annual flowers. Low-growing, spreading plants cover themselves with blossoms. Colors range from red, pink, purple and blue to white and pale yellow. Many two-toned types are available, some with contrasting "stars," others with fringed margins of different colors ("picotee"), still others with contrasting venation. Single and double-flowering types are available. "Multiflora" types produce greater quantities of smaller flowers, while "grandifloras" produce fewer, but larger, flowers. Best used in

GERANIUM

CALIFORNIA POPPY

PETUNIA

FLOWERING TOBACCO

GERANIUM

massed plantings of single colors or in pots or hanging baskets. Also excellent as low flower bed border. Seed is very fine and should only be planted in carefully controlled greenhouse conditions. Nursery transplants are the best means of starting petunias. Tolerate light frosts and should be planted in fall or early spring in southern third of Texas, in very early spring in the northern two-thirds of the state. Most varieties will complete their growth and blooming by the arrival of hot summer weather.

Portulaca
MOSS ROSE (Rose Moss, Portulaca)

Sun. Height: 4 to 8 inches. Extremely tolerant of high temperatures, bright sunlight. Foliage resembles a succulent moss. Blooms from spring through first frost, although individual plants may complete life cycles within three to four months. Reseeds freely, though hybrid types will not "come true" from seeds. Colors: refreshing sherbet colors, including orange, raspberry-rose and pineapple yellow, also white, pink and bright red. No plant cools down (or cheers up!) a hot summer day any better than portulaca. Good in massed plantings of mixed or single colors, also in pots and baskets. Plant from seed or started nursery transplants. Many new hybrid types are now available, including varieties with more and larger flowers, more double flowers, blooms that remain open later in the day (older types close by mid-afternoon on hot summer days), and more prostrate habits. Space plants 6 to 8 inches apart in beds, closer together for quicker show in containers.

Rudbeckia
GLORIOSA DAISY

Sun. Height: 18 to 36 inches. Outstanding warm season flower, actually improved forms of the native black-eyed Susan. Best used as background flower or in massed plantings. Endures heat well, blooming from late spring well into summer. Some types are perennial. Colors: yellow, orange-gold, brownish-red. Flower size varies from 3 to 5 inches. Grow from started nursery transplants set out in spring after danger of frost has passed. Space plants 14 to 18 inches apart.

Salvia
SCARLET SAGE

Part sun to shade. Height: 8 to 18 inches. Nationally, one of the most popular warm-weather sun annual flowers, but somewhat less adapted in Southwest due to extreme heat (hence recommendation of less than full sunlight). Plants are rather upright, bearing flowers in spikes. Colors: intense and brilliant red, also purple and pastel pink, white. Good in massed beds and in patio pots. Start from nursery transplants set into garden once danger of frost has passed. Space plants 8 to 12 inches apart, depending on mature height of the variety.

Note: see (Chapter 9,) *Perennials* for other salvias.

Tagetes
MARIGOLD

Sun. Height: 8 to 36 inches. Among the most popular of all warm season flowers. Native to Southwest U.S. and Mexico, so well adapted to hot, dry conditions. Best used in low borders and containers (dwarf types) and in massed plantings (taller varieties). Nurseries and seed houses offer dozens of varieties, most double-flowering, in shades of yellow, orange, mahogany-red and even near-whites. Spider mites are a serious hot weather pest on marigolds. Marigolds are said to repel nematodes, but only if all other nematode-prone plants are kept out of the area for several years while the marigolds are being grown there. Can be started from seed or nursery transplants. Plant in early spring, after danger of frost has passed, for summertime color. Replant in mid-summer for fall marigolds. They'll develop intense . . . spectacular . . . fall colors! Space plants 8 to 18 inches apart, depending on the variety.

Thunbergia
CLOCK VINE, BLACK-EYED SUSAN VINE

Sun. Height: 6 to 10 feet. Fast-growing vine with multitudes of yellow, orange or white blooms during summer and fall. Plants require support of fence, wall or post. Can also be grown in hanging baskets and patio pots, though will require frequent shaping. Spider mites can be problem during hot weather. Sow seed directly into garden, or set out started transplants. Space plants 2 to 4 feet apart on supports.

Tropaeolum
NASTURTIUM

Part sun. Height: 8 to 12 inches. Popular flower farther north, it requires more special care in Texas. Not adapted to hot summer weather or to freezing temperatures, so seed must be planted two to four weeks before average date of last killing freeze. Afternoon shade will prolong its blooming season, but only for a few weeks. Grow in rather infertile ground, and avoid high-nitrogen fertilizers that could over-stimulate leaf production. Colors: yellow, orange and red. Space plants 6 to 8 inches apart.

Verbena
VERBENA

Sun. Height: 4 to 12 inches. Trailing plants grown for their numerous flower heads, in shades of red, pink, purple and white, many with attractively two-toned flowers. Well adapted to hot, sunny locations. Best used in massed bed plantings and in patio pots and hanging baskets. Spider mites may be problem during warm weather. Grown from started transplants set out once danger of frost has passed in spring. Space plants 12 to 16 inches apart.

Note: perennial ground cover types of verbenas are available. Several types are also native Texas wildflowers, for naturalized plantings.

GLORIOSA DAISY

NASTURTIUM

MOSS ROSE

SCARLET SAGE

MARIGOLD

Viola
PANSY

Sun. Height: 6 to 10 inches. Fragrant flowers in shades of yellow, white, purple, lavender and mahogany-red. Many of the blossoms are attractively marked with contrasting colors and unusual blotches. Best used as low border or in massed plantings. For most dramatic impact, mass like colors in beds, rather than planting mixed colors. Should be planted in fall in southern two-thirds of Texas (keep plants well watered during cold snaps and use a shallow one-inch layer of mulch such as shredded bark or compost to lessen cold damage). Plant in very early spring (two to four weeks before average date of last killing freeze) in North Texas. Can be planted from potted nursery transplants or from bundles of bare-rooted plants. Space plants 8 to 10 inches apart. Keep old blooms picked off for better flower production. Use hybrid varieties whenever possible.

Note: Two closely related groups of flowers, the violas and Johnny Jump-ups, bloom more profusely than pansies. Flowers are quite similar, though smaller. Care is essentially the same as for pansies.

Zinnia
ZINNIA

Sun. Height: 6 inches to 3 feet. One of most popular warm season annual flowers. Heat-tolerant and adapted to all parts of the state. Flower size varies from 1 to 5 inches, depending on the variety. Most varieties produce double flowers, though single types are available. Great advances have been made in variety improvement in recent years. New hybrid types offer greater flower production on more vigorous plants. Colors: red, yellow, pink, orange, white and even green. Two-toned fringed and freckled types are also available. Dahlia-flowering types offer formal petal arrangement, while cactus-flowering types are shaggier, less formal. Best used as massed color planting (shorter types) or as tall background flower. Powdery mildew on foliage is about the only problem of any concern. Grown from seed sown directly into garden or from started nursery transplants. Plant in spring, once danger of frost has passed. *For even more spectacular color, plant zinnias in mid-summer, to bloom during fall's cooler weather. You simply won't believe the brilliant colors!* Space plants 8 to 24 inches apart.

VERBENA

ZINNIA

ZINNIA

PANSY

Chapter 9

Perennials

Botanically, perennials are plants that live more than two years. That's compared to annuals (plants that live one year or part of one year) and biennials (plants that complete their life cycles in two years). That's the botanical meaning of the word "perennial."

To a gardener, though, perennials are a salvation. They're plants you can count on, plants that will come back to grow and bloom year after year just like clockwork. They're plants for the front flowerbed or the edge of the alleyway. They're for the intimate garden or the freeway median.

Perennials have learned how to fight. Many face hostile conditions sometime during their year: heat, cold, drought. Sounds like Texas! They combat those conditions by strategic retreat to fleshy bulbs or tuberous roots. A few remain evergreen, but simply quit growing. Given minimal care, however, all return to bloom the following year.

Perennials just may be the most overlooked group of landscaping plants throughout Texas . . . and for no good reason. Few plants provide so much color for so little effort.

Give perennials a chance to work their magic at your place! The following pages contain a starter kit for success with perennials in Texas. You'll find tips for choosing, planting and caring for this great group of plants. You'll likely agree that they're some of the most versatile plants you've ever grown!

GETTING THE MOST OUT OF
YOUR PERENNIALS

As great as perennials are, there are several ways to get more for your time, effort and money. As long as you're turning the earth, setting out plants, watering, weeding and feeding, you might as well maximize the returns.

Spring

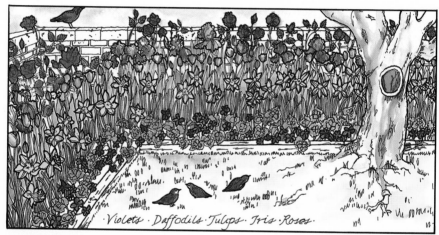

Violets · Daffodils · Tulips · Iris · Roses.

Summer

Gaillardia · Phlox · Gloriosa Daisy · Day Lily · Rose Mallow

Fall

Fall Crocus · Spider Lily · Chrysanthemum · Michaelmas Daisy

Tips

1. Plan your plantings carefully. Know each plant and where it should be planted for maximum effectiveness.

2. Plan for best overall color display by massing colors. Even a small bed of yellow daffodils or red cannas will show up better than a large planting of mixed colors.

3. Plan for a succession of blooms. It's easy to have color in the spring. The challenge comes in providing color in the summer, fall and especially winter.

4. Prepare the soil carefully prior to planting. It may be several years until you're able to work the soil again. Do it right the first time!

5. Care for your plants. Just because they're perennials doesn't mean they can withstand neglect.

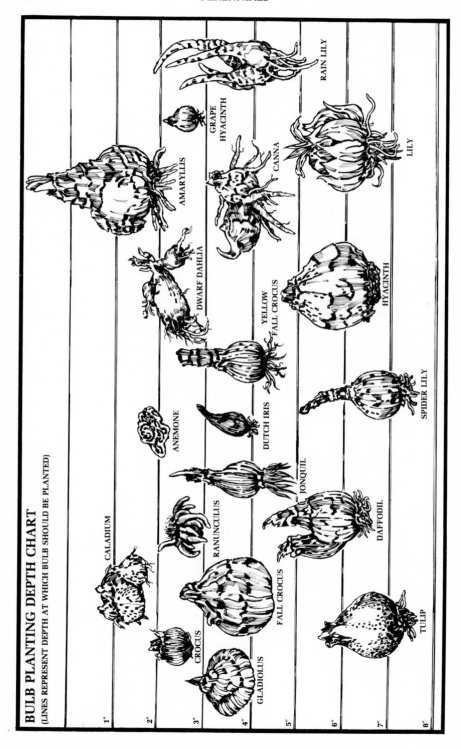

BULB PLANTING DEPTH CHART
(LINES REPRESENT DEPTH AT WHICH BULB SHOULD BE PLANTED)

1"
2"
3"
4"
5"
6"
7"
8"

CALADIUM
CROCUS
GLADIOLUS
RANUNCULUS
ANEMONE
FALL CROCUS
DUTCH IRIS
JONQUIL
DAFFODIL
TULIP
AMARYLLIS
DWARF DAHLIA
GRAPE HYACINTH
CANNA
YELLOW FALL CROCUS
HYACINTH
SPIDER LILY
RAIN LILY
LILY

HOW TO PLANT PERENNIALS

Good care at planting is the real key to success with perennials. They'll be growing in the same soil for years, so give them the best you can offer . . .

1. Full sun and good drainage are essentials for most perennial plants.

2. Raised planting beds ensure adequate drainage. A six to eight-inch elevation would be ideal. Railroad ties and masonry retaining curbs are two possibilities.

3. Remove weeds and grass from new bed area, roots and all.

4. Add a four to-five inch layer of peat moss, compost, shredded bark or other organic matter on top of the soil.

5. Washed brick sand can also be added if you are trying to improve a clay soil, but it must always be used in combination with the organic matter.

6. Rototill to a depth of eight to 12 inches, mixing the organic matter and sand with the soil thoroughly. Several passes across the area may be required.

7. Rake the area smooth, removing rocks, roots and other debris.

8. Apply a soil fumigant prior to planting, to eliminate problems of nematodes, weeds already growing in the area, and soil-borne insects and diseases. Read and follow the label directions carefully, to avoid damage to nearby trees and shrubs.

MOST COMMON QUESTION

"When should I transplant my perennials?"

Gardeners are generally asking about one perennial in particular, be it daffodils, daisies, daylilies . . . or whatever. The answer is simple: if it blooms in the spring, transplant it in the fall. If it blooms in the fall, transplant it in the spring. There will be occasional exceptions.

HOW TO "NATURALIZE" YOUR PERENNIALS

Plan carefully if you expect a woodland effect from your perennial plantings. Choose types that will grow and multiply year after year.

• Choose an area that is not completely covered with turf grass. Lawns must be mowed in the spring, weeks before the bulbs' leaves have finished their work of making and storing food for next year's bloom. Best areas for naturalized plantings are in rock gardens, in ground cover beds, and under large deciduous trees where turf grass is somewhat sparse.

• Getting the naturalized effect: gently "sow" the bulbs by tossing them onto the ground in a sweeping motion. Plant where they fall.

TEXAS TIP
Spring bulbs such as jonquils and the smaller narcissus, species tulips and grape hyacinths are some of the best for naturalizing in Texas landscapes, since they have the ability to increase and rebloom for years.

CARE TIPS FOR YOUR PERENNIAL PLANTINGS

We've said it before . . . perennials require less care than most other sources of landscaping color. But that doesn't mean you can neglect them. Follow a few routine guidelines and you'll ensure repeat bloom.

Watering

• Keep soil moist throughout the year, even though most perennials go dormant at one season or another.

• Soak beds thoroughly, especially during periods of active growth just before flowering.

• Whenever possible, avoid overhead irrigation. You'll lessen chance of disease invasion and reduce damage to flowers.

• Best watering tools: soaker hose or trickle irrigation equipment.

Fertilizing

• For beds filled strictly with flowering perennials, apply 1-2-1 ratio fertilizer such as 10-20-10, one to two pounds per 100 square feet monthly during periods of active growth. Fertilize bulb beds prior to emergence of foliage, both to promote better blooms for the current year, and to encourage vigorous growth and food storage for subsequent seasons.

• For beds of mixed flowering and foliar perennials, apply 1-1-1 ratio fertilizer such as 8-8-8 or 12-12-12, one to two pounds per 100 square feet monthly during periods of active growth.

• Follow all fertilizations with a thorough watering.

• Remember that some perennials will grow most actively during the spring, others in summer and still others in the fall. Gear your feedings accordingly.

Pest Control

• Insects will occasionally attack your perennial plants. Learn to recognize their symptoms and treat at first sign.

• Diseases should be a minor problem with most of the adapted perennial plants. Should a disease develop, identify it and control it with the appropriate chemical before it ruins your plantings.

Mulches

• Apply mulches around perennial plants, both for conventional mulching benefits (reduce weeds, retain moisture, control erosion), and to protect crowns of plants during their dormant period. Best mulches: bark chips, well rotted compost, tree leaves.

Weed Control

• Whenever possible, eliminate weeds prior to planting by applying soil fumigant.

• Some pre-emergent weed killers can be used safely around perennial plants. Dacthal, balan and betasan can all be used, provided you read and follow label directions.

• To control existing weeds, spot treat with a post-emergent weed killer where possible. Otherwise hand dig.

PLAN FOR COLOR

One of the joys of blending nature's colors together is that they seldom clash with one another. Still, it's good to know what you might expect from every plant in your landscape. Our color wheel will help you know all the resources you have to draw on ... perennial plants and their colors.

Amaryllis (Hippeastrum)	Gaillardia (Gaillardia)	Pinks (Dianthus)
Anemone (Anemone)	Gladiolus (Gladiolus)	Ranunculus (Ranunculus)
Canna (Canna)	Hollyhock (Alcea)	Rose (Rosa)
Carnation (Dianthus)	Iris (Iris)	Rose Mallow (Hibiscus)
Chrysanthemum (Chrysanthemum)	Lily (Lilium)	Spider Lily (Lycoris)
Dahlia (Dahlia)	Michaelmas Daisy (Aster)	Tulip (Tulipa)
Daylily (Hemerocallis)	Peony (Paeonia)	Yarrow (Achillea)
Foxglove (Digitalis)	Phlox (Phlox)	

Amaryllis (Hippeastrum)	Fall Crocus (Crocus)	Oxalis (Oxalis)
Anemone (Anemone)	Foxglove (Digitalis)	Peony (Paeonia)
Bergenia (Bergenia)	Gladiolus (Gladiolus)	Phlox (Phlox)
Canna (Canna)	Hollyhock (Alcea)	Pinks (Dianthus)
Carnation (Dianthus)	Iris (Iris)	Rainlily (Zephyranthes)
Chrysanthemum (Chrysanthemum)	Lantana (Lantana)	Rose (Rosa)
Dahlia (Dahlia)	Lily (Lilium)	Rose Mallow (Hibiscus)
Daylily (Hemerocallis)	Michaelmas Daisy (Aster)	Spider Lily (Lycoris)
		Tulip (Tulipa)

Butterfly Weed (Asclepias)	Daylily (Hemerocallis)	Lantana (Lantana)
Canna (Canna)	Gaillardia (Gaillardia)	Lily (Lilium)
Chrysanthemum (Chrysanthemum)	Gladiolus (Gladiolus)	Ranunculus (Ranunculus)
Dahlia (Dahlia)	Gloriosa Daisy (Rudbeckia)	Rose (Rosa)
		Tulip (Tulipa)

Basket of Gold (Alyssum)	Gaillardia (Gaillardia)	Rain Lily (Zephyranthes)
Canna (Canna)	Gladiolus (Gladiolus)	Ranunculus (Ranunculus)

Column 1	Column 2	Column 3	Column 4	Column 5
Daylily (Hemerocallis) **Foxglove (Digitalis)**	(Foliage) Aspidistra (Aspidistra) Bergenia (Bergenia)	Anemone (Anemone) Crocus (Crocus)	Anemone (Anemone) Chrysanthemum (Chrysanthemum) Crocus (Crocus) Dahlia (Dahlia) Daylily (Hemerocallis) Foxglove (Digitalis)	Amaryllis (Hippeastrum) Anemone (Anemone) Candytuft (Iberis) Carnation (Dianthus) Chrysanthemum (Chrysanthemum) Crinum Lily (Crinum) Crocus (Crocus) Daffodil, also jonquil (Narcissus) Dahlia (Dahlia) Daylily (Hemerocallis)
Michaelmas Daisy (Aster) **Peony (Paeonia)**	Elephant's Ear (Caladium) Ferns (various species) Hosta (Hosta)	Grape Hyacinth (Muscari) Iris (Iris)	Gay Feather (Liatris) Gladiolus (Gladiolus) Hollyhock (Alcea) Hosta (Hosta) Iris (Iris) Michaelmas Daisy (Aster)	Foxglove (Digitalis) Gladiolus (Gladiolus) Grape Hyacinth (Muscari) Hollyhock (Alcaea) Iris (Iris) Lantana (Lantana) Lily (Lilium) Michaelmas Daisy (Aster) Oxalis (Oxalis) Peony (Paeonia)
Yellow Fall Crocus (Sternbergia)	Lamb's Ear (Stachys) Santolina (Santolina) Sedum (Sedum)	Michaelmas Daisy (Aster) Sage (Salvia)	Peony (Paeonia) Phlox (Phlox) Purple Coneflower (Echinacea) Rose (Rosa) Sage (Salvia) Tulip (Tulipa) Violet (Viola)	Phlox (Phlox) Pinks (Dianthus) Rain Lily (Zephyranthes) Rose (Rosa) Rose Mallow (Hibiscus) Shasta Daisy (Chrysanthemum) Spider Lily (Lycoris) Tulip (Tulipa) Violet (Viola) Yarrow (Achillea)

SEASON OF BLOOM CHART *

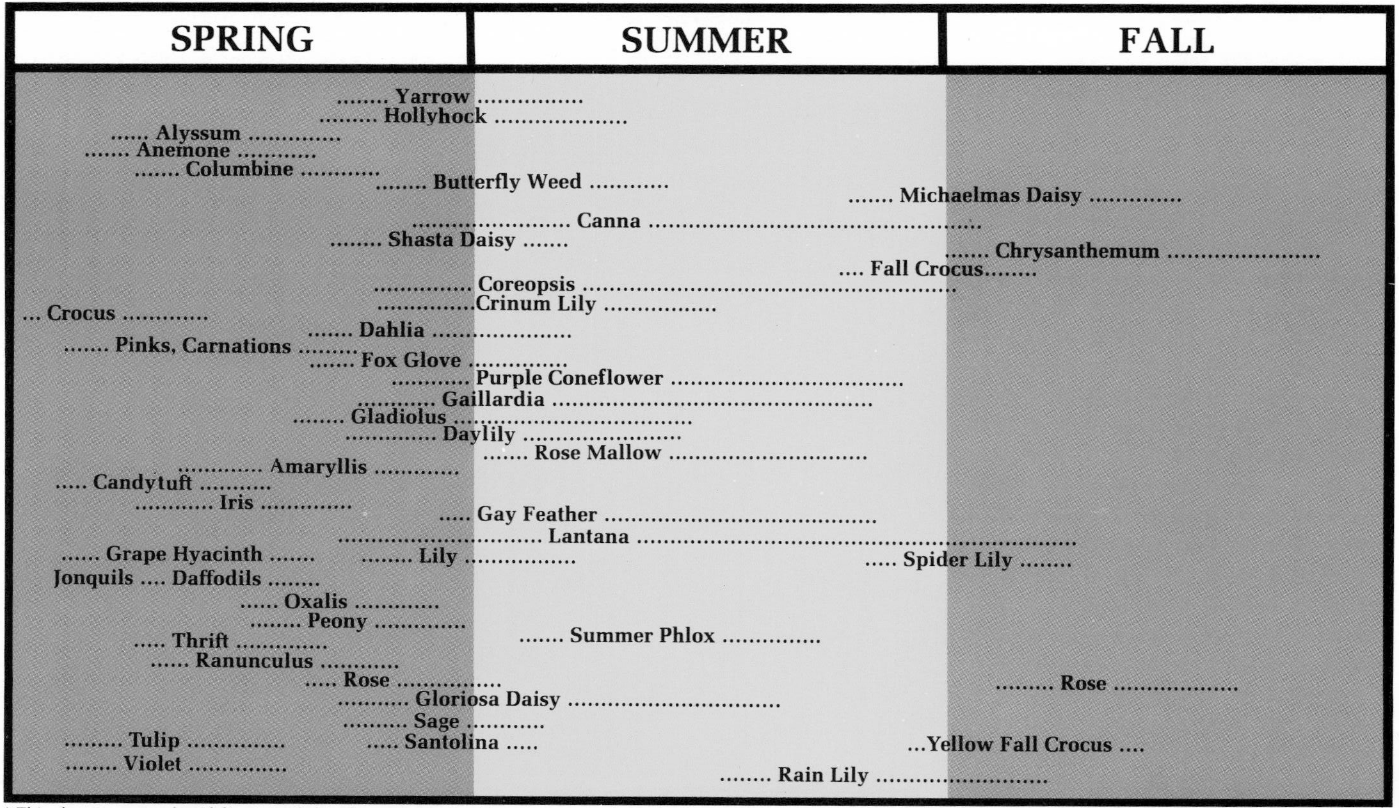

SPRING	SUMMER	FALL

Yarrow
Hollyhock
Alyssum
Anemone
Columbine
Butterfly Weed
Shasta Daisy
Canna
Coreopsis
Crinum Lily
Michaelmas Daisy
Crocus
Dahlia
Pinks, Carnations
Fox Glove
Purple Coneflower
Gaillardia
Gladiolus
Daylily
Rose Mallow
Fall Crocus
Chrysanthemum
Amaryllis
Candytuft
Iris
Gay Feather
Lantana
Spider Lily
Grape Hyacinth
Lily
Jonquils .... Daffodils
Oxalis
Peony
Summer Phlox
Thrift
Ranunculus
Rose
Gloriosa Daisy
Sage
Santolina
Rose
Tulip
Violet
Rain Lily
Yellow Fall Crocus

* This chart is a general guideline intended to show comparative blooming seasons by varieties. Exact timing will depend on local conditions, planting sites and specific varieties chosen.

RULE OF GREEN THUMB: If you expect your perennials to bloom again next year, leave their foliage intact until it turns brown. It is essential in food manufacture and storage. Cutting it prematurely weakens the plant.

TEN OVERLOOKED AND UNDERPLANTED PERENNIALS FOR TEXAS

Some would contend that most perennials have been overlooked by Texas gardeners. That tide, however, seems to be turning. Still, there are some dandies, plants that cry out to be tried. Listed below are 10 sure-fire winners for Texas landscapes. Check through the whole group and read their descriptions in the pages that follow.

Basket of Gold *(Alyssum saxatile)*
Butterfly Weed *(Asclepias tuberosa)*
Heartleaf Bergenia *(Bergenia sp.)*
Golden Wave *(Coreopsis sp.)*
Blanket Flower *(Gaillardia grandiflora)*
Gayfeather *(Liatris sp.)*
Beard Tongue *(Penstemon sp.)*
Gloriosa Daisy *(Rudbeckia sp.)*
Yellow Fall Crocus *(Sternbergia lutea)*
Rain Lily *(Zephyranthes sp.)*

PERENNIALS A TO Z

If the idea of a colorful plant that lives from year to year appeals to you . . . if you'd like to perk up your plantings . . . if you want something really showy, better plan on perennials.

Though there are hundreds of types, we've selected the best for Texas conditions. You'll find a garden of winners on the pages that follow.

Achillea
YARROW

Sun. Height: 2 to 3 feet. Dwarf form also available to 12 inches. Blooms spring and summer: yellow, red or white. Flowers are 3 to 4 inches across, shaped like umbrellas. Flowers are long-lasting and are often dried and used in permanent arrangements. Foliage gray or green. Plant in fall or spring from divisions or potted seedlings. Space plants 15 to 18 inches apart. Very durable plant, well suited to rock gardens.

Alcea
HOLLYHOCK

Sun. Height: 2½ to 4 feet in newer varieties, to 6 to 8 feet in older types. Blooms spring and early summer on vertical spikes. Flowers red, pink, white, yellow and lavender, single and double. Start from seed or started nursery transplants. Shorter types often bloom the first year from seed if planted early. Short-lived perennial often grown as biennial. Good as background flower.

Alyssum
BASKET OF GOLD

Sun. Height: 10 to 15 inches. Blooms in spring: brilliant yellow. Plant in fall or very early spring from started nursery transplants. Space plants 12 to 15 inches apart. Does not resemble low-growing annual alyssum. Durable, well suited to perennial beds and rock gardens. Easily grown.

Anemone
ANEMONE, Windflower

Sun. Height: 10 to 15 inches. Blooms spring: red, pink, blue and white. Plant in fall or late winter, 2 inches deep. Soak tubers overnight before planting, then space 3 to 4 inches apart in beds. Use old leaf scars to identify tops of tubers. Among the most colorful of all spring perennials. Does not rebloom well the second year, so best treated as annual flower.

Asclepias
BUTTERFLY WEED

Sun. Height: 1 to 3 feet. Blooms spring, early summer: bright orange, sometimes yellow. Plant in fall or spring from started nursery transplants. Space plants 15 to 18 inches apart. Tuberous-rooted native wildflower.

Aspidistra
ASPIDISTRA, Cast-Iron Plant

Shade. Height: 18 to 30 inches. Grown for its strap-shaped green leaves that emerge singly from ground. Plant in fall or spring from divisions or started nursery plants. Requires mulching in northern half of Texas to prevent winter damage. Striking plant.

Aster
MICHAELMAS DAISY

Sun. Height: 2 to 4 feet. Blooms late summer and fall in shades of purple, blue, pink and white. Purple and blue types most common, best suited to Texas conditions. Plant in spring from started nursery transplants. Space plants 3 feet apart in beds. Showy and dependable.

Bergenia
HEARTLEAF BERGENIA

Shade. Height: 12 to 18 inches. Pink flower stalks in spring, but grown primarily for showy foliage: large, rounded, dark green and glossy. Plant from started nursery plants, either in fall or spring. Use as border or clumping rock garden plant, spacing plants 15 to 18 inches apart. Evergreen in warmer climates. Semi-evergreen in northern half of Texas.

*Caladium**
ELEPHANT EAR

Shade. Height: 3 to 4 feet. Grown for luxuriant green leaves, often reaching 3 to 4 feet in length. Plant bulbs in spring, once soil warms. Larger bulbs produce larger leaves and taller plants. Plant 4 to 6 inches deep, depending on size of bulbs. Dig bulbs in northern parts of Texas once foliage has died back to ground. Store dry at 55 to 60°F until soil warms the following spring. Mulch bulbs in southern half of state over winter.

   *see also: Chapter 8, *Annuals*

Canna
CANNA

Sun. Height: 2 to 5 feet. Blooms late spring through fall: shades of red, yellow, orange, pink and white. Some types also grown for foliar color — variegated foliage marked purplish-red. Often used as a background flower. Most effective when massed in beds of single colors. Plant in early spring from root divisions spaced 15 to 18 inches apart. Apply general purpose insecticides as needed to control leaf rollers. Prune out old flowers to encourage additional blooming all season long. Varieties include Pfitzer dwarfs (30 to 36 inches), the Seven Dwarfs series (18 to 24 inches) and taller types such as The President (brilliant red), City of Portland (rosy pink), Red King Humbert (orange-red) and Richard Wallace (yellow).

Chrysanthemum
SHASTA DAISY

Sun. Height: 18 to 24 inches. Bloom spring, early summer. Most types are white, many single types with contrasting yellow centers, other varieties fully double. Start from nursery transplants in early spring or by dividing established clumps in fall. Space plants 15 to 20 inches apart. Most popular varieties include Alaska (large single white flowers with yellow centers), Marconi (frilly double white), Roggli's Super Giant singles and Diener's Giant Double (last two types grown from seed). A dwarf form, Little Miss Muffet, grows to 12 inches.

CANNA

SHASTA DAISY

BUTTERFLY WEED

BASKET OF GOLD

Chrysanthemum
CHRYSANTHEMUM

Sun. The most popular fall-blooming perennial (will occasionally rebloom in spring), mums will repeat beautifully year after year when given regular care. They are best used in full-sun locations, in rock gardens, mass plantings and as low borders.

Flower forms:

Each "flower," or more properly, flower head, consists of hundreds of individual flowers, or florets. Two types are common: flattened or elongated with a "petal" appearance (ray florets); and shortened, tufted, often in the center of the head (disc florets).

Anemone: one or more rows of ray florets around the edge. Center disc florets are conspicuously raised and tufted.

Decorative: ray florets are long and wide and overlap like shingles. This is the most common standard chrysanthemum.

Incurve: large flower heads with broad ray florets curving up and in toward the center of the flower.

Pom pom: rounded, very regular flowers with flat or quilled ray florets. They are generally small, with diameters under three inches.

Single: single row of ray florets surrounding yellow center of disc florets. They resemble single shasta daisies, but are available in many colors.

Spider: ray florets distinctly rolled and elongated, often for several inches. The rays are cupped at the end, like fish-hooks. The spoon form is similar, though generally fuller and less droopy.

Planting is best done in late spring or early summer, provided you can locate plants in nurseries. Plants set out earlier will become overly lanky and tend to be more succulent in hot summer weather. Prepare the soil carefully before planting, then space new plants 16 to 24 inches apart. Spacing depends on the variety and its growth habits. Whenever possible, specify "garden" mums at the nursery. Those types have been selected for their compact, spreading growth habits.

Established clumps of chrysanthemums can be divided in early spring, just as they start to grow. Dig them so that you have three or four growing shoots in each clump. Plant them just as you would transplants from the nursery. New plants can also be started from cuttings taken in May or June.

Water chrysanthemum plantings frequently during the growing season, but be sure they're growing in well drained soil. Good drainage reduces the threat of stem and root disease.

Fertilize mums with a complete and balanced plant food every six to eight weeks during the growing season. Switch to a high-phosphate fertilizer from late summer on to promote better flowering.

Prune mum plants by pinching the growing shoots off each of their stems every three to four weeks from spring through early August. Pinching encourages branching, which keeps the plants compact. The garden mums will branch more freely naturally, eliminating the need for much of this hand work.

To grow large mum flowers, you need to remove all of the side buds on each flowering stem when they are about the size of a b-b. Simply roll them out with your thumb, leaving the tip, or terminal, bud to develop.

Aphids and thrips will visit mums' foliage and flowers. Both can be controlled with any general purpose insecticide such as malathion or diazinon. Use benomyl or captan to control stem and root diseases. Either can be mixed as a spray, or poured around the plants as a soil drench. Try to treat early. Once these diseases get started they are difficult to control.

Chrysanthemums flower according to the length of the night. When nights reach a certain length, the plant's hormonal shift stimulates bud formation. As you plant mums, be careful not to locate them where light from streetlights will fall on them. Otherwise, you may never see any blooms.

Colchicum
FALL CROCUS, Meadow Saffron

Sun or part sun. Height: 12 to 18 inches (foliage), 4 to 6 inches (blooms). Flowers late summer, fall: pink, white or lavender. Foliage is produced in spring but dies to ground by midsummer. Plant when bulbs are available in local nurseries, generally late summer. Good for perennial beds, rock gardens.

Coreopsis
COREOPSIS, Golden Wave

Sun. Height: 1 to 2½ feet. Flowers spring and summer, predominantly single yellow blooms. Plant in spring from started nursery transplants or divide established clumps in fall. Space clumps 15 to 20 inches apart. Easily grown and durable. Shorter types less invasive. Improved form of native Texas wildflower.

Crinum
CRINUM LILY

Filtered shade. Height 2 to 3 feet. Showy white lily-like flowers in summer. (Pink forms also available.) Plant in fall or early spring from divisions of established clumps or from nursery transplants. Plants are large, so space 2 to 3 feet apart. Leaves are long, strap-shaped and glossy green.

Crocus
CROCUS

Sun or part sun. Height 3 to 8 inches. Blooms extremely early in spring: white, blue, purple and yellow, also striped. Plant bulbs late fall or very early spring, 2 to 3 inches deep and a similar distance apart. Best used in foreground plantings. Repeat reasonably well year after year.

Dahlia
DAHLIA

Sun or part sun. Height: 1 to 2 feet (taller types will be offered in seed catalogs, but are better adapted in northern climates). Dwarf types flower late spring through fall: pink, red, yellow, white and lavender. Plant from tubers or started nursery transplants set out in spring. Space plants 12 to 18 inches apart. Mulch dwarf types and they should return the following spring.

DAHLIA

CROCUS

COREOPSIS

CHRYSANTHEMUM

Dianthus
PINKS, CARNATIONS

Sun or afternoon shade. Height 8 to 20 inches. Bloom late winter through early summer. Flowers of most types are fragrant, shades of red, pink, white, orchid. Plant in fall or very early spring from started nursery transplants. Spacing varies with type, generally 10 to 15 inches apart. Sweet Williams are a closely related biennial type. See listing under "Annual Flowers" for other types.

Digitalis
FOXGLOVE

Morning sun. Height: 3 to 6 feet. Bloom in spring, early summer. Flowers are white, yellow and purple, borne in spikes. Plant in fall for best bloom. Shorter types are more dependable, since they flower reliably their first spring. Though technically a perennial, most Foxgloves are best treated as cool season annuals in Texas.

Echinacea
PURPLE CONEFLOWER

Sun. Height 18 to 30 inches. Blooms spring, summer with daisy-like purple flowers resembling gloriosa daisies. Start in early spring from nursery transplants. Space plants 18 to 24 inches apart. Showy background flower. Best treated as annual or short-lived perennial. *(Photo page 317)*

Gaillardia
GAILLARDIA, Blanket Flower

Sun. Height: 1 to 3 feet. Blooms late spring through fall: red, orange or yellow with contrasting bands marking most blooms. Single and double-flowering types available. Start from small transplants in early spring or by dividing established clumps in fall. Plant 1 to 2 feet apart. Improved form of native Texas wildflower, well adapted to rock gardens and perennial beds.

Goblin: best dwarf variety. An excellent rock garden plant reaching height of 12 to 14 inches. Red flowers bordered in yellow, 2 to 3 inches in diameter.

Torch Light: taller, to 30 inches. Torch Light flowers reach 5-inch diameter. Red with yellow bandings. Showy background.

Gladiolus
GLADIOLUS

Sun. Height: 18 to 60 inches. Flower late spring-summer: white, cream, yellow, orange, red, rose, lavender, purple and even green. Flowers are produced on spikes, making glads suitable as background flowers. Plant corms from early to mid-spring for a succession of blooms. Plant in well prepared garden soil, 4 to 6 inches apart and about 4 times as deep as the corms are tall. Stake larger types at planting, while corms are still visible. Corms can be dug and stored dry during winter, or, provided soil is well drained, can be left in ground through winter in southern two-thirds of state. Mulch well to protect against cold.

Hemerocallis
DAYLILY

Sun. Height: 1 to 5 feet, depending on variety. Blooms late spring to midsummer, sporadically to frost. Flowers yellow, orange, red, pink, near-white and purple. Both single and double-flowering types are available. Many of the newer types are tetraploid, containing twice the normal number of chromosomes and resulting in larger, stouter plants and blooms. Plant daylilies in fall or early spring, either from divisions or from nursery plants. Depending on the size of the variety, space plants 15 to 24 inches apart. Dig and divide the clumps as they become crowded, generally every 3 to 5 years. Versatile in landscapes. Used in rock gardens, bank plantings (to hold soil), perennial gardens and in specimen landscape settings. Deserving of a place in everyone's garden!

Hibiscus
ROSE MALLOW

Sun. Height: 3 to 6 feet. Flowers late spring through summer. Blooms are very large, 10 to 12 inches in diameter, shades of red, pink and white. Flowers last but one day, but are produced in multitudes. Available as individual colors or as mixtures such as Mallow Marvels and Southern Belle. Plants are hardy to temperatures well below zero (unlike tropical hibiscus). Clumps die to ground with first hard freeze, then come back following spring. Plant from divisions or from started nursery transplants.

Hippeastrum
AMARYLLIS

Part sun (afternoon shade). Height: 18 to 24 inches. Flowers red, pink, white and striped in spring. Large flowered hybrid types that are often sold during Christmas season are less hardy than standard red type. Plant in spring, before bulbs start to grow. Space plants 12 to 15 inches apart. Set bulbs shallowly, half out of soil.

Hosta
HOSTA, Plantain Lily

Shade. Height: 15 to 30 inches. Grown for its luxuriant foliage with large, heart-shaped green leaves, many types variegated white. Most types also produce attractive white or lavender flowers late spring and summer. Requires moist, highly organic soil. Plant nursery transplants in early spring. Plants die to ground with first hard freeze, return following spring.

Iberis
CANDYTUFT

Sun. Height: 6 to 10 inches. Snow-white flowers early spring. Flowers last 4 to 6 weeks. Plant in very early spring from started nursery transplants. Excellent low border or rock garden plant. Improved varieties include Snowflake and Little Gem.

ROSE MALLOW

GAILLARDIA

GLADIOLUS

ROSE MALLOW

HOSTA, PLANTAIN LILY

DAYLILY

DAYLILY

CANDYTUFT

Iris
IRIS

Sun or light afternoon shade. Height: 8 to 48 inches. Popular spring-blooming perennials, irises are well suited to borders, backgrounds, rock gardens and massed plantings. Dozens of types and thousands of varieties are available, all characterized by pointed, upward facing foliage. Most types have upright petals ("standards") and downward-facing sepals ("falls").

Most types should be planted in late summer or early fall. Bulbous types, such as Dutch Iris, should be planted four inches deep, while rhizomatous types such as bearded iris and Louisiana iris should be planted nearer to the soil surface. Most types do best in well-drained garden soils, though some types are adapted to poorly drained locations. Bulbous types can be dug and stored during hot summer months, but rhizomatous types should be left undisturbed for three to five years. Dig and divide their clumps as they become crowded.

Fertilize rhizomatous irises with a complete and balanced plant food in the early spring as plants start to grow, after they finish blooming and again before the flush of fall growth. Fertilize bulbous types with a high-phosphorous fertilizer at planting in the fall and again in early spring.

Some of the types are . . .

Bearded Iris: Height: 8 to 48 inches. The most popular group, these are characterized by having a "beard," actually tuft of hairs, on each of the falls. This type is well suited to Northern and Central Texas, but somewhat limited by warm winters and disease along the Gulf Coast.

Thousands of varieties are available in almost all colors except true red. They bloom from early spring into summer, some again in fall depending on the variety. Plant rhizomes 16 to 20 inches apart.

Dutch Iris: Height: 18 to 24 inches. A favorite bulbous type, Dutch iris blooms in mid-spring with three to four-inch flowers on straight 18 to 24-inch stems. Yellow, white, blue, purple, pink and bicolors are available. Plant bulbs four inches deep and four inches apart. Mulch to protect bulbs from extreme cold and heat.

Louisiana Iris: Height: 2 to 4 feet. A form of a very adaptable native flower, the Louisiana iris comes in an array of colors: white, blue, purple, yellow and red. This type of iris is adapted to poorly drained soils, but it will grow well in normal locations, too. It blooms in mid-spring.

Liatris
GAYFEATHER

Sun. Height: 2 to 3 feet. Blooms summer and early fall in tall spikes of white, lavender and purple. Plant in fall or early spring, spacing plants 12 to 18 inches apart. Unusual plant well suited to rock gardens and background plantings. Close relative of native Texas wildflower.

Lantana
LANTANA

Sun. Height: varies with types, 1 to 6 feet. Flowers from spring through fall. Multitudes of small flower heads cover plants, shades of orange, red, yellow, white, pink and lavender. Start from cuttings or started nursery transplants in spring, after danger of frost has passed. Plants may survive winter intact in South Texas, die to ground and return following the spring in Central Texas or die out entirely in North Texas. Mulching will help protect plants from extreme cold. Among the most durable, heat-tolerant plants we can grow. Great source of summertime color!

Lilium
LILIES

Morning sun, afternoon shade. Height: 18 to 36 inches, depending on variety and location. Blooms late spring-early summer, with colors ranging from yellow and white to pink, orange and red. Plant bulbs in fall or early spring in deep, rich garden soil. Best types for Texas include Enchantment (orange-red), Madonna (white) and Regal (white). Others are worthy of trying given good growing conditions.

Lycoris
SPIDER LILIES

Sun. Height: 12 to 18 inches. Bloom early fall. Generally red, but pink and yellow forms are also available. Plant in late summer, when bulbs are offered in nurseries. Plant 3 to 4 inches deep and 6 to 8 inches apart. Foliage will precede blooms by several months, then die down. Showy in masses.

Muscari
GRAPE HYACINTH

Sun. Height: 4 to 6 inches. Blooms early spring. Flower spikes are intensely blue (white form also available). Plant in fall. Small bulbs should be planted in masses, 2 inches deep and 1½ to 2 inches apart. Will naturalize beautifully, spreading freely through the years.

Narcissus
DAFFODIL, also jonquil

Height: 6 to 24 inches. Among the best of the spring-blooming perennials, is adapted to all areas of Texas. Flowers yellow, white, orange and pale pink. Types vary from tiny tubular jonquils to large trumpeted daffodils. Double and short-trumpeted types are also available.

Daffodils are best used in massed plantings, as low borders, in containers, naturalized in the lawn or in ground cover beds and in rock gardens. Plant the bulbs two to three times as deep as the bulb is tall. Space the bulbs four to eight inches apart, depending on the size of the variety you are growing and the effect you are trying to achieve. Incorporate one tablespoon of bone meal or some other high-phosphorus fertilizer in the soil around each bulb at the time of planting.

Water daffodils regularly during the winter and spring if rains are infrequent. Keep their soil moist during the summer to prevent heat damage to the bulbs. Fertilize established plants in the fall and again in the very early spring with a high-phosphorus fertilizer.

If you find your daffodil plantings are "playing out," they may have become overcrowded. Dig and divide the bulbs in the early fall, resetting them to allow ample room for growth. Smaller flowering types, such as many of the jonquils, will bloom better year after year. Larger types like King Alfred and the several double-flowering types soon go entirely to leaves, producing their best flowers in the first year.

SPIDER LILY

DAFFODIL

LANTANA

LILY

GRAPE HYACINTH

Oxalis
OXALIS, Wood Sorrell, Shamrock

Part shade. Height: 8 to 12 inches. Blooms in spring: pink, white, rose or yellow. Plant in fall or early spring from started transplants, divisions or, in some types, from small bulbs. Good for low borders, in rock gardens. Control spider mites in summer with kelthane.

Paeonia
PEONY

Afternoon shade. Height: 18 to 30 inches. Bloom mid-spring in shades of red, pink and white. Plant in fall, setting roots quite near the soil surface, so they'll receive maximum cold during the winter. Pile snow and ice over roots whenever possible during winter. Best adapted to northern parts of Texas.

Phlox
THRIFT, Moss Phlox

Sun. Height: 6 to 8 inches, spreading to 2 to 3 feet. Blooms over extended period in spring. Flowers range from intense hot pink to rosy-pink, lavender and white. Plant from nursery transplants in early spring, spacing plants 18 to 24 inches apart. Useful in edgings, rock gardens, low borders.

Phlox
SUMMER PHLOX

Light afternoon shade. Height: 2 to 4 feet. Blooms summer in tall sprays of red, pink, rose, purple, lavender and white. Plant in fall or early spring from nursery transplants or by dividing established clumps. Space plants 15 to 18 inches apart in beds. Best used in masses.

Ranunculus
RANUNCULUS

Sun. Height: 12 to 18 inches. Flowers spring: shades of red, pink, yellow and white. Plant in fall in South Texas, in early spring in North Texas. Plant tubers 2 to 3 inches deep and space them 6 to 8 inches apart. Plant with pointed ends down. Best treated as annual, since reblooming in successive years is modest. Good border or short background plant. Cheerful!

SUMMER PHLOX

RANUNCULUS

THRIFT

Rosa
ROSES

The all-time favorite perennial flower. Blooming season begins in spring and runs throughout summer and fall, with peaks in mid-spring and mid-fall. Roses, in their different forms, are useful as small bedding color, borders, shrubs and vines. Colors include orange, red, pink, yellow, white and lavender.

Types of Roses are . . .

Hybrid Teas Height: 3 to 5 feet. This is the most popular rose category. It's "THE rose" people think of. Flowers are large and beautifully proportioned. Many are also fragrant. Plants have glossy, dark green foliage. Hundreds of varieties are available and new and exciting introductions are made each year.

Grandifloras Height: 5 to 8 feet. Plants in this group can closely resemble hybrid teas. Flowers are borne on long stems, singly or in clusters. They make good background plants.

Floribundas Height: 2 to 3 feet. Also known as "landscaping" roses because of their neat, compact habit. These roses are borne in clusters of several to many flowers. Their height makes them ideal for low borders and massed plantings.

Climbing Roses Though not actually vines, these are useful on fences and trellises. They are vigorous growers that provide color all season. Climbing roses require training and tying to the support. All standard rose colors are available as climbers. More conventional large-flowering roses are available in climbing ranks, as are smaller-flowering types such as Lady Banksia rose.

Miniatures In all respects — foliage, buds, flowers — these are just miniature forms of larger roses. They can be planted outside in a garden or left as potted plants. Container plants will need protection in sub-freezing weather.

Selecting Rose Plants

Always buy your roses from a reputable nursery. Roses are graded as Numbers 1, 1½ and 2. Number 1 bushes will be the best, with sound roots and vigorous canes. Number 1½ will be intermediate, and Number 2 plants will be weak and slow to produce good blooms. Though they may cost a dollar or two more, Number 1 bushes are by far the best buy.

Packaged bare-root rose bushes will be available during mid-winter, either from local nurseries or from large mail order houses. Many nurseries are now offering container-grown plants in bloom in the spring and early summer. This allows you to buy plants when you can see their flowers, and it lets you be sure the plants are healthy and vigorous. Be sure, though, that your plants are growing in at least a 2-gallon (preferably a 5-gallon) container for best root development.

You may also see a tag indicating that your rose is an "All America Rose Selection." That means it has been tested alongside other similar roses at test gardens all over America. To win the AARS designation, it had to outperform those other varieties under an assortment of soils and climates. Generally, AARS winners are good investments.

Planting

The best planting season for roses is in mid to late-winter, four to six weeks before the average last killing freeze for your area.

Select a planting site that receives full or nearly full sunlight. Shady locations promote lanky growth, poor flowering and disease.

If poor soil or lack of drainage is a problem, plant your roses in raised beds. Use masonry or railroad ties as an edging to allow a 6 to 8-inch rise above surrounding soil.

ROSES

Rose garden soil should be loose and well drained, preferably a sandy loam. Incorporate a 4 to 6-inch layer of peat moss, shredded bark, compost or some other form of organic matter, and till to a depth of 10 to 15 inches. Rake out all rocks, roots and other debris. Use a soil fumigant such as vapam if weeds or nematodes are a known problem.

Ask your nurseryman or check the plant tag or catalog description when you buy your rose bushes to determine proper spacing. Generally, though, floribundas can be spaced 30 to 36 inches apart, while hybrid teas and other larger types will require 4 to 5 feet.

Set the new plants so their bud unions are slightly out of the soil. Generally you will be able to see the height at which they were growing in the nursery. Try to duplicate that planting depth. Remove any damaged roots as you plant the bushes. Apply a root-stimulating fertilizer and plenty of water immediately after planting.

Watering

Keep your roses well watered all season. Spring and fall watering ensures good blooming. Summer watering obviously keeps the plants alive, and midwinter watering protects the roots from cold weather injury. Use mulches to conserve water.

Whenever possible, keep irrigation water off your rose leaves. Use soaker hoses, slow-dripping hoses or trickle irrigation systems to water your plants. Moisture on the foliage promotes disease.

Fertilizing

Start feeding your roses as they begin growing in the spring. Continue feeding them every 4 to 6 weeks through late summer. Most serious rose growers use a complete and balanced fertilizer such as 12-12-12, or one that is slightly higher in phosphorus, such as 10-20-10. Many specialty rose fertilizers are available. Apply one half to one pound of fertilizer per 100 square feet of bed space, making applications on 4 to 6-week intervals except in the heat of mid-summer.

Spraying

The number 1 problem of roses is a fungal disease called "black spot." Most varieties are susceptible to it to some degree. Several new fungicides have proven very effective in controlling it when used on a regular basis. Provide good air circulation and keep water off the foliage to lessen its effects.

Many roses will also develop powdery mildew, a white crusty fungal organism that looks like flour dusted on the leaf surface. Most fungicides that control black spot will also control powdery mildew.

Various insects will visit rose bushes during the year, including aphids during cooler weather and leaf-cutting bees during summer. Use a general-purpose insecticide to control them. Regular spraying (include insecticide with your disease controls) will prevent insect damage.

Spray in evenings to lessen chance of damaged, "burned" foliage.

Pruning

Much of your roses' health and vigor will depend on your pruning program. Remember that pruning is an ongoing thing, to be done several times every year. Most bush roses are pruned in mid-to-late winter 4 to 6 weeks before the last killing freeze for the area. Climbing roses should be pruned immediately after their flush of spring blooms.

Prune Hybrid Tea and Grandiflora roses by removing all weak, spindly stems, or canes, and by reducing the overall height of the bushes to 18 to 24 inches. Always cut right above a bud that faces away from the center of the plant, so the branching that develops will be spreading away from the crown of the plants. Seal the cut ends with clear shellac or with white wood glue. Prune, too, through the growing season. Keep old flower heads and weak growth removed.

Floribundas should be pruned less severely. Again, though, you should remove weak growth. Prune the entire planting, if it is all the same variety, to a uniform height for better landscape appearance.

Climbing roses will be pruned differently. Head back the most vigorous canes to 4 to 5 feet. Remove the weak, spindly twigs that develop along the stems. And remember, prune climbers after they flower. Winter pruning would remove all the flowering wood.

Rudbeckia
GLORIOSA DAISY

Sun. Height: 18 to 30 inches. Blooms spring, summer and into fall. Flowers are daisy-like, mostly golden yellow with mahogany markings, brown centers. Single and double-flowering types are available. Plant in early spring, from started nursery transplants. Space plants 12 to 16 inches apart. Heat and drought tolerant. Should be more widely planted. Good massed in beds.

Salvia
SAGE

Sun. Height: 18 to 36 inches. Blooms late spring, summer. Flowers borne in spikes are blue or purple. Plant in early spring from started nursery transplants. Useful as background flower, contrasting with brighter colors of other flowers.

Santolina
SANTOLINA, Lavender Cotton

Sun. Height: 12 to 18 inches. Grown primarily for its bright green or gray-green foliage, but also produces bright yellow blooms in late spring (blooms should be removed immediately after flowering to keep plants compact). Requires perfect drainage. Good low border plant, also useful in rock gardens.

Stachys
LAMB'S EAR

Sun or filtered shade. Height: 6 to 10 inches. Grown for appealing gray-green fuzzy foliage. Blooms are light purple, not showy. Good edging plant, but should be sheared occasionally to keep it in bounds. Prune off old flower stalks to keep plants compact.

Sternbergia
YELLOW FALL CROCUS

Sun. Height: 4 to 8 inches. Blooms late summer-early fall with bright yellow crocus-like flowers. Plant bulbs in late summer, 4 inches deep and 4 to 6 inches apart. Unusual plant that should be tried more commonly.

Tulipa
TULIPS

Sun. Height: varies with different types, generally between 6 to 36 inches. Colors: red, pink, orange and yellow to white, purple and near-black. These popular, spring-blooming bulbs are best adapted to colder climates, but can be grown in Texas if given an artificial winter. Store bulbs 4 to 6 weeks in the vegetable bin of your refrigerator (about 40 degrees F). Plant the bulbs in late December or early January. The planting site should be in a well drained location. Plant the bulbs 2 to 4 times as deep as the bulbs are tall. Keep them well watered, especially as the leaves and buds are emerging and growing. Use a high-phosphorus fertilizer at the time of planting and as growth starts in the spring for best flowering.

Most types of tulips are best treated in Texas as annual flowers. Though they will produce new bulbs, most types will not flower reliably the second year in the garden. The bulbs, instead, should be dug and discarded to make room for more productive flowers. Possible exception: the species tulips (described later in this section).

A tulip trick: Nowhere are color massing and close planting more beneficial than with tulips. Plant all the same color and pack them tightly (4 to 8 inches between bulbs).

Tulip Types
(Many other types are also available . . . these are merely the most common. They are listed in their general order of blooming.)

Single Early: Large bright flowers on 16-inch stems.

Double Early: Flowers 4 to 5 inches across, peony-shaped, bright colors.

Mendel: Single flowers on 20-inch stems. Available in shades of red, yellow, white and orange.

Triumph: Single flowers on strong 20-inch stems. These are useful in providing color between bloom season of early tulips and Darwins.

Darwins: Most popular tulips, growing on tall, strong stems to a height of 30 inches. Flowers are egg-shaped with square bases. Darwins are available in all tulip shades. Darwin hybrids are the result of crosses between Darwin and another large, brilliant type, *T. fosterana*. Hybrids bloom slightly before Darwins and reach a height of 22 to 28 inches.

Breeder: Among the tallest of all tulips, breeders reach 30 to 36 inches. These tulips are grown for their unusual colors: orange, purple and mahogany-red.

Lily-flowered: With long, tapered buds, this type of tulip looks very graceful, available in all tulip shades, reaches a height of 20 to 26 inches.

Cottage: Resemble Darwins, but bloom later.

Rembrandt: Multi-colored tulips with brightly contrasting colors. Variegation results from a virus infection, so do not plant them near species types you intend to save for more than one year.

Parrot: Like Rembrandts, Parrot tulips should not be planted near perennial species tulips.

GLORIOSA DAISY

TULIPS

YELLOW FALL CROCUS

SAGE

TULIPS

Parrots offer large, ruffled and fringed blooms. They are unusual in appearance and flower late in the season.

Species: Actually, there are many species types of tulips, including Clusiana, Praestans, Kaufmanniana and Greigii. Most are shorter growing and early-flowering. Most are well suited to rock gardens and border plantings, where they can be left undisturbed to come back year after year. These are some of the best tulips for Texas gardeners.

Viola
VIOLETS

Shade. Height: 6 to 8 inches. Flower in spring: lavender, white and purple. Blooms fragrant. Plant in fall or early spring from started nursery transplants or by dividing established clumps. Space plants 10 to 12 inches apart. Protect plants from spider mites in summer by spraying undersides of leaves with kelthane.

Zephyranthes
RAIN LILY

Sun. Height: 8 to 12 inches. Bloom summer and fall following rains. Flowers yellow, pink and white. Plant as bulbs are available in nurseries and from mail-order houses. More commonly you'll have to mark native plants while they're flowering and return later to dig them. Rain lilies can also be started from seed collected from nature and planted carefully into good garden soil.

Chapter 10

Fruit
and Nut Crops

Texas is a fruit-growing state! In fact, few other states offer the diversity of crops ... citrus to cherries, persimmons to pomegranates ... the list is almost all-inclusive.

The challenge, then, comes in knowing just which crops will grow where. They're not all adapted to every part of the state. And, it's no easy matter to contend with our heat, the bugs and the diseases. You have to know what you're doing, and you have to know when to do it.

Given these considerations, fruit growing can be fun and rewarding. Here's hoping the pages that follow will help you enjoy it to the maximum!

SELECTING THE SITE
FOR YOUR FRUIT PLANTINGS

Where you locate your fruit plantings makes a great deal of difference. Here's a shopping list. Try for as many of these features as possible.

Essential

1. Full or nearly full sunlight. (Although strawberries and blueberries will tolerate some afternoon shade, particularly during the summer.)
2. Good drainage. Otherwise, "plant high," slightly above surrounding grade.

Highly Advisable

3. Deep, rich soil. Ideally, three to four feet for fruit, six feet or more for pecans. Minimum: 18 to 24 inches for fruit, three to four feet for pecans.
4. Good air circulation. This is especially important in protecting early-flowering varieties from early spring frosts. Avoid low, still locations.
5. Proximity to water.

HOW AND WHEN TO BUY FRUIT TREES

If you're starting an orchard . . . or if you're just planting one single fruit tree, plan on doing it during the winter. That's when the trees will be dormant. Since most fruit and nut trees are sold bare-rooted, winter planting gives them a chance to get their new roots established before warm weather arrives.

The trees are dug after the first frost, packed in moist sawdust and enclosed in moisture-retaining packaging. Hopefully they've been stored in a cool, shady location at the garden center. Try to select your tree as soon after it arrives as possible, and plant it immediately to minimize transplant shock.

RULE OF GREEN THUMB: Remember that biggest isn't always the best . . . at least not with new fruit and nut trees. If you're buying bare-rooted trees, you're better off with a good medium-sized tree. It will be large enough to prove it isn't a runt, yet small enough to recover quickly from the transplanting. Large trees may take extra years to reach peak production. Good sizes: three to five feet for fruit trees, four to six feet for pecans.

Be sure the tree you're selecting is alive. There are three simple checks:

1. Twigs should be supple and easily bent, not dry and crisp.

2. Buds should be moist and green, not dry and shrivelled.

3. Wood just under bark should be moist and green. Scratch lightly with your thumbnail.

MOST COMMON QUESTION

"We don't have a lot of room for a big fruit garden. Which types are the most productive? Which will we get the best return from?"

Obviously, that varies with the locale. Texas' climates hit extremes, from El Paso to Beaumont and Brownsville to Amarillo. Some of the best for almost all of the state include blackberries, figs, grapes, peaches, pears, pecans, plums and strawberries.

Productivity depends greatly on the variety selected. Some types don't stand a chance of ever setting fruit well. Be sure the type you select is adapted to your area. (See listing at the end of this chapter.)

DETERMINING TREE SPACING

When you're buying small bare-rooted fruit trees, it's a real temptation to plant them too close together. You need to lay the orchard out on paper. Make a list of the types you want to grow, and determine your planting pattern. Listed below are the optimum spacings for home garden fruit production. These spacings assume maximum care and regular pruning. Commercial spacings would, in many cases, be farther apart.

Tree	Preferred Spacing		
Apple (standard)	25	to	30 feet
(dwarf and semi-dwarf)*	8	to	16 feet
Apricot	15	to	18 feet
Cherry	15	to	18 feet
Citrus	15	to	25 feet
Figs	15	to	20 feet
Grapes	8	to	12 feet
Muscadines	15	to	20 feet
Peaches	18	to	25 feet
Pears	25	to	30 feet
Pecans	35	to	45 feet
Persimmons	15	to	25 feet
Plums	15	to	18 feet

*spacing depends on dwarfing rootstock used, expected size of plant. Dwarf fruit varieties not generally recommended for Texas because of soil limitations.

TEXAS TIP

It's not always easy to find all the best varieties of fruit and nut trees. Even some of the types listed later in our individual crop listings may be a little hard to locate.

Fortunately, more and more Texas nurseries (both local retailers and mail-order houses) now stock the desirable types. Your local county Extension agent probably has an up-to-date referral list of sources. Give him a call or write, requesting a listing of sources of varieties recommended for your part of Texas.

WHEN YOU SHOULD PLANT A SECOND
VARIETY FOR CROSS-POLLINATION

Not all fruit trees are self-fertile. That means that they either don't produce pollen, or that they're sterile to their own pollen. Whatever the reason, if you expect fruit from that variety, you'll have to plant a second tree *of a different variety* that blooms at the same time, and that produces viable pollen.

Two special notes: first, you can't go wrong planting a second tree. If in doubt, plant a second one, just to be sure both get pollinated. Also, remember that your neighbors also have trees. You can generally count on pollen being carried for a block or two, perhaps even a quarter mile or more, by bees (fruit trees, berries) and by the wind (nut trees).

Crop	self-fertile	partially self-fertile*	self-sterile*
Apples			x†
Apricots		x	
Blackberries	x		
Blueberries			x
Cherries	x		
Citrus	x		
Figs	x		
Grapes	x		
Nectarines	x		
Peaches	x		
Pears		x†	
Pecans		x	
Persimmons	x		
Plums		x†	
Strawberries	x		
Walnuts		x	

*Planting of second variety recommended for best pollination.

†Fertility varies between varieties. See listings under specific crops at the end of this chapter.

MOST COMMON QUESTION

"We saved the seeds from some really good peaches. Can we grow trees from those?"

The answer to this question also applies to every other fruit and nut crop. While you can grow fruit and nut trees from seeds, it's a poor investment of time, effort and space. Problem is: fruit and nut trees are hybrids. Their seeds will not reproduce the variety you ate. There's a good chance that the seedling you get won't bear fruit for many years. When they finally do start bearing, the fruit may be of terrible quality. And, another drawback: you lose the special rootstock the budded varieties have. It's better adapted to Texas soils. Seedlings don't have it.

To put it bluntly . . . you should never plant a fruit or pecan seed in the hopes of getting a producing tree. It's just not worth the few dollars you'll save!

FRUIT CROPS — YEARS TO FIRST HARVEST

We all want our fruit crops to start producing the first year they're planted. In most cases, that just won't happen. For instance, it can take up to 10 years for some types of pecans. There are some tips, though, to help speed up the process.

1. Buy varieties adapted to your area. Plants that aren't happy may never bear fruit.

2. Buy quality plants. Ideally, they shouldn't be overly large. A good medium-sized plant is preferable. Be sure they're healthy and vigorous. Be sure they're fresh if they're bare-rooted. If they're in containers, be sure they're established.

3. Plant them in the best possible site, and plant them immediately. Don't let them dry out.

4. Give them the best possible care . . . water, feed, prune and spray them. Keep them growing vigorously.

5. If necessary, provide a second tree . . . a pollinator variety. Make sure when your trees do reach the age of production that there's pollen available. (see page 355 for those types requiring cross-pollination.)

Having done all that, here's the time range you need to expect before you get a good harvest from the various fruit crops.

Fruit Crop	Years to First Harvest		
Apples	3	to	4
Apricots	5		
Blackberries	2		
Blueberries	4		
Cherries	5		
Citrus	4	to	5
Figs	2	to	3
Grapes	3		
Muscadines	4		
Nectarines	3		
Peaches	2	to	3
Pears	5		
Pecans	6	to	10
Persimmons	4		
Plums	2	to	3
Strawberries	½	to	1

CHILLING REQUIREMENTS OF THE VARIOUS FRUIT CROPS

Most deciduous fruit crops have a sort of biological clock-thermostat that measures dormant season exposure to cold. Fruit growers call that clock the plant's "chilling requirement."

Specifically, what the plant is measuring is its exposure to cold below 45°F and above freezing. Each fruit variety has its own specific needs . . . a minimum number of hours' exposure to those temperatures . . . that it must have before it can bud and bloom in the spring.

Page 358 shows Texas and the amounts of chilling various parts receive. Locate your area to determine its average winter exposure. Plant only fruit varieties that generally coincide with that figure. (See crop and variety listings at the end of this chapter.) You must meet the requirement. Plant a type with a much higher chilling requirement and it will, most years, fail to bud and bloom properly. It may not even leaf out and grow. Plant a variety with a much lower chilling requirement and it will bloom too early almost every year. Its cold needs will have been met just part way through the winter. Then, when the weather warms up prematurely (and temporarily), it'll try to bloom, only to be frozen later.

Chilling requirements of the fruit crops vary, even within the same type of fruit. Peaches, for example, have generally had high chilling requirements — 800 to 1,000 hours. Research over the last several decades has resulted in types that need as little as 250 hours of chilling. These are adapted, quite obviously, to South Texas, even the Rio Grande Valley. Specific needs of each variety will be in its description at the end of this chapter.

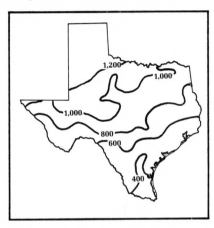

Minimum number of hours of chilling temperature (below 45°F and above 32°F) expected in Texas.

MOST COMMON QUESTION

"Why does my pear tree bloom in the fall? Did I do something wrong? Will it hurt the tree?"

Pears will frequently bloom sporadically in the fall, and that is no real cause for concern. However, if your tree has been hurt badly by fungal leaf spot disease or by drought, causing almost complete defoliation during the summer, fall bloom may be much heavier. The tree will think its chilling requirement has been met and will respond by flowering. Such a fall bloom is more serious, since it saps the tree's reserves and leaves it more vulnerable to winter and disease damage. Use general-purpose fungicides to control the leaf spot in advance, and keep the tree well watered throughout the summer to lessen the problem.

HOW TO PLANT FRUIT TREES

Since most fruit and nut trees are sold either bare-rooted or in "packaged balls" (tree is dug bare-root, then put into a machine-made soil ball), planting techniques will be the same for all varieties.

1) Plant the tree as soon as possible. If there will be any delay, store the tree in a cool, shady location (but out of extreme cold). Keep its roots moist.

2) Dig the planting hole large enough to accommodate the tree's root system comfortably. It should be wider than absolutely necessary, but no deeper.

3) Prune off any broken, damaged roots.

4) Set the tree at the same depth at which it grew in the nursery. You'll be able to see soil lines on its trunk. Be sure the bud union is above grade.

5) Use a mixture (equal parts) of the soil you removed from the hole and organic matter (such as peat moss and compost) to fill in around the roots. When the hole is half filled, water the tree thoroughly.

6) After the water has drained away, fill the remainder of the hole and pack the soil lightly.

7) Prune the tree to compensate for roots lost during the digging . . . 40 to 50 percent for most bare-rooted trees. This pruning can also be the initial training for limb structure . . . see specific crop for details at the end of this chapter.

8) You may choose to wrap the trunk, either in paper tree wrap or aluminum foil, to lower limbs. This protects against rabbit damage, also prevents trunk from being sunscalded. Generally, however, it is not required.

9) Apply a root-stimulating fertilizer once a month during the growing season for the entire first year. Begin regular fertilization the second year. Keep tree well watered all through the growing season.

(See illustrations that follow.)

1.

2.

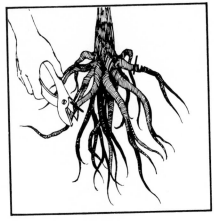

3.

4.

5.

6.

PRUNE
HERE →

7.

8.   9.

HOW TO WATER FRUIT PLANTINGS

Water is the chief constituent of all fruit. Add to that the fact that most parts of Texas don't get adequate rainfall during the times the fruit is forming, and you have perfect reason to develop some type of irrigation system.

The amount of water your crops will require depends on several factors, including size and vigor of the plants, soil type, temperature, wind, rainfall, humidity and fruit load, among others. The figures below are general guidelines of the mature plants' needs as their fruit is developing, particularly during the hot, dry weather of early summer. Use these only as guidelines, however. Always check the soil daily. Don't water if it's still wet. Water immediately if it's dry three to four inches deep.

Fruit Crop	Gallons of Water Per Plant Per Day		
Apples	15	to	20
Apricots	15	to	20
Blackberries	2	to	3
Blueberries	5	to	7
Cherries	15	to	20
Citrus	10	to	25
Figs	10	to	15
Grapes	5	to	10
Peaches	15	to	20
Pears	15	to	20
Pecans	25	to	100
Persimmons	10	to	15

Fruit Crop	Gallons of Water Per Plant Per Day		
Plums	15	to	20
Pomegranate	10	to	15
Strawberries	½	to	1
Walnuts	20	to	25

Watering Equipment

All you absolutely need to water your fruit trees is a hose and a faucet to hook it up to. However, there are more sophisticated systems available that are much easier and perhaps even more reliable.

A: If you're watering fruit trees simply with a hose, construct a soil berm 15 to 18 inches out from tree trunk to retain water. Let hose run slowly to fill berm. Remove basin once trees are established or if prolonged rainy weather threatens to cause root problems.

B: Drip irrigation systems allow you to water slowly, evenly ... and, automatically! The equipment can be either above or below the ground. Emitters installed below grade may become clogged, a major problem. By positioning the drip irrigation emitters uniformly all around your trees, or all through your berry plantings, you'll have the kind of even watering your plants will love. Talk with a reputable dealer handling drip irrigation equipment and let him tailor-make a system for your needs. Several brands are also available by mail. Either way, you'll be amazed at the convenience, the dependability and the rewards of a drip irrigation system. Because of its water conservation and uniform application, it's the best way to irrigate fruit crops.

WHAT TO DO FOR SPRING FROSTS

Your fruit trees are all blooming. The temperature's dropping. They're forecasting a frost. What do you do?

First, evaluate the flowers. If they're freely breaking bud and showing color, or if they're already in full bloom ... or even in fruit ... your trees are at the most vulnerable stage. Tight buds can withstand several degrees more cold, so evaluate carefully.

Let's assume, then, that something has to be done to protect the flowers, and, ultimately, the fruit.

One option is to cover the plants. If they're not too big and if you have plenty of quilts, blankets or sheets, drape them over the trees. Put a light bulb or heat lamp under the cover, but be sure it's kept away from contact with water. *Do not use plastic!* It traps the heat too quickly in the morning, causing serious problems to the tender new tissues.

Second option is to spray the plants continuously with water. A fine mist applied from the time the temperatures drop below 36 to 38°F, and continued until all ice has melted the following morning, will protect the tender flower tissues from the cold. You must not stop the spraying until temperatures warm or you'll lose all your flowers. Surprisingly, the ice won't harm the plant so long as new ice is forming. Be sure you don't apply enough water to break limbs should ice form.

Finally, a "Don't" . . .

Whatever you do, *don't* start any type of fire under your trees. The intense heat could be the end of their limbs. At best, the flowers and foliage would be lost.

HOW FRUIT RIPENS

Sometimes, because of insects, diseases or weather, it's helpful to harvest fruit crops a day or two early. That may cause some problems, however, because some crops stop ripening the moment they're picked from the plant. Know what you're facing before you harvest the fruit.

Crops That Continue to Ripen After Harvest	Crops That Ripen Only on Plant
Apples	Blackberries
Avocados	Figs
Pears	Grapes
Persimmons	Peaches
Plums	Strawberries

CONTROLLING INSECTS AND DISEASES

Pests are frequent visitors to Texas fruit gardens. In fact, there's hardly a season that you won't need to spray for some type of a problem. You need to take a page from the growers' notebook: keep ahead of the problems . . . get on a regular *preventative* spray program. Don't let the insects and diseases ever get started.

Each fruit crop will have its own set of pest problems. As a result, you'll find those problems dealt with later, in the plant-by-plant listings.

There are some general guidelines that you must follow in treating any fruit crop:

• Identify the problem. You can't be sure you're applying the right material until you know what type of a pest you're attacking. If you can't identify it, seek help.

• Choose the appropriate control. *Read its label carefully!* Be sure the pest and the fruit crop are both listed on the label. If you misapply a chemical (for example, one that's not registered for the crop) to a fruit crop, there's not a soul on this earth who can legally tell you it's safe to eat. Also from the label: be sure you have adequate time before harvest . . . every label must list the waiting period required between treating and eating.

• Use a sprayer that applies the chemical uniformly over the entire plant. You may need high-pressure equipment to reach the tops of tall trees. (see Chapter 12: *Insects and Diseases* for various spray equipment options.) Be sure the sprayer has never been used for applications of weed killers, particularly broadleafed (hormone) types that might leave a harmful residue.

• When spraying during the blooming season, spray early or late in the day, while bees aren't actively flying.

• Use standard safety precautions. (see Chapter 12, *Insects and Diseases* applying the pesticides.) Though types available to home gardeners are reasonably safe, care should always be exercised when dealing with any type of chemical.

Cultural Guidelines: Pesticide sprays can do a good bit toward solving pest problems, but you also need to keep the plants healthy and vigorous.

Let that start at the time of planting by choosing varieties resistant to common insect and disease problems.

You also must practice good sanitation. Keep dead leaves and fruit picked up. Prune out any damaged or decayed wood.

BEST FRUIT AND NUT CROPS FOR TEXAS

Variety selection is the single most important factor in your fruit-growing success. To get good results, you need to start with a winner. The listings that follow cover, crop-by-crop, the best fruit and nut varieties for each part of Texas and how to grow them to perfection.

The opposite map will serve as a guide in determining best types for your area. Each variety will be keyed, by letter, to its best areas of adaptation. Locate your area on the map, then find the best types for your plantings.

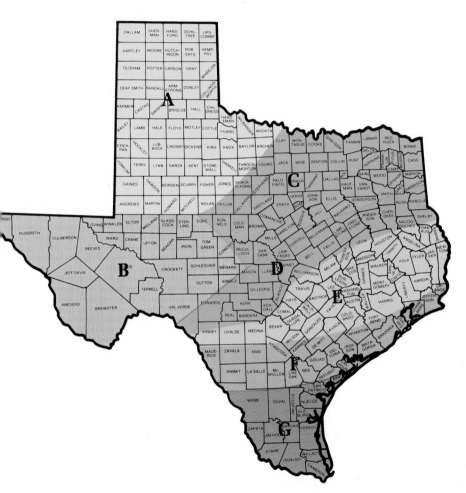

Map shows area of adaptation for fruit growing in Texas.

APPLES

Through the research and development of new apple varieties, most Texas gardeners can now grow at least some type of apple. Only the southern parts of the state are left out, and perhaps that will change in the near future.

There are a couple of oddities, though, about Texas apples. Most varieties will ripen during the summer, and the heat may cause some of the fruit to fall prematurely. Also, that fruit which remains may fail to develop red coloration, since it's ripening without fall's cooler weather. All things considered, apples are worth a try in many Texas gardens.

Plant Size

Varies with variety and with rootstock used in budding. Some rootstocks permit normal growth, to 25 to 35 feet, while others keep the trees as short as 5 to 6 feet. Space trees accordingly. Intermediate and taller types generally show better adaptation to Texas soils.

Pollinator Needed?

Yes, generally. Many apples are self-sterile. Varieties Golden Delicious and King David work well as pollinators.

Soil and Site

Apples are quite susceptible to root problems, most especially cotton root rot. Plant them only in perfectly drained soils, and in soils having no prior history of the cotton root rot fungal organism.

Size to Buy

Bare-rooted: 4 to 6 feet tall; containers: 5-gallon.

When to Plant

Bare-rooted: winter. Container: anytime.

Training and Pruning

First Year: Remove one-third to one-half of the whip at planting, leaving central leader at three to four feet in height. Encourage branches and vigorous growth first season.

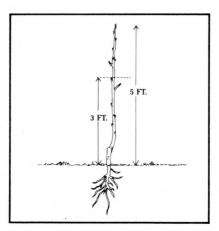

5 FT.

3 FT.

Pruning at planting

Second Year: Select central stem and three or four side (scaffold) branches. Scaffold branches should be evenly spaced around trunk, with none directly above another. Choose scaffolds that have a wide angle attachment to the trunk. The bottom branch should be on the south side and should be 26 to 30 inches from the ground.

Subsequent Years: Little regular pruning will be required for apples after their shape and habit have been established initially. Remove damaged or rubbing limbs as needed. Retain the tree's scaffold branching system by pruning back flush with the main limbs ... don't leave stubs. Do all pruning during winter.

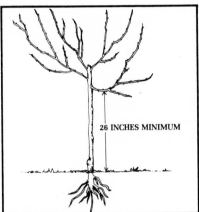

Pruning second season

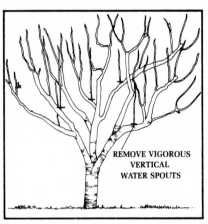

Subsequent years

Watering:

Apples develop most of their mature fruit size during late spring and early summer. If rainfall is lacking at those times, soak the tree regularly and deeply. Inadequate watering is one of the chief causes of premature fruit drop. Water as needed to keep the soil moist the remainder of the season.

Fertilizing

Apple trees should be fertilized with high-phosphorus, root-stimulating plant foods their first year.

From the second year on, apply a complete and balanced plant food such as 12-12-12, one pound for each inch of trunk diameter. Apply the fertilizer in early spring, before growth and blooming begin. Avoid high-nitrogen fertilizers that might stimulate succulent leaf growth (susceptible to fire blight). Nitrogen also discourages development of fruit color.

Pest Control

Regular spraying with an insecticide-fungicide combination on a 10 to 14-day interval during the spring will aid in preventing pest problems.

Apple scab: fungal leaf spot coupled with deteriorated, corky spots in fruit. Worse in wet weather. Fungicide such as benomyl.

Fire blight: Bacterial disease that attacks new branches, twigs. Leaves are scorched almost as if they've been hit with a blowtorch. Leaves remain attached to tree. Prune out infected wood (disinfect pruning equipment *between every cut* with 10 percent chlorine bleach solution, to prevent spread). Spray with streptomycin antibiotic spray while in full bloom.

Harvest

Trees should come into good production by fourth year. Most varieties will ripen during summer. Fruit can be picked once it has reached full size. Most red types fail to develop customary red coloration during heat.

Varieties

GOLDEN DELICIOUS Good pollinator variety. Quality golden fruit ripens September. Adapted northern half of state. Good yields. (Zones A-D.)

HOLLAND Established red variety for Texas. Ripens August. Adapted northern half of state. Good fresh or cooked. (Zones A-D.)

JONATHAN Red apple, medium-sized fruit with tart flavor. Good pollinator variety. Matures August, but fails to develop intense red color. (Zones A-D.)

MOLLY DELICIOUS Red variety adapted to south central Texas (area where other apples don't receive satisfactory chilling). Matures late July, early August. Fruit quality good. (Zones D-E.)

STARKRIMSON DELICIOUS Best of the red Delicious types for Texas conditions. Ripens early September. Adapted northern half of state. Productive, with quality fruit. (Zones A-D.)

EIN SHEMMER, ANNA and DORSETT GOLDEN New low chilling apples for South Texas. Worthy of trial in southern areas. (To date, exact zones have not been determined.)

APRICOTS

Attractive trees with one major fault: they bloom too early each spring. Flowers and immature fruit are frozen and yield will be sporadic. You may suffer through three years of nonproductivity for every year you get fruit.

Plant Size

Apricots grow to be medium-sized, rounded trees, 12 to 18 feet tall and wide. Space trees 15 to 18 feet apart.

Pollinator Needed?

Advisable.

Soil and Site

Deep, rich and well-drained soils are best. Avoid low, sheltered sites where frost will be more likely due to poor air circulation and settling of colder air.

Size to Buy

Bare-rooted: 4 to 6 feet tall; containers: 5-gallon.

When to Plant

Bare-rooted: winter. Container: anytime.

Training and Pruning

First Year: Remove one-third to one-half of whip at planting. Encourage root growth and beginning of top growth first year.

Subsequent Years: Develop strong scaffold branching system of 3 to 5 limbs radiating around trunk. Lowest limb should be on south side and from 24 to 30 inches off ground. To keep trees shorter and to admit more sunlight to ripening fruit, prune annually to maintain 3-branch scaffold system. Do all pruning during winter.

Thinning

Fruit should be, on average, 5 inches apart on limbs. Thin as soon as fruit are visible.

Watering

Fruit forms during spring and early summer. Supply ample moisture during periods of drought to encourage large fruit. Water as needed during periods of drought remainder of year.

Fertilizing

Apply complete and balanced plant food such as 12-12-12, one pound per inch of trunk diameter, in very early spring, before growth and blooming begin.

Pest Control

Several insects and diseases attack apricots. Treat regularly, on schedule similar to peaches and plums.

Brown rot: fungal disease of fruit. Protect by regular spraying with benomyl from flowering until harvest.

Plum curculio: worm common to plums and peaches also attacks apricots. Apply malathion or zolone from bud stage through harvest according to label directions.

Harvest

Trees should begin to produce (weather permitting) by fifth year. Harvest when fruit has reached full size and has started to soften slightly.

Varieties

BRYAN Most consistent producer under Texas conditions. Good quality fruit, but highly susceptible to brown rot. Ripens early June. Adapted northern half of Texas. (Zone A-D.)

MOORPARK Good quality fruit on large, vigorous tree. Adapted to northern half of Texas. (Zone A-D.)

BLACKBERRIES

Blackberries are one of the best adapted and most productive of all fruit crops grown in Texas gardens. They require less space than tree fruits, they're adapted to widely varying soils, and they're highly resistant to insects and diseases. In short, they should be a part of everyone's plantings.

Plant Size

Established blackberry clumps will be 4 to 6 feet tall. Space plants 3 feet apart in the rows, with rows 10 to 12 feet apart commercially or 6 to 8 feet apart in the home garden.

Pollinator Needed?

No. Blackberries are self-fertile.

Soil and Site

Blackberries do best in rich, well-drained soil, though they're tolerant of moderately acid to slightly alkaline soils. Provide them a permanent planting site in your garden, preferably along an edge where they can grow undisturbed for many years.

Size to Buy

Root cuttings (3 to 4 inches long) are available during winter. Some nurseries offer one and two-year-old plants, some even in one-gallon containers.

When to Plant

Root cuttings: midwinter. Plant root cuttings 2 inches deep. Container plants: anytime, but spring is preferable.

Training and Pruning

First Year: Allow young plants to develop strong canes for next year's crop.

Second and Subsequent Years: Blackberries bloom and fruit only on wood that was produced the preceding year. To keep your plants productive you must remove all fruiting canes in early summer, *immediately after harvest.* Use long-handled pruning shears to cut the just-fruited canes back to the ground. Allow the new canes that are emerging from the ground to develop into the next year's producing wood. Tip-prune those new canes as they reach 36 to 48 inches, to encourage side branching and to keep canes erect.

Watering

Blackberries develop during the spring. If rainfall is lacking at that time, water slowly and deeply. Water as needed the remainder of the year. Drip irrigation is an ideal way of watering blackberries.

Fertilizing

Apply a complete and balanced plant food such as 12-12-12, one-quarter cup per established plant, just as growth starts in the spring. Repeat the application immediately after the post-harvest pruning. Keep the fertilizer off your plants' foliage. Water thoroughly after feeding.

Pest Control

Few pests bother blackberries, which is perhaps why they're so good for Texas gardens. Among those that may:

Anthracnose: A fungal stem disease characterized by sunken purplish spots with gray centers. Control with benomyl or other fungicide, spraying regularly during the spring. Prune out badly infected canes.

Thrips: Small insects inhabiting fruit. May cause some deterioration of fruit quality. Control with malathion or zolone applied as fruit is developing.

Harvest

Blackberries will begin producing their second year. Most varieties ripen during late spring and early summer. Fruit should be allowed to reach full maturity (dark color, slightly softened) on the plant. Use short stick to "comb" your way through the thorny vines as you search for all the fruit. Do not leave mummified fruit hanging on vines, as a disease preventative.

APRICOTS

BLACKBERRIES

APPLES

Varieties

Many blackberry varieties are offered, particularly from out-of-state mail-order houses. Most are not suited to Texas conditions. Each of the following was introduced by Texas A&M University following years of testing and research. They will perform in your garden!

BRAZOS Well adapted to eastern three-fourths of the state. Vigorous plants produce quantities of large berries. Quality fruit, with acid taste. Well suited to desserts and jellies. Standard commercial variety. (Zones A-G.)

BRISON Fruit almost as large as Brazos. Very good quality, productive. Best suited to southern half of state. (Eastern parts: C-F.)

ROSBOROUGH Introduced at same time as Brison and Womack, but well suited to larger portion (most) of state. Fruit almost as large as Brazos and of higher quality. (Zones A-G.)

WOMACK Perhaps best current variety for northern half of state. Excellent production, quality on vigorous plants. (Zones A-C.)

Note: Dewberries are a trailing form of blackberry. As judged by the hundreds of miles of dewberries growing in the state's ditches and pastures, they're equally well adapted to our area. However, cultivated dewberries (variety Austin is best) produce much less per equal area when compared to upright blackberries. Space plants 3 to 4 feet apart in the rows, with 6 to 8 feet between the rows. Grow on trellis or fence to keep fruit off ground. Otherwise, care for them as you would upright blackberries. (Zones A-D.)

Also, Dorman red raspberries, introduced by Mississippi State University, are the only raspberries adapted to most Texas conditions. Their fruit is of less than ideal flavor and quality, but they at least are adapted to central third of Texas. No other raspberries are. (Zones C-D.)

BLUEBERRIES

Yes, you *can* grow blueberries in Texas! They're well adapted to the eastern third of the state, provided you give them perfect soil preparation and select your varieties carefully. The types to grow: improved forms of a native southern blueberry, the rabbiteye blueberry. Read the directions carefully, though . . . they're not the easiest crop by any means.

Plant Size

Rabbiteye blueberries develop into large shrubs, 10 to 15 feet tall and across. Space plants 8 to 10 feet apart.

Pollinator Needed?

Yes. Plant two or three different varieties.

Soil and Site

This is the point at which blueberries make it or break it in Texas. They must have an acid soil mix! It must be in the range of pH 4.0 to 5.5, preferably below 5.0. Prepare their planting bed much as you would for azaleas and camellias. Work in generous amounts of peat moss, compost or other organic matter. If your native soils are neutral or only slightly acid, you may want to plant the blueberries in raised beds filled completely with Canadian sphagnum peat moss. Be sure, too, that the soil drains well. Blueberry roots are shallow and sensitive to overwatering. At the same time, they're also delicate and are easily damaged by drought. Simply put, prepare their soil perfectly if you hope to have any success growing blueberries in Texas. Use mulches generously to conserve soil moisture and to reduce soil temperatures.

Size to Buy

Most blueberries are sold as two-year-old transplants. Many nurseries are also offering blueberries in gallon containers.

When to Plant
Bare-rooted transplants: winter; container plants: anytime.

Training and Pruning
Set bare-rooted transplants one inch deeper than they grew in the nursery. Prune top growth back by 40 to 50 percent at planting. As the plants develop they will require little regular pruning. Prune them to remove diseased and decayed wood, and to direct growth into a somewhat horizontal habit, for easier harvesting.

Watering
Water your blueberries carefully. Too much means root death and decay. Too little water also causes root damage, and possible loss of the plant altogether. Keep the soil mix moist at all times. Drip irrigation works well in meeting the plants' needs.

Fertilizing
Do not feed blueberries their first year. Use only acid-forming fertilizers on your blueberries from that time on. Special azalea-camellia-gardenia foods work well, and you can add supplemental nitrogen with ammonium sulfate (if needed) after harvest, to stimulate new growth.

Pest Control
No major pest problems.

Harvest
Harvest in late spring-summer. Average yield from established plants: 12 to 15 pounds. Harvest when fruit is fully ripe. Test one or two fruit before harvesting large numbers.

Varieties
WOODARD Popular large, vigorous type with quality fruit. One of finest for our state. Ripens early, light blue. (Eastern portions: C-E.)

TIFBLUE Large fruit on vigorous plants. Late fruiting, cold hardy. Should be included in plantings. (Eastern portions: C-E.)

CHERRIES

Because of their winter chilling requirements in excess of 1,200 hours, cherries are limited to far North Texas. Even there, the sour cherry is the better adapted type.

Plant Size
Cherry trees grow to 15 to 20 feet, with a rounded habit of growth. Space trees 15 to 18 feet apart.

Pollinator Needed?
No. Cherries are self-fruitful.

Soil and Site
Plant cherries in deep, rich garden soil. As with other fruit crops, good soil drainage is essential.

Size to Buy
Bare-rooted: 4 to 6 feet tall.

When to Plant
Bare-rooted: winter.

Training and Pruning
Train young tree to main trunk. Allow to develop natural shape. Encourage strong limb growth, with lowest limbs at 27 to 32 inches from ground. Little regular pruning will be required once tree is established. Prune in winter.

Watering
Water regularly as fruit is developing and as needed throughout year.

Fertilizing
Apply complete and balanced plant food such as 12-12-12, one pound per inch of trunk diameter, in early spring.

Pest Control
Fungal leaf and fruit diseases are most common problems, especially during prolonged rainy weather. Apply fungicide such as benomyl to control.

Harvest
Fruit ripens in early summer. Harvest when fully ripened, slightly soft to touch.

Variety
MONTMORENCY Best adapted variety to North Texas conditions. Fruit is large and red, tart. Used in pies and preserves. (Zone A.)

CITRUS

Limited by their cold sensitivity, most citrus crops are confined strictly to South Texas and the Rio Grande Valley areas. Nonetheless, several types can provide attractive trees and good yields where winter temperatures stay above 18 to 22 degrees.

Plant Size
Small, full trees to 10 to 18 feet. Space 15 to 25 feet apart.

Pollinator Needed?
No. Citrus are self-fruitful.

Soil and Site
Citrus varieties are adapted to both sands and clays, so long as the soil drains well. In areas with frequent heavy rains or high water tables, plants should be set on slight mounds to provide better drainage. In colder areas, shelter plants from north winds when possible.

Size to Buy
Balled-and-burlapped, also container: 3 to 4 feet.

When to Plant
Anytime. Avoid fall plantings in colder areas.

Training and Pruning
Citrus trees require only occasional pruning to direct growth of limbs. Light pruning may be done at any time. Heavier pruning and reshaping should be done during the winter dormant season.

Watering
Keep citrus trees well watered throughout the year. Be sure plants don't go into periods of extreme cold in drought conditions.

Fertilizing
Apply one pound of complete and balanced fertilizer such as 12-12-12 per inch of trunk

diameter in early spring and again in early summer. Water thoroughly after feeding.

Pest Control

Scale insects: Affix themselves to stems, leaves, even fruit. Control with summer-weight oil sprays.

White flies: Small (pinhead-sized) insects that feed on citrus leaves. Generally present in large numbers. Their honeydew exudate promotes growth of black sooty mold, which can cause a shading effect on foliage. Control white flies (and hence the mold) with summer-weight oil or general fruit spray.

Cold Protection

Keep trees healthy and vigorous. Water prior to hard freezes and cover the plants with blankets or quilts (not plastic) if at all possible. Place a lighted bulb or heat lamp for added protection. Wrap trunks with blankets, insulation batts or other fibrous material to protect bud union.

Harvest

Allow fruit to remain on plant until fully ripened.

Varieties

For areas of the Texas Gulf Coast, where winter temperatures regularly fall below freezing, choose from Meyer lemon, Chang Chau tangerines, Satsumas and Nagami kumquats. (Zones F-G.)

For Rio Grande Valley plantings, choose from Navel and Valencia oranges, Ruby Red and Star Ruby grapefruit, tangerines, tangelos and lemons. Consult with a local nurseryman for most precise recommendations for your exact locale. (Zone G.)

FIGS

Vigorous fruit crop adapted, due to sensitivity to cold, to southern two-thirds of Texas. Attractive landscape tree or large shrub adapted to wide assortment of soils. Productive and tasty, both fresh and preserved.

Plant Size

Mature fig plants reach 15 to 25 feet tall and 15 to 20 feet across. Space 15 to 20 feet apart in rows.

Pollinator Needed?

No. Fruit is seedless, does not require pollination.

Soil and Site

Figs should be planted in deep, well-drained soil. Avoid areas known to be infested with root knot nematodes, one of figs' most serious problems. Plant on south side of buildings in northern regions to lessen chance of winter damage.

Size to Buy

Bare-rooted: 18 to 24 inches tall; balled-and-burlapped: 24 to 36 inches; container: 1, 2 or 5-gallon.

When to Plant

Bare-rooted: late winter. Balled-and-burlapped: late winter, spring. Container: spring, summer, early fall. Avoid planting dates that might not allow plants time to become established before cold weather.

Training and Pruning

Allow young plants to develop as shrubs, with several main trunks arising from ground. Mature plants will require little if any regular pruning. Should winter damage occur, remove it in early spring, when its extent can be determined.

Watering

Large fig leaves demand frequent and deep watering. If leaves wilt during afternoon heat, or if fruit is dropping freely, you may not be watering enough. Keep soil thoroughly moistened, particularly as fruit is forming. Beginning in early fall start cutting back on water to allow plant to go dormant. Plants that have slowed their growth for fall suffer less cold weather injury. Mulch around plants with grass clippings or compost, both to conserve moisture and to protect against winter damage to trunks.

Fertilizing

Figs have relatively low fertility needs. In poorer, sandy soils, feed in spring with a complete and balanced plant food such as 12-12-12, one pound per inch of total trunk diameter. Water thoroughly after feeding. Otherwise do not apply commercial fertilizers to fig plantings.

Pest Control

Dried fruit beetle: This tiny insect causes fruit to become "soured" and inedible. The insect invades the fruit just as it ripens, through the open "eye" at the end of the fruit. The insect infects the fruit with microorganisms that cause its deterioration. Select a variety with a "closed" eye to avoid the problem.

Nematodes: Microscopic soil-borne worms that are particularly fond of figs. Roots develop knots where nematodes have fed, cutting off water and nutrients to leaves. Grow plants adjacent to house and roots that grow under house will likely have few nematodes. Avoid areas suspected of having nematodes. Otherwise, just assume your mature plant has them and care for it accordingly . . . like you would a sick child. No chemicals are available that will give good control around existing plants.

Harvest

Pick fruit just as it ripens. It will not develop further once it's been harvested. Remove all deteriorated fruit to prevent spread of insects and disease.

Varieties

Both of the following have "closed eyes" to lessen chance of insect invasion.

CELESTE Small, dark, high quality fig that ripens in June. Vigorous and productive. Well-adapted to all Texas fig areas. Good preserved and fresh. (Eastern half of B; C-G.)

TEXAS EVERBEARING Medium-to-large fruit, good quality, ripening in late June and for a continuing period thereafter. Vigorous plant. (Eastern half B; C-G.)

GRAPES

Interest in fresh fruit and wine-making have made grapes one of the most popular of all home garden fruits in recent years. Interestingly, of all the species of grapes in the world, over half are native to Texas. That doesn't mean, however, that all grapes grow well in our state. You must choose the best types for your area and grow them according to specific guidelines.

If your fruit-growing space is limited, grapes may be just the answer. Grown on trellises or fences they take little horizontal space. Put them up and over the patio roof and they can add shade while they're producing their fruit.

GRAPES

BLUEBERRIES

FIGS

CITRUS

CHERRIES

Plant Size

Grapes are large plants ... vigorous vines. Allow them 10 to 15 feet to grow and sprawl. If you're planting the vines along a trellis or wire support, space them 8 feet apart.

Pollinator Needed?

No. Grapes are self-fruitful.

Soil and Site

Choose a deep, well-drained soil, preferably sand or sandy loam. However, grapes can be grown on a variety of soil types. Reduce the chance of disease by planting where air circulates freely. Grapes should have full sun to grow and fruit to their maximum.

Size to Buy

Most grapes are sold bare-rooted (usually packed in sawdust and wrapped in plastic bags), with sizes ranging from 12 to 24 inches. Plants may be purchased by age in nursery row (one-year or two-year plants). One-gallon nursery stock is also available, from 15 to 24 inches tall.

When to Plant

Bare-rooted: winter. Container: anytime.

Training and Pruning

First Year. On Wire Trellises: Start by establishing the wire trellises at 42 and 72 inches from the ground. Use No. 10 or No. 12 smooth galvanized wire stretched between heavy fence posts and supported by wooden stakes. Use one heavy fence post for every 10 plants. Put a stake at each planting site . Install stout anchors at each end of the trellis.

Trim root systems to 4 inches prior to planting. Remove top growth to leave 1 or 2 buds above the soil line. Allow plants to grow unchecked the first year.

Second and Third Years. On Wire Trellises: Prune each vine back to two buds before second growing season. Select the more vigorous shoot and tie it to the stake as it grows. Allow the stem or trunk to reach the top of the stake and then prune its top out. Encourage four branches to develop from the center stem, one going each way on each of the two wires.

Before the third growing season prune the four shoots back to 2 to 3 buds each. Allow only one cluster of fruit per bud. Remove all others in early May.

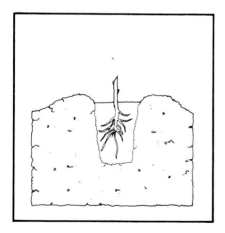

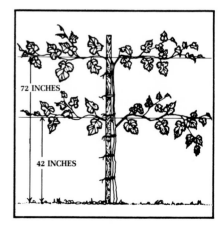

72 INCHES

42 INCHES

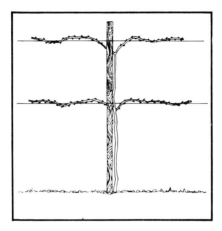

Subsequent Years: Probably no other fruit crop requires such heavy and regular pruning as established grapes do. The amount of growth a grapevine makes in any year determines how much fruit it can carry the following year. That means that the number of buds you leave on a plant when you prune it is determined by the amount of wood that was produced the preceding year. All pruning is done during the winter.

At that point you get out the scales. Leave 30 buds distributed on the vine's four branches for the first pound of wood you remove. For each additional pound you remove, leave 10 more buds. It may sound confusing, but you'll soon get the knack of it. Just remember, regular pruning is absolutely essential to the success of a grape planting.

Thinning

Removing part of the fruit load is an important part of pruning your grapes. Thin 3-year old vines to 8 to 12 clusters, 4-year old plants to 16 to 24 clusters and older vines to 40 to 80 clusters. Don't allow your plants' fruit load to overtax their capabilities. Thin the clusters in mid-spring, while they're still young.

Watering

Use basins or drip irrigation systems to keep your grapes well watered all year long, especially during prolonged summer droughts.

Fertilizing

Apply a complete and balanced fertilizer such as 12-12-12, one pound per inch of stem diameter at ground level. Fertilize in early spring. Water thoroughly after fertilizing.

Pest Control

Black rot: Attacks grape clusters, also leaves and stems. Causes fruit to become black and mummified. Often only a few of the fruit in a cluster are affected. Control by spraying in early spring with benomyl, zineb or captan.

Pierce's disease: Serious ailment of many grape varieties when grown in warm, humid climates. Disease is spread by leafhopper insect and is uncontrollable chemically once plants are affected. Leaves develop tip die-back and eventually dry completely. Canes show dead lesions. Spraying for insects may offer some help, but selection of adapted varieties with resistance to the disease offers more hope.

Harvesting

Harvest grapes when desired taste has been reached. Immature fruit will have a puckering astringent taste. As crop matures it will become sweeter. Grapes being grown for wine-making should be harvested somewhat earlier, before sugar content reaches its maximum.

Varieties (I)

Many of the conventional grape varieties we know from the grocery are not well adapted to large parts of Texas. Include in that list Thompson Seedless and Concord. Primarily because of disease problems, these are adapted only to the arid areas of far West Texas. Elsewhere they should not be planted. Instead, try the following:

AURELIA Large white fruit of excellent quality. Vigorous, productive. Not recommended along Gulf Coast. Excellent for fresh eating at table. (Zones A-D.)

BLACK SPANISH (Lenoir) Small black fruit in full, compact clusters. Vigorous, productive. Resistant to Pierce's disease, but susceptible to black rot. Good for jelly, juice and wine. Adapted to central portion of Texas. (Zones B-F.)

CHAMPANEL Large black fruit borne in loose clusters. Vigorous, productive and resistant to heat and diseases. Adapted to heavy soils, also along Gulf Coast. (Zones A, C-F.)

FREDONIA Large black berry with large, compact clusters. Vigorous and durable. Useful in juice, jellies and fresh. Adapted to areas from Central Texas northward. (Zones A, C-D.)

SEIBEL 9110 White grape forming large, compact clusters. Very durable, one of Texas' best varieties. Almost seedless, good for wines and jellies. Excellent fresh. (Zones A-D.)

Muscadine Grapes

Native to much of the South, muscadines are adapted to areas of high humidity and hot weather. Since they do best with acid soils, muscadines are adapted to much of East Texas. When grown in alkaline soils the plants will grow more slowly and will require regular applications of soil acidifier and iron supplements. Muscadines can be grown in zone 7 and southward . . . where temperatures do not go below 5 to 10°F.

Muscadine grapes are used both fresh and in jellies. Their berries are borne in loose clusters. The plants are quite vigorous and are grown in much the same way as the other grapes just discussed. You may want to train them to a single wire trellis placed 60 inches above the ground. Space plants at 20-foot intervals along the trellis. You can also use muscadines on fences, arbors and patio roofs by training to a single main cane with two or three main branches.

Prune your established muscadines annually, leaving short spurs, or side branches, along the major branches. The spurs should be approximately 6 inches apart on average, with 2 to 3 buds per spur.

Harvest muscadines when the individual fruits ripen, picking one at a time until all have been gathered.

Varieties (II)

Some muscadine varieties produce only female (pistillate) flowers. Since these have no pollen, a second (pollinator) variety that does produce pollen must be planted.

Other varieties produce "complete" flowers, with both male and female parts. No pollinator is needed for these. In fact, these can be used as pollinators for other types.

All of the varieties listed below are vigorous and disease-resistant under proper Texas growing conditions.

CARLOS Small bronze with medium-sized clusters. Complete flower. (Eastern half: C-F.)

COWART Large black with large clusters. Complete flower. (Eastern half: C-F.)

HIGGINS Large reddish-brown with large clusters. Requires pollinator. (Eastern half: C-F.)
JUMBO Large purple-black with long productive season. Requires pollinator. (Eastern half: C-F.)
MAGNOLIA Medium-sized bronze with medium-sized clusters. Complete flower. (Eastern half: C-F.)
SCUPPERNONG Oldest muscadine variety. Bronze fruit with delicate, distinctive flavor. (Eastern half: C-F.)

PEACHES

One of the more important fruit crops for Texas. Many thousands of acres across the state are planted commercially with peaches and millions of trees are grown in home gardens as well.

Though there are several keys to peach-growing success, in no crop is variety selection so critical. You have to buy a type that's adapted to your area.

You also must care for your peaches regularly. Pruning and pest control are two of the most important responsibilities. Check through the details and be sure you stay ahead of the problems.

Plant Size

Mature trees, properly trained, will be 8 to 12 feet tall, with a spread of 15 to 18 feet. Space the trees 18-25 feet apart. Dwarf types are also available and may be of value to gardeners with extremely limited areas. Some types can even be grown in containers, though yield is not always good.

Pollinator Needed?

Rarely needed. Most varieties are self-fruitful. However, planting of several varieties not only guarantees good pollination of all, but also lengthens harvest season.

Soil and Site

Peaches produce best in sandy well drained soils. They can succeed in either sands or clays, provided they have good drainage. Ideally their soil should be 2 to 3 feet deep. To protect buds and flowers, avoid low, sheltered sites where frost is most likely to form in early spring cold snaps.

Size to Buy

Bare-rooted: 2½ to 4 feet tall; containers: 5-gallon.

When to Plant:

Bare-rooted: winter. Container: anytime.

Training and Pruning

First Year: Your objective in training peaches is to develop a vase-shaped tree with 3 or 4 strong scaffold branches arising from the main trunk between 20 and 24 inches from the ground.

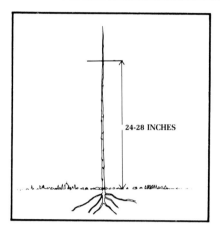

24-28 INCHES

You begin to form that branching system by pruning the new tree back to 24 to 28 inches immediately after planting. Buds and branches below the cut will then start to grow. As these new shoots have developed to 6 to 10 inches in length, remove all but 3. These will be the plant's permanent scaffold branches and should radiate out from the trunk like spokes on a wheel ... no two directly above one another. Allow these to grow the remainder of the first year.

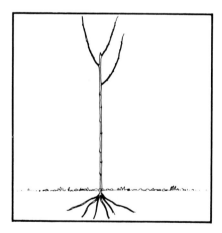

Second Year: As these 3 main scaffold branches grow and develop during their second year, prune them back to 30 to 34 inches, to encourage lateral growth. Let additional branches form, but try always to train growth away from the center of the tree, to keep the plants more horizontal and to allow more sunlight to reach ripening fruit. Accomplish this by pruning above outward-facing buds and twigs. Do not allow sub-scaffold limbs to start within 18 to 24 inches of trunk. Remove any strong vertical shoots ("water sprouts").

Subsequent Years: Once the tree has its scaffold branching system established, pruning will be a rather routine winter occurrence. Remove about 40 percent of the twigs and limbs each winter. Remember your objective is keeping the tree horizontal, with maximum sunlight penetrating in from above. Always prune just above an outward facing bud or limb. Remove strongly vertical limbs and those that hang decidedly downward. If one branch now shades another, remove the weaker of the two. Always prune flush with a remaining limb . . . don't leave stubs that could invite borer and disease invasion.

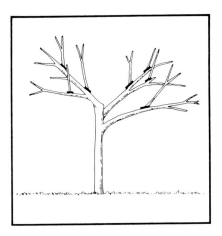

Thinning

You must thin normal fruit set if you expect best production from your peach tree. Aim to leave an average of 5 to 6 inches between fruit (use the greater spacing for larger and later types). Fruit should be thinned when it reaches marble size. Failure to thin does not increase total yield, but it does reduce quality of the fruit. Thinning prevents limb breakage on peach trees and greatly increases fruit size.

Watering

Water peaches regularly, particularly as the fruit is developing. Mature fruiting trees may need as much as 15 gallons of water daily during warm summer weather.

Fertilizing

Apply one pound of complete and balanced plant food such as 12-12-12 per inch of trunk diameter at ground level. Fertilize in early spring, before blooming and growth begin. Water trees thoroughly after feeding.

Pest Control

Several serious insect and disease problems threaten every peach planting in Texas. Spray regularly to prevent them.

Peach tree borer: Adult beetle lays eggs on tree trunk during warm months. Larvae hatch and begin burrowing in wood of tree, primarily near ground level. Sticky sap flows out of wounds and congeals at points of entry. Borers continue to damage internal tissue, causing weakening of entire tree. Insect is difficult to cure, easier to prevent in the first place. Use borer sprays on 4 to 8 week intervals during summer and early fall (mid-August treatment is critical) to prevent initial borer invasion. Read and follow label directions carefully when applying borer remedies to trees that are carrying fruit.

Plum curculio: This is the worm that invades the fruit of peaches, plums and other stone fruits. Control with malathion or zolone applied when buds are pink (before opening), when three-fourths of the petals have fallen and again on 10 to 14 day intervals for 3 to 5 more applications.

Brown rot: Fungal disease that causes deterioration of fruit. Mummified fruit on tree and ground is prime source of invasion. Remove and destroy. Include fungicide such as benomyl or captan with each insecticide application during spring. These treatments will also eliminate peach scab, another serious disease.

Scale insects: Several types attack the trunk and limbs of peaches. Insects are attached directly to tree's bark and may be difficult to see. Control with application of dormant oil during winter.

Stink bugs: Bugs sting ripening fruit leaving deteriorated spot that often decays. Adult stink bug is very mobile and difficult to control. Regular spraying for other insects as discussed will generally reduce populations.

Peach leaf curl: Bacterial infection most evident on succulent new growth in early spring. Leaves are greatly misshapen, often puffed and folded like accordions. Prevent by applying bordeaux mixture or other copper material in fall, as leaves drop.

Harvest

Check each fruit individually before picking, since peaches will not continue ripening once harvested. Fruit should be very slightly softened and should have lost its green coloration before picking. Harvesting of a particular variety may extend over 10 to 15 days, so check the tree several times.

Varieties

Each part of Texas has its own best peach varieties, depending on the amount of chilling temperatures it receives (see explanation, p. 357). To buy the best type for your area you must know how many hours of proper chilling your trees will receive. (See map p. 358). Buy varieties that match that number, at least within 200 hours. That way you'll avoid the problems of failure to bloom (lack of sufficient chilling) and premature blooming, before spring arrives (variety requiring far less chilling than your area receives).

Numbers listed in parentheses indicate chilling requirements in hours. (Varieties are arranged in order of ripening.)

Note about Elberta peaches: Many new gardeners specify "Elberta" peaches when buying trees. Certainly it's a familiar variety name. However, Elberta peaches lack many of the qualities of more recent introductions. Commercially it has become a very minor part of Texas' orchards. Similarly, it should not be planted in home gardens. Choose, instead, from the following list:

SPRINGOLD (700) yellow fleshed cling, good production of small fruit, reasonable quality for early peach. Ripens early May. (Zones C-E.)

EARLY AMBER (350) cling, fair to good quality, medium-sized. (Southern half of F; G.)

RIO GRANDE (450) semi-cling, large fruit of fair quality, dependable producer. (Zone F, Northern half of G.)

JUNE GOLD (650) yellow fleshed cling, good production of quality fruit. Ripens late May. One of the best performers for South Texas. (Zone E; Northern half of F.)

DIXIRED (950) larger cling, moderate crops of good quality. Ripens early June. (Zones A-C.)

SAM HOUSTON (500) freestone, good production, fair quality. (Zones E-F.)

SENTINEL (800) semi-freestone, excellent quality, yields well. Ripens mid-June. Increasingly popular. (Zones C-E.)

RED HAVEN (950) semi-freestone, excellent quality, good crops. (Zones A-C.)

RANGER (900) freestone, excellent quality, good production, medium-sized. Resistant to late freeze damage. (Zones A-C.)

HARVESTER (750) freestone, excellent quality, good commercial variety, disease-resistant. Ripens late June. (Zones C-D; Northern half of E.)

REDGLOBE (850) freestone, good quality, productive. Ripens early July. Susceptible to bacterial spot. (Zones A-D.)

LORING (750) large freestone, excellent quality, disease-resistant. One of the largest peaches grown. (Southern half of C; D, Northern half of E.)

REDSKIN (750) freestone, excellent quality, fine variety. Ripens Elberta season. (Zones C-D, Northern half of E.)

DIXILAND (750) cling, fine quality, very late season, dependable producer. Used for pickled peaches. Ripens in August. (Zones A-E, Northern half of F.)

FRANK (750) freestone, one of the best quality peaches, ripens with Redskin.

Note about two peach relatives:

1. Almonds: Not generally adapted because of low chilling requirements (bloom prematurely in spring).

2. Nectarines: Smooth-skinned selection of peaches. Highly susceptible to brown rot fungus. Should only be tried in Western sections.

PEARS

Pears rate as some of the best fruit trees for Texas landscapes and gardens. Given the proper varieties, they're dependable and they're attractive. They can even be used as dual-purpose fruit and shade trees.

Plant Size
Upright trees to 20 to 30 feet, 15 to 25 feet wide. Space trees 25 to 30 feet apart.

Pollinator Needed?
Required for most varieties.

Soil and Site
Pears flower early and should be planted where early spring frosts won't damage buds and blooms: away from low and wind-sheltered spots where frost might develop more readily. Provide deep, well-drained soils. Trees may show iron deficiency in alkaline soils.

Size to Buy
Bare-rooted: 4 to 6 feet tall. Container: 5-gallon.

When to Plant
Bare-rooted: winter. Container: anytime.

Training and Pruning
Pears are upright trees at maturity, and will start developing a central trunk from the outset. If your tree was transplanted bare-rooted, remove 40 to 50 percent of its top growth immediately after planting, to compensate for roots lost during the digging.

As new growth develops the first year, select one shoot to be the central leader trunk. Remove side growth below 24 inches. Allow other branches to develop into major scaffold limbs. Your pear will come into production years sooner if you'll promote lateral growth. Use weights, blocks or wires to pull lateral branches out of their decidedly upright habit.

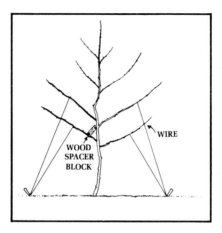

Mature pear trees will require little regular pruning except to repair insect, disease and storm damage. Rubbing or competing limbs should also be removed entirely. Whenever possible, confine pruning to the winter months.

Important note in pruning pears: always disinfect your pruning tools between every cut to prevent spread of fire blight, pears' most serious disease problem. Use a 10 percent solution of chlorine bleach. When finished, wash your pruning tools, dry and oil them to prevent corrosion damage to metal surfaces.

Watering
Water pears regularly, especially during fruiting season and during prolonged droughts. Avoid continued excessive water that might stimulate soft, succulent growth that might be damaged by fire blight.

Fertilizing
Avoid high-nitrogen fertilizers that might stimulate soft, succulent growth. Fire blight is most prevalent on that type of tissue. Use only a root-stimulator fertilizer (high in phosphorus) for the first year. Beginning the second year you can apply a complete and balanced fertilizer such as 12-12-12 in early spring, before growth starts. Apply one pound per inch of trunk diameter.

Pest Control
Pears have few insect and disease problems, however you should learn to recognize them before it's too late. One can cause serious harm.

Fire Blight: Kills entire limbs back almost overnight, as if they'd been hit with a blowtorch. Leaves turn black and remain attached to the limb. Diseased lesions can sometimes be seen along limb, at farthest point of die-back. Disease can spread to kill entire plant. It is spread during blooming season and by pruning with contaminated equipment (see guidelines above). Control by removing it by pruning, and by spraying while plants are in full and total bloom in the spring. Use streptomycin, bordeaux mixture or fixed copper sprays. Avoid highly susceptible varieties like Bartlett except in far West Texas.

Stink Bugs: Insects sting ripening fruit causing black deteriorated spots. Pest is difficult to control because of its size and mobility. Regular spraying with zolone or malathion will keep populations in check.

Harvest

Most pear varieties will continue to ripen following harvest. In fact, flavor and texture will improve if the fruit is given 5 to 7 days on a counter or windowsill before it's eaten. Kieffer requires additional time. Its fruit should be wrapped in paper and stored at room temperature for 2 to 4 weeks.

Varieties

Resistance to fire blight varies between varieties. Avoiding Bartlett (except in far West Texas) because of its susceptabililty, choose from the following more resistant types.

AYERS High quality small fruit with few grit cells. Good fire blight resistance. Best adapted to northern two-thirds of state. Pollinator recommended. (Zone A-E.)

KIEFFER Old popular variety. Fruit hard, of fair quality. Good fire blight resistance. Good in northern three-fourths of state. Pollinator recommended. (Zone A-F.)

LeCONTE Very high quality fruit with fine texture. Good fresh and preserved. Susceptible to fire blight, so best adapted to western parts of state. Pollinator required. (Zone A-B; western half of C-E.)

MAXINE Medium-sized fruit of good quality for fresh eating. Good fire blight resistance. Vigorous tree, recommended for northern half of Texas. Pollinator recommended. (Zone A-E.)

MOONGLOW Newer variety with good fire blight resistance. Fruit has good texture and flavor. Bears at early age. Self-fruitful, also makes good pollinator variety. (Zone A-E.)

ORIENT Almost immune to fire blight. One of the best pears for Texas, large fruit of good quality. Attractive landscape tree. Good in northern three-fourths of state. Pollinator recommended. (Zone A-F.)

PECANS

In addition to being our official State Tree, pecans are also among our finest large landscaping shade trees. The fact that they also produce a delectable by-product is the reason they end up in this chapter on fruit. All things considered . . . good looks, fruit production, overall durability, adaptability to all parts of the state . . . pecans are perhaps the best all-around trees we can grow.

Plant Size

Pecans are very large trees, attaining heights of over 60 feet at maturity. Growth habit is rounded, so a comparable spread can be expected. As a result, pecans should be planted at least 35 to 40 feet from other trees. That means that in an urban landscape you may just want to plant one or two trees.

Pollinator Needed?

Yes. See variety lists for specific details.

Soil and Site

Being large trees with strong-growing tap roots, pecans do best in deep, rich soil. For commercial production, 4 to 6 feet of soil is a minimum. Home gardeners, because of their more intensified care, can grow very satisfactory trees in 3 to 4 feet of soil. Regardless of the soil depth, though, good drainage is a requirement.

Size to Buy

Bare-rooted: 4 to 6 feet tall (taller trees will suffer more transplant shock, require more time to begin bearing).

Balled-and-burlapped: not commonly available, but 8 to 12 foot sizes transplant well when dug carefully with good soil ball.

When to Plant

Bare-rooted: winter. Balled-and-burlapped: winter or very early spring.

Training and Pruning

First Two Years: Pecans are grown with one central trunk. Training from the outset should be directed toward that end. To compensate for roots damaged during digging, and to help the tree develop a strong trunk, remove half of the top (stem) growth at planting. Encourage the growth of several side shoots, but pinch them back to 8 to 12 inches from the main trunk. Their foliage will help sustain the trunk, causing it to thicken and grow stronger. Watch for one main leader to develop into new trunk. Should you have two, remove the weaker.

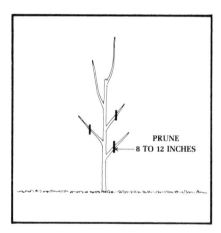 

PRUNE
8 TO 12 INCHES

Third and Subsequent Years: Once the tree has an established and strong trunk you can select 3 or 4 main scaffold branches at 5 to 6 feet from the ground. Keep all shoots lower than 5 feet headed back to 8 to 10 inches to encourage the new scaffold limbs to grow and develop into a full tree. The cut-back limbs below the main scaffolds will be removed in the third or fourth growing season. Little regular pruning will be required of established pecans, other than to repair damaged limbs and to remove rubbing or otherwise competing limbs.

All major pruning of pecans should be done during the dormant season.

Watering

Being large trees, pecans will demand large quantities of water, sometimes over 50 gallons per tree per day. That, of course, is especially true during hot summer weather. Water if it's been over two weeks since the trees last received some type of watering. Be especially mindful of watering as nuts are expanding (early summer) and filling (late summer). Drip irrigation works well in developing pecan orchards.

Fertilizing

Pecans are, among fruiting crops, an oddity. Research has shown that best yields occur when high-nitrogen fertilizers are added. Apply 1 pound of ammonium nitrate (33-0-0) per inch of trunk diameter to the soil around the tree in late winter, concentrating your feeding around the drip line (under the outer canopy of leaves). Water thoroughly after feeding. Repeat the feeding in May. If the tree is in a lawn area where it is also receiving high-nitrogen lawn fertilizers, omit the second (May) application of ammonium nitrate.

Pecan rosette, a die-back of twigs and limbs, is caused by a deficiency of available zinc in alkaline soils. It is a problem in the western two-thirds of the state, and can seriously diminish pecan production. Control rosette by spraying with zinc sulfate or other zinc additive. Trees in the western two-thirds of Texas will respond noticeably to 5 or 6 applications of zinc during the growing season (it can be included with insecticide and fungicide applications). Even East Texas trees will benefit from 2 or 3 applications during the spring. Be sure to spray the zinc onto the foliage. Soil applications will be inactivated by the soil's alkalinity and will be wasted.

Pest Control

Pecans are bothered by a dozen or more common insects and diseases. Many attack only the fruit and do not alter the tree's usefulness as a shade tree. Others attack the foliage and threaten the health and vigor of the tree itself. Label directions will give you specific guidelines, but here are the most common problems.

Pecan scab: Fungal disease that invades in early spring. Leaves are affected first, but disease is most noticeable in fruit, which turns black and falls prematurely in late summer and early fall. Control with benomyl or other registered fungicide. Spray as leaves emerge and regularly remainder of season. Most serious in humid portions of East Texas. Some varieties are more resistant than others.

Pecan nut casebearer: Small larval insect that feeds on developing shoots, young fruit. A serious insect pest all over Texas. Spray schedule varies from place to place and even from year to year. Consult your local County Extension office in mid-spring for more exact timing. Spray with zolone, malathion or other registered insecticide. Repeat spraying in 6 weeks for second generation.

Pecan phylloxera gall: Small insects cause leaves to develop warty galls in spring. Galls break open in late spring and thousands of insects emerge. Control with a dormant oil spray in the winter.

Twig girdler: Twigs and small limbs die and fall from tree, looking as if they'd been cut loose with a pocket knife. Damage is result of adult twig girdler beetle. The female lays her eggs on twig, then chews around and around it. Limb eventually dies and falls and young girdlers are left to feed on the decaying wood. Control by removing dead twigs and destroying ... that's where the eggs are.

Aphids: Small pear-shaped insects that suck plant juices. Insects then secrete a sticky honeydew that coats the leaves and everything below. Black pecan aphid attacks trees in late summer and leaves much of foliage mottled yellow. Control all aphids with applications of malathion, zolone or others as needed.

Webworms: Ravenous foliage eaters. One webfull of worms can strip an entire limb in a matter of days. Webs are also unsightly. Treat with malathion or zolone, but include a few drops of a liquid detergent to help the spray penetrate into the web. You can also prune the webs out of the tree.

Borers: Healthy, vigorous pecans seldom are invaded by borers. If you suspect borers, be sure first that it isn't sapsucker damage (regularly spaced holes around trunk, as opposed to the more sporadic holes caused by borers). Should you find that borers are there, treat with borer control spary. Note, too, that bark falling away from a pecan trunk isn't evidence of borers or other serious problems. Bark is a dead tissue and as a pecan tree grows and swells, it can only crack and fall away. New bark will replace it.

Pecan weevils: Larval form of insect invades fruit in late summer, feeds on developing kernels. By harvest there is no meat left in the pecans. Control with a mid-August spraying of sevin.

Hickory shuckworm: Larvae invade shuck surrounding the pecan, tunneling through it. In their feeding, they cut off water and nutrient supply lines to kernels. Pecans don't fill out properly, also fail to separate from the shucks and fall in late autumn. They may still be hanging on the trees after the winter. Control at same time you spray for pecan weevils (mid-August), using either malathion or zolone.

Harvest

Pecans will start to fall by October and harvest should be completed within 4 to 6 weeks. Once nuts have ripened and shucks have split, the pecans can be harvested by shaking or thrashing the limbs with poles. Rake or blow the leaves away to expose the nuts lying on the ground.

A note about yield: some varieties produce good crops every other year (alternate bearing). That's not good if you enjoy pecans every year. The solution: plant a variety that produces regularly (see the listing that follows), and keep your trees vigorous. Keeping the foliage on your trees until the first frost helps promote a heavy crop the following year.

Pecan Zone Map

Unlike other fruit crops, pecans' adaptability is split by a line running north and south across the state. Prime reason for the division is a disease called pecan scab. Some varieties such as Western and Wichita have poor resistance to it and must be grown in drier climates, where it is not a problem. These are termed "western" varieties and should never be grown east of the dividing line.

Other varieties such as Desirable, Kiowa and Shawnee should be grown only east of the line, to a large degree because of intolerances to calcareous (high levels of calcium) soils in the western parts of the state. These are classed as "eastern" varieties.

Still others are resistant to the scab disease and are also tolerant of growing conditions west of the line. These are suitable in both eastern and western regions.

Varieties will be labelled as E or W, for their area(s) of adaptability.

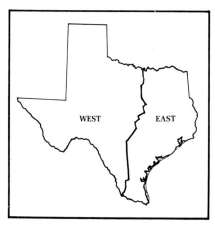

Line separating eastern and western regions of pecan growing in Texas. Varieties planted east of the line should be resistant to pecan scab fungal disease.

Varieties

There are scores of pecans in common production in Texas. Many are older varieties, and others have met with limited favor. Most have thin shells and would qualify for the designation "papershell." Outlined below are the best for our state, along with specific guidelines for each. Note that some varieties produce the male flowers (with pollen) first, while others produce the female flowers (with nutlet) first. To ensure good cross-pollination (done by wind), you should either have several other pecan trees near your tree or you should plant one of each type.

CHEYENNE Medium-sized pecans, trees productive at early age, generally after 5 years. Good disease resistance. Good kernel quality. Pollen first. (Zone E or W.)

CHOCTAW Large pecans, outstanding quality. Tree is vigorous and disease resistant. Thin shell, with attractive and tasty kernels. Nutlets first. (Zone E or W.)

DESIRABLE Large pecans, of very good quality. Produces regularly. Less likely to bear in alternate-year cycles. Disease resistant and somewhat weak-wooded in winds and ice. Long-standing commercial variety. Pollen first. (Zone E.)

KIOWA Large pecan, good quality. Productive at early age, good disease resistance. (Zone E.)

MOHAWK Large pecans of good quality. Produces early (6 years to first crop). Attractive and strong landscape tree. Keep well fertilized and watered to ensure regular crops of good quality pecans. Nutlets first. (Zone E or W).

SHAWNEE Medium-sized pecans of good quality. Very productive and resistant to pecan scab disease. Nutlets first. (Zone E.)

SIOUX Small pecans of outstanding quality. Strong tree that begins bearing after 6 years. Nutlets first. (Zone E or W.)

WESTERN Medium-sized pecans of fair quality. Old standard commercial variety for West Texas. Produces early and abundantly. Not disease resistant, hence adapted to western part of Texas. Pollen first. (Zone W.)

WICHITA Medium-sized pecans of very good quality. Very productive, starting at early age. Not disease resistant, hence best adapted to western two-thirds of state. Must have regular zinc applications. Nutlets first. (Zone W.)

Say "No!" to these varieties: Burkett, Mahan and Stuart have all been replaced by better varieties. Given the time, space, effort and money you'll pour into your pecan, there's no reason to use these older types. At all costs avoid the variety Success, since it has developed a physiological disorder that keeps it from producing.

Pecan Variety Comparisons[1]

Pecans vary greatly, both in size and quality. Research to develop new pecan varieties takes many years of constant attention, as evidenced by the following chart.

Variety	Years tested before release	Year released	Number nuts per pound	Percent of nut that's kernel
Burkett	—	1901	46	57
Caddo	46	1968	60	58
Choctaw	13	1959	34	59
Desirable	28	1930	33	56
Mohawk	19	1965	33	60
Shawnee	19	1968	45	60
Sioux	19	1962	59	60
Stuart	—	1870	45	48
Wichita	19	1959	40	62

[1] *Pecan Culture*, Brison, F. B., Texas Pecan Growers Association, Drawer CC, College Station, Texas

PERSIMMONS

PEARS

PEACHES

PECANS

PERSIMMONS

Few fruit trees are as attractive in landscapes as oriental persimmons. Their dark green foliage turns bright colors in the fall, providing lovely combination with the orange-red ripening fruit. They're adapted to a variety of soils and climates, being suitable to almost all of the state. From a fruit standpoint, they're productive, tasty and nutritious.

Plant Size

Mature trees vary from 10 to 40 feet in height. Their growth habit is relatively upright and the trees can be spaced 15 to 25 feet apart.

Pollinator Needed?

Persimmons vary greatly in pollination requirements. Many varieties must have pollinator (See below). Seedless fruit will be produced by some varieties in the absence of cross-pollination.

Soil and Site

Persimmons will grow in most moderately deep, well drained soils.

Size to Buy

Bare-rooted: 3 to 4 feet tall; containers: 5-gallon.

When to Plant

Bare-rooted: winter. Container: anytime.

Training and Pruning

Prune bare-rooted trees back 50 percent immediately after planting. Little pruning will be required for container-grown trees following planting. Persimmons grow, by nature, into attractive trees. Prune to remove damaged or mis-directed growth. Otherwise, leave the trees alone.

Watering

Keep all persimmons well watered during prolonged periods of summer drought. Apply a layer of compost or straw as mulch under the trees. Fruit drop will occur when trees are allowed to get dry.

Fertilizing

Feed established trees with a complete and balanced plant food such as 12-12-12, one pound per inch of trunk diameter, in early spring, before growth starts. Water heavily immediately after fertilizing.

Pest Control

One of persimmons' big selling points is that few insects and diseases bother them. About the only common one is the fall tent caterpillar, which can be removed physically before it damages the plant extensively. You can also spray to control it, using either malathion or zolone, with 2 or 3 drops of liquid detergent added to help the spray penetrate into the web.

Harvest

Persimmons, being very attractive fruit, add a great deal of interest to any landscape. Fortunately, leaving them on the tree past the first frost also helps diminish their puckering effect. You can wait until after the first frost or freeze to harvest your persimmons. The exposure to cold won't hurt them.

Varieties

EUREKA Medium-sized tomato-shaped red fruit. Small tree, self-fruitful. Excellent quality fruit. Most widely grown variety in Texas.

FUYU Medium-sized flattened red fruit of good quality. Self-fruitful and can be used, if desired, to pollinate all other varieties.

HACHIYA Large heart-shaped seedless orange-red type. Trees are upright and vigorous. Excellent landscape tree.

TAMOPAN Large orange flattened fruit. Excellent landscape variety. Largest tree of all Japanese persimmons.

TANE-NASHI Medium-sized heart-shaped seedless orange fruit. Tree is vigorous, upright. Good in landscapes.

PLUMS

Plums are among the most productive and easiest of all Texas tree fruit crops. The trees are compact and the showy white blooms, in early spring, make plums attractive for use in the landscape. The fruit is tasty and can be used either fresh or in jellies.

Plant Size

Mature plum trees are 10 to 15 feet tall, with spread of 12 to 18 feet. Space the trees 15 to 18 feet apart.

Pollinator Needed?

Advisable. See variety listing.

Soil and Site

Plums are quite tolerant of a variety of soils. Good drainage, however, is essential.

Size to Buy

Bare-rooted: 3 to 4 feet; container: 5-gallon.

When to Plant

Bare-rooted: winter. Container: anytime.

Training and Pruning

First Year: Aim to train plums much as you would peaches, to a vase shape with an open center that admits sunlight to the ripening fruit.

Begin training the tree at planting. Aim to remove 50 percent of the top growth of bare-rooted trees at planting. If the main stem is taller than 27 inches, top it at that level. Select 3 or 4 branches and train them to become the tree's scaffold system. Ideally they should each emerge from a different side of the tree. Allow the scaffold branches to develop at their own rate the first year. Remove all other branches that develop.

Subsequent Years: Once your plums have developed a strong scaffold system you must remove 25 to 35 percent of their top growth each year. Concentrate on strongly vertical shoots and limbs that rub or compete for sunlight. Prune above buds that face away from the center of the tree, to encourage more lateral growth. All major pruning of plums should be saved for mid-winter.

Watering

Keep plants well watered, particularly as fruit is developing. Water as needed throughout the year during periods of extended dry weather.

Fertilizing

Apply a complete and balanced fertilizer such as 12-12-12, one pound per inch of trunk diameter in early spring. Water thoroughly after feeding.

Pest Control

Peach tree borer: Apply borer spray to prevent borer invasion. See peach pest controls for details.

Plum curculio: This worm burrows through fruit, virtually ruining it. Control with malathion or zolone with sprayings starting while buds are showing color, again when three-fourths of petals have fallen and repeatedly on 10 to 14-day intervals until two weeks before harvest.

Bacterial stem canker: Jelly-like sap oozes from lesions along stems. No chemicals offer much help. Prune out diseased wood and keep tree as vigorous as possible. Prune and thin fruit as recommended to reduce drain on plant.

Bacterial leaf spot: Causes leaves to develop "shot-hole" effect in spring. Control by spraying with zineb as buds are breaking and again on 7 to 10-day intervals throughout spring. Plant resistant varieties.

Harvest

For best flavor, leave fruit on tree until it becomes slightly soft when squeezed. Fruit will continue to ripen for several days following harvest if picked slightly prematurely.

Varieties

BRUCE Large red plum, commonly used in commercial plantings. Productive variety used for fresh eating and, especially, for jams. Requires variety Methley as pollinator. Suited to northern three-fourths of Texas. Very early variety, ripens late May. (Zones A-F.)

METHLEY Medium-sized deep purple plum with red flesh. Excellent both fresh and in jams. Self-pollinating, can also be used to pollinate other varieties. Adapted to northern three-fourths of Texas. Ripens early season. (Zones A-E; Northern half of F.)

MORRIS Very large, bright red plum with red flesh throughout. Good flavor and high sugar content. Fruit retains high quality for extended period. Introduced by Texas A&M University. Increasingly popular, an excellent variety. Cross-pollination advisable. Adapted to northern half of state. Ripens late June to early July. (Zones A-D.)

OZARK PREMIER Large yellow and red fruit with yellow flesh. Excellent flavor. Tree is moderately productive. Self-pollinating. Suited to northern half of state. Ripens late season. (Zones A-D; Northern half of E.)

POMEGRANATES

Pomegranates are an unusual fruit, almost completely filled with seeds. The fruit comes wrapped in a leathery covering which must be peeled away. For those who enjoy their unusual flavor and texture, pomegranates are an easily grown fruit crop. Even if you don't care for the fruit, the plant is an outstanding large deciduous landscaping shrub. The bloom is attractive in late spring and the fruit is colorful in late summer and fall. Fruitless ornamental types are even available.

Plant Size

Mature fruiting pomegranates can attain heights of 8 to 14 feet. Since the plants are relatively upright, they can be spaced 8 to 10 feet apart in rows.

Pollinator Needed?

No.

PLUMS

STRAWBERRIES

POMEGRANATES

Soil and Site
Pomegranates are adapted to almost any type of soil so long as it is well drained. In the northern portions of Texas they may benefit from protection from north wind.

Size to Buy
Bare-rooted: 18 to 24 inches; container: 1 or 5-gallon.

When to Plant
Bare-rooted: late winter. Container: anytime (avoid late fall and winter plantings in northern half of state).

Training and Pruning
No special attention will be needed. Allow plants to grow into full shrubs. Prune as needed to repair damage.

Watering
Pomegranates endure heat and drought well, but your plants will do better kept moist at all times. Water slowly and deeply.

Fertilizing
Apply a complete and balanced fertilizer such as 12-12-12 in early spring, with a second application in early summer (1 to 2 pounds/inch of trunk diameter/application).

Pest Control
Almost no insects or diseases bother pomegranates, either plant or fruit.

Harvest
Pick fruit after it has developed rich red coloration, generally late summer and fall. Will hold at peak of maturity for several weeks on bush. Harvest before fruit splits (accelerated by excessive soil moisture).

Variety
"Wonderful" is most common variety available. (Zones B-G.)

STRAWBERRIES

Most of the fruit crops we grow here in Texas are produced on trees. Strawberries are one tiny stronghold among them. They're low growing, ground hugging sources of sheer delight. And, in addition to producing some fantastic fruit, they're also attractive when used as ground covers in landscaping.

Plant Size
Strawberries occupy little garden space for the yield they return. Depending on the growing system used, plants will be set 12 to 18 inches apart.

Pollinator Needed?
No. Strawberries are self-fruitful.

Soil and Site
Strawberries do best in a raised, well-drained planting mix. Ideally it should be half sand, one-fourth peat moss, well-rotted compost or shredded bark soil conditioner and one-fourth native soil. To insure drainage it should be raised 4 to 6 inches above the surrounding grade. If weeds, nematodes or soil-borne diseases are a known problem, the bed should be fumigated

with vapam 3 to 4 weeks prior to planting. Incorporate a complete and balanced fertilizer such as 12-12-12, 1 to 2 pounds per 50 square feet of bed space before planting.

Since strawberries grow so low to the ground, and because they flower quite early, you should be sure they're planted in an area with good air circulation to lessen the likelihood of frost damage. Full sun is best, though plants will tolerate 2 or 3 hours of afternoon shade.

Strawberries can also be grown in special pots, called "strawberry jars," tubs, pyramids and other containers. Use the same general soil mix, but be prepared to water and fertilize container plants much more frequently than you do plants in the ground. They may also require protection from hard freezes.

Size to Buy

You will be buying clumps of small bare-rooted transplants or small potted plants. Depending on the cropping system you choose you will need to buy your transplants either in fall or very early spring. Buy only from a reputable nurseryman, or from one of the mail-order houses that specialize in strawberries. The dealer should guarantee his plants to be true to variety and free of insects, diseases and nematodes. Don't use transplants given to you by well-meaning friends, since they're likely to be infested with pest problems.

When to Plant

Because of our great temperature variations, Texas is divided into two strawberry cropping systems.

If you live in the southern third of the state you'll want to grow your plants by the annual system, planting in October and early November (harvest the following spring).

If you're in the northern two-thirds, use the matted row system, setting the plants in late January or February (harvest 14 months later).

Training and Pruning

Annual System: Build a bed 42 inches wide and at least 6 inches deep. Set plants 12 inches apart in two rows down the center of the planting bed. Since plants are being set in late fall, runners will not be freely produced. Any that do develop should be pinched off.

Keep plants well watered and mulch with compost, pine needles or dried grass clippings. Allow all fruit to develop the following spring. In spite of your temptations to save the plants for years, you'll get the best production by discarding the plants after harvest and replanting elsewhere in your garden the following fall.

Matted Row System: Because winters are too cold and too long, gardeners in the northern two-thirds of Texas should use this technique. Start with the same bed size and amendments as described for the annual system. Set plants (late winter) 18 inches apart in a straight row down the center of the bed. As the plants begin to grow, select five runners 8 to 10 inches long and peg them down in a regular pattern. Train the growth into a solid mat 20 inches wide. Mulching will help retain soil moisture as well as retarding weed growth.

Pick all flower buds off the plants the first spring. Let all buds develop the second year, for harvesting in April and early May. Though commercial growers will generally remove the plants after the first bearing season, you can leave the plants in the ground as long as they're productive. Generally you'll see the yield dropping off sharply by the third or fourth year, at which time you need to have another bed elsewhere in the garden coming along, so that you can remove the original planting.

Watering

Strawberries need moisture, yet drainage is also important. Use a drip irrigation system to supply the needed water to the beds. Water regularly, particularly as fruit is developing. Protect your plants against heat damage by watering deeply and frequently.

Fertilizing

In addition to the fertilizer you apply at planting, apply a complete and balanced fertilizer such as 12-12-12, one pound per 50 square feet of bed space, just prior to growth starting in the spring. This applies to either cropping system, annual or matted row.

Pest Control

Fungal leaf spots: disfigure leaves, especially during cool, wet weather. Control at first sighting with benomyl, captan or other general-purpose fungicide. Do not apply water by overhead irrigation if leaf diseases occur.

Mites: near-microscopic pests that feed on leaves causing them to lose dark green color, turn brown and crisp. Apply kelthane or other miticide to both top and bottom leaf surfaces.

Soil-borne diseases, nematodes: should these serious problems develop it's probably best just to replant elsewhere in your garden with certified clean stock from one of the nation's strawberry specialists. Destroy the existing planting and fumigate the entire bed with vapam. Don't plant strawberries back into the area for several years.

Harvest

Allow all strawberries to ripen fully on the plants. If birds are a problem install bird netting over the garden. Sevin dust or sevin baits can be used to discourage slugs, snails and pillbugs from feeding on the fruit. Apply the sevin on the ground, away from the fruit itself. Your harvest season will begin 3 to 4 weeks after the last frost and will continue for 3 to 6 weeks, depending on the varieties you've planted.

Varieties

For Annual System (Southern half of E; F-G.)

SEQUOIA Very large, with outstanding color and flavor. Fruit is too soft for shipping required by commercial production, but is outstanding for home gardens.

TIOGA Productive large berry of excellent quality, though plant is not resistant to leaf spot diseases.

For Matted Row System (Zones A-D; Northern half of E.)

CARDINAL Medium-sized fruit of excellent quality, texture. Resistant to stem diseases. From University of Arkansas.

POCAHONTAS Large berries, good texture, tart flavor. Vigorous grower, resistant to leaf spot diseases.

SUNRISE Medium-sized berry. Resistant to several stem, leaf diseases. Tolerant of heat, low humidity and, to a degree, drought.

Note: Everbearing varieties such as Gem and Ozark Beauty may be used in West Texas and the South and High Plains, where standard varieties are erratic in performance.

WALNUTS (Black Walnuts)

Black walnuts are large growing native trees well adapted to a variety of soils and climates. Planting of improved variety Thomas gives quicker, better production. Trees are generally sold bare-rooted from specialty mail-order nurseries. Buy 3 to 4-foot size and plant during dormant winter season. Allow 30 to 40 feet between trees. Train much as you would a pecan, to a central trunk and strong side branches. Water regularly during the growing season. Fertilize in early spring with a high-nitrogen fertilizer similar to what is used on pecans. Insects and diseases will attack walnuts, though less commonly than they attack pecans. Controls will be the same as for pecans. Gather nuts as soon as they have fallen from the tree. (Eastern half of C-E.)

Chapter 11

Vegetable Gardening

A trend over the last several years has been to grow much of what our families eat. That's just as important here in Texas as it is anywhere else. Gardening here, though, varies from other parts of the country. Ask any local grower . . . someone who's been at it for more than a year or two. Our soils, rainfall (or lack of it), late freezes and blazing summers all add to the challenge.

This chapter presents the basic guidelines you'll need to succeed with Texas vegetable gardening. You'll find planting tips, care suggestions and harvesting pointers. You'll find specific guidelines on particular crops, including pest problems.

Read it, and may your garden grow well! Who knows? You may end up on the gardening bandwagon with the millions of other Texans who've found gardening a great form of family relaxation, exercise and "getting back to nature."

SELECTING THE SITE
FOR YOUR VEGETABLE GARDEN

It's not always easy to find the right spot for a vegetable garden, particularly in today's more cramped urban lifestyle.

Luckily, though, it needn't take acres. Many vegetables, as you'll see in the following pages, are actually quite ornamental. Incorporate them into the landscape. To utilize empty patio space, put some in containers. Grow them up fences and walls, on wires and trellises. Or do it the conventional way: stake out a plot and start planting.

Do consider a few basics however:

• Full sun is best, particularly for fruit-producing vegetables (such as tomatoes and beans). Leaf and root crops can succeed in partial shade.

• All vegetables require good drainage. Plant in raised beds. Use railroad ties, masonry or similar retaining structure to elevate your planting site six to 12 inches. You'll be able to control the soil mix better, plus you'll provide perfect soil drainage, a must in vegetable gardening.

• Good air circulation diminishes disease problems.

• Your site should be convenient to the house and to the water faucet.

• Since vegetable gardens aren't attractive year 'round, you might want to locate yours in the "out-back" . . . out back of the fence, or out back by the garage.

How Large Should Your Garden Be?

Wondering how much space you should devote to your garden? Well, take the words of a weeder. Start small! You can always increase the size following initial successes. Start too big and you may get discouraged.

Avoid the space gobblers if your gardening area is limited. Corn and melons take too much room to be space-effective in small urban gardens.

Want two to three times the garden space at little additional expense or effort? It's simple: keep the place planted. Don't let it lay idle. When you're through with one crop, plant another. Follow cool season crops with late spring plantings of the warm season vegetables (for example, beans after lettuce and spinach). Interplant fast-growing crops such as lettuce and radishes between slower growing vegetables such as tomatoes and peppers. And plant a fall garden . . . all in the same area. Rotate your crops from one part of the garden to another to prevent accumulations of soil-borne insects and, especially, diseases.

Garden plantings change with the seasons. Keep your space planted and productive.

Spring

Summer

Fall

WHICH CROPS TO GROW?

When you're choosing your crops, consider these:
• Plant vegetables your family enjoys. There's no point in growing something no one will eat.
• Plant crops that give the best return for the area and time required.
• Grow types you have trouble finding . . . vegetables you enjoy but can't buy at the grocery.
• Plant types adapted to your area. Don't waste space on vegetables with limited productivity in Texas (such as rhubarb, celery, large tomatoes). And be sure you're planting at prime time. Give a vegetable the wrong climate and it'll be gone in a flash.
• Try the All America Selections varieties. They're varieties that have been tested all across America, including gardens in Texas. They've compared very favorably with other varieties of their type, and you can be reasonably sure they'll succeed for you.

TIME TO MATURITY

30 to 60 Days	60 to 80 Days	80 Days or More
Beets	Broccoli	Brussels Sprouts
Bush Beans	Bush Lima Beans	Bulbing Onions
Leaf Lettuce	Carrots	Cabbage
Mustard	Cherry Tomatoes	Cantaloupe
Radishes	Chinese Cabbage	Cauliflower
Spinach	Cucumbers	Eggplant
Summer Squash	English Peas	Garlic
Turnips	Green Onions	Irish Potatoes
	Kohlrabi	Parsnip
	Okra	Pole Lima Beans
	Parsley	Pumpkins
	Peppers	Sweet Potatoes
	Pole Snap Beans	Tomatoes
	Sweet Corn	Watermelons
	Swiss Chard	Winter Squash

GETTING THE GARDEN READY . . . SOIL PREPARATION

We've said it before: good soil is the foundation of good gardening. How well your plantings do depends to a large part on the type of soil preparation you give them.

Recipe for a productive garden plot . . .

1) Start with a sunny location with good surface and sub-surface drainage.

2) Have the soil tested through your county Extension office.

3) Incorporate a three to five-inch layer of organic matter (peat moss, rotted compost, shredded bark) and, if you're working with a clay soil, include a one to two-inch layer of washed brick sand.

4) Rototill to a depth of eight to 12 inches.

5) Rake out all rocks, roots and other debris. Re-till as needed, until all soil clumps are no larger than golf balls.

6) If nematodes, weeds or soil-borne insects and diseases may be or have been a problem, fumigate the area with vapam three to four weeks prior to planting (most effective in warm soils).

7) Cultivate the soil frequently through the growing season and incorporate additional organic matter every year or two.

3.

4.

TEXAS TIP

Rotate your vegetable crop planting sites. It's no secret our state has more than its share of soil-borne diseases and nematodes. By planting in different parts of your garden each year you'll lessen the chance of pest build-up. For example, plant lettuce where tomatoes were last year, beans where the radishes were, and so on.

5.   **6.**

DIRECT SEEDING OR TRANSPLANTS?

Some crops can be planted directly from seed into the garden. Others really should be started elsewhere, under more protected conditions before being planted out into the ground.

Transplants offer some obvious advantages:

• Plants can be started earlier for quicker yields.

• Seeds may be too small for uniform sowing, or they may wash too deeply into freshly tilled soil. Soil may crust, causing small seedlings problems in germination.

• Young plants may be susceptible to soil-borne diseases and insects, including damping-off and cutworms.

Vegetables most commonly planted from started nursery transplants: tomatoes, peppers, eggplant, cabbage, onions, cauliflower, broccoli, Brussels sprouts and herbs. Also: lettuce, melons, cucumbers and others. Note, too, that some vegetables are planted from roots and stems: potatoes, sweet potatoes, asparagus.

Planting started transplants can reduce time to vegetable production by four to six weeks.

MOST COMMON QUESTION

"Can I save my vegetable seeds for another year?"

There are actually two answers to that. First, if you're talking about saving seeds from your current produce . . . like the seeds out of your tomatoes . . . you'd better be sure they're not from a hybrid variety (as opposed to an inbred type). Hybrids do not "come true" from seeds, that is, they don't reproduce the same variety.

If you're talking about storing excess seeds, you most definitely can. Keep them cool (40 to 45°F) and dry. Some types will last longer than others. You can expect five years or more from beets, cucumbers, eggplant, cantaloupe and tomatoes. Seeds you can store for three to five years include most of the cole crops (cabbage, broccoli, Brussels sprouts and cauliflowers), beans, lettuce, okra, peas, pepper, radishes, spinach, turnips and melons. Some seeds last but a year or two, incuding onions, parsley and corn.

If you're in doubt about the viability of a seed packet, moisten a paper towel and lay several seeds out on it. Fold it back to cover the seeds and keep it moist. Check back in seven to 10 days to see how many have sprouted. You can estimate germination percentages from that.

Getting It Growing

Vegetable seeds are packets of magic. One single seed can provide almost an entire meal, be it broccoli, corn or green beans. But that only happens if you get the seedling off to a good start. Plant it carefully and help it along.

Seeding Techniques:

Seed can be planted directly into garden. Large seeds can be placed singly.

Seed can also be spaced either with a mechanical seeder or simply by creasing the packet and tapping the seed out directly in place, one seed at a time.

Large gardens can be planted with specialized tools. Note various discs for different sizes of seeds.

Seeds vary greatly in size. However, as a rough rule of green thumb, plant all seeds two to three times as deep as the seed is thick. Use a loose garden soil to cover seeds.

Plant the seed two to three times as close as you ultimately want the plants to stand. Then, once the seedlings are up and actively growing, thin them to the desired spacing. Don't neglect this or you'll seriously reduce your crops' yield.

Seeding into narrow bands of commercially prepared potting soil or vermiculite can hold moisture better and help seedlings establish root systems faster.

MOST COMMON QUESTION

"My seed packets say I should plant some types of vegetables in 'hills.' Are these actually raised spots in my garden? Just what is a hill?"

That's a misnomer, at least for Texas conditions. Planting seed atop small hills results in slow starts because of a lack of available water . . . it just drains away too fast. Raised planting beds are a good idea for most parts of Texas, but only if the entire root area is raised uniformly, for example, by using railroad ties around the entire garden. Basically, you'll want to plant seed in rows, as outlined in the crop descriptions that follow.

FERTILIZING THE GARDEN

When you consider the whole scheme of vegetable crops, you find that we eat every plant part.

We eat roots of carrots and radishes, stems of asparagus, onions and potatoes, leaves of lettuce, cabbage and spinach, flowers of broccoli, fruit of tomatoes, squash and watermelons and seeds of peas and corn.

That means that we have to consider each of our crops' fertilizer needs individually. Get in the habit of reading the fertilizer bag. Look for the three-number analysis. It's your guarantee of what that bag contains.

High-nitrogen fertilizers — If the first number of the analysis is larger than the other two, you can expect that plant food to stimulate leaf and stem growth. Use a high-nitrogen fertilizer on leafy vegetables.

High-phosphorus fertilizers — If the middle number of the analysis is larger than the other two, you can expect that plant food to stimulate roots, flowers and fruit. That means you'd use a high-phosphate fertilizer on all root and fruit crops.

Potassium — The third number in the fertilizer analysis, improves hardiness to heat and cold. It should be present in any fertilizer you apply to the garden.

Complete and balanced fertilizers — If you're growing a variety of vegetables it may be more expedient for you to apply a plant food that contains relatively equal amounts of each of the three elements. Obviously, you won't get good leaf growth in leafy vegetables without a good root system, and conversely, you won't get good flowers and fruit if your plants don't have good leaves.

There are many good general-purpose vegetable garden fertilizers on the market today. Each will give suggestions for use and directions of application. With your soil test results in one hand, fertilize your vegetables as needed.

MOST COMMON QUESTION

"How often should I fertilize my vegetable garden?"

That varies a lot with the crop, the soil and the season. If the soil is loose and well drained, or if it's been raining a great deal (and washing fertilizer minerals out of the soil), or if your plants are large and actively growing, you may need to feed them every three to four weeks. At other times a five to six-week interval may be sufficient.

Ways to Feed Vegetables

1) Broadcast fertilizer over entire garden, generally done by hand. Weigh fertilizer and apply carefully for uniform feeding. Keep off foliage. Water thoroughly afterwards.

2) Side dressing of fertilizer in rows along plantings assures its proximity to plants' roots. Be careful not to apply in excess or roots will be damaged. Soak thoroughly afterwards.

3) Place fertilizer in sunken pots or gallon-sized nursery containers. Apply one or two tablespoons, then fill container with water.

4) Feed through injector system, either using siphoning proportioner or special drip irrigation equipment.

1.

2.

3.

4.

MOST COMMON QUESTION

"Should I fertilize my garden when I plant the seeds?"

If your soil test report shows nitrogen or phosphorus to be extremely lacking in your garden plot, you could apply an appropriate fertilizer prior to planting. Be careful, though, to keep it away from the planting row so you don't burn the sensitive new roots as they develop. Otherwise, wait until the plants have been up and growing for two to three weeks.

MEETING THE WATER NEEDS

Water is the chief constituent of most vegetable crops. Without it your garden soon fails. Yet there's a delicate balance between proper and improper watering.

Signs of improper watering . . .
too wet:
• wilting, even though soil remains moist, leaves are yellowed over entire plant
too dry:
• wilting, soil dry to touch;
• scorched leaves, generally from tips or margins (points farthest from water source) inward;
• small fruit, often cracked;
• bitter or hot-flavored produce

Tomato leaves roll in water stress conditions.

Blossom-End Rot results from fluctuations in soil moisture levels.

MOST COMMON QUESTION

"How often do I water my vegetables?

Water your garden when the soil surface is dry to the touch. Watch for early signs of moisture stress, especially slight wilting, then soak the soil thoroughly. Don't ever try to do it on a calendar basis . . . the intervals will change with the seasons, and as your crops mature.

Ways to Water Vegetables

Run hose slowly in furrows or basins, saturating root zone around plants.

Use drip, or trickle, irrigation to supersaturate soil in small patches. Roots will grow toward the wet soil.

Fill one-gallon nursery cans sunk flush in ground.

Use overhead irrigation, but only when absolutely essential. Keeping foliage wet promotes disease.

MOST COMMON QUESTION

"Why do my tomato plants wilt? They keep growing, and I know they're moist enough."

Tomato plants wilt frequently, often for no apparent reason. Commonly, though, it's because they've been exposed to several days of cool, rainy weather. When the sun finally returns, the tomatoes wilt in the heat of the afternoon. If they spring back once the sun goes down you have no cause for concern. Be sure you keep them moist.

At the other end of the spectrum, no garden plant is more susceptible to over-watering than tomatoes. Let them stand in waterlogged soil for two or three days and you can expect them to fade. You'll likely even see hundreds of roots trying to develop along their main stems. Open up their furrows . . . anything to eliminate the standing water.

Nematodes are also a possibility. Check roots for signs of knots or other abnormalities, or have soil tested for nematodes through county Extension office. Fumigate with vapam between crops, and plant successive tomato crops in another part of your garden. Plant nematode-resistant types.

RULE OF GREEN THUMB: Don't apply chemicals to food crops until you read the entire product label. Once I received a call from a man who used roach spray to kill bugs on his crepe myrtles. He not only killed the crepe myrtles, but also the tomatoes behind them. There are proper controls for pests that can be applied safely to produce. Know them *before* you spray your crops. (See details at end of this chapter.)

MULCHING PAYS OFF

Nowhere will mulches do more for your plantlife than in your vegetable garden. Consider these advantages:

Mulches conserve moisture for better quality, tastier produce; retard weed growth, reduce its competition;

improve soil as they decay (organic mulches);

reduce soil temperature extremes, particularly helpful in summertime heat;

and reduce chance of erosion.

So what types of mulches are the best? Basically, any type of coarse organic mulch. The list includes: well-rotted compost, shredded bark, dried grass clippings, shredded leaves, pine needles, and even newspaper or specially treated paper mulch.

Black polyethylene plastic makes a fine mulch, particularly in controlling weeds. However, it retains all the water that penetrates its seams. Watering becomes a much more difficult task. (Be sure you provide good drainage below it.) You also need to cover it with some other type of organic mulch to hold it in place. Left uncovered, it soaks up the sun's heat (a decided advantage in early spring, when the soil is cool, but a drawback in the summer). Overlap it by four to six inches to keep weeds from growing up and through it. Remove it by late spring to keep the soil from overheating.

Mulches are invaluable in gardening, resulting in increased quantity and quality of produce.

Start mulching early in each crop's life. Once your plants are four to six inches tall you need to start putting the mulch up around their stems. Leave the mulch in place as long as the crop is still actively growing.

PROTECTING YOUR PLANTINGS FROM COLD

Late spring and early fall frosts are too often a trademark of Texas vegetable gardening. Such a shame, too, because it doesn't have to ruin your plantings. There are things you can do to protect those tender plants . . . to extend their productive season:

Hotcaps retain warmth of sun, allow it to be released from soil inside canopy during nighttime hours; also keep frost from settling on tender parts of new plants.

Cut-off milk cartons provide same benefits. Use dowel sticks and plastic twist-ties to hold securely in place.

Spraying plants with mist during periods of near-freezing weather can protect flowers and foliage from light frosts.

Wrap plants in quilts or burlap to protect against early fall frosts. Do not use plastic film since it provides limited protection from cold, and absorbs heat too rapidly the following morning.

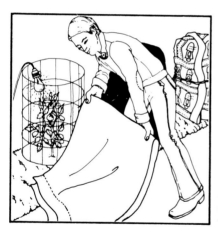

Light bulb (60-100 watt) placed under cover will provide one or two degrees' worth of protection during light freezes.

GOOD EATS AND GOOD LOOKS

Major league managers like players who can handle more than one position. They call them "utility" ball players.

Well, turn the tables to gardening. How'd you like a "utility" vegetable? A plant with two purposes?

That's the way it is with this list ... plants that are great both for eating and looking. All are vegetable plants that can also add to the landscape. Consider most any leaf lettuce (especially variety "Ruby"), Swiss chard (especially the variety "Rhubarb"), red cabbage, also flowering cabbage and flowering kale, most peppers, Tiny Tim tomatoes, purple kohlrabi and most of the herbs. To a plant, they're landscaping winners!

Purple kohlrabi and Rhubarb Swiss chard make attractive twosome, good both as landscape plants and food crops.

DATES OF FIRST AND LAST FROSTS

The average dates of the first and last frosts for an area are two of the most important climatic factors a gardener contends with. Find your county on the map below and plan your garden activities accordingly. For example, if you're starting your own tomato transplants indoors for the spring, figure back four to six weeks to determine the sowing date. For your fall garden, check the variety's description to determine how many days are required from planting to first harvest. Allow an extra four to six weeks for peak production. *To illustrate:*

1. If the average first frost date for your area is November 15 . . .

2. And if you're growing a tomato variety that requires 70 days to first harvest (need to add 10 to 15 days because of fall's cooler weather) . . .

3. Then you would, figuring backwards, have to plant a vigorous transplant of that variety by mid-August just to pick the first fruit. But, let's say you wanted more than just the one fruit for your effort . . .

4. Allow an extra eight weeks for production, and that brings your planting date back to mid-to-late June.

5. By knowing your crops, their cold tolerances, their time requirements and your local climate, you can soon figure back for all other plantings.

Know average date of first frost for your area (see map).

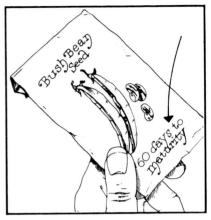

Each seed package will tell you how many days will be required for first harvest.

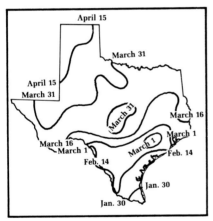

Average date of last killing frost in spring.

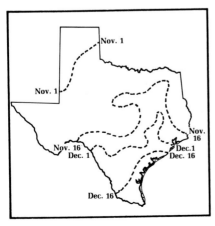

Average date of first killing frost in fall.

Count backwards from first frost date, allowing extra eight to 10 weeks for maximum production, to determine planting date.

Fall Garden Guidelines

All the talk about figuring the proper planting date for a fall garden opens up an important subject. Most Texans, unfortunately, still think that spring is the only time to garden.

TEXAS TIP

Fall may just be the best gardening season in Texas.

Luckily, that knowledge is spreading. There are some advantages to growing your plants in fall's cooler weather:
- Produce matures over prolonged period, for sustained production.
- Produce ripens in cooler weather, suffers less from sunburning and sunscalding.
- Color, texture and flavor are all at their peaks in fall weather.
- There are fewer insects and diseases in the fall.

GETTING KIDS INTO GARDENING

Whether you have a son or a daughter, there's something beautifully special about a child with a garden. While watching the seed-planting ritual, a youngster seems to suddenly discover the meaning of life. Gardens teach responsibility and patience. Here are some tips to make your youngster's garden a hit.

Start modestly. For the first year, 50 to 100 square feet will do. You can always expand later.

Plant the varieties your child likes best, but be sure your selections are reasonably dependable. Beans, lettuce, squash and tomatoes are all good.

Let the child paint a sign: "Brian's Garden," "Todd's Tomatoes," "Erin's Area" and so on. Put it right in the middle, where everyone can see.

Help your child with the basics of good gardening: Soils and seeds, planting and caring, picking and pest control.

Include a few flowers. Periwinkles, marigolds, moss roses and zinnias are all dependable.

The flowers of tomorrow are in the seeds of today. Garden with a child today and you'll improve his or her life forever.

GROW AS A GROUP!

Estimates are that 10 to 20 percent of the gardens in America are community gardens. Yet, here in Texas, the figure is much smaller.

Folks in other parts of the country have learned to save money, energy and space by gardening together. Parcels of five to 25 acres are set aside. In most of the gardens the land is plowed with farm equipment, the whole area at once. It's then marked off and leased to urban gardeners who match the plot size to their time and ambition. Seed, fertilizer and chemicals may be bought in bulk by the organization to lower the total cost to participants. Classes may even be taught.

We Texans could learn from their lessons. Community gardening is a great idea. Let folks at the office, boy scout troops, area apartment dwellers — whatever the group — garden together.

Community gardening utilizes otherwise useless space, provides folks who otherwise couldn't garden, because of space limitations, to "get back to nature."

CONTAINERIZED GARDENING

If you have room for a flowerpot, you have room to vegetable garden! The days of the two-acre farm garden are long gone for urban homeowners. Today, it's often most practical simply to grow vegetables in pots.

It's a great trend, too, since container gardening offers some decided advantages:

• They're totally portable. You can move the plants in and out of the sunshine. You can move them into protection from frost. You can get them out of strong winds.

• You have complete control over the soil mix. You can provide exactly what your plants will require. You have almost complete control over the plants' environment.

• Container gardens take little ground space. You can hang plants from the walls or grow them in baskets. You can put them on the patio and turn it into a regular produce market.

Pick the Best Pot

Both clay and plastic pots work well with vegetable plantings. For that matter, you can even use old nursery containers, bushel baskets and old trash cans.

The important thing isn't the type of pot so much as whether it has a drainage hole. If it doesn't you must drill one immediately, to prevent waterlogged soils and accumulations of soluble mineral salts.

The pot should also be properly sized. It's better to repot a plant periodically rather than going directly to the large sizes. Over-potted plants have a hard time coping with the large volumes of soil. It's too easy to over-water.

Soil Mix Most Crucial

Believe it or not, your soil isn't the greatest for gardening! You're better off to buy a commercially prepared nursery potting soil (be sure it's relatively coarse — particles larger than b-b's) or mix one yourself. Start with raw materials like peat moss, perlite, vermiculite and sand . . . just like the commercial growers do. Mix your own soil.

Beginning Blend for An Artificial Soil Mix

50% organic matter, at least half of that peat moss, the remainder finely shredded bark or compost;

25% perlite or vermiculite for drainage and aeration;

25% washed builders' sand for weight. (Modify the blend as desired . . . you'll gain from experience.)

Feeding and Watering

Plants grown in containers have more limited soil reservoirs, so they need more frequent watering and feeding.

It's entirely possible that you'll have to water these plants daily, maybe even twice daily, during the summer. And when you do water them, soak them thoroughly.

Use a complete and balanced plant food for most of your container plantings. Select one with trace elements . . . the things your soil-less potting mix won't be able to provide. There are several types available. Some are water-soluble or liquid and should be used each time that you water. Others are in timed-release form as capsules or stakes.

Best Container Vegetables

If you're looking for the most productive crops to grow in your container garden, choose from tomatoes (five-gallon or bushel basket minimum container size); peppers, eggplant, cabbage and cucumbers (three to five gallon size minimum); lettuce, onions, radishes, carrots, spinach and other smaller vegetables (eight to 12-inch pot minimum). Herbs are also ideal in container gardens.

MOST COMMON QUESTION

"What vegetables can I grow in pots indoors during the winter?"

Remember that leaf and root crops do best in shady spots outdoors. For indoors, I'd suggest you stay with leafy herbs, lettuce, spinach, endive and other similar plants. If you have a really bright garden room you might try some of the miniature tomatoes, peppers and cucumbers, among others.

HERB GARDENING

Herbs have been in our gardens almost longer than bugs have! Fact is, they predate many of the common vegetables we grow today. We grow them for fragrance, for flavors and just for plain fun.

If you made a list of all the plants we call "herbs," you'd need several sheets of paper. Just about any plant that has flavorful roots, stems, leaves, flowers or seeds is grown somewhere for seasoning or for use as a perfume. Some types are universally grown, while others are of localized interest.

Where to Grow Herbs

Most herbs grow best in partial shade ... with protection from the afternoon sun. Almost all types require good drainage. Other than that, you can include herbs with almost any of your plantings. Some types grow large and unruly. They'll need the space of the back row of your vegetable garden. Others are far more refined and can even be grown in flower beds, patio pots and hanging baskets. Use parsley to edge beds and plant chives in the rock garden. Mint is great in moist, shady spots and sage is the perfect contrast to evergreen ground covers. You can use herbs almost anywhere. Just one suggestion ... use them where people are. Let them get in the way, where folks will have to brush against them to get past.

Soil Preparation for Herbs

Herbs are no different than any other plant that you grow. They need a rich, loose, well-drained soil that's free of harmful diseases and competing weeds. If you're growing your herbs in pots or other containers, use one of the commercially prepared potting soils or mix your own. Use a combination of half Canadian sphagnum peat moss, one-fourth perlite or vermiculite and one-fourth washed brick sand. If you're planting the herbs in beds, incorporate a three to four-inch layer of peat moss, compost or shredded bark soil conditioner prior to planting. Fumigate the soil with vapam two to three weeks before planting.

Getting Herbs Started

Many of the more popular herbs are offered as small potted starter plants in the early spring. You can dig and divide many perennial types and you can start most annual types from seed. Many reseed themselves freely, coming back year after year.

Care During the Growing Season

For the best flavors and fragrances, keep your herbs growing. Water them whenever their soil is dry to the touch, and fertilize every six to eight weeks during the growing season with a complete and balanced plant food analysis. Watch for insects and diseases and treat as needed. Read and follow the label directions carefully.

Harvesting Herbs

Once your herbs are mature you'll want to preserve them for use in the off-season. Some types, like basil, dill, chives, parsley and tarragon, are better frozen. Cut healthy stems or leaves and tie a string around them. Rinse the leaves and pick out any dead or diseased ones. Then dip the bundles in boiling water for one minute. Hang onto the string so you can pull them back out. Rinse, then dry the leaves and pack them in freezer bags. Place them in the freezer as quickly as possible.

If you'd rather dry the leaves, cut them still attached to the stems. Gather them in bundles and tie them, then hang them upside down where air can circulate freely around them. Keep them out of direct sunlight. They'll be dry within a couple of weeks, at which time you can break them off and store them. Just keep them dark and dry until you use them.

If you're drying seeds, use frames that will hold the seeds and allow air to circulate. Make the frames square, six or eight inches on a side, and use window screen for the bottoms. Once the seeds have dried you can separate them from the unwanted leaf and stem parts by blowing gently across the frame. The heavier seeds will stay put, while the chaff will blow away.

Popular Herbs

As already stated, there are hundreds of herbs. Here are growing details on some of the more common types:

Basil Sweet basil is a short bushy annual plant grown for its leaves and small growing shoots. Both green and purple-leafed types are available. Keep plants' shoots pinched back to encourage full, bushy growth. Good in pots. Grow from seed or started transplants.

Chives These are small clumping perennials related to onions. Their foliage is harvested all season long, chopped and used as a flavorful topping to vegetables, meats and salads. It can also be dried and stored. Chives are exceptionally easy to grow, and are attractive additions to the landscape. Grow from started transplants.

Coriander Annual herb growing one to two feet. Plants can be harvested in 6 to 8-inch size, or leaves can be removed and used fresh or dried. Coriander is used to season sausage and other dishes.

Dill This is a large annual herb, grown both for its seeds and its foliage. Plant in rows three to four feet apart, with plants 12 to 18 inches apart in the rows. Best in full sun. Harvest by tying plastic bag over seed head before it reaches maturity. Grow from seed sown directly into garden.

Marjoram Tender perennial growing to one to two feet. Small oval light green leaves. Grow in full sun or afternoon shade, either from seeds or nursery transplants. Attractive in containers. Used in seasoning meats, salads and other dishes.

Mint There are several common types of mints grown in Texas gardens. Some are annuals and reseed freely, while the common spearmint is a shade-loving perennial. Does best in moist conditions. Harvest and use leaves fresh. Grow from transplants or from runners collected from established plants.

Oregano Medium-sized perennial (to two to three feet) grown for its leaves. Best used fresh, but can be dried. Keep plants pruned back to keep them compact. Grow from started nursery transplants or from divisions.

Parsley Attractive low-growing annual (will survive winter, but blooms second season), to one foot tall and wide. Good low border and container plant. Harvest leaves individually as plant becomes large enough to replenish the supply. Start from nursery transplants.

Rosemary Tender perennial (hardy in southern half of Texas) with attractive gray-green foliage and low spreading growth habit to two to four feet. Leaves are used in seasoning. Start from small nursery transplants. Sometimes available in one-gallon containers.

Sage Low growing sub-shrub to two to three feet tall. Gray-green foliage contrasts nicely with other green herbs and vegetables. Good in rock gardens, pots and along walks. Grown for its leaves. Start from nursery transplants, seed, cuttings or divisions.

Thyme Several types, all low perennials grown for their leaves. Attractive in pots and as low border plants. Grown from nursery transplants, cuttings and seeds.

VEGETABLE PLANTING GUIDE FOR TEXAS GARDENS

If you're excited about gardening, but need some particulars on a specific crop, check through the pages that follow. Arranged in alphabetical order, you'll find planting and how and when to harvest, tips for recommended varieties, plus control measures for insects and diseases. We've outlined, plant-by-plant, the cultural tricks to making them thrive here in Texas. You'll see a lot of similarities in the growing techniques . . . but watch out for the differences. They'll be subtle . . . and crucial!

Note: Under each vegetable listing you'll find planting rates and spacings. Some crops will show seeding rates, while others will refer to transplants, roots, sets and other means of starting plants. Decide how much space you can devote to the crop, then use these guides to determine how much to buy.

A seed packet ("pkt.") generally represents the smallest amount of seed of a particular variety that's offered for sale. Unless you have a particular love for that vegetable, or unless you intend to can or freeze large amounts of it, a seed packet will generally offer sufficient quantity for the average family's needs.

ASPARAGUS
plant on 18-inch centers
65 plants/100 feet

Increasingly popular vegetable. Quick-growing, attractive large plants with ferny foliage. Can be used as background plant for landscape beds or planted in rows along perimeter of garden . . . anywhere it can grow undisturbed for many years. Best suited for northern half of state, where colder winter weather allows longer dormant period. Resulting spears will be larger and of better quality than those produced in areas with longer growing season.

Asparagus is a perennial vegetable, planted in mid-to-late winter from bare-rooted 1 to 3-year-old roots. Buy a disease (rust) resistant variety such as Mary Washington, and be sure roots are fresh and moist. Plant as soon as possible to prevent drying. Depending on your family's tastes, 10 to 30 plants should provide generous harvests.

Prepare asparagus beds carefully, since your plants will be productive 10 to 20 years, perhaps even more. Prepare trenches 12 to 15 inches deep and 4 to 5 feet apart. Be sure adjacent soil and internal slope of trenches allow good drainage.

Prepare a planting soil consisting of at least 50 percent peat moss, compost or other organic matter. Put a 2-inch layer of the mix in the bottoms of the trenches. Place the new crowns on top of the mix, 18 inches apart in the rows. Be careful to spread the roots out evenly. Remove any that are damaged or decayed. Cover the crowns with 3 inches of the planting mix and water them thoroughly. As the shoots begin to grow, gradually fill the trenches, 2 to 3 inches of soil mix at a time until you've brought it back to the original grade.

Fertilize asparagus beds with a complete and balanced plant food twice per year: just before growth starts in the spring and again immediately after you complete harvesting. Keep plants well watered at all seasons. Mulching will help conserve moisture during summertime.

Harvest
New shoots will emerge in very early spring. Harvest regularly, using either special asparagus knife or sharp paring knife, when spears are 6 to 8 inches tall. No spears should be cut for first two years, regardless of age of original roots. Once plants are established spears can be harvested for 4 to 6 weeks each spring.

Following harvest, allow all growth to develop until the first frost of the fall. Once tops have frozen and turned yellow you can remove the old growth and apply additional mulch. If prolonged warm-weather growing season in South Texas keeps plants from going dormant in the fall, withhold water until tops have yellowed, then proceed as above.

Varieties
Mary Washington is most commonly available, also Waltham Washington.

BEANS
pkt. sows 25 to 35 feet
½ to 1 pound/100 feet

Ranking near the top in Texas garden popularity, beans are easy, even for young and beginning gardeners. They're productive, delicious and nutritious. Available in many types, sizes and colors, both as bush and vine types. Bush snap beans are among the easiest, limas are among the more difficult.

Warm season vegetables, beans should be planted 7 to 10 days after average date of last killing freeze. Earlier planting merely encourages seed rot. Make subsequent plantings on 2 to 3-week intervals until mid-spring. Fall plantings, particularly of bush types, also yield well.

Space rows 24 to 36 inches apart for bush types and 36 to 48 inches apart for pole beans. Plant seed 1 to 1½ inches deep, 2 to 3 inches apart in rows (thin seedlings to stand 4 to 5 inches apart in rows). Soil must be loose and non-crusting, so seedlings can emerge easily.

Though beans, like other legumes, have nitrogen-fixing bacteria which allow them to provide their own supply of usable nitrogen, the plants will still respond well to an application of a complete and balanced garden fertilizer every 4 to 6 weeks. Keep plants well watered, particularly as they begin to come into production. Avoid water stresses especially while plants are blooming.

Problems
INSECTS
Aphids: feed on tender new growth (diazinon, malathion)

Mexican bean beetle: feed on plants (malathion)

Spider mites: turn plants tan, mottled and crisp (kelthane)

DISEASES

Powdery mildew: causes dusty growth on leaves (control with benomyl)

Fungal leaf spots: several types attack beans, cause irregular brown spots (control with benomyl, captan, maneb)

Nematodes: a frequent problem of beans (control with vapam fumigation between crops)

Harvest

Pick all types of snap beans when the pods are slightly more than half their mature length (generally 4 to 6 inches long) and before the seeds start their rapid swelling. Do not allow overly mature beans to hang on the vine or they'll cause a rapid decline in production.

Varieties

Bush Snap Beans: Contender, Topcrop, Tendercrop, Executive, Blue Lake Bush, among others.

Pole Snap Beans: Kentucky Wonder, Blue Lake, Romano.

Bush Wax Beans: Golden Wax, Black Wax.

Bush Lima Beans: Jackson Wonder, Henderson, Fordhook.

Pole Lima Beans: Florida Speckled.

Dry Beans (allow to hang on plants until dried): Horticultural, Pinto, Red Kidney.

Southern Pea (actually types of beans, grown in warm season): Blackeye, Crowder, Purple Hull.

Novelty: Purple Royalty bush, Yardlong pole.

BEETS
pkt. sows 25 to 30 feet
1 oz./100 feet

Dual-purpose vegetable grown for its tender young top growth and, later, for its fleshy roots. Beets are a cool season vegetable that should be planted 2 to 4 weeks before the average date of last killing freeze. Fall plantings should be made 8 to 10 weeks prior to average date of first killing freeze.

Beets must have a loose, well-drained soil to develop good roots. Unlike most crops, they do best in a slightly alkaline soil. Sow seed in rows 14 to 24 inches apart, with the plants 2 to 3 inches apart in the rows.

Fertilize beets with a complete and balanced plant food, 1 to 2 pounds per 100 square feet every 4 to 6 weeks. Keep the plants well watered and actively growing.

Problems

Few insects and diseases bother beets. Boron deficiency, however, may cause black corky spots throughout root. Should that occur, apply 4 ounces of grocery store borax per 1,000 square feet. Apply it in a water solution to the entire planting bed.

Harvest

Harvest the first of your beet plantings when the roots reach the size of golf balls. Allow every other root to remain, so they can develop to 2 inches in diameter. Do not allow roots to become large and tough. Harvest tops as long as they remain tender and mild-flavored.

Varieties

Detroit Dark Red, Golden Beet, Early Wonder, and, primarily for its tops, Green Top Bunching.

BROCCOLI
space plants 16 to 24 inches apart
¼ oz. seed/100 feet or
50 to 60 plants/100 feet

Broccoli has enjoyed a rapid increase in popularity, both with Texas gardeners and with gourmet diners, over the past several years. It's a hardy, easy crop that everyone should include. Seed or transplants can be planted 2 to 4 weeks before average date of last killing frost in spring. Fall plantings of transplants should be made 10 to 12 weeks prior to average date of first killing frost. Allow 3 to 4 extra weeks if you intend to sow seed directly into garden. Broccoli, like its relatives cabbage, Brussels sprouts, kale and cauliflower, is quite hardy and will produce even after the first freeze.

Seed should be sown into loose soil on 3 to 4-inch spacings and ½-inch deep. Rows should be spaced 2 to 3 feet apart. Thin seedlings to stand 16 to 24 inches apart. If you are using transplants, set them at the same 16 to 24-inch distances.

Fertilize broccoli every 4 to 5 weeks with a complete and balanced plant food to keep it actively growing. Apply 1 to 2 pounds per 100 square feet of bed space. Water following the feedings as needed throughout the growing season.

Problems
Cabbage loopers: will chew holes in leaves of broccoli and other cole crops. Control with *Bacillus thuringiensis* ("Bt") biological worm spray. Allow spray 12 to 36 hours to kill worms.

Aphids: congregate in tender new growth, particularly around flower heads (malathion or diazinon).

Harvest
Harvest broccoli as buds reach full size, but before yellow florets open. Cut through stem just below flower head with sharp knife and allow side shoots to develop for several subsequent harvests.

Varieties
Premium Crop, Green Comet, Cleopatra, Calabrese, Waltham 29.

BRUSSELS SPROUTS
space plants 18 to 24 inches apart
¼ oz. seed/100 feet or
50 to 60 plants/100 feet

Another relative of cabbage, Brussels sprout plants produce several dozen tiny cabbage-like heads along their main stems. Best treated as a fall crop in Texas, since best quality sprouts are produced in longer, cooler growing conditions.

Plant seed 14 to 16 weeks prior to average date of first killing freeze, or preferably, use small transplants set out 12 to 14 weeks prior to that date. Spring plantings, (not usually successful) when tried, should be made 2 to 4 weeks before the average date of the last killing freeze for your area. Only potted transplants should be used in the spring.

Transplants should be spaced 18 to 24 inches apart in the rows, with 2½ to 3 feet between the rows. Shelter the tender new plants from late summer sun with shingles or cardboard for 5 to 7 days, until they become adjusted to light. Seed, if used, should be planted ½-inch deep into loose garden soil with 3 to 6 inches between seeds. Thin seedlings to stand 18 to 24 inches apart.

BEETS

BEANS

BRUSSELS SPROUTS

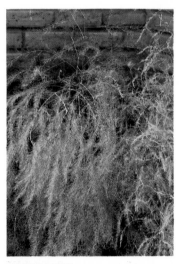

ASPARAGUS

BROCCOLI

Fertilize Brussels sprouts with a complete and balanced plant food once a month, 1 to 2 pounds per 100 square feet. Keep the plants well watered, since they must grow quickly and vigorously.

Remove lower leaves when sprouts become visible, to encourage their growth. To speed the growth even more remove terminal (tip) bud of plant. This latter process may reduce total yield somewhat.

Problems
Cabbage loopers: feed on Brussels sprouts and other cabbage relatives. Control with *Bacillus thuringiensis* biological worm spray or dust.

Aphids: may appear on tender new growth during cooler seasons (malathion or diazinon sprays).

Harvest
Cut off Brussels sprouts while the heads are still tight. Most heads will be in the 1 to 1¼-inch range. Four or five plants will keep a family well supplied.

Varieties
Jade Cross hybrid, Long Island Improved.

CABBAGE
space plants 16 to 24 inches apart
¼ oz./100 feet or
50 to 60 plants/100 feet

Most popular of the cole crops, cabbage is grown for use fresh, cooked and preserved. Given good growing conditions and protection from loopers, it's dependable in both spring and fall gardens.

Cabbage is best started from either potted or bare-rooted nursery transplants set out 2 to 4 weeks before the average date of the last killing freeze in the spring or 12 to 14 weeks before the average date of the first killing freeze in the fall. Plant in loose, well-drained garden soil. Space plants 12 to 14 inches apart in the rows, with rows 2 to 3 feet apart.

Fertilize cabbage once a month using a complete and balanced garden fertilizer, 1 to 2 pounds per 100 square feet of bed space. Keep plants well watered to prevent hot weather damage, but don't allow soil to remain waterlogged.

Problems
Cabbage loopers: small worms riddle leaves and heads of cabbage plants. Control with biological worm spray, *Bacillus thuringiensis.* Allow the Bt 12 to 36 hours to kill worms.

Aphids: prevalent in cool weather, congregating in tender new growth (malathion).

Harvest
Cut your cabbage anytime after heads are size of grapefruit until they reach total mature size. Don't wait too long, though, or heads may sunscald or split.

Varieties
Green: Earliana, Early Jersey Wakefield, Emerald Cross, Harvester Queen, Stonehead.
Red: Red Head, Red Acre.
Savoy: Savoy Ace, Savoy King.
Chinese Cabbage (best in fall garden): Michihli.

CARROTS
pkt. sows 25 to 30 feet
½ oz./100 feet

Not an important garden vegetable in Texas, due partly to tight clay soils prevalent in many parts of the state, and because good quality carrots are reasonably inexpensive in most supermarkets.

Carrots must have a loose and deep soil if you expect long, slender roots. As a margin of safety, most Texans would do well to plant the shorter, stubbier types listed here.

Sow seed ½-inch deep and one inch apart in the rows. Thin to stand 2 inches apart, with the rows one foot apart. Plant carrots 6 to 8 weeks before the average date of the last killing freeze in your area. For a fall crop, plant 8 to 12 weeks prior to the average date of the first killing freeze. Additional plantings can be made at each season for a month or more.

Fertilize carrots with a complete and balanced garden fertilizer, 1 to 2 pounds per 100 square feet of bed space once a month. Keep them moist (not wet) at all times to ensure continuous and vigorous growth. Active plants have better flavor.

Harvest
Harvest carrots when they're less than half of their expected mature length. Letting them grow to mature size merely decreases flavor and makes them more fibrous.

Varieties
Danvers Half Long, Chantenay.

CAULIFLOWER
space plants 16 to 24 inches apart
¼ oz./100 feet or
50 to 60 plants/100 feet

Cauliflower is yet another cabbage relative grown with much the same care. It is best suited to the fall garden, where it can produce its head during cooler growing conditions. Cauliflower is a good investment of garden space . . . just compare costs at the market.

Plant cauliflower transplants in loose, well-drained soil 12 to 14 weeks before the average date of your area's first fall killing freeze. Space the plants 16 to 24 inches apart in the rows, with the rows 2 to 3 feet apart. Protect the young plants from the sun's rays for their first 5 to 7 days with an A-frame made out of shingles or cardboard.

Fertilize cauliflower with a complete and balanced garden plant food once a month, 1 to 2 pounds per 100 square feet of bed space. Keep the plants well watered to encourage vigorous growth.

Once the cauliflower head starts to form, tie the top leaves up and over it (a process called "blanching"). That will keep the head a pure white. Otherwise green and even brown tissues may develop.

Problems

Cabbage looper: devours leaves of all cole crops, including cauliflower. When worms and their holes start to appear, spray at once with *Bacillus thuringiensis* biological worm spray (dust form also available).

Aphids: common on tender new growth during active growing season (malathion or diazinon).

Harvest

Cut cauliflower with a sharp knife when heads are in the 4 to 8-inch range, before they begin to deteriorate.

Varieties

Snowball, Early Snowball, Snow King, Snow Crown, Royal Purple.

CHARD
pkt. sows 25 to 30 feet
2 oz./100 feet

Swiss chard is one of the most ornamental of all vegetables. Add to that its versatility and dependable production, and it's a plant for everyone's garden.

Since chard is hardy to mild freezes, seed should be planted 2 to 4 weeks before the average date of the last spring freeze. Fall plantings should be made 10 to 12 weeks prior to the average first frost date.

Plant the seed ½ to 1 inch deep in well-prepared soil, 3 to 4 inches apart in rows. Chard is one of our larger leafy vegetables and its rows should be spaced 18 to 30 inches apart. Just as they start to crowd, thin the seedlings (use those you've thinned in salads) to stand 6 to 8 inches apart in the rows.

Fertilize chard every 2 to 3 weeks with a complete and balanced garden fertilizer, 1 to 2 pounds per 100 square feet. Water it frequently to keep the leaves vigorously growing. Let them slow down and you run the risk of bitter flavor.

Harvest

Harvest the outer leaves while they're still developing . . . before they become tough and bitter. Hand pick the leaves, so some will be left to keep the plant growing.

Varieties

Lucullus: leaves are broad, thick and crumpled. Veins very pale green, almost white. Excellent flavor, texture.

Rhubarb: leaves broad, crumpled, dark green, heavily marked with intense red. Leaf petioles (stems) resemble rhubarb in appearance. Spectacular in landscape or garden.

COLLARDS
pkt. sows 25 feet
¼ oz./100 feet

Another cabbage relative, collards actually look like a headless type of cabbage. Plants continue to grow season after season, eventually becoming 2 to 3 feet tall. It is a popular and nutritious vegetable common in Texas gardens.

CHARD

CAULIFLOWER

CARROTS

CABBAGE

Very hardy, it can be planted in early spring 4 to 6 weeks before last killing freeze. Late summer plantings will mature during cooler weather, for better leaf flavor and quality.

Sow seed 3 to 4 inches apart and 1 inch deep in well prepared garden soil. Thin as plants start to crowd, leaving plants 12 to 20 inches apart, 24 to 36 inches between rows.

Fertilize collards monthly with a complete and balanced garden plant food, 1 to 2 pounds per 100 square feet. Water frequently enough to keep the soil from drying excessively.

Problems

Cabbage loopers: white butterflies lay eggs which develop into looping worms that devour leaves. Apply *Bacillus thuringiensis* dust or spray for control.

Harvest

Harvest leaves while still relatively small.

Varieties

Georgia, Vates.

CORN
pkt. sows 60 to 80 feet
2 to 3 oz./100 feet

Sweet corn is a space-consuming vegetable that should be reserved for medium-to-large sized gardens. It should always be planted in square or rectangular blocks rather than long singular rows to insure good pollination and full ears. Corn produces best in warm weather, so it is best suited to the spring garden. Plant it once all danger of frost has passed.

Prepare the soil to a depth of 8 to 12 inches, then plant the kernels 1-inch deep and 3 to 4 inches apart in the rows, with the rows 2 to 3 feet apart. Once the seedlings are 6 inches tall thin them to stand 12 inches apart in the rows.

Fertilize corn with a high-nitrogen plant food as seedlings reach 6 to 10 inches tall. Apply a complete and balanced garden fertilizer 3 to 4 weeks later.

Cultivate the soil shallowly to avoid damaging the roots that are right under the soil surface. You may want to incorporate the plant food at the time of cultivation, then water heavily. You may also want to pull fresh soil up around the corn stems 4 to 6 inches deep. Corn produces prop roots near the ground line and piling new soil there will help it hold itself erect.

Water whenever the soil surface is dry, and especially if the leaves are also rolled. Soak the soil deeply each time that you water. Be especially careful to water thoroughly while the kernels are developing, otherwise your corn may end up with poorly formed ears.

Problem

Corn earworm: adult moth lays eggs on the corn silks during flowering. Resulting larvae crawl into ear and start feeding on developing kernels. Controls: put drop of mineral oil on silks after they're fully developed. Mineral oil smothers earworm eggs. Can also use sevin or other garden insecticide applied to mature silks.

Harvest

Pick corn when the kernels squirt a milky juice when pressed with your thumbnail. Ears will generally be at prime quality for only 2 to 3 days, so check often. Try to harvest the corn as close to the time you'll eat it as possible, so its sugars won't start converting to less tasty starches.

Varieties
Calumet, Golden Cross Bantam, Merit, Bonanza, Silver Queen, Xtra-Sweet hybrid, Candy Corn.

CUCUMBER
pkt. sows 30 feet
½ oz./100 feet

Among our more prolific vegetables, only a handful of cucumber plants will provide all you need for fresh eating and pickling.

Cucumbers are warm season vegetables and should be planted 1 to 2 weeks after the average date of the last killing frost for your area. Fall plantings should be made 12 to 14 weeks before the average date of the first frost.

Sow seed 1 to 2 feet apart in the rows, with the rows 4 to 6 feet apart. Plant the seeds ½-inch deep, 5 or 6 to a planting site. You may also want to plant them adjacent to a fence where they can climb, to conserve valuable garden space. Soil should be loose and friable for best germination and growth.

Fertilize cucumbers with a complete and balanced garden plant food every 3 to 4 weeks, 1 to 2 pounds per 100 square feet. Water regularly. Allow your plants to become dry and you'll have bitter, misshapen cucumbers. Keep water off foliage whenever possible to lessen chance of disease.

Note that cucumbers, like squash and other melons, bear both male and female flowers on the same plant. Female flowers have a swollen stem that develops into the fruit. You can expect the males to fall off without fruit.

Problems
Cucumber beetles: striped or spotted insects that chew holes in plant leaves (malathion or sevin).

Squash bugs: gray shield-shaped insect, congregate along stem, deplete food reserves (sevin for young bugs, thiodan for adults).

Spider mites: cause tan mottling, leaves turn crisp and lifeless. (kelthane).

Mildew: dusty growth on leaf surface, causes wrinkling and distorted growth (benomyl).

Harvest
Harvest pickling cucumbers early, before they reach maturity. Sweet pickles require 2 to 3-inch fruit, while dills can be made from 4 to 6-inch cukes. Fresh-eating cucumbers are generally harvested at 6 to 8 inches length. Do not allow overly ripe cucumbers to stay on the vine or you'll cut into the total production.

Varieties
Pickling: Crispy, Patio Pik, Burpless and others.
Fresh: Improved Long Green, Straight 8, Poinsett, Burpless, Marketer and others.

EGGPLANT
space plants 18 to 24 inches apart
50 to 60 plants/100 feet

Relative of tomatoes and peppers, eggplants are also warm season vegetables. In many respects their care will resemble that given their relatives.

Eggplants grow best once the soil has warmed in the spring, so try to delay plantings until 1 to 2 weeks after your last frost. Loose garden soil containing a good portion of organic matter is best, as is a sunny location.

Transplants of better varieties are available at proper planting time and should be spaced 24 to 36 inches apart in the rows, with rows 2 to 3 feet apart.

Fertilize eggplant monthly with a high-phosphate garden fertilizer. Read and follow label application directions. Keep the plants well watered to prevent off-flavored fruit.

Problem

Spider mites: serious problem of eggplant, causing leaves to turn brown and crisp. Biggest problem is that there are few controls that can be used on food crops and that won't kill sensitive foliage of eggplants.

Harvest

Harvest when fruits are about half mature size, usually 4 to 6 inches long . . . before they lose their gloss.

Varieties

Black Beauty, Black Knight, Florida Market, Long Tom, Morden Midget, White Beauty.

HORSERADISH
plant 12 inches apart

Horseradish roots planted in spring will be ready for harvest by fall. Use root cuttings from the nursery, planting them 2 inches below soil surface, small end down. Fertilize on 6 to 8 week intervals through the growing season with a complete and balanced plant food, ¼ cup per plant scattered over soil surface. Keep plants well watered.

Growth will be most vigorous in late summer and fall, so delay harvest until October and November. Use a pitchfork to remove roots as needed (freshly dug roots have best flavor). You can remove one or two roots per plant and still leave the parent plant intact.

JERUSALEM ARTICHOKE
plant tubers 15 to 18 inches apart

Novelty vegetable gaining in popularity, actually first cousin to sunflowers (often sold as "sunchokes"). They're rank growing, attaining a height of 6 to 8 feet and should be confined to the background of the vegetable garden or landscape. Plants die to the ground with the first freeze but reemerge from the tubers each spring.

Plant tubers in spring (can use part of a tuber as long as it has 2 to 3 growing points, or "eyes"), 2 inches deep. Begin harvesting the following fall. Store the harvested tubers in refrigerator and use them as crisp, low-calorie snacks and in salads. Save enough tubers for replanting the following spring, or leave a portion of the bed undisturbed during harvest.

KALE
pkt. sows 25 to 35 feet
¼ oz. per 100 feet

One of the oldest of all vegetable crops, kale is especially well suited to fall gardens in Texas. Plant it 10 to 12 weeks before the average date of the first killing frost.

Sow seeds ½-inch deep and 1 to 2 inches apart in the rows, later thinning the seedlings to stand 8 to 10 inches apart. Rows should be 18 to 24 inches across.

Fertilize monthly with a complete and balanced plant food analysis and keep the soil moist at all times.

Problems
Treat as needed for cabbage loopers with *Bacillus thuringiensis*.

Harvest
Harvest leaves in late fall and early winter. Flavor is better after exposure to frosts. Plants are totally hardy to Texas winters and will remain productive for some time.

Varieties
Blue Curled Scotch, Dwarf Siberian Curled. Ornamental, colorfully leafed types are also available for use in landscapes.

KOHLRABI
pkt. sows 25 to 35 feet
¼ oz./100 feet

Curious little relative of cabbage and other cole crops. Grown for its fleshy storage stem which is produced right above the ground line. Flavor is sweet and similar to cabbage and turnips. Plants are productive and interesting. Both white and purple types are available.

Plants are hardy to late winter cold. Sow seed directly into garden 4 to 6 weeks before average date of last killing freeze. Plant in late summer or early fall for fall crop. Space seed 1 to 2 inches apart in rows (½-inch deep), later thinning seedlings to stand 8 to 12 inches apart.

Fertilize with a complete and balanced plant food on 3 to 4-week intervals and keep plants well watered.

Problems
Control cabbage loopers, should they become a problem, with *Bacillus thuringiensis*.

Harvest
Harvest kohlrabi while the stems are less than fully grown, preferably in the 2 to 3-inch range.

Varieties
Early Purple Vienna, Early White Vienna, Grand Duke.

LETTUCE
pkt. sows 20 to 25 feet
¼ oz./100 feet

Productive, attractive and tasty. Three great attributes for any crop. Lettuce is easy and dependable, so long as you confine your efforts to leafy and loose-headed types.

Plant lettuce to mature in cool weather. High temperatures cause premature bolting (flowering), also bitter flavor. Spring plantings should go in 2 to 4 weeks before the average date of the last killing freeze. Fall plantings should be made 8 to 10 weeks before the average date of the first killing freeze.

Sow seed ½ to 1 inch apart (⅛ to ¼-inch below surface) in rows, with 15 to 18 inches between the rows. Thin them later to stand 2 to 3 inches apart. Do not allow lettuce to remain crowded, or yield and quality will suffer greatly.

LETTUCE

KOHLRABI

CUCUMBER

EGGPLANT

CORN

Fertilize lettuce every 2 weeks with a complete garden fertilizer, preferably a 2-1-1 or similar ratio. Work the fertilizer into the soil alongside the row and water it in thoroughly. Irrigate the planting regularly to keep the lettuce vigorous. Allowing it to slow its growth rate will result in bitter flavor.

Harvest
Pick partially matured leaves around the outside of the plants by cutting or pinching them loose, one leaf at a time. Leave the small new growth and some mature foliage to keep the plants productive. In late fall, on night of first hard freeze, clear-cut all good leaves and refrigerate them for use in the following 1 to 2 weeks.

Varieties
Leaf: Black Seeded Simpson, Oakleaf, Ruby, Salad Bowl.
Butterhead: Buttercrunch, Bibb, Summer Bibb.
Romaine: Paris White, Valmaine.

MELONS
space 5 to 8 feet apart
1 oz./100 feet

Melons are large-fruiting members of the cucurbit group, first cousins to squash, cucumbers and gourds. Like the others, they prefer sandy soil, warm weather and plenty of water. Most types are large, vining plants that really eat up small urban gardens. Some new miniature types are available.

Plant seeds in groups of 3 to 5, allowing 5 to 8 feet between planting sites. Thin seedlings to 2 or 3 per site as soon as they've started growing vigorously.

Fertilize melons once or twice during the growing season. Use a complete and balanced plant food, 1 to 2 pounds per 100 square feet of bed space.

Most melons have an ultra-high water content. Provide that water regularly, by thorough deep soakings.

If fruit fails to set, remove male flowers (straight stems) and use to dust pollen liberally onto female flowers (swollen stems).

Mulch melon beds with straw or compost, so fruit won't come in contact with soil, also to conserve moisture and to retard weed growth.

Problems
Most melons, being cucurbits, are affected by the same insects and diseases as cucumbers. Controls will be the same.

Harvest
Harvest melons according to the following guidelines:

cantaloupes: stem slips away easily from fruit, blossom end softens slightly and netting becomes more conspicuous.

watermelons: veteran gardeners all have their own ways of testing for ripeness. Some use white spot under melon. When it turns yellow they harvest the melon. Other folks use the two tendrils that are on the stem adjacent to the melon. When they turn brown and dry, melon is probably ready. Tap the fruit with your fingernail. If it makes a dull sound, melon is probably ready. If it's a high-pitched ping, wait several more days.

honeydew, casaba: wait for blossom end to become somewhat softened. Honeydews will turn from pale green to yellowish. Rind of casabas will be yellow at maturity.

Crenshaw and Persian: ripe aroma will become obvious at blossom end at maturity.

Varieties

Watermelon: Sugar Baby, Golden Midget, Yellow Baby, Super Sweet Seedless, Crimson Sweet, Charleston Gray, Black Diamond.

Cantaloupe (muskmelon): Perlita, Hales Best, Samson Hybrid; also Israeli (Oghen) melon, casaba, Crenshaw, honeydew, Persian.

MUSTARD
pkt. sows 40 to 50 feet
¼ oz./100 feet

Cool season leafy vegetable for early spring and fall. Plants begin to flower with first warm weather. Leaves also develop strong peppery taste when grown in warm conditions.

Sow seed near average date of last freeze for your area. Plant in early fall for fall gardens. Space seed 2 to 3 inches apart in rows, later thinning to allow 6 to 10 inches between plants. Cover seeds with ½-inch of soil and space rows 12 to 18 inches apart.

Mustard grows quickly if fertilized and watered regularly. Apply a complete garden fertilizer, preferably slightly higher in nitrogen (2-1-1 or similar ratio), 1 to 2 pounds per 100 square feet of bed space, on 3 to 4 week intervals. Keep soil uniformly moist at all times.

Problems

Control cabbage loopers with *Bacillus thuringiensis* biological worm control.

Harvest

Your first harvest should come 4 to 5 weeks after planting. By taking leaves from the stem, leaving the growing shoot intact, you'll have continued production.

Varieties

Florida Broadleaf, Southern Giant Curled, Fordhook Fancy, Tendergreen ("Spanish Mustard").

OKRA
pkt. sows 15 to 20 feet
2 oz./100 feet

Heat-loving, deep rooted vegetable well adapted to Texas conditions. Related to cotton. Grows tall, so plant at north side of garden, where it won't shade other crops. Very sensitive to cold . . . wait until soil is warm to plant. Okra should be your last crop to plant in the spring, going in 2 to 4 weeks after the average date of the last killing freeze.

Sow seed 6 to 8 inches apart and 1 inch deep in rows spaced 3 to 4 feet apart. Thin the young seedlings to stand 1 foot apart in the rows.

Fertilize okra with a complete and balanced plant food, 1 to 2 pounds per 100 square feet of bed space applied every 4 to 6 weeks. Water the plants deeply to encourage vigorous root growth.

Problems

Nematodes: okra appears stunted, has gall knots on roots. Fumigate area with vapam prior to replanting.

Cotton Root Rot: plants die suddenly, leaves remain attached. Roots may show very fine webbing attached to outer surface. Incorporate organic matter and soil acidifier. Move okra plantings to another part of garden.

Assorted insects: list includes leaf-footed bug, stink bug, ants, others. Few do major damage. If you're concerned, though, an application of a general-purpose insecticide should stop problems.

Harvest

Harvest okra regularly. Pods will mature quickly. Try to gather them before they exceed 3 to 3½ inches in length (while they will still snap from plants). Leaving them on the plant longer reduces production greatly.

Varieties

Clemson Spineless, Louisiana Green Velvet, Dwarf Green, Red River, Emerald.

ONIONS

100 plants for 20 to 25 feet row
400 to 500 plants/100 feet
1 oz. seed/100 feet

Among the most popular of all vegetables in Texas gardens, onions can also be among the most confusing. You must plan your plantings carefully and know the varieties well.

If you expect good bulbing onions you must choose varieties with short day requirements:

Varieties

White or yellow: Bermuda, Granex, Early Grano, Sweet Spanish, Excel, Texas Grano 502, Eclipse.

Red: Burgandy and Tropicana.

Short-day varieties can form bulbs during Texas springs, while temperatures are still cool. Long-day types must have 14 to 16 hours of daylight each day to form bulbs. Those varieties won't meet your needs for bulbing onions here in the South, where it simply gets too hot before those day lengths are met. They are useful, however, for green onion plantings.

Plant onions in well-drained garden soil. Plant so final spacing can be 2 to 3 inches between bulbs, with rows 16 to 24 inches apart.

Plant nursery transplants as soon as they become available in the early spring. These will produce the best bulbs fastest, generally within 2 to 3 months. Sets (small hard onions) can also be used, though the variety selection won't be as great.

You can also grow your own transplants from seed sown thickly but shallowly in beds in September, October or November. Protect from extremely low temperatures. Transplant into the final garden site in January, as plants reach pencil size in diameter.

Keep onions growing vigorously. Any delay may cause them to bolt into flower, diminishing the quality of the bulb. Fertilize with a complete and balanced fertilizer on 3-week intervals throughout the growing season. Apply one pound per 100 feet of row beginning when the onions have reached the 5-leaf stage. Water thoroughly, but be certain soil drains well.

Problems

Thrips: chewing insects that damage foliage, causing elongated brown spots and decline of plants (diazinon or malathion).

Pink Root: fungal disease causing stunting of bulbs. Can be identified by pink coloration of young feeder roots. Plant resistant varieties such as Excel, Eclipse, Granex, Texas Grano 502, Beltsville Bunching.

Harvest

Harvest green onions from spring plantings as bulbs begin to enlarge and plants become crowded. Bulbing onions should be harvested in late spring, once two-thirds of the tops have died to the ground. Break the remaining leaves to hasten bulbs' maturation. Dig bulbs and lay them on top of ground to dry. Cover bulbs lightly with plants' dried foliage. Be sure not to injure them, and get them inside if there's threat of rain. Store them cool and absolutely dry, preferably in open containers or mesh bags for best air circulation.

Green Onions: Also called "multiplying" onions, can be planted from seed in fall. Will produce during fall, winter and even into spring. Beltsville Bunching and Evergreen White Bunching are two common types. Green onions can also be grown from sets, including varieties White Lisbon and Ebeneezer.

Shallots: Plant shallowly in fall using sets from nursery, seed house or grocery. Harvest tops and use as substitute for chives. Plants will form small bulbs in spring. Separate bulb clusters and allow bulbs to dry for 3 to 4 weeks after harvest before using.

Garlic: Plant cloves 1 to 2 inches deep. Plant in fall in Texas, fat base downward. Space cloves 2 to 4 inches apart in rows 14 to 18 inches apart. Harvest in spring. Hang cloves in well ventilated garage to dry.

Leeks: Plant in fall in loose, well-prepared soil. Space seedlings 3 to 4 inches apart in rows, with 8 to 15 inches between rows. Plants will require 6 to 8 months to mature. As they grow taller, pull the loose soil up around the stem to blanch it. Harvest when the stems are ½ to 2 inches in diameter.

PEAS
pkt. sows 25 feet
1 pound/100 feet

English peas require a moist, cool growing season to do their best. Though they may not be quite as spectacular in Texas as they are in points farther north, nothing beats the taste of fresh garden peas . . . it's a treat few Texans have enjoyed.

Plan your plantings so the peas will mature during cool weather. For spring plantings that means you'll have to plant extra early, 3 to 6 weeks before the average date of the last killing freeze. For fall plantings, have them in the ground 10 to 12 weeks prior to the first frost.

Space the seed 1 to 2 inches apart in the rows (1 inch deep), with 3 or more feet between rows, so you can work in between the supports. Once the plants are actively growing and before they begin to crowd, thin to allow 2 to 3 inches between plants.

Peas require some type of support, be it a fence, a wire cage, or some type of garden netting. The vines are heavy, so build your support well.

Fertilize peas with a complete and balanced plant food analysis every 3 to 4 weeks. Keep the plants well watered, but try to keep the moisture off the foliage to lessen the disease problems.

Problem

Powdery mildew can be controlled with benomyl, also by keeping water off foliage whenever possible.

Harvest

Harvest your peas when the pods have swollen to a rounded appearance. Pick the peas frequently to be sure no overly mature ones remain on the plants and cut into production.

Varieties

Special Note: **Sugar Snap English Pea** was introduced to Texas and U.S. gardeners as an **All America Selection.** In its first year of availability it became one of the top vegetable varieties of all time. It's that good! Best of all, it does well in Texas conditions. Use it three ways: as a snap pea, much as you'd use a green bean; shell it and eat the peas (the husk is the sweetest); or, perhaps best of all, eat it fresh, in salads or as a snack. It's a winner!!!

Other types: Wando, Alaska, Little Marvel.

(See "BEANS" for Southern peas)

PEPPERS
space plants 18 to 24 inches apart
50 to 60 plants per 100 feet

There's a pepper for everyone! Whether you're hot or you're cold, there's a pepper to meet every whim. And, best of all, they're remarkably easy to grow. They're equally at home in pots or out in the garden.

Peppers are warm season vegetables and should be planted 1 to 2 weeks after the average date of your area's last spring killing frost. Fall plantings should be made 12 to 15 weeks before the expected first frost.

Use started nursery transplants spaced 18 to 24 inches apart in rows, with rows 2 to 3 feet apart. Protect fall garden plantings from late summer sun with A-frames erected from a pair of old shingles, boards or even cardboard. Remove in 5 to 7 days.

Fertilize peppers with a complete garden fertilizer, preferably one that's higher in phosphorus (middle number of the analysis). Apply 2 tablespoons to ¼ cup of the plant food per plant at 3 to 4-week intervals. Keep plants well watered and active.

Many of the larger peppers, especially the bells, will quit setting fruit when temperatures exceed 90 to 92°F. Keep the plants healthy during the summer and they should return to good productivity during the fall.

Problems

Aphids: congregate on tender new growth, cause distorted leaf tissues (malathion or diazinon).

Blossom-end rot: part of fruit farthest away from stem dries up and dies, leaving concave dead area. Indication of improper watering, generally too little too seldom.

Harvest

Harvest your peppers as soon as they reach their desired size and color. Bells can be harvested slightly immature or left on the plant to turn red or yellow. Other types will also turn from green to red or yellow as they mature.

Varieties

Bells: California Wonder, Yolo Wonder, Keystone Giant, Bell Boy, Golden Bell, Early Prolific.

Other Sweet Peppers: Sweet Banana, Pimiento.

Hot Peppers: Long Red or Thin Cayenne, Jalapeno, Chili, Hungarian Yellow Wax, Tabasco.

SWEET BANANA PEPPERS

PEAS

PEPPERS

ONIONS

POTATOES
8 to 12 pounds/100 feet

Productive and easy cool season vegetable, suited to both spring and fall garden. Even small plantings of 10 to 15 feet can provide plenty for immediate use. Larger plantings will provide potatoes for storage and later use.

Buy only certified seed potatoes (grocery store potatoes intended for human consumption may have been sprayed with a growth inhibitor to retard sprouting). Nurseries generally have their supplies by late winter. Cut the seed potatoes into sections containing 2 to 4 eyes (growing points, visible on surface of potato). Lay the cut sections out on newspapers for 2 to 3 days to allow them to form a thin callous layer over the cut edges. That will retard decay once they're placed in the soil.

Plant potatoes while the soil is still cool, 2 to 3 weeks before the average date of your area's last killing freeze. Space the sections 12 to 15 inches apart in rows, with 2 to 3 feet between the rows. Plant 3 to 4 inches deep in loose, well-drained garden soil. Plants will do best in slightly acid soil that has a high percentage of organic matter. Early shoots will be susceptible to freeze damage and should be covered with compost, newspapers or burlap if temperatures are expected to fall into the 20's.

Fertilize potatoes with a complete and balanced plant food once, when plants are about a foot tall. Work the fertilizer into the soil shallowly, then water deeply. Keep plants well watered all season long, but be sure soil does not become waterlogged, or roots will deteriorate rapidly.

Mulch potato plantings with compost or straw 3 to 5 inches deep around the plants. Some gardeners even grow their potatoes directly in composted mulch in shallow, well-drained trenches. That makes it easier, both to check on the development of the tubers and to harvest them once they're ready.

Problems

Colorado potato beetle: common and serious potato pest, feeding on foliage. Black and yellow stripes lengthwise along ⅜-inch body (sevin or diazinon).

Aphids: cluster around tender new growth (malathion or diazinon).

Potato scab: fungal organism causing corky, rough spots. Problem mainly in alkaline soils. Control with application of soil acidifiers.

Nematodes: cause distorted root growth, usually with galls. Fumigate area with vapam prior to replanting.

Harvest

Pick new potatoes when plants have reached or just passed peak flowering. (If your plants reach mature height of 18 to 20 inches and fail to flower, dig carefully around crown of several typical potatoes to check progress of potato formation.) For baking-size potatoes, wait until tops have fallen to ground. Dig potatoes carefully, lifting out of the garden soil with a spading fork inserted well to the side of the plants. Store them cool (65 to 80°F), dark and dry. Do not wash tubers until ready to cook. Save small potatoes (golf-ball-sized and slightly larger) for late summer plantings for fall garden, since certified seed potatoes will be hard to find at that time.

Varieties

Many garden centers merely label their potatoes as "certified seed potatoes," however, specific varieties are sometimes offered. Best types for Texas include: (white) Irish Cobbler; (red) Norland, LaSoda.

PUMPKINS
space plants 4 to 6 feet apart
½ oz./100 feet

Large plants, often spreading 10 or 15 feet in all directions . . . not practical for small urban plot. Easily grown, however, and popular with children when space permits.

Pumpkins are a warm-season crop, so plant 1 to 2 weeks after average date of last spring killing frost. Pumpkins planted then will mature during early to mid-summer. For pumpkins around Halloween, sow seed during mid-summer. Calculate time required for your variety to produce fruit to determine best planting time.

Sow seed 1 to 2 inches deep in well prepared garden soil. Rows should be 6 to 8 feet apart, and the seeds should be planted 2 to 3 feet apart in those rows, later thinned to stand 3 to 4 feet apart.

Fertilize pumpkin plants with a complete and balanced garden fertilizer, 1 to 2 pounds per 100 square feet applied on monthly intervals. Water deeply following feeding and regularly throughout the season. Ample water promotes good fruit size.

Problems
Vine borers: feed inside stem, cutting off flow of water, nutrients to leaves. Sevin, malathion will be of some help.

Squash bugs: cause plants to wither and dry (sevin dust for young bugs, thiodan dust for mature insects).

Mildew: a problem in cool, moist weather (benomyl, coupled with surface, not sprinkler, irrigation).

Harvest
Harvest pumpkins when the fruit has changed color, the skin toughened and the vines dried. Do not leave them exposed to hard freezes. Leave 2 to 3 inches of stem attached to the fruit for longer storage life.

Varieties (listed by category, generally in order of increasing size):
Bush types: (spreading 4 to 6 feet) Spirit, Cinderella.

Vining types: (spreading 8 to 15 feet) Small Sugar, Big Tom, Jack O'Lantern, Big Max, Connecticut Field, Hungarian.

Novelty type: Lady Godiva (seeds have no hulls, ideal for roasting).

RADISHES
pkt. sows 20 to 25 feet
1 oz./100 feet

Among the quickest growing of all vegetables, can be harvested within a month of planting. Tastes best when grown in cool weather of early spring or late fall.

Plant seed in loose, well-drained garden soil 2 to 4 weeks before average date of last spring frost. Make subsequent plantings on 1 to 2-week intervals for a month. Fall plantings should be made 6 to 10 weeks prior to the average date of the first frost.

Plant seeds ½-inch deep and ½-inch apart in rows, with rows 8 to 12 inches apart. Thin seedlings to stand 1 to 1½ inches apart in the rows. Plants that produce luxuriant top growth but little or no roots often are too crowded (or have been given excessive nitrogen).

PUMPKINS

POTATOES

RADISHES

Fertilize radishes with a complete and balanced plant food soon after they germinate, 1 pound per 100 square feet. Keep plantings well watered. Any slowing of radish root growth will result in hot, bitter taste.

Harvest
Pick radishes early, before they even approach full mature size. Large old radishes are hot and woody.

Varieties
Many types are available, and each should do reasonably well. However, Cherry Belle, Champion, French Breakfast, Sparkler, Early Scarlet Globe and White Icicle are all good.

SPINACH
pkt. sows 25 to 30 feet
1 oz./100 feet

Increasingly popular as a fresh salad vegetable, spinach must be grown during cool weather. Plant 3 to 4 weeks before average date of last spring frost. Fall plantings should be made 8 to 10 weeks prior to average date of first frost. Plant seed 1 to 2 inches apart and ½-inch deep. Space rows 16 to 24 inches apart, and thin seedlings to stand 3 to 4 inches apart in rows. Make successive plantings as long as cool weather persists.

Keep plants actively growing for best size and flavor. Fertilize with a complete, high-nitrogen fertilizer (2-1-1 or similar ratio), 1 to 2 pounds per 100 square feet, on 2 to 3-week intervals. Water regularly, keeping soil uniformly moist at all times, never waterlogged and never dry to the wilting point.

Aphids will congregate on tender new spinach leaves. Either spray with malathion or diazinon or remove by washing with hard stream of water.

Harvest
Pick spinach leaf by leaf, selecting those that are only partially matured. When the plants begin to bolt into flower, remove all remaining foliage and refrigerate it immediately.

Varieties
Melody, America, Hybrid Number 7, Bloomsdale Long Standing.

New Zealand spinach: a related and similar vegetable. It stands heat better than the others listed.

SQUASH
space plants 4 to 5 feet apart
summer squash: 1 oz./100 feet
winter squash: ½ oz./100 feet

Two distinctly different types of vegetables are classed under one crop name:

Summer squash generally grow as bushes. Their fruit is harvested while still growing, at ⅓ to ½ mature length, and is eaten whole: skin, flesh, seeds and all.

Winter squash are slower to mature and generally grow on wide-spreading vines. Their fruit is allowed to reach full maturity before harvest. Seeds are scraped out and only the flesh is eaten.

An important note: the terms "summer" and "winter" squash are misleading. Both types can be planted in spring, 1 to 2 weeks after the last frost. Summer types, including crooknecks, zucchini and scallops, will be ready for harvest from early to mid-summer. The so-called "winter" types, including acorn, hubbard and butternut, will take more time, maturing in mid-summer. Since northern growing seasons start later and are shorter, the winter types generally don't mature there until fall. The squash are stored for several weeks, even months, hence the name "winter."

Plant squash seeds 1 to 2 inches deep, three or four in a group, with 3 to 4 feet between the planting sites in the rows. Space rows 4 to 5 feet apart for summer squash and 6 to 8 feet apart for winter types. Once the seedlings are visible, thin to leave 2 plants per site.

Fertilize squash once or twice during their growing season. Use a complete, high-phosphorus fertilizer (1-2-1 or similar ratio) to avoid excessive leaves, 1 to 2 pounds per 100 square feet of bed space. Water regularly. Don't let the plants wilt for long periods or poor fruit quality will result.

Remember that squash flowers, like other members of the cucurbit family, are either male or female. Both types will eventually be present on each plant. Don't be alarmed, then, if you get no fruit set the first two weeks your plants bloom. Those are just male flowers (straight stems), sent early to ensure pollination later. Female flowers (swollen stems) are produced later. Bees are the main method of pollination for squash and other cucurbits. If they aren't present, the flowers won't get pollinated. You may need to help in the pollination by removing a male flower and using it to hand pollinate the female blooms.

Problems

Squash bug: very difficult pest to eliminate. Grey bugs feed on foliage, sap life from plant. Treat young bugs with sevin dust. Use thiodan dust on mature bugs. Remove as many bugs as possible by hand, along with egg clusters on leaves. Lay boards on edge under plants. Squash bugs will congregate under them during heat of day. Remove boards and kill bugs.

Spider mites: turn leaves tan and crisp (kelthane).

Fruit rot: fruit turns soft and black at blossom-end, often with conspicuous mold growth. Remove diseased fruit and spray plant with benomyl, maneb or captan.

Mildew: both downy mildew and powdery mildew will attack squash, particularly during moist, cool weather. Spraying with benomyl or folpet will help.

Harvest

Harvest crookneck and zucchini squash when 4 to 6 inches long, before seeds become woody. Scallop (Patty Pan) squash should be picked while still small and green, before it turns white.

Winter types should be harvested once their skins have become hardened and as the vines die out. Cut them from the vines, leaving a 2 to 3-inch stem attached to prolong storage life.

Varieties

Summer squash: (yellow) Butterbar, Yellow Crookneck, Dixie Straightneck, Golden Zucchini.

Zucchini: (green) Aristocrat, Cocozelle, Greyzini, Gold Rush, Ambassador.

Scallops: Patty Green Tint, Scallopini.

Winter squash: Butternut, Hubbard, Table King, Table Ace.

Novelty: Spaghetti squash has fluffy string-like flesh that can be removed after boiling and used as substitute for spaghetti.

Male Flower (bottom) Female Flower (top)

Peel petals away from
male (pollen) flower.

SCALLOP SQUASH

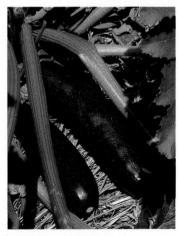

ZUCCHINI SQUASH

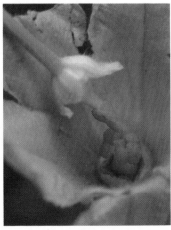

Transfer pollen from male flower to
female flower.

SWEET POTATOES
75 to 100 plants/100 feet

Warm-season vegetable, more closely related to morning glories than to Irish potatoes. Large vines require ample garden space. Sandy soil is decidedly preferable.

Buy sweet potato slips in mid-spring from nurseries or feed stores. Set them 12 to 16 inches apart in the rows, with rows 36 to 48 inches apart.

Fertilize prior to planting and once or twice during the growing season with a high-phosphorus fertilizer. Avoid high-nitrogen plant foods to prevent excessive leaf growth at the expense of root formation. Water plants regularly, since sandy soil will drain freely.

Diseases
Diseases affecting sweet potatoes are often associated with the soil and especially with poor drainage. Prepare a good planting bed and fumigate with vapam if problems become severe.

Harvest
Harvest sweet potatoes in the fall. Dig carefully around one or two plants to check the development of roots. Once they've reached full size dig them and lay them out on newspaper in the garage to dry for 10 to 14 days. Store them cool (50 to 55°F) and dry for best "shelf life."

Varieties
Centennial, Goldrush, Jewel, Vineless Puerto Rico, Nemagold and others.

TOMATOES
space 2 feet apart in rows
50 plants/100 feet

By far the most popular vegetable in Texas, tomatoes are grown in over 90 percent of all the gardens in our state. And it's no wonder. The fruit you'll produce will be of spectacular quality and flavor. You'll save money, too. An expenditure of just a few cents for a transplant can return many dollars' worth of fruit in spring, summer and into the fall.

Prepare your tomato garden plot carefully, mixing in a 4 to 5-inch layer of peat moss or compost. Rototill and rake out all roots, rocks and other debris. Plant tomato transplants in well-prepared garden soil, on the average date for the last killing freeze for your area. Be prepared to protect them from light frosts by covering with hotcaps or cut-off milk cartons.

When you're buying your spring tomato transplants, remember that biggest isn't always best. Look for those that are stout-stemmed, preferably with a purplish coloring to the stems and leaf veins (indicates hardening to cold). If they're taller than you'd really like them to be, don't plant them vertically. Dig a shallow trench for each plant and lay it on its side, with just the tip emerging out of the soil. The stem will form roots where it's submerged, further aiding the plant.

Keep track of the types that you buy. You may find your family prefers one variety over the others. For best results, it's always a good idea to plant two or three varieties. That way, you're likely to have more sustained production, plus you'll have protection should some odd insect or disease ruin one type.

Important advice in variety selection: it's generally better to stay with the small and medium-sized fruit. Varieties producing large fruit (Big Boy, Beefsteak, Ponderosa and others) have a very short productive season in most parts of Texas. They're reluctant to set fruit in cool weather and they quit setting when daytime temperatures climb over 90°F.

Best Tomatoes for Texas

Standard types to choose from include (hybrids) Early Girl V, Spring Giant VF, Better Boy VFN, Super Fantastic VFN, Bigset VFN, Spring Set VF, Terrific VFN, Bonus VFN and (inbred) Homestead 24.

Cherry, or "salad" tomatoes to plant include (hybrids) Sweet 100, Small Fry VFN, (inbreds) Red Cherry, Porter and Yellow Pear.

Important coding to gardeners: those letters V, F and N are significant. They indicate resistance to Verticillium Wilt, Fusarium Wilt and Nematodes. Some varieties also now carry designations T and A, for resistances to tobacco mosaic virus and Alternaria disease.

Gardeners still ask, too, for "low-acid" tomatoes . . . types that won't bother their digestive systems. Recent research shows that we've apparently been fooling ourselves. Most tomatoes are quite similar in their acid content. Some types just have a higher sugar content, to mask the acidic flavoring.

Fertilize tomatoes with a complete fertilizer slightly higher in phosphorus (middle number of the analysis), preferably a 1-2-1 ratio. Keep the plants constantly fed by applying the material at 3 to 4-week intervals. Several brands of special tomato fertilizer are also available.

Water is a real key to tomato success. Obviously, tomatoes are mostly water. Cut off the supply and fruit will quit developing. In fact, blossom-end rot, a serious problem of some types of tomatoes during the summer, is brought on almost exclusively by underwatering. Get in the habit of watering often . . . "read" your plants. They'll let you know when they're dry.

Train your tomatoes to grow inside wire cages. Some nurseries sell prefabricated cages, but most are too short for tomatoes in the long growing season of the Southwest. You need a cage made from concrete reinforcing wire. Sections cut 60 inches long will, when tied into a cylinder, give an 18-inch diameter cage for the tomatoes to grow in. Drive a stake against the inside wall of the cage to keep it erect. Allow all side shoots to develop, but keep them trained within the cage. Not only will they shade the developing fruit, but they also will eventually flower and bear fruit of their own.

Tomatoes in Pots

Tomatoes are well suited to container culture. Select a 5-gallon can (or larger) and fill it with a loose, well-drained potting soil mix. Choose a determinant variety such as Spring Giant (Patio is also used frequently) that will stay compact without frequent pinching. Fertilize each time that you water, using a water-soluble high-phosphorus fertilizer.

Fall Tomatoes

There are some pretty compelling reasons to grow tomatoes in the fall garden. First, they'll have the finest quality and flavor, since they'll be ripening in fall's cooler weather. You can also expect fewer insects and diseases. They're a super investment of time, space and effort.

If you'd like to extend your tomato season clear up to frost, replant with new transplants 12 to 16 weeks before the average date of your first killing freeze. It's pretty tough to pull old, tired plants through the heat of a Texas summer and convince them they need to bear heavily again in the fall. It's time for new blood . . . vigorous new transplants set out during the summer.

Plant the fall crop in another part of your garden, away from the prior tomato location. Protect the young seedlings from the hot blazing sun by covering them with a couple of old shingles or cardboard for their first week or so in the garden. Keep them well watered until they establish deep roots.

If you have trouble finding tomato transplants in the middle of the summer, you might try growing your own, either from seed or from cuttings from your best spring plants. Tomato seeds can be started indoors, then transplanted out to the garden, and the cuttings will root readily in a good, moist potting soil mix. You *can* do it!

Thumping blooms for pollination

TOMATOES

Caging tomatoes for support

SWEET 100 TOMATOES

Problems

Spider mites: most serious "insect" pest problem of tomatoes (actually a mite, not an insect). Plants will turn brown and crisp from bottoms up. Fine webbing will often be present. Mites will be visible on very close inspection (almost microscopic). Control with kelthane spray.

Tomato hornworm: large green worms with harmless horn on back end. Feed voraciously on foliage, are hard to locate. Hand pick or spray with malathion, diazinon, sevin or *Bacillus thuringiensis.*

Tomato fruitworm: feed in developing fruit. Control with sevin spray.

Aphids: early-season visitors to tomatoes, congregating on tender new growth. Spray with malathion or diazinon.

Leaf blights: cause leaves to become spotted, die and drop, particularly from base of plant upward. Control with maneb or captan.

Soft rot of fruit: fruit turns watery, hangs like water-balloon on vines. Putrid odor. Remove all affected fruit, spray with zineb.

Nematodes: cause plants to become stunted, wilt easily. Roots show visible signs of galls. Fumigate area with vapam, move tomatoes to another part of garden, and start growing varieties resistant to the pest.

Leaf roll and wilting: these are normal reactions of tomato plants to strained growing conditions. Plants will wilt on first sunny day following long cloudy, rainy spell. Leaves (starting with lower leaves) will roll under when exposed to continued heat. If leaves roll upward and develop long, pointed tips, your plants have either been in the drift area of a broadleafed weed killer or they have tobacco mosaic virus. It's especially important that you never handle your tomato plants after smoking without first washing your hands.

Harvest

Harvest your tomatoes regularly. Don't leave overly-ripe fruit on the vine or you'll reduce total production. It also can serve as a source of disease contamination.

If sunburning, cracking and splitting are common with your ripening tomatoes, pick them when they're just starting to turn pink or white. Place them on a bright windowsill or counter to ripen. They'll lose no flavor or nutritional value.

If it's about to freeze for the first time in the fall and you're left with 10 bushels of tomatoes, wondering which will go ahead and ripen, you might use this rule of green thumb: select several representative tomatoes and slice through them with a sharp knife. If the knife passes the seeds, pushing them out of the way, that fruit would ripen. If the knife passes through the seeds, then that fruit is too immature and should be used immediately in relish.

MOST COMMON QUESTION

"Why do tomatoes fail to set fruit?"

Absolutely the most common question asked about Texas' most popular vegetable.

Often it's directly attributable to the variety choice. Large-fruiting types won't set in extreme heat, or when temperatures fall below 55 to 60°F. Change to one of the other varieties listed.

It may also be a lack of pollination. Tomatoes are self-pollinating. Their flowers shed pollen when vibrated. If your plants are back in a corner where the wind doesn't hit them, better thump all the flower clusters every day or two. The agitation will cause much better pollination.

Feeding and watering may be the culprits. You have to keep tomatoes well nourished and moist. Don't overdo the nitrogen or you'll get all leaves and no flowers.

Nematodes or other pest problems may be weakening the plants enough that they just can't stay alive and produce fruit, too.

TURNIPS
pkt. sows 25 feet to 35 feet
½ oz./100 feet

Grown both for its fleshy root and for its fresh leaves. Turnips are a cool-season vegetable and should be planted 2 to 4 weeks before the average date of the last frost. Fall plantings should be made 6 to 10 weeks prior to the average date of the first killing freeze, though plants are frost-hardy.

Sow seeds ½-inch deep, 1 to 2 inches apart in rows, thinning seedlings to stand 2 to 4 inches apart. Rows should be spaced 15 to 18 inches apart. Soil should be loose and well drained.

Fertilize with a high-phosphorus fertilizer if you're interested primarily in turnips as a root crop. Use a complete and balanced analysis food if you're also interested in fresh green leaves. Water as soil becomes dry to the touch.

Problems
Control aphids with either malathion or diazinon; cabbage loopers with *Bacillus thuringiensis*.

Harvest
Harvest greens while still small, preferably under 5 to 6 inches. Roots should be pulled when they reach 1½ to 3 inches in diameter, depending on the variety. Roots will store well.

Varieties
For greens and roots: Tokyo Cross Hybrid, Just Right Hybrid, and Purple Top White Globe.
For greens: Seven Top.

Chapter 12

Insects and Diseases

Are your shade trees drab and dreary? Are your fern fronds turning brown? Is your bug load on the increase? Do plant diseases have you down?

If you can answer YES to any of these, then you'll want to read this chapter . . . quick! It's devoted, as a final wrap-up to Texas gardening, to the plant problems we face. You don't garden too long here in the hot Southwest before insects and diseases move in to threaten your plantings.

Learn to diagnose those problems promptly and accurately. The pages that follow will identify the most common insect and disease problems in Texas. You'll find suggestions for controlling those problems and tips for getting the best results for your effort.

You'll find, in reading through these pages, that there's no point in sharing your plants and your produce with the insects and diseases.

. . . May these pages help you to happier gardening!

TIPS FOR SOLVING PLANT PROBLEMS

The first step in solving any problem is to recognize and understand it. So it is with your plants. You should study your plants regularly and carefully. Watch for subtle changes indicative of new problems.

> **RULE OF GREEN THUMB:** Identify the plant first when trying to solve its plant pest problems. Plant problems are rather specific. What attacks one species likely won't bother another. Knowing exactly what type of plant you have will narrow your choices considerably.

Study the Symptoms

Analyze the symptoms of your plant's problems. Each will have its own characteristic appearance. Learn to recognize them. Here are some of the more common:

Insects

Symptoms: Visible damage to stems, flowers and especially leaves. Insects may still be present so check closely, both on top and bottom leaf surfaces. The type of damage varies with the insect. Leaves may be chewed, mottled or cupped.

Diseases

Symptoms: Plant diseases are caused by fungi, bacteria, viruses and nematodes.

Disease symptoms caused by fungi are numerous, including seedling stem diseases, root rot, leaf spots, leaf curl, cankers and wilts.

Bacterial disease symptoms appear as blights, galls, wilts, leaf spots (often with "shot hole" effect) and soft rots (often with putrid odor from deteriorated tissue).

Virus disease symptoms include mosaics, leaf spotting, stunted growth, streaks, curly top, ring spots and yellows — several of the symptoms are so descriptive that they're used in naming the virus diseases.

Nematode symptoms include root knots, stubby roots, stunted plant growth, often with yellowing or loss of color and lack of vigor. Nematodes will even (rarely) feed on stems, buds and leaves.

Fertility and pH

Symptoms: Plant growth is not vigorous. Two most common causes: (1) nitrogen deficiency — leaves pale green, lower leaves first, and (2) iron deficiency — leaves yellow, usually with dark green veins, newest leaves first.

Root Damage

Symptoms: Plant growth is not vigorous. Leaves may wilt even though soil is moist. Brown "scorched" margins may develop around leaves. Leaves may turn yellow and drop, generally affecting all leaves. Common causes include: excess fertilizer, over-watering, grub worms, root rot fungi, mechanical injury and addition of excessive fill soil.

Weed-Killer Damage

Symptoms: Erratic, distorted growth (new tissues primarily), yellowed leaves, or burning of existing tissues. Symptoms usually are evident within one to two weeks after herbicide application, but can take up to six to eight weeks.

Transplant Shock

Symptoms: Plant fails to leaf out and grow normally. New growth lacks vigor, and leaves are much smaller than normal. Especially a problem when transplanting large plants. Shock will persist one or more growing seasons after transplanting.

Miscellaneous Growth Problems

Symptoms: Plant grows well for short period of time, then develops problems. Growth may be scorched, lanky or otherwise affected. Common causes include: excessive shade or sunlight, overcrowding, underwatering, and the use of varieties poorly suited to your area.

Defining Some Terms

Insecticide: Product is intended to kill insects and other related pests, including snails, slugs, pillbugs, scorpions, spiders, mites and ticks.

Fungicide: Chemical used to control or prevent fungal plant diseases. Some are intended for use on bacterial diseases as well.

Nematicide: Product used to kill nematodes (microscopic soil-borne roundworms that feed on plant roots and cause distorted growth).

Herbicide: Product used to control weeds. Includes both pre-emergent (prevents annual weed seeds from germinating) and post-emergent (kills existing weeds) types.

Fumigant: Product used to control wide range of pests, including insects, diseases, weeds, nematodes. Often used in soil preparation to eliminate soil-borne problems prior to planting.

MOST COMMON QUESTION

"Can I mix an insecticide with a fungicide when I spray?"

Yes, in many cases. Product labels will often tell you whether their contents can be combined. Remember, though, that you're mixing two different chemicals. Include water, which in some parts of Texas has strong chemical properties of its own, and an undesirable chemical reaction may occur causing the spray to be changed chemically into some other material. Thick precipitates may even form. When in doubt, keep them separate.

WHAT TO LOOK FOR ON THE PESTICIDE LABEL

All products claiming to kill insects, diseases, weeds or nematodes must be sold with a complete label attached. That label is a carefully structured legal document that outlines very important information, including specific instructions for the safe and effective use of the product. As an active gardener you must become familiar with each product's label. It will identify:

A. Product or brand name.
B. Active ingredient, by common or chemical name, or both
C. Net contents shown in U.S. units, perhaps also metric units
D. EPA registration number and factory identification
E. Manufacturer's name and address
F. Directions for use
G. Pests controlled

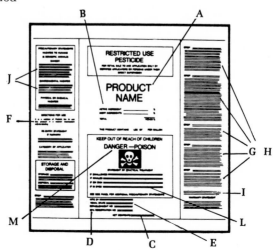

H. Plants on which product can be used safely
I. Warnings of plants that could be damaged by product
J. Other environmental hazards
K. Special application techniques
L. Statement of treatment for accidental poisoning
M. Signal word identifying order of toxicity.

Any product aimed at killing pests is toxic. It must be to do its intended job. Some are more toxic than others. The "signal" word indicates the relative toxicity.

Danger identifies a highly toxic product. Such products must also carry the skull and crossbones and a physician's guide for treating accidental poisoning.

Warning is required on all products of moderate toxicity as defined by government regulation.

Caution is the word placed on products of low toxicity.

All products will carry the warning "Keep out of reach of children."

SIX WAYS GARDEN CHEMICALS ARE SOLD

If you're trying to keep plant pests in check, you can choose from several forms of pesticide products. Each has its own advantages. You must choose the best means for your needs.

Emulsifiable Concentrate. (E.C.) Concentrated liquid form of the chemical. To be diluted (generally with water) before application.

Wettable Powder. (W.P.) Product comes dry, in powdered form. It is intended to be mixed with water, agitated and sprayed onto plant. Material may actually dissolve, or it may merely stay in suspension in water. Label may suggest frequent agitation for the latter.

Dust. Product comes in dry, dust form. Should be applied with some type of garden duster for most uniform coverage. Useful because dust will remain effective on plant longer than some sprays. Unexpected showers may wash dust off plants prematurely.

Aerosol. Product is either put under pressure or is sold in pump applicator bottle. In both situations, it is ready to apply with no mixing. Useful for small spraying jobs, particularly for plants inside the house.

Granules. Chemical is sold in pelletized form, to be applied with conventional fertilizer spreader. Limited, therefore, to soil applications such as turf pest control. Easier to apply in breezy weather than sprays, dusts.

Bait. Active chemical is impregnated on material which attracts insects. As they devour the bait they also ingest the poison and die. Useful for pillbugs, snails, slugs and cutworms, but be careful in treating areas with edible crops, since a few of the baits are not registered for use in gardens.

Not all insects are harmful. Some are the gardener's friend as the praying mantis.

MOST COMMON QUESTION

"Is it better to buy a stronger formulation of a garden chemical? For example, is a product with 50 percent of the chemical in it better than one with 25 percent? How can I compare the two?"

It doesn't matter. Both will do the job if you end up with the specified amount of the active chemical ingredient on the plant, fighting the pest. It just takes more of the less concentrated material. In fact, if you were to read the label directions in the example carefully, you'd probably find that you must use twice as much of the less concentrated product. That means that a bottle of it, to be comparable in cost, should be half as expensive as a bottle of the 50 percent product. If it costs more than half, then the stronger material is the better buy.

TYPES OF PESTICIDE APPLICATORS

There are many types of plant pests. Some climb, some crawl, some fly and some don't move at all. Some are subterranean, while others live high up in trees. Obviously, you must use different types of equipment to deliver the pest control products. Outlined are some of the most common choices. It's entirely possible that you'll want to include each in your pest-fighting fortress.

Hose-end Sprayers. Attach quickly to water hose. Disperse chemicals over large area quickly, giving reasonably good coverage, uniform concentrations at varying volumes. Special types available for reaching into trees. Not recommended for applying broadleafed weed killers adjacent to trees and shrubs (danger of drift, injury to desirable plants). Relatively inexpensive.

TEXAS TIP

It's a proven fact that Texas is blessed with more than its share of insects and diseases. So how do you know when to start spraying? Well, get in the habit of looking at every plant every time that you mow. That way you'll give them at least a weekly inspection. Look for changes in color and vigor. Watch for signs of abnormalities and treat accordingly. Keep ahead of the problem. Don't let the bugs and diseases get the upper hand!

Compression Sprayers. Best for uniform coverage. Spray can be adjusted from fine mist to coarse droplets as needed. Particularly effective in applying weed killers and in spraying undersides of low-growing foliage. Somewhat heavy to carry when applying large amounts of materials. May deliver chemicals more accurately than hose-end sprayers, but more expensive to buy and requires more time for the application. Plastic, galvanized metal and stainless steel types are available.

RULE OF GREEN THUMB: Once you use a sprayer for an application of a broadleafed weed killer, it should never be used for any other type of chemical after that. Have two sprayers: one for broadleafed weed killers and one for everything else (such as insecticides and fungicides).

Dusters. Many types available, some with plungers, others with rotary discharge. Buy a quality duster for long tool life and uniform distribution of the chemicals. Look for a type with optional long-throw discharge chute that allows you to stand back out of the dust. Dust when air is calm.

Trombone Sprayers. A special type of compression sprayer that allows you to siphon the chemical from a bucket and spray it 30 to 35 feet into your trees. Inexpensive way of spraying tall plants.

Atomizer Sprayers. Many inexpensive types available. These are particularly suited to small spraying jobs . . . isolated outbreaks of plant pest problems. Some have top-mounted plunger, others use trigger.

Baits. These products require no special equipment. Most brands come in shaker cans. Others can be measured and scattered around by hand under the plants.

Spreaders. Most useful in applying granular pesticides. Buy a type which gives uniform coverage. Rotary types are generally best.

Power Sprayers. Frequent large spraying jobs may justify the expense of power spray equipment. All sizes and styles are available. Contact an agricultural products dealer for more details and descriptions of different power equipment.

Many rental shops also offer these products. However, if you'll be spraying plants that might be injured by weed killers, ask the dealer if there might by any residues left in the sprayers from previous rentals. Broadleafed weed killers are especially persistent.

Hose-end Sprayer

Compression Sprayer

Duster

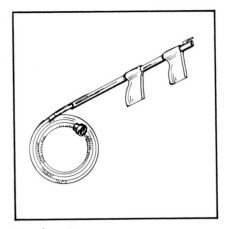

Trombone Sprayer

Atomizer Sprayer

Bait

RULE OF GREEN THUMB: Spray at the first signs of an insect or disease invasion. The pests are usually less mature and there usually are fewer of them. The result: less damage done to your plants by the pests and less chemical required to control them.

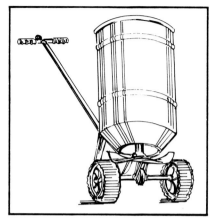

Spreader

Power Sprayer

HOW TO USE PESTICIDES SAFELY

As we've already pointed out, pesticide labels contain a great deal of information. Many folks are intimidated by their first reading of one of the product labels. The warnings are enough to discourage even the most dedicated gardener.

Realize, though, that those warnings are intended to protect us from our own carelessness. Properly used ... according to label directions ... pesticides available to the retail gardening trade are safe, both to the gardener and to his environment.

Still, it's a good idea to follow these few simple steps:

• Mix the materials according to label directions. Don't "double up" on the dosage ... use it just as it says.

• Avoid direct contact with either the concentrate or the mixed material. Wear rubber gloves when mixing. Wear long-sleeved clothing and long pants when spraying. Wear a wide-brimmed hat and a respirator. Don't touch your mouth, nose or eyes while you're applying the pesticide.

• Wash your hands and face immediately after treating. Better yet, take a bath and wash your clothing.

• Don't spray on a windy day, and don't spray directly above your head, where sprays could drift down on you.

• Don't store mixed sprays for more than 15 to 20 minutes. They may change form chemically.

• Never store pesticides in anything other than their original containers. That is a violation of both the label restrictions and common sense. And store chemicals out of extreme heat and cold.

• Rinse sprayer with hot, soapy water to remove pesticide residues. Pump and spray the suds mixture to clean nozzle and wand.

• If you detect any abnormalities in your physical capabilities as you're applying pesticides, stop at once. Contact a physician as necessary.

MOST COMMON QUESTION

"How long do I have to wait after spraying before I can put my dogs back in the yard?"

To a degree, that depends on the material you've used, but generally the pets can return once the spray has dried on the foliage. Under normal weather conditions that should be under two hours.

TEXAS' TOP 25 INSECTS

Illustrations of each insect are provided on pages 478-481.

Asterisks indicate those which are not true insects, but have been included because damage and control measures are similar.

Ants

size: ⅛ to ¾-inch, depending on species.
color: black, brown, red, yellow.
plant hosts: generally not plant pests. May be seen feeding on honeydew secreted by aphids. May build nests inside tree bark or in decayed areas. Generally more of a problem in turf areas.
season: warm months.
damage: several types inflict painful stings, most especially the imported fire ant (small dark ant that makes mounds of fresh soil. Thousands of ants "boil" from hill when disturbed. Bites usually become infected, leave scars).
controls: Diazinon, Dursban. [Fire Ants: Diazinon, Dursban, Amdro.]

Aphids

size: ⅛ to ¼-inch.
color: black, brown, green, white, yellow, red.
plant hosts: common on tomatoes, photinias, crepe myrtles and roses, but any tender new growth is susceptible.
season: primarily cool months, but may be found year 'round.
damage: suck plant sap, cause distorted growth, spread diseases, leave sticky honeydew residue.
controls: spray at first signs of invasion with Malathion, Diazinon, Orthene or Meta Systox-R.

Bagworms

size: 1 to 2 inches long when full grown (may be as small as ¼-inch in early spring).

color: case brown from dried leaves, larvae dark green to brown.

plant hosts: junipers, arborvitaes, cypress, cedars and occasionally broadleafed plants.

season: late spring-early summer.

damage: strip foliage from twigs, girdle twigs and small branches with bags.

controls: treat worms while they're still young and actively feeding. Use Malathion, Diazinon, Orthene, Sevin. Hand-pick old bags.

Borers

size: worms range from ½ to 1 inch . . . many species.

color: larvae usually light tan, cream color.

plant hosts: common in cottonwoods, willows, peaches, plums, apricots, ash, other soft-wooded trees. Can occur in any tree that has been weakened by other insects, diseases, transplanting, storm damage, etc.

season: year 'round.

damage: cut off supply lines for water and nutrients. Plant declines, may eventually die.

controls: keep trees as vigorous as possible through good plant maintenance. Wrap trunks of newly transplanted trees. Spray with Lindane or Dursban during growing season. Use Ethylene dichloride product to control existing borers.

Cabbage Loopers

size: 1 to 1½ inches long.

color: green.

plant hosts: cabbage, broccoli, cauliflower, Brussels sprouts, other cole crops.

season: spring-fall.

damage: loopers chew holes in leaves, heads, ruin crop.

controls: Bacillus thuringiensis biological worm spray.

*Chiggers

size: microscopic (1/150-inch).

plant hosts: usually found in turf, weeds. Do not feed on plants.

season: mid-spring through first frost.

damage: extremely irritating bites that show up 12 to 48 hours after exposure.

controls: Use insect repellent when working outdoors, particularly on feet and legs, under tight-fitting clothing. Treat turf, low-growing shrubs with Diazinon or Dursban spray.

Chinch Bugs

size: ⅛ to ¼-inch.
color: body black, with white wings.
plant hosts: primarily St. Augustine lawns.
season: late spring, summer and early fall.
damage: turf looks dry, yet fails to respond to watering. Starts in small patches near sidewalks, curbing (hot, sunny locations first). Grass ultimately dies.
controls: Diazinon, Dursban.

Cutworms

size: 1 to 2 inches.
color: grayish-brown to black.
plant hosts: tender new seedlings.
season: early spring.
damage: cut seedlings off at the ground.
controls: Diazinon, Sevin. Encircle plants with bottomless tin cans for added protection. Remove cans once plants are growing.

Elm Leaf Beetles

size: beetles ¼-inch long, larvae ½-inch.
color: beetles yellowish-green, larvae yellowish-green with dark stripes.
plant hosts: Siberian ("Chinese"), American elms.
season: late spring-early fall.
damage: larvae devour leaf tissue between veins, leaving foliage skeletonized, tan.
control: Diazinon, Malathion, Sevin, Orthene. Spray on 3 to 4-week intervals during summer.

Fleas

size: 1/16-inch.
color: black.
plant hosts: live in turf, low-growing foliage.
season: year 'round.

damage: do no damage to plants, but inflict annoying bites to humans, pets.

controls: Diazinon, Malathion, Dursban, Sevin sprays. Use 5% Sevin dust to control fleas on pets.

Grasshoppers

size: ½ to 3 inches.
color: green, yellow, brown.
plant hosts: all tender growth is susceptible.
season: summer, fall.
damage: strip foliage, often devouring all existing leaves.
controls: Diazinon, Malathion, Sevin.

Lacebugs

size: ⅛ to ¼-inch.
color: lacy wings give insects almost transparent appearance.
plant hosts: pyracantha, sycamores, elms and others.
season: late spring through early fall.
damage: suck plant sap from leaves. Leaves turn mottled tan, then completely tan. Black waxy specks visible on bottoms of leaves.
controls: spray at first signs of mottling with Diazinon, Sevin, Malathion, Orthene. Repeated sprayings will probably be needed.

Leafrollers

size: adults are moths of varying types; larvae are ½ to 1½ inches long.
color: larvae range from green to gray and brown, depending on species.
plant hosts: pyracantha, sweet gums, cannas, tomatoes and many others.
season: spring-fall.
damage: strip foliage and/or attach leaves together with silken threads to form protective housing.
controls: Malathion, Diazinon, Sevin, Orthene. Must spray at first signs of invasion. Control is difficult once leafrollers are encased in dried foliage.

Mealybugs

size: ⅛ to ¼-inch.
color: creamy white.
plant hosts: common on coleus, succulents, crotons. More common indoors and in greenhouses.
season: year 'round.
damage: suck plant sap, cause weakened plants with messy appearance.

controls: Diazinon, Malathion, Orthene. Spray regularly for total control.

Pecan Nut Casebearers

size: moth ¾-inch, larvae ½-inch.
color: moth dark gray, larvae olive green.
plant hosts: chiefly pecans.
season: late spring-summer.
damage: devour pecans, and bore into tender shoots in early spring, before pecans appear in tree. One of the most devastating pecan insects in Texas.
controls: apply Malathion or Zolone pecan spray. Timing is extremely critical ... check local authorities for exact date for your area, generally early May for South Texas and late May for North Texas.

Scales

size: 1/16 to ¼-inch, depending on species.
color: white, brown, yellow.
plant hosts: common on euonymus, camellias, hollies, fruit and shade trees, house plants.
season: year 'round.
damage: suck plant sap, cause gradual decline of plants' vigor.
controls: apply dormant oil spray during winter, Orthene, Malathion or summer-weight oils during warmer weather.

*Snails, Slugs and Pillbugs

size: ½ to 1½-inch long.
color: light gray or white.
plant hosts: tender foliage of flowers, vegetables, shrubs.
season: year 'round, especially spring.
damage: Strip foliage, leave large holes in leaves.
controls: Sevin bait, Sevin dust, other baits.

*Spider Mites

size: 1/60 to 1/16-inch.
color: often red, also white and yellowish-green.
plant hosts: common on marigolds, tomatoes, beans, cucumbers, melons and dozens of other plants outdoors; scheffleras, crotons, palms and others indoors. One of most prevalent plant problems in Texas.
season: worse during warm months outdoors, year 'round indoors.

damage: suck plant sap, cause drying and death of leaf tissues. Webbing may be present.
control: Kelthane.

Squash Bugs

size: ⅔-inch.
color: gray.
plant hosts: squash, melons, cucumbers, pumpkins.
season: late spring-fall.
damage: bugs suck plant sap from stems, leaves. Plants decline rather rapidly.
controls: difficult to eradicate. Use Sevin dust on young bugs, Thiodan on adults. Lay a board or shingle on its side under the plants. Bugs will congregate there during heat of midday. Lift up the board and kill the squash bugs.

*Ticks

size: ⅛ to ½-inch.
color: red, gray, brown.
plant hosts: do not feed on plants. Found in turf, weeds, low-growing foliage.
season: warm months, especially spring and early summer, into fall.
damage: Irritating bites, spread of disease in pets, humans.
controls: Use insect repellent when working outdoors, particularly on feet and legs. Bathe as soon as possible after coming indoors. Treat outside areas with Diazinon or Dursban. Use 5% Sevin dust on pets and in their quarters.

Webworms (also tent caterpillars)

size: 1 to 1½ inches long when full grown (may be as small as ⅛-inch).
color: creamy white to pale brown.
plant hosts: pecans, mulberries, persimmons, walnuts, other shade and nut trees.
season: late spring through fall.
damage: strip foliage off major limbs. Leave ugly webs hanging from limbs.
control: prune webs out of trees, destroy. Spray with Diazinon, Sevin, Malathion. Include liquid detergent or spreader-sticker to help spray penetrate web.

White Grubs (larval form of June beetle)

size: ½ to 1 inch.

color: creamy white with brown head.

plant hosts: common problem in lawn grasses, including bermuda, St. Augustine, tif bermuda. Also a problem in ornamental plantings, vegetable gardens.

season: in soil year 'round, but bulk of damage done late summer through mid-spring.

damage: sever plant roots, especially turf grass. Badly infested turf may lay dead on top of ground, like a piece of carpet.

controls: Diazinon granules. Apply 6 weeks after major flight of June beetles in your area. Timing of treatment varies with year, generally from early summer in South Texas to mid-late summer in North Texas. Eggs will be hatching at that point, and the small grubs will be more easily killed.

Whiteflies

size: 1/12 to 1/20–inch long.

color: white.

plant hosts: ligustrums, privet, gardenias, gerbera daisies, tomatoes and many others.

season: spring-fall.

damage: do minor damage, however they're a great annoyance.

controls: spray every 5 to 7 days with Malathion, Diazinon or Orthene. Regular spraying is essential for complete control, since young whiteflies will be constantly hatching.

Ant

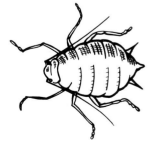

Aphid

Bagworm

Borer

Cabbage Looper

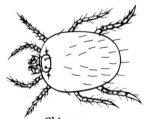

Chigger

Chinch Bug

Cutworm

Elm Leaf Beetle

Flea

Grasshopper

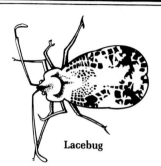

Lacebug

Leafroller

Mealybug

Pecan Nut Casebearer

Scale

Snail,

Slug

Pillbug

Spider Mite

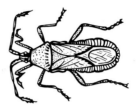

Squash Bug

Tick

Webworm

White Grub

Whitefly

MOST COMMON QUESTION

"We just lost a shade tree and want to replace it. What's the minimum distance away from the old tree's hole that the new tree must be?"

If the tree that died was a large tree I'd stay at least six to eight feet from it. If cotton root rot or other soil-borne disease problems were the main culprit, better get even farther.

TEXAS' TOP 13 DISEASES

Photographs are provided for each disease on pages 485—488.

Anthracnose

Disease group caused by several different fungi. Most common example is on sycamores, where entire trees can suddenly turn a tan-coppertone. Leaf deterioration follows vein patterns. Remove dead wood, disinfecting tools as with fire blight. Spray as leaves emerge in spring with Bordeaux mixture.

Bacterial Leaf Spots

May start as small dark green water-soaked spots. These then turn brown and dead spots may fall out altogether leaving holes all through leaves. Prime plants: tomatoes, plums, many other landscape and fruit plants. Control: Bordeaux mixture.

Brown Patch

Cool weather fungal disease of St. Augustine. Grass turns brown quickly. Leaves pull loose from runners with slight tug. As spot enlarges center may return to vigorous green growth. Not fatal, but weakens turf badly. Control with Terraclor, Maneb, Benomyl or Daconil.

Cotton (and Mushroom) Root Rot

Most common in alkaline soils. Affected plants die suddenly. Roots, on close inspection, show fine fungal strands. Many of the plants Texans grow are susceptible to this disease. Unfortunately, there is no chemical control. Where cotton root rot is a known problem, it's best simply to plant resistant plants: hollies, pecans, oaks, cedar elms, redbuds . . . generally the native plants.

Crown Gall

Relatively infrequent problem. Generally attacks trees and shrubs, including roses, euonymus, fruit trees, pecans, other landscape plants. Affected plants cannot be treated. It's best to dig and destroy affected plants and plant a resistant species in its place.

Damping Off

Seedling disease caused by a variety of organisms. Plants fall over as if their stems had been pinched with hot tweezers. Sow seed thinly to avoid overcrowding. Use only sterilized potting soil and keep the plants only moist, not wet. Soil drench of Captan will give some measure of control.

Fire Blight

Disease of plants in rose family. Twigs and entire limbs die back suddenly, almost as if they'd been scorched by a blow torch. Leaves generally remain attached to plant. Pear leaves turn black. Loquat, cotoneaster and pyracantha foliage turns a coppertone brown. Remove dead and dying wood by pruning back into healthy growth. Disinfect pruning tools between cuts by dipping them into a 10-percent chlorine bleach solution. Spray for fire blight while plants are in full flower (spring for most, late fall for loquats). Apply Streptomycin once or twice during the blooming season.

Fungal Leaf Spots

Dying spots start randomly over leaf surface. There generally is a yellow or light tan halo surrounding the dead spot and a black spore mass may be present in the spot's center. Spots may enlarge and grow together. Leaf ultimately dies. Prime plants: lawn grasses, food crops and landscape plants. More common in cool, moist weather. Controls: Benomyl, Captan, Maneb, Zineb, Folpet.

Nematodes

Nematodes are the ghosts of the garden . . . invisible invaders that ruin your crops. They're microscopic soil-borne worms that sting plant roots and inject digestive enzymes into them. The roots respond by forming swollen galls that ultimately cut off the flow of water and nutrients. Though nematodes are actually small animals, their damage appears more like diseases. Affected plants weaken and may ultimately die. Plants most commonly affected include tomatoes, beans, boxwood, ajuga, gardenias, figs and okra. If you detect special problems with these or any other plants in your landscape and garden you may want to have your soil tested through the county Extension office to see if nematodes are present. Fumigate the area with vapam prior to replanting. If other plants are in the area, you'll not be able to use vapam. Your only recourse then will be to plant resistant species.

Pecan Scab

This fungal disease is responsible for brown spots on the foliage and black spots on the shucks. This disease can cause kernels to be shrivelled and may cause premature drop of pecans in late summer and early fall. The disease invades in early spring and can be controlled by combining a fungicide such as Benomyl with all of your pecan insect and zinc sprayings.

Powdery Mildew

White or light gray powdery fungal growth over top and bottom leaf surfaces and flower buds. Growth may become puckered and disfigured. Prime plants: zinnia, crepe myrtle, euonymus, photinia, melons. Control: Benomyl, Acti-dione PM, Karathane, Sulfur. Read labels before applying to edible crops . . . not all have label clearance.

St. Augustine Decline (SAD)

Virus disease of St. Augustine that first shows up as yellow mottling. Grass gradually fades away until you're left with bermuda or weeds. There is no chemical control for the disease. Some of the newer varieties such as Floratam and Raleigh are resistant to this disease. Inquire about their availability and suitability for your area.

Sooty Mold

Black fungal growth on leaves of gardenias, ligustrums, citrus and other plants frequented by aphids, scale and whiteflies. Mold is not harmful to plant (other than shading leaf surface). It merely exists in honeydew secretions left behind by the insects. Can be washed off with soapy water. To prevent recurrence of problem, spray to control insects.

Anthracnose

Bacterial Leaf Spot

Brown Patch

Cotton (and Mushroom) Root Rot

Damping Off

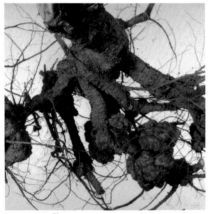

Crown Gall

Fungal Leaf Spot (*Black Spot of Roses*)

Fire Blight

Nematode

Pecan Scab

Fungal Leaf Spot

Powdery Mildew

St. Augustine Decline

Sooty Mold

Sooty Mold

TEXAS TIP

Insects and diseases often get their start in old plant debris left around existing plants. Remove dead leaves, spent flowers and mummified fruit. Keep decayed tissues pruned out to lessen spread of the disease. Good sanitation measures will help lessen spread of disease. Keep'em growing!

Index

Names in *italics* are proper botanical or scientific names; cross references are made from the scientific name to the most common name. Page numbers in **bold face** indicate illustrations.

V-W

X-Z